THE COMMITTED SELF

THE COMMITTED SELF

AN INTRODUCTION TO EXISTENTIALISM FOR CHRISTIANS

VICTOR A. SHEPHERD

BPS Books
Toronto & New York

Published in 2015 by
BPS Books
Toronto and New York
www.bpsbooks.com

A division of Bastian Publishing Services Ltd.

ISBN 978-1-77236-000-4 paperback
ISBN 978-1-77236-001-1 ePDF
ISBN 978-1-77236-002-8 ePUB

Cataloguing-in-Publication Data available from Library and Archives Canada.

Cover: Daniel Crack, KD Books
Text design: Pressbooks

To
Maureen & Matthias Benfey
and
Deborah Sawczak
in gratitude for their unfailing
encouragement, generosity, and affection

Contents

Preface

It is my thesis, and the premise of this book, that greater exposure to the philosophy of Existentialism[1] will assist Christians in coming to terms with their world, with the faith they uphold, and, finally, with themselves. I maintain that Existentialism has much to say to Christians with its understanding of what it is to be a human being; how diverse forces operative in the world and in the psyche shape human self-awareness; and the manner in which radical commitment forges and forms that "self" that is nothing less than a new birth. An acquaintance with Existentialism will aid Christians in negotiating the minefield they think life has become.

Of course, Existentialism itself is a bit of a minefield for Christians. Anyone who listens to formal media interviews or overhears informal conversations at social gatherings is aware of how the philosophy of Existentialism is praised or blamed for an outlook on life that some people relish and others abhor. Christians in particular are frequently nervous at the mention of this philosophy, fearing it to be no more than a contemporary legitimization of that "selfism" traditionally associated with sin. On the other hand, people who hail secularism as release from the restraints of religious arbitrariness welcome the philosophy's emphasis on freedom, authenticity, and uncompromising confrontation

---

1. Inasmuch as I have focused, in this book, on Existentialism strictly conceived as a school of philosophy articulated by specific recognized proponents, I have capitalized it to distinguish it from its subsequent derivatives in the social sciences and its ongoing reflection in literature, the arts, popular culture, and so on. For consistency, I have treated similarly most references to other "isms."

with life's unavoidable (albeit often semi-consciously denied) anguish, uncertainty, unfairness, and death.

In addition, ready access to electronic communication has brought the world not merely into North American living rooms but above all into North American minds: to learn how people elsewhere live, think, and behave, and not least to learn what they are prepared to defend, has left many of us Christians more aware than ever that Christendom has retreated—never to return, we fear. No one can pretend that it is easy, if even possible, to claim that "our" way has to be the right way, if only because it is the only way.

In response to this state of faith and intellectual affairs, some Christian denominations attempt to reassure members that the disappearance of Christendom is not a liability but may even be God's way of calling the church to a profounder understanding of its essence and mission. The same denominations, however, no longer speak with anything resembling a unified voice on matters pertaining to doctrine, ethics, or politics. Within the church the philosophy of Existentialism is hailed for having helped us shed the shackles of cloying traditionalism; or else it is cursed for having fostered a subjectivism that gleefully rejects reasoning as rationalization, convention as groundless, and propriety as the death rattle of social privilege.

What are we Christians to do in this welter of uncertainty as to how life is to be both understood and lived? I maintain that we can benefit from probing the philosophy of Existentialism as we recognize its core tenet—self-commitment—as akin to the biblical notion of faith, the faith by which one becomes a new creature in a renewed cosmos. To be sure, while such an affinity between such thinkers as the theologian Luther and the philosopher Kierkegaard is plain (the latter, we should note, was a lifelong Lutheran), the repudiation of any such affinity in an Existentialist like Sartre is stark. Nevertheless, by reading Existentialist thinkers we will find ourselves asking repeatedly, "Wherein is Existentialism one of the unpaid debts of the church? Why did Nietzsche, whose father and grandfather were pastors, vehemently repudiate the gospel? What is it about the church's articulation that compromises the credibility of its message?"

The seeds for this book were sown decades ago in a course I took from Professor Emil Fackenheim at the University of Toronto. Fackenheim was, at that time, according to many, the brightest luminary in the university's Department of Philosophy. The year-long course was concerned chiefly with Hegel, but in the last few weeks attention was directed to the anti-Hegelian protests of Kierkegaard, Marx, Nietzsche, Heidegger, and Sartre.

While Hegel intrigued me (not least because he considered his philosophy to be the self-articulation of reality itself, and therefore the terminus of philosophy), it was the protesters who electrified me. Fackenheim reminded us frequently that the Existentialist protest was always concerned with the *difference* philosophy made to life *lived*, as opposed to abstractions merely thought. In other words, it addressed the whole person in all of life's opportunities, threats, and contradictions.

Years later, at an informal social gathering, I casually asked Fackenheim, "Whom do you regard as the greatest thinker in Christendom?" I expected him to favour either Augustine or Aquinas, but without hesitation he named Kierkegaard. I thought this was at least in part because of Fackenheim's decades-long immersion in European philosophy and his reputation as an expert in Hegel. Whenever I repeated this remark to colleagues, however, they were quick to assure me otherwise. And then one day in the course of leisure reading I came upon the opinion of Ludwig Wittgenstein, the Cambridge philosopher who, unlike Fackenheim, made no religious profession and whose work in philosophy pertained to other orbits; Wittgenstein, too, maintained Kierkegaard to be the pre-eminent Christian thinker. Obviously Kierkegaard was too important to be ignored, and those who dismissed him with borrowed clichés ("He's nothing more than a subjectivist who affirms truth to be whatever you think it to be") had simply not taken the trouble to understand him.

Kierkegaard, of course, carefully distinguished subjectivism from subjectivity. Far from being the arbitrary elevation of one's own thoughts as truth, subjectivity was the transformation of the person, born of radical commitment, ultimately, to the God who summons us to an existence no less absurd than that of Abraham on Mount Moriah. For there Abraham came face-to-face with *the* absurdity: the contradiction between God's promise (descendants as numberless "as the sand which is on the seashore"[2]) and God's command: "Take your son, your only son Isaac, whom you love…and offer him there as a burnt offering…."[3] If Abraham declined to obey, he would have no descendant *in faith* (and, in light of the covenant, therefore no descendant at all); if he obeyed, he would just as surely lack even one descendant. Thrilled by Kierkegaard's subtle, anguished discussion of this event—and its contrast with, for example, the suffering of the person who dies out of loyalty to an ethical cause—I read more widely in Kierkegaard, and have never stopped.

More recently Tyndale University College & Seminary, where I teach, asked me to offer a course dealing with the Existentialist roots of Postmodernism, the *Zeitgeist* that has prevailed since World War II ended the "modernity" that began with the Renaissance. The features of Postmodernism, indisputably the "ism" operative in our culture, are well-known. The most salient of these features are the loss of confidence in technoscience as unmitigated blessing; loss of confidence in human progress; loss of confidence in reason; the disappearance of truth (or at least an acknowledgement of the arbitrariness and non-universality of truth-claims); and the rise of consumerism, as well as the tacit understanding of its implications concerning the human. Social scientists readily point out that "reality" is socially configured. Philosophers have no difficulty illustrating that the concept of "nature" is not scientifically determined but rather socially constructed. (We need only think of the widely differing views of nature as "mother" or as "red in tooth and claw"; as a "great teacher" or as that which "teaches" nothing except, perhaps, survival of the fittest.) Philosophers and social scientists alike recognize that reasoning is subject to countless determinations: social, for instance, as well as economic, intrapsychic, religious, and historical. It is indisputable, Postmodernists maintain, that reasoning is the servant of any number of extra-rational ends. All of these features of

---

2. Genesis 22:17. Unless indicated otherwise, all biblical quotations are from the Revised Standard Version (Oxford: Oxford University Press, 1973).

3. Genesis 22:2.

Postmodernism have their seeds in Existentialism, a relation I sought to make apparent in my course lectures at Tyndale.

This book represents, with some modifications, the content of that course. It makes no claim to a new angle of vision on any of the thinkers it discusses, nor does it pretend to offer the expertise that graduate-level philosophy students look for. It aims rather at acquainting relatively uninitiated readers with the characteristic aspects and major proponents of Existentialism. At all times it compares and contrasts, whether in the body of the text or in the footnotes, a biblical orientation with that of Existentialist philosophers who either endorse the logic of Scripture (e.g., Kierkegaard and Buber) or depart from it (e.g., Nietzsche and Sartre).

Having taught many courses in the last two decades, I am always aware of the difficulty of finding a text suitable to the needs and abilities of the class, with readings adequate for week-by-week lectures and discussions, at a price students can afford. The book I selected for my course was *Existentialism: Basic Writings*.[4] The four philosophers expounded in it are Kierkegaard, Nietzsche, Heidegger, and Sartre. Wanting students to be aware that biblical faith did not disappear from Existentialism after Kierkegaard's death in 1855, I added Martin Buber, whose best-known book, *I and Thou*, is referred to repeatedly by many who exhibit no grasp at all of Buber's biblically-informed Existentialism. Not least, the classroom lectures included an exposition of two remarkable essays on Buber by none other than my primary mentor, Emil Fackenheim; I wished to expose the class to the subtlety and rigour of a Jewish thinker who has penetrated my mind and heart as few others have.

I hope this book will provide readers with an introduction to an important tradition in Western philosophy, as well as help them understand features of Postmodernism that some people deplore and others welcome. Above all, I hope this book will move many to, or confirm them in, the self-forgetful faith of Abraham, who trusted God to fulfill God's promise *in this life* when obedience to God's command

4. Charles Guignon and Derk Pereboom, eds., *Existentialism: Basic Writings* (Indianapolis: Hackett Publishing Company, 2001).

could only render that promise void. Jesus of Nazareth is said to have startled hearers with his "Those who find their life will lose it, and those who lose their life for my sake will find it."[5] As Kierkegaard aphoristically put it, "Only he who raises the knife gets Isaac."[6]

---

5. Matt. 10:39 (NRSV).

6. Søren Kierkegaard, *Fear and Trembling*, trans. Howard V. Hong and Edna H. Hong (Princeton: Princeton University Press, 1983), 27.

1

What Is Existentialism?

Introduction: Existentialism as a Mode of Philosophizing

The first thing to note about Existentialism is that, unlike many other philosophies, it begins with the human person. It does not begin where the Aristotelian tradition begins, where Realism begins.[1] But neither is it a type of Idealism. Unlike Idealism, which begins with the human person but is interested primarily in mental processes, Existentialism is interested in the whole range of human existence. Spanish philosopher Miguel de Unamuno said, "It is the man [or woman] who philosophizes."[2] In other words, it is the *whole person who philosophizes*, not just the head. Other schools of philosophy, the Existentialists maintain, reduce humankind to a severed head; but it is not a severed head that philosophizes, it is the human self in the totality of its existence. Existentialism begins with the person, not as thinking subject engaged in detached reflection, but as existent—embodied, in the world, and having to act in the theatre of life where decision cannot be suspended.

Existentialism represents a departure from two major streams of traditional philosophy, Realism and Idealism. Idealism, in capsule form and for the purpose of distinguishing it from other schools of thought, is the notion that reality is mind-correlative or mind-coordinated: objects are not independent of the minds that perceive and categorize and think about them, but exist only in some way correlated to those mental

1. For the briefest discussion of Idealism and Realism I am indebted to *The Cambridge Dictionary of Philosophy,* 2nd ed. (Cambridge: C.U.P, 1999), 412, 562-3.

2. Miguel de Unamuno, *The Tragic Sense of Life,* trans. J. E. C. Flitch (New York: Barnes and Noble, 1990), 28.

operations. Kant and Hegel are Idealists. Kant maintained that we never know any object as such but only as it is "for us," as it appears to us, through categories engendered by our own minds and by which we order the welter of sense-perception. All we can know is appearances, because the structure of knowing is determined by the mind.

The other tradition, Realism, is the notion that objects exist independently of our own existence or our knowledge of them, and have properties independent of the concepts through which we understand them or the language we use to describe them. The whole Empiricist tradition, the tradition of scientific investigation arising largely from the Enlightenment, is Realist.

Generally speaking, Plato is an Idealist, while Aristotle is a Realist. According to Aristotle, there is nothing in the mind that was not first in the senses; all mental operations presuppose sense perception of some sort. Plato, by contrast, insists that there is a great deal in the mind that is not in the senses, because the intellect can apprehend the world of eternal forms—the good, the true, and the beautiful. The eternal forms may be embodied in material objects perceived by the senses, but the philosopher, at least, can apprehend the forms as such through the process of the intellect.

Existentialism is neither Realist nor Idealist. Unlike Realism, it does not consider persons and other things as existing somehow discretely, independent of one another. At the same time, it finds Idealism one-sidedly and unrealistically cerebral. The key point for an Existentialist is that it is the _whole person_ who philosophizes, not just the head.

Existentialism also represents a departure in terms of its main themes or concerns. Traditionally, Western philosophy has been preoccupied with epistemology, that is, questions of knowing: What is it that we know? How can we know? What are the limits and conditions of knowing? In fact, epistemology has been the preoccupation not only of philosophy in the West but also of theology: What is it to know God? How do we know God? Is God knowable at all? If so, what are the limits of that knowing?[3] Existentialism, on the other hand, eschews such

---

3. This takes it into a doctrine of revelation, of course, which has been a primary concern of theology from the Reformation onward.

speculations. It is concerned with matters of concrete human existence, such as the anguished and ambiguous ethical choices we regularly face, the prevalence of the absurd in life, the overwhelming arbitrariness of what is, and our inescapable mortality. It is preoccupied not with mental abstractions but with the inescapable conundrums of living, aspects of human existence that no reflection can forestall, deny, or avoid.

From Descartes on, a central concern of Western philosophy has been the self as thinking subject. Everyone has heard of the Cartesian *cogito ergo sum,* "I think, therefore I am." The senses deceive all the time, said Descartes, but the one thing beyond doubt is the fact or truth that I am thinking. Even if I am reflecting on a deception produced by my senses, at least I can know for sure that I am thinking. Descartes therefore defines the human being as a thinking thing: the human is that which thinks (animals apparently not sharing humankind's capacity for thought).

The Existentialist regards Descartes' reasoning and conclusion, first of all, as shallow or one-dimensional. Human beings do many things that animals do not, such as cook their food and mate all year round. Why not say, then, that to be a human being is to be a cooking thing, or a copulating thing? Why not say, "I bury my dead, therefore I am"? Moreover, in saying, "I think, therefore I am," Descartes is presupposing an "I"—a massive presupposition. The Existentialist asks, "Who is the I that thinks?" And as soon as you try to answer this question by reflecting on the I that thinks, the I is no longer the I that thinks, but an object of thought. Any attempt to get behind this introduces an infinite regression; by definition, no amount of reflection will disclose the I who is the subject and condition of that reflection. Then is the I that thinks the same as the self that acts? Does Descartes' "I" allow us to know what sort of I it is? Sartre, for example, says that Descartes' conclusion, "I am," from an examination of self-consciousness, is logically unjustified; Descartes could have concluded only that *there is thinking*—a conclusion that gets us nowhere.[4] Existentialists, then, find the Cartesian *cogito* to be indefensible as the starting point for philosophy.

4. See Jean-Paul Sartre, *The Transcendence of the Ego,* trans. Forrest Williams and Robert Kirkpatrick (New York: Noonday Press, 1957), 45f.

From a theological perspective, we would say that the "I" that I am is what God has created and addressed. The characteristic of the living God is that he speaks, and his address *constitutes* me as "I," a subject. But for a philosopher who disregards this theological notion, where and how does the I or self arise? Existentialism is preoccupied with this discussion.

All Existentialists are also characterized by their refusal to sidestep the tragic or absurd element in life, the contradictions of human existence. In our youth we may not notice these contradictions, but the more we see of the world, the more we recognize that life abounds with absurdities and contradictions. Take, for example, the fact that the problem of infertility occupies the cutting edge of medicine, while at the same time medical ethics seeks to rationalize feticide and even (to all intents and purposes) infanticide as medical procedures: in a partial-birth abortion, a child whose head and body are extruded can be killed as long as its feet have not yet emerged. In one tragic instance, a woman who was pregnant with twins, one of which was found to have a serious defect while still in the womb, decided to abort the twin with the defect and carry the other to term; but the wrong twin was aborted. A newspaper account of the error persisted in using the word *fetus* for the unwanted twin that remained alive in the womb, while the defect-free twin that had been aborted was a *baby*, even though it was never born. There is an undeniable absurdity here of the kind that abounds everywhere in life. Existentialism refuses to sidestep such absurdities or rationalize them away.

"Nothingness" is another concern of Existentialists. Sartre, for instance, is best known for his work *Being and Nothingness* (*L'Être et le Néant*). Heidegger, too, says much about nothingness: "*Das Nichts nichtet*," he writes; that is, nothing brings to nothing, or nothing reduces to nothing. Before anyone dismisses this as a near-pointless observation, we should note that Christian thought is also concerned with nothingness. For example, we believe that creation was fashioned by God out of nothing—not out of some kind of formless "stuff," or out of his own being, but out of nothing at all. We find this notion difficult to grasp; we keep wanting to imagine some sort of raw material out of which God made the universe. But creation out of nothing is a central doctrine for people of biblical faith, because it establishes both the independence of God from creation and his lordship over it.

Or take the commandment not to bear false witness, not to lie. A lie is a statement to which there corresponds nothing; there is no reality to which the statement refers. Is a lie something, then, or nothing? What is its ontological status? If a lie is strictly nothing, completely vacuous, then telling a lie must be no different from remaining silent. But telling a lie *is* different from remaining silent. When we tell a lie, have we not told something? Lies have terrifying power; they ruin people and reputations. Obviously a lie is nothing, in one sense, yet it is also something that can have tremendous effect. In the same way, is a vacuum something or nothing? By definition it is nothing, yet it has the power to suck in everything around it. Is nothingness *ever* merely nothing, then? Or is nothing also, somehow, something?

Existentialism is also concerned with finitude. God may be infinite, if he exists, but everything else is finite. Even the universe, though immeasurably large, is nonetheless finite. We humans are also finite, and this finitude—not only our inexorable mortality, but the limitedness of our power, understanding, and experience—is existentially problematic for us. No less so are guilt, alienation, and despair, all of which are characteristic concerns of Existentialism.

One of the most prominent themes for Existentialists is freedom, which they regard as essential to human existence. Animals may be biologically determined without remainder, but humans are not. We are, of course, subject to a certain degree of biological determination (among other kinds): if the level of our blood sugar falls, we faint; and if someone drives an ice pick into our brain, invariably we think differently (and likely are found to have a different "personality"). Yet biological determination is not definitive in human beings; nor are the many other determinations to which we are subject, such as gender or psychology or nationality. We always remain more than any one such determination or even the sum total of them. We are characterized by our ability to *choose*; and this freedom is what underlies our responsibility.

We might say of a person who is acting shabbily that he is behaving inhumanly. Someone might rebuke him with the words, "For goodness' sake, be a man!" as though he were not one. We never reproach any other creature in this way—for example, by saying to an alligator that is dismembering another animal, "Be an alligator!"—because other creatures cannot be anything else. But somehow, you and I can be human yet fail to be human at the same time. This seems paradoxical, like the nothing that is also something. Can we really be human and yet not be human? From a theological point of view we cannot, because the *imago Dei* can never be forfeited; it can be denied, contradicted, and defaced, but it can never be effaced or forfeited. The Existentialist, on the other hand, speaking philosophically, would say that if we forfeit or abdicate our freedom, our existence is not *authentically* human. Freedom, decision, integrity, responsibility, authenticity: these are the core of personal being, and hence central concerns of Existentialism.

Existentialism is concerned with the affective or emotional dimension of human existence. Most schools of philosophy tend not to be concerned with this, as philosophers like to think of themselves as affect-less, uninfluenced by emotion. The affective dimension has traditionally been assigned to psychology; psychology is interested in how people *feel*, whereas philosophers want to know how people *think.* This is a false dichotomy, however, because our thinking and feeling are bound up together to a far greater extent than we like to imagine. It takes very little to alter the way someone thinks in a given situation: all you have to do is threaten their self-interest or sense of security, or offend their pride. Touch their emotions, and their thinking changes accordingly. After all, in the long run do we not all think and act in conformity to what we *love?*

Once feeling or affect has been relegated to psychology, it moves into the social sciences as an object of quasi-scientific analysis. Existentialism, however, includes the emotional not as material for social science, but as an aspect of the lived human. Existentialist philosophy is always concerned with the human, not simply as detached thinker, but as *lived* human, involved and committed. Recognizing that our affective dimension has much to do with our self-commitment—that is, our involvement in others and in the world at large—Existentialism is concerned especially with the feelings that hamper that self-commitment, such as anxiety, boredom, and "nausea."

"Nausea," it turns out, is another key theme in Existentialism, but not as the uncomfortable sensation in your stomach that makes you want to vomit. Nausea is the condition of feeling overwhelmed by the superfluity and sheer arbitrary givenness of what is. This is a big theme in Nietzsche's work, and an even bigger one in Sartre's: in Sartre's famous novel *La Nausée*, the distressing issue is that there is no reason for what is, and no meaning to it; it just *is*. The sheer superfluity of being, inherently meaningless, spills over everywhere. Why should that tree behind me be a pine tree rather than a maple? And why should it be there instead of ten feet to the left, or ten feet to the right? And why is there anything at all? Ultimately, there is no reason. There is simply a randomness, a glut of meaningless being, of *facticity*,[5] that the Existentialist finds overwhelming.

Existentialism Contrasted with Other Philosophies

It will help to understand Existentialism if we put it side by side with other major schools of philosophy and see how they differ.[6] Take Empiricism, for example. Its method is detachment for the sake of observation. You as scientific observer are detached from the peanut in front of you, the object you are looking at. Moreover, as an observer you are concerned particularly with nonhuman things: rocks, microbes, reptiles, weather—or, in the case of the social sciences, the human with humanness subtracted, the human made quantifiable. Just as you can measure blood pressure and cell multiplication, you can measure how many people in a group do X or Y, and whether that figure is higher or lower in a crowd, in a prison, or on a ship. The social sciences deal with things that are quantifiable, but to the extent that behaviour is quantifiable, you have abstracted humanness from the human. In other words, the Empiricist, who is concerned with objectivity and measurement, never deals with humans in their *humanness*.

5. The notion of facticity will be explored more fully below.

6. In the following paragraphs I have been stimulated by John Macquarrie, *Existentialism* (London: Penguin Books, 1973), 26–34.

Existentialism is just the opposite: it is *always* concerned with what is specifically, uniquely human—not what we share with animals, not the behaviour of nameless people in a crowd, and not what we are in terms of the sum total of our biological, economic, and social determinations, but the specifically, irreducibly human self.

According to Russian philosopher Nikolai Berdyaev, Empiricism triumphs wherever Existentialism is ignored,[7] with unfortunate results. The first result is that the object is estranged from the subject. The best instance of this today is the environmental crisis, where human beings are experiencing the terrifying consequences of hundreds of years of estrangement from the rest of nature. Second, the unrepeatably particular person is absorbed in the universal; the individual human disappears into the mass of humanity, the social class, or the nation. Third, freedom is crushed and concealed, and multiple determinisms are deemed definitive.

We must acknowledge, of course, that (as noted earlier) there *are* multiple determinations, operative for every one of us: I am a male; I have no perception at all as to what it is to be a woman, because I cannot get out of my maleness. A gender determination is operative there. I also happen to be white, in a society in which it is easy to be white: there is a racial determination to me that I, at least, find non-problematic. I am a Christian and a clergyman, so I am subject to a religious and professional determination. I am socially influenced by the fact that I belong to the middle class. All of these determinations are operative, but they are not *definitive*: I cannot be reduced to the sum total of these determinations. Berdyaev says that where Existentialism is ignored, people are *reduced* to their multiple determinations, which then become determinisms.

The fourth consequence of the triumph of Empiricism, says Berdyaev, is the destruction of character through socialization. Social existence finally comes down to what we share with the crowd and how our behaviour is formed by the crowd: how the mob renders us moblike so that we fit into the mould. Character is submerged. In short, everything championed by Existentialism—human self-commitment, particularity, freedom, character—is buried by Empiricism.

7. Referred to in Macquarrie, *Existentialism*, 27.

The relationship of Existentialism to Humanism is a little more complex. Humanism is not, strictly speaking, a philosophy. Renaissance Humanism, which prevailed from approximately 1450 to 1650, signalled the end of the Middle Ages and the beginning of modernity, which was followed by the Enlightenment. Renaissance Humanism was primarily a literary movement, crowned by poetry (there was a chair of Poetry in every humanist university), and it produced very little philosophy as such—in fact, its contempt for Aristotle, and for the stifling metaphysical hair-splitting characteristic of medieval philosophy, gave it a distinctly counter-philosophical tone. But it did become a worldview. Sartre has famously asserted that Existentialism is a kind of Humanism.[8] However, Existentialist philosophers find the usual expression of Humanism too one-sidedly rosy, even Pollyannaish, and insufficiently critical in its understanding of the human being. Humanism magnified human richness, especially as nourished by literature and the arts; it saw the human being in a positive, optimistic light, and regarded human existence as eminently sensible. Existentialists, by contrast, see human existence as immersed in contradiction and absurdity. They are more intent on wrestling with evil, alienation, despair, and death, and with the way that death in the future reaches back into the present to unhinge everything.

Pragmatism has certain features in common with Existentialism: like Existentialism, it protests against abstract intellectualism, and maintains that the demands of concrete life force us to make decisions before we can complete a rational analysis of them or arrive at theoretical grounds for them. We must make decisions every day without being able to gather all the information we would like. What we would all like to do when faced with a major decision is suspend it until we have more information. But how much is more, and how much is enough? The truth of the matter is, we have no way of knowing how much relevant information is available, or whether any of it is available. Yet these decisions ultimately concern our total existence, and avoiding them is

8. Sartre, *Existentialism and Humanism*, trans. Philip Mairet (London: Methuen & Co., 1948). Note that for Sartre, Humanism entails atheism. This was not the case with Renaissance Humanists, many of whom were Christian.

not an option: we may be unable to make up our mind, but we cannot help making up our life, because we will end up doing something (or nothing—which, remember, is a kind of something). If we say, "I can't decide whether or not I should study tonight; I just can't make up my mind," then we have already made it up: we will not be studying. Some people say they are unable to decide whether to marry or remain single, but as long as they dither, they have made up their life: they are single. It is impossible not to decide, say the Existentialists. Even if you decide to suspend your freedom for now, and let whatever happens happen, that, too, is a decision that you make freely. Moreover, it is an ignoble decision, because it means that you are living in bad faith,[9] pretending that you are not free.

But whereas Pragmatists agree with Existentialists about the unavoidability of deciding, the Pragmatists' criteria for decision-making are biological and utilitarian, with virtually no concern for what Existentialism calls "inwardness." Inwardness sounds like a highly abstract, semi-Romantic, psychological notion, but it is a dimension of human being that deeply concerns Existentialist philosophy, although different philosophers understand it differently. For Kierkegaard, who was a Christian, inwardness is one's relation to oneself before God.[10] Not only do I relate to my neighbour, to my family, and to the world at large, but I also relate to myself. I think about myself; I relate to myself. The way that I relate to myself *before God* is what Kierkegaard calls "inwardness." Obviously, nontheistic Existentialists will have a different understanding of the concept, but it figures largely in the thinking of all of them. To eschew inwardness is to live in shallow phoniness. Eight hours a day spent mindlessly in front of the TV, for example, would involve minimal inwardness; anyone who did that would be considered a pitiful instance of a human being by Existentialists. What can a person be after hours of TV, except little more than a ghost or phantasm, a shallow phony? Moreover, insists the Existentialist, such a person is

9. Exactly what is meant by "bad faith" will be specified below, especially in the chapter on Sartre.

10. Søren Kierkegaard, *Concluding Unscientific Postscript to Philosophical Fragments*, ed. and trans. Howard V. Hong and Edna H. Hong (Princeton: Princeton University Press, 1992), 390.

accountable for being a shallow phony; no one twisted his arm into watching TV. He could have turned it off, or pulled out the plug. But Pragmatism, knowing nothing of inwardness, does not trouble itself with such issues.

Like Humanism, Pragmatism tends to be more optimistic than Existentialism. Pragmatism was developed by Charles Sanders Peirce at the turn of the twentieth century in America. It was easy to feel positive about humankind in that place and time; Americans had had no devastating war in their own nation since the Civil War. But those living in Europe fifty years later, in the time and place where Existentialism arose, had had war after war after war on their own soil—especially World War I and World War II, followed by the Cold War. People in Europe at mid-century did not feel so unqualifiedly positive about human existence; on the contrary, they had discovered that *having* to act as a true human was excruciating. Existentialism maintains that acting in truth is painful and disruptive, and may even involve martyrdom. It costs everything to be authentic, and nothing to belong to "the herd."[11] Pragmatism does not understand this cost.

Nihilism, on the other hand, is extreme skepticism, the denial of meaning and truth. The word *Nihilism* comes from the Latin *nihil*, meaning "nothing." According to the Nihilist, there is no substance to traditional social, political, moral, or religious values; they are meaningless. Certain Existentialists are sometimes called Nihilists, particularly Camus, Sartre, Heidegger, and Nietzsche, because they offer a fundamental critique of traditional value systems. In fact, however, all of these Existentialists *deny* Nihilism, because they advance a philosophy that promotes human integrity and authenticity. Obviously they find meaning somewhere for human existence. On the other side of seeming Nihilism, they see new possibilities for existing, a new understanding of truth, and a "transvaluation of values."[12]

The above is an expression frequently used by Nietzsche, who maintains that Western values, which are a carryover from Christianity, need to be "transvalued" because they are degrading: they

---

11. See chapters 6 and 7 for Nietzsche's use of "the herd."

12. For more on Nietzsche's use of this expression see chapters 6 and 7.

promote self-loathing, exalt weakness, and lead to bitterness and resentment. He points out that the earliest Christians (for example, in Corinth) came from the lowest classes of society, including the slave class, resulting in a slave mentality in Christian ethics: we cower before God as "miserable offenders,"[13] believing that we deserve condemnation, and grovel for forgiveness. It is a pathetic valuation of human existence, says Nietzsche. Moreover, because the earliest Christians were from the underclass, they envied and resented the privilege of their social superiors. This resentment[14] seeped into the Western tradition: there is, says Nietzsche, a characteristic contempt in Christian ethics for worldly success, for wealth, for the power others wield; historically, Christians have paraded this contempt as virtue when it is nothing more than thinly disguised resentment. Even the convention of kneeling to pray was repulsive to Nietzsche. It is ostensibly a sign of submission to God, but he explained it as merely a holdover from the peasantry kneeling before their earthly superiors, a humiliation which was then projected onto God.[15] The Christian value system is an exercise in human self-rejection; it promotes self-loathing as virtue, and should be jettisoned.

Nietzsche has identified something important here. Christians tout humility as paramount, but they frequently express it in terms of self-belittlement: "I am nothing; I am a worm, I am a miserable wretch." Genuine humility is not self-belittlement or self-rejection, but self-forgetfulness. As long as you are belittling yourself, you are preoccupied with yourself; you may say you are nothing, but in insisting on your own nothingness you remain self-preoccupied and so make yourself everything. Moreover, so-called humility is often a cover for abdicating proper human initiative; it degenerates into lack of resolve, and ends up

13. Nietzsche would bristle at this language in the *Book of Common Prayer*. At the same time he would have failed to grasp what it has in mind.

14. *Ressentiment* in Nietzsche's writing; he wrote in German, but retained this French word.

15. For this reason the Puritans, who repudiated that humiliation, refused to kneel for prayer. Jews also do not kneel to pray; they stand, believing that prayer is a response to the God who has spoken to us, and that his address dignifies us. Occasionally people in the Bible are said to kneel at prayer, but this is a sign of overwhelming distress and not the usual posture. Jesus knelt in Gethsemane, and Daniel knelt in exile because he was devastated by the situation of his people. But normally, Jews have stood to pray, right up to the present day.

exalting weakness. Hence Nietzsche and other Existentialists—including Kierkegaard—said that the values in Christian Western culture need to be transvalued. But it was not as Nihilists that they said so.

Distinctive Features of Existentialism

The whole philosophical tradition stemming from Plato privileges essence over existence. Reason ignores what is changeable, contingent, and particular in favour of what is unchanging, eternal or necessary, and universal. Traditionally, therefore, philosophy has concerned itself with humankind in general rather than with individual human existence. But Existentialism is concerned with the concrete specificity of the individual's existence, which it considers more real than humankind or any putative human "essence." Humankind is an abstraction; some people would even say it does not exist. We have all met specific persons, but has anyone ever met humankind? If not, then does it exist at all? And if it does not exist, why are we preoccupied with it? Existentialism, on the other hand, always insists on the priority of existence over essence, reversing or inverting the philosophical tradition. For Plato, the form of something, in the eternal world of forms, has a reality more profound than that of the object which embodies it. Existentialist tradition inverts this: it is the concrete, the particular, that is real.

To exist—*existere* in Latin, literally "to stand out"—is specifically to stand out from *nothing*, because *nothing* threatens us at every moment. We are always tempted to surrender our freedom—as if we could—because it is too great a burden. We want to surrender our responsibility, because we would rather not be answerable for our actions. *Nothingness* laps at us every moment, and to exist is to stand out from that nothingness. There is an old Christian hymn that says, "Oh to be nothing, nothing…Only to lie at His feet."[16] All Christians, of course, want to be rendered useful to God, but what is he to do with nothing? Of what use to him is nothing? For the Existentialist, an aspiration to

16. Georgiana M. Taylor. Each of the three stanzas begins, "Oh, to be nothing, nothing!" *Victorious Life Hymns* (Dayton, OH: Heritage Music Press, 1975), #45.

be nothing is a complete abdication of being human. To exist is to be someone, to be self-enacted, to stand out from nothing.

We are back again to the question of nothing, because it is so important in Existentialist thought. What do we understand by nothing? If nothing is nothing, can there be anything in it to understand? We can understand a chair, a pop can, or a rock, because it is something; but can we understand nothing?

We can ask the same question about evil, another preoccupation of Existentialism. What is it? Everyone has been, at some point, a victim of evil, and everyone has been a perpetrator of evil; we know that it is something, and that it is terrible. But if God is good, and his creation is good, what is the origin of evil? Does it have any ontological status at all? Is it amenable to our understanding? People say that evil is the corruption of what is good. We can understand that; we can understand a corrupted good. But surely evil as such, evil for the sake of evil, cannot be thus explained or understood. One aspect of evil's evilness is its incomprehensibility, its sheer unintelligibility. To just the extent that an event can be understood, it fails to be evil; if it can be understood, then there is a reason for it. Influential everywhere, evil appears to be something, yet as "nothing" it is utterly un-understandable, groundless, and meaningless.

Non-Existentialist philosophies aim at an intellectual grasp or conceptualization of reality. Existentialist philosophy, on the other hand, maintains that reality cannot be intellectually grasped. The only thing that can be grasped intellectually is that which is artificially abstract; what is concrete can never be intellectually grasped; it can only be lived. The difference is like that between being married and reading a book on marriage: the reality of marriage is the interpenetration of two specific lives committed to each other in a relationship they aspire to let nothing terminate except death. No amount of reading a book on it will yield the reality, just as no amount of reading a book on swimming will make you a swimmer: at some point, you must let go of assorted securities and risk all by jumping into the deep end of the pool.

If reality cannot be grasped intellectually, neither can it be conveyed by direct communication. We can directly communicate statements, truths, propositions, principles—but not reality. For that, indirect communication is essential. Think about the difference between fiction, or literature generally, and philosophy as traditionally practised. The abstraction that is in my mind I endeavour to communicate to your mind; we sit and discuss Plato's theory of the forms, or Kant and the transcendental unity of apperception, and try to finesse the concepts so as to make clear by our words and arguments what we mean. We ask one another, "Do you see? Do you understand?" and answer one another, "Oh, yes, I get it." We are communicating directly something that is itself no more than a concept, and a highly abstract one at that.

But fiction, or poetry, communicates indirectly by inviting us into a reality that we *live* by means of the imagination. As a philosophy student I took only one course in English literature in my entire university career, but I often ate lunch with students who were majoring in English literature. I thought they were soft in the head: I was a philosopher, a rigorous thinker, whereas they merely filled their heads with emotional mush spewed onto a page. And then in 1963 I read Northrop Frye's informative little book *The Educated Imagination*, in which he describes how literature functions.[17] Literature creates a world, and the writer invites your participation: you will not understand what the novel is about unless you step into that created world and live in it. Once I perceived this, the world of literature was suddenly delivered into my hands.

I also started reading parts of the Bible besides the epistles. The epistles are highly abstract: "In Christ God was reconciling the world to himself." "Therefore being justified by faith, we have peace with God through our Lord Jesus Christ."[18] But in the gospels, Jesus walks along, engaging living persons in the course of his daily encounters, some of whom accost him with questions like: "Why do you eat with ne'er-do-wells?" Jesus never answers them with an argument or explanation. He does not say, "I'll tell you why; here's the reason." Instead he spins a yarn beginning, "Once upon a time a man had two sons. And he said

17. Northrop Frye, *The Educated Imagination* (Toronto: CBC Publications, 1963).

18. 2 Corinthians 5:19 and Romans 5:1, respectively. Unless indicated otherwise, all biblical quotations are from the Revised Standard Version (Oxford: O.U.P., 1973).

to one…" and so on. The parables of our Lord are pure fiction, but they are his favourite means of communicating. He never communicates directly, because the reality of the Kingdom of God is such that while it can be pointed to, described, and commended, it cannot be conveyed intellectually and so known at a distance, from the outside; it cannot be known until we step into it. The traditional philosopher thinks we can know something while remaining detached from it, and would even say that detachment from it is the *condition* of knowing it; the Existentialist, by contrast, says that commitment to something is the condition not only of knowing it, but also of knowing oneself as transformed by it. Jesus' answer seems to confirm this. To those who will not commit themselves to the Kingdom until the Master has proved its nature and presence, he only says, "You want a sign of the Kingdom so that you can decide in advance whether it is worth entering or not. There is no sign. Either you abandon yourself to it, or you will never know. To commit yourself unconditionally to the Kingdom is to know both Kingdom and self; to withhold such surrender is to know neither."

The conversation in John 10 is another good example. People say to Jesus in John 10:24, "How long will you keep us in suspense? If you are the Christ, tell us plainly." Jesus does not take pity on these people who are uncomfortable being kept in suspense, and say to them, "All right. I'll tell you if I am the Christ or not. Listen up.…" Rather, he insists he will not tell them. And the reason is that if he tells them he is the Christ, they will say, "Oh, good, because some of us thought you were." And if he tells them he is not the Christ, they'll say, "Oh, too bad; some of us thought you were." But either way they are no different. The only way they will ever know whether Jesus is the Christ is through committing themselves to him.

Again, ponder Mark 8:12. Jesus asks, "Why does this generation seek a sign? Truly, I say to you, no sign shall be given to this generation." People want a sign; that is, they want Jesus to authenticate himself to them independently of their commitment to him. He refuses. He says, "I will not authenticate myself to you and leave you detached from me. The only way you will know who I am is if you abandon yourself to me. As long as you do not abandon yourself to me, you will never know who I am, no matter what I say or do." Prior to a commitment to Jesus, no sign is sufficient; following such a commitment, all signs are superfluous.

Once I moved past my inexcusable prejudice against imaginative literature (thanks to Northrop Frye), the gospels came alive for me—and so did the Old Testament, because so much of it is cast in the form of story. Nearly all evangelical preaching comes out of the epistles, because their explicit reference to concepts like justification or reconciliation makes them seem like an easier way to communicate than preaching from the gospels or the Old Testament narratives. But Jesus invites us to *live in* the reality of justification by telling us the story of two men who go to the temple to pray: it is the second one, the reprehensible person devoid of moral merit, who goes home justified. Similarly the truth of reconciliation is grasped existentially through Jesus' action as he pulls the contemptible Zacchaeus out of the tree and invites himself over to lunch in Zacchaeus' house—the outcome of which is that Zacchaeus is rightly related to God.

In short: reality, according to Existentialism, can be pointed to, commended, or urged on others, but it cannot be communicated. Martin Luther said that everyone has to do his own believing, just as everyone has to do his own dying. Similarly, Jesus says that only you can enter the Kingdom of God for yourself. And only you, says the Existentialist, can exercise your own unforfeitable freedom so as to become an authentic self.

The question that metaphysics asks is: What is real? Metaphysics asks about reality abstractly and speculatively. But the question that Existentialism asks is: On what am I willing to stake my life? And none of us is going to stake our life on an abstraction. We stake our life only on that which is utterly real for us. Neither abstraction nor speculation nor mere concept meets that criterion.

The reality that Existentialism commends is not unknowable. It can be known, but it is known by experience, and the evidence of this knowledge is personal transformation. Here we encounter another distinctive feature of Existentialist philosophy. If I were to ask you, "Do you know pain? Do you really know pain?" I would not be asking whether you have a scientific understanding of the neurophysiology of pain, how it works, what sort of thing is likely to cause it, and what its function is. I am asking, first of all, whether you have had much experience of pain; and secondly, whether that experience of pain has been so intense and profound as to make you forever different. You know pain to just the extent that it has made you different.

Similarly, what does the prophet mean by the question, "Do you know God?" It is not a question whether you can pass a Systematic Theology examination. The prophet is really asking, "Have you encountered God? Do you have an experience of God? And is your life forever different as a result?" When Isaiah says on behalf of God, "This people, Israel, does not know me," he is not complaining that they lack theological information—the Israelites are the best theologians in the world—but that their lives remain unaltered by an experience of God. They remain unaltered because, despite their theological sophistication, they have yet to meet the One of whom theology speaks, the One to whom it points. They do not know God.

For the Empiricist, to know is to have information about the properties of something. But knowing persons, or knowing God, is never a matter of acquiring information about properties; it is a matter of being transformed by an encounter with someone. Martin Buber's writing is characterized by this notion, as we shall see. I have been married forty-five years, and if you were to ask me whether I know my wife, I could tell you that she is five feet tall, weighs hundred and five pounds, and speaks French, all of which is true. I would be giving you information about her, the same information that is knowable by anyone, but I would not be answering your question. The question, "Do you know your wife? What do you know of your wife?" is answered in this way: "What I know of my wife is exactly the difference that living with her has made to me." If I have lived with her for forty-five years and am no different for it, then I do not know her at all, regardless of how much information I have. In an Empiricist or Enlightenment model of knowing, knowledge is information gained from detached observation of an object, but in an Existentialist model, knowledge is personal transformation undergone through the commitment of a subject to another subject. There is no object; knowledge involves the commitment of a subject to another subject.

Note that knowing of this kind is no less *knowing*. There is more than one form of knowing. We live in a society so infatuated with scientism[19] that we tend to assume an Empiricist model as the *only* model of knowing. It is indeed one kind of knowing, and an important kind, but not the most important kind. What is the information gained about any object, compared to the transformation of yourself through intimacy with a fellow human? Our society is reluctant to use the word *knowledge* for this. But the Existentialist says that, on the contrary, it is the only kind of knowledge worth anything. Kierkegaard faults the church relentlessly for having substituted intellectual apprehension of doctrine for intimacy with the One of whom doctrine speaks. To be sure, we should never minimize the place of doctrine, for doctrinal truths describe the Lord who is Truth (in the sense of "reality," as in John's gospel). Yet however much doctrine *describes* Jesus Christ and *points to* him, it can never *convey* him. Only the Holy Spirit conveys Jesus Christ to us, and does so only in the course of our abandoning ourself to him.

Moreover, real knowledge, according to the Existentialist model, arises only with the radical commitment of the *whole person*. Intellectual commitment is necessary, but it will never suffice. Knowledge of reality arises only through the radical commitment of the whole person, because it is only in such commitment that reality itself occurs. In other words, strictly speaking, we do not come to know an already-existing reality; rather, the reality *arises only in the instant of our knowing it*. This is different, of course, from all Empiricist models: if you are examining the properties of aluminum in a laboratory, says the Empiricist, the aluminum exists independently of your knowing it and is unchanged by your knowing it. But in an Existentialist model of knowing, the reality is not that which you apprehend; rather, the reality *occurs* or *arises* in the course of your commitment.

Buber, a Jewish Existentialist thinker, presses this point with respect

19. Scientism is (among other things) the illegitimate encroachment of the scientific method into non-empirical areas of life, with the result, for instance, that scientific knowing is deemed to be the only mode of knowing.

to God. On the one hand, God exists independently of us. However, says Buber, we have no access to God in himself independent of our engagement with him; in fact, we do not even know there is a God to engage with until we engage with him. Reality for Buber is what he calls "the between." It is the encounter, the engagement between God and us, the small-s subject with the capital-S Subject.

We have noted that for all Existentialists, theistic or not, reality is not simply apprehended; strictly speaking, it *occurs* in the moment of self-commitment. Reality, in this view, is not the same thing as actuality. The objects in our environment are elements of actuality. To say that a desk is actual is to say that it is not imaginary or mythological. But is it *real*? From a Christian perspective, reality is the effectual presence of Jesus Christ in his engagement with us, drawing us into intimacy with himself. From a nontheistic Existentialist position, reality is the transformation that occurs in our existence in the course of our self-commitment to someone or something. This squares with Buber's understanding of what it means to know someone, according to which the measure of our knowledge of someone else is precisely the difference made in us by our unreserved engagement with that person. In other words, in an Existentialist model, to know is always to be transformed, and that process of transformation is reality.

Consider the Hebrew notion of תשובה (*teshuva*), or repentance. In the Christian tradition, as Nietzsche liked to remind us, repentance has typically meant feeling wretched about oneself. But in the Hebrew, *teshuva* means to make a 180-degree turn, to turn around, to make an aboutface that re-orients us towards God in fresh commitment to him. Fallen human beings do not seek God, although they think they do; we have to be turned around to face God. Since we customarily flee God, repentance is a turn back towards him. The Hebrew Bible has three major metaphors for repentance, and every one of them has to do with relationship, with reviving one's commitment to another person. The first is an adulterous wife returning to her husband (we could just as easily say, an adulterous husband returning to his wife); the second is idolaters returning to the true and living God; and the third is rebel subjects returning to their rightful ruler.

The adulterous wife who returns to her husband has violated him and disgraced herself, but she returns to long-standing, patient, freely-accepting love. When idolaters put away their idols to worship the Lord, they are turning from what Hebrew calls "the nothings" (literally) to the real, true, living God.[20] And when rebel subjects return to their rightful ruler, they turn from disorder and chaos to order and integrity. The Bible understands all of these radical transformations as commitments to a relationship. While I am not suggesting that a straight line can be drawn from Existentialist philosophy to the Hebrew Bible or to the ministry of Jesus, there are clearly more than a few affinities.

We have observed that, according to the Existentialist, knowing is transformative and is impossible without radical commitment. The next crucial point to note is that, in the course of such a radical, transformative commitment, the self is forged. Before that, you are a pre-self, a non-self, a sub-self, or a ghostly self. The self is "forged" according to Sartre, and "chosen" according to Kierkegaard, but for both, it arises from commitment. Recall that Existentialism opposes all forms of Essentialism, which sees the self, or human nature, as given. It is not the case, say the Existentialists, that everybody has a self: rather, one *becomes* a self. Nor is there a human nature that determines our behaviour: for Existentialists, blaming human nature is an indefensible evasion. Nobody *has* to behave in a particular way. There is no generalized, universal human nature which is given, only a self that you enact. That is why Existentialists speak of the human 'condition' rather than of a human 'nature.'

It is true, of course, that things in our personal history, especially our childhood, have shaped us to some degree. There are many things about my childhood and my upbringing that I relish and want to perpetuate, and many other things that I want to avoid duplicating in my own parenting. The Existentialists would call all such matters "facticity." These are things we cannot change, but we can always choose the way we respond to them.

---

20. Incidentally, this brings us back to the Existentialist preoccupation with nothingness. An idol is by definition nothing, in that no deity corresponds to it. But just like a lie, it is a 'nothing' that is also, in some sense, something, and exerts power over people.

Facticity also includes external circumstances. For example, you may be out hiking one day and come upon a steep hill.[21] A variety of responses are possible. You may decide the hill is too steep and the day too hot, and turn back. Or you may say to yourself, "This is a wonderful challenge! I wonder how fast I can run up that hill?" Or you may reflect on the fact that the purpose of your hike was to get to a village five miles away, and the hill is no more than a minor impediment on the way. But the one thing you cannot say is that the hill made you turn back, or that it defeated you, or that it made you do anything at all, because the hill is non-essential; it is mere facticity. You did not have to respond to it in the way you did. Of course, neither could you have moved the hill, or reduced its size. The Existentialist would maintain that, like the hill on your hike, many features of the world are unchangeable aspects of our facticity; after all, only a deranged person believes he can create a world of his own imagining. But we do have an irreducible, inalienable freedom with respect to our response—and therefore responsibility with respect to that response.

Responsibility is a heavy burden. Sartre did much of his writing during the German occupation of France, where people who were found to have joined the Resistance movement were tortured and executed. Many people were sympathetic to the Resistance movement, but stood on the sidelines and did not join; they collaborated with the Nazi occupation instead. "What choice did we have?" they said. "We just wanted to survive until the war ended. And if this meant capitulating to Nazism for the time being, what alternative did we have?" Others, however, belied this rationalization by making a different choice. Jacques Ellul, a lawyer, sociologist, historian, and Protestant Christian thinker, joined the French Resistance even though the British strongly urged people not to do so because the cost outweighed the return in terms of helping the war effort: the Resistance actually accomplished very little in turning the tide of the war, and its members were tortured and killed if discovered by the Nazis. After the war, Ellul

---

21. Sartre has made this illustration notorious. He refers to it and examples like it throughout Part Four, "Having, Doing and Being," of *Being and Nothingness*, trans. Hazel E. Barnes (New York: The Citadel Press, 1965).

was asked why he had joined. He replied that if he had not, he could not have lived with himself; he would not have known who he was, would not even have *been* a self. The military efficacy of the Resistance, and the risk of torture or death, did not finally matter as much to him as the significance of that choice in becoming a self.

We *always* have a choice, says Sartre, though it may carry a heavy price. That is something we often prefer not to hear. In many situations, we would rather pretend that we have no choice, that our background and past experiences have deprived us of the ability to choose. The Existentialist will have none of that. Existentialism, far more than most philosophy, is concerned with the self and the forging or choosing of the self, and maintains that it is only in committing oneself that one becomes a self.

Notice again the similarity here with biblical teaching—especially in the terms used by Kierkegaard, who was a Christian. Kierkegaard spoke of self-abandonment, or surrender of the self, as the condition of becoming a self. What else is Jesus saying when he declares that you gain your life only when you lose it, and that whoever tries to preserve his life forfeits it? Kierkegaard even goes so far as to say, paradoxically, that self-abandonment *is* the self. Only in the act of radical commitment do we become the self we then recognize, in the light of which we also recognize the non-self we were before. Peter says to Jesus, "We have left everything and followed you."[22] Here Peter anticipates the Existentialist, because until we make that commitment of leaving everything, of self-abandonment in the midst of what others regard as radical insecurity, we are not a self at all.

Socrates is an illustration of this kind of commitment, even though he was not a Christian; he lived in the pre-Christian era, and there is much in his philosophy that a Christian cannot agree with. Socrates was imprisoned by the Athenians for his teaching, and was told that his life would be spared if he recanted. He refused. His friends, seeing that he would not recant, offered to sneak him out of jail and into another country, and so save his life. He refused that as well. These two choices, his refusal to recant and his refusal to escape, indicate that he was so

22. Mark 10:28.

utterly committed to the reality of which he spoke that he *was* that reality. He had staked his very self on it.

One might well ask, at this point, whether it matters at all to the Existentialist that we abandon ourselves to one thing or person rather than another. That is, are all commitments of similar value? Given equal levels of commitment, is the mobster as authentic as the missionary? Existentialist ethics, as will be seen in the chapter on Sartre, maintains that the exercise of my freedom ought not to curtail anyone else's; and, no less telling, that the choice I make concerning myself I implicitly make for all.[23] One thing we can say on behalf of the Existentialist is that even a commitment to what someone else regards as an improper end is nonetheless a self-forging and a self-forming. We choose the self we become. It is not that we choose among alternative available selves, like a child at an ice cream counter looking at all the flavours and choosing the one she fancies. Rather, in the act of self-commitment the self arises for the first time in our lives.

Presuppositions of Existentialism

Obviously, Existentialism rejects determinism. We are free to make decisions, in the sense that we are not finally determined biologically, psychologically, politically, and so on. We are all subject to many kinds of determinations; but these manifold determinations do not add up to determinism.

Second, Existentialism holds freedom to be inalienable. We are condemned to be free, says Sartre; we cannot repudiate our freedom. Anyone with Christian theological training will recognize two different understandings of freedom here; in any case, however, according to Existentialism freedom is something we cannot abdicate. We are entirely responsible, and cannot blame anybody or anything for our decisions. Nor can we avoid deciding: not to decide is itself a decision.

Third, meaning does not inhere in things independently. Meaning is not given to us by features of the thing we are contemplating, nor created by an articulation of concepts; rather, meaning is brought forth

---

23. This concept is explained further in chapter 11.

by our response. The meaning of an event, encounter, or opportunity is forged in a response-as-commitment, and is disclosed in the transformation of the person who experiences it. That which makes no difference to one's *life* has no meaning, no *human* significance.

In light of the above, it is less important to try to understand something, such as evil, than to respond to it. As was noted earlier, to the extent that evil is meaningful, it is not evil. Consider the Holocaust, for example, and the millions of people who were gassed and whose remains were incinerated in the crematoria, or the millions of children who were simply thrown *alive* into the crematoria. To claim to have found meaning in it is to trivialize the event and demean its victims. One of the mythologies of our society is that everything in the world must ultimately be made transparent to our understanding. For Existentialism, however, meaning always pertains more to response than to understanding. Hence the question we ought to be asking about evil is not: What does it mean? but rather: What are we going to do about it? What is our response to horror that paralyzes comprehension even while our responsibility in the face of it is undeniable?

The features and assumptions we have been talking about can be illustrated in the following way. Consider the statement, "All humans are mortal."[24] Everybody agrees with that; we all know we're going to die one day. But now suppose you are told, "You are going to die today." This bites a little more, because there is a turning from the universal to the particular, from the objective to the personal, and from the abstract to the concrete. And if Jesus says to you, "Fool, this night your life is required of you," that bites even more, because now there is a turning from mere statement of fact to a call to responsibility. And now, suppose you decide to change your priorities because of this, to do certain things and speak to certain people in your life: this is a turning from detached reflection to committed response. These five turnings capture the heart of Existentialist thought. In this fivefold turning, for the first time in your life, your *self* appears, because it now *is*; it can appear only once it has come to *be*. Prior to that, you were a potential self, a putative self, a

24. For several illustrations I am indebted to Roger L. Shinn, *The Existentialist Posture* (New York: Association Press, 1959), 15–18.

semi-self, or a ghostly self, but you were never real. Only now, in this fivefold turning, have you become real.

When the Existentialists say that you were not real before this fivefold turning, they are not denying your facticity or actuality. There was always an actual you, weighing so many pounds, living in this or that place, member of a certain social class, and so on. These things are not nothing, but they are not *you*, they are not the *real* you, your self. Until this fivefold turning occurs, the real you has not appeared, because it has not yet been forged.

How one understands the foregoing hinges on whether one is a Christian (theistic) Existentialist or a secular (atheistic) Existentialist. From the point of view of biblical theology, fallen human beings are nevertheless human; they have not become something less than human, or some other kind of creature. But there is something grossly defective about the fallen human being. The image of God in which we were created can never be forfeited or effaced, but it can be tarnished, and it can be defaced. Every fallen human being is made in the likeness and image of God, but that image is so pathetically defaced that it provides no transparent insight into God's nature. My brother is made in the image and likeness of God, and that image cannot be forfeited; therefore I have no excuse for ever treating him as less than fully human. But the image of God in him is not evident, and in that sense one might describe it as "nothing"; it does not correspond to the reality it is intended to reflect. There is a recognition in Christian Existentialism that, while no human being is a nothing, we become our real self—we find our real identity—only in the act of abandoning that self to Christ in radical commitment.[25]

Threats to Selfhood

Existentialists are keenly aware of threats to selfhood. One such threat

---

25. C.S. Lewis' discussion of hell gives an insight into the Christian notion of selfhood, or lack of selfhood. He talks about hell as the state wherein one becomes radically depersonalized—not psychologically, in the sense that one *feels* depersonalized, but in an ontic sense, so that one exists somehow only as a subperson in a sort of shadowy existence. See C.S. Lewis, *The Great Divorce* (Glasgow: Fontana Books, 1972).

is the common identification of human beings as machines, as neurologically programmed. The growing edge of psychology today is neuropsychology, which often risks reducing psychological states and events to neurological impulses in the brain by a sort of neurobiological determinism. If this is the last word about the human, then we are mechanistically determined, whether we like to think so or not. This understanding is reflected in the current aim of technological innovation to approximate ever more closely the thinking and decision-making of a human being. If, to all intents and purposes, we are machines, what is the self?

Another threat to selfhood is our tendency to seek comfort above all else. A great deal of so-called common sense is mere comfort-seeking. What people mean when they say, "Well, it only stands to reason..." is that we understand the behaviour of anybody who promotes her own comfort, and find irrational the behaviour of someone who is not preoccupied with her own comfort. If we are fundamentally comfort-seekers, there is no place for guilt, anguish, or sacrifice, whereas these things are key to what Existentialism is finally all about: they are the furnace in which the self is forged.

Yet another threat to selfhood is the view of the human as commodity, as a thing that supplies labour to the process of production, rather than as a person who labours. We all recognize Karl Marx as the thinker who most notably exposed this threat. Marx thought that, prior to the revolution, people exist in a kind of subhuman, shadowy state, thoroughly determined by their capitalistic overlords, and that only through revolutionary activity do they become selves. He maintained that by collapsing ourselves into our labour, we reify, objectify, or "thingify" ourselves, so that we become depersonalized and alienated from ourselves. And once reified and self-alienated, we can become a self only through radical commitment to the revolution. Marx was not considered an Existentialist thinker, but there is enough overlap to conclude that he is at least a semi-Existentialist: certainly he shares Existentialism's criticism of Hegel.

Then there is the view of humans as animals. There is more than a little truth to this view. In the biblical story of Creation, human beings and warm-blooded animals are made on the same day; they are both "sixth-day creatures," as it were. Moreover, we are not the only creatures whom God loves, because God also loves the animals; he protects them and provides for them. If it is not the love of God that distinguishes human beings from animals, what does? According to Scripture, it is the *address* of God: everywhere in the Bible, human beings are the only creatures to whom God speaks. We are the only creature to whom God relates via *word*. We do not know how he relates to the other animals, but he relates to humans by means of word, and pre-eminently in the Word become flesh.

There are very significant commonalities between animal psychology and human psychology. Those who think they are wonderfully superior to the beasts do not know whereof they speak; they are denying their own creatureliness. If we are deprived of certain physical requirements, for example, we become very suggestible—a fact exploited by cults in their methods of indoctrination. People who are kept hungry or denied access to the toilet will believe anything they are told, and people who are not allowed to sleep will soon lose their ability to think properly. Casinos commonly do not have windows, so that patrons cannot see when it is getting late; they continue to gamble, because they lose their sense of the passage of time. The air is superoxygenated, keeping everyone unnaturally alert so that there are no bodily cues (such as fatigue) to tell them they should stop gambling and return home. In short, we are biologically influenced to an extent that is easily taken advantage of.

Some people use this commonality as grounds for declaring that we are no more than animals, but that is not true from a Christian perspective. Christians and theists would say that human beings differ from animals in that we are made in the image of God and are the recipients of God's address. Existentialists who are not theists would say that we are distinguished by our self-consciousness, which gives us the capacity for reflection and abstraction. An animal has consciousness, but it does not have the neural complexity that supports self-consciousness. It may even be able to recognize words of human language: the most intelligent dog has a vocabulary of about 200 words, but they are all words that pertain to things in its immediate environment, like *slipper*, *newspaper*, *walk*, and *water*. A dog has no capacity for reflection or abstraction. The shift from consciousness to self-consciousness is huge, and for many Existentialists, it is in that shift from consciousness to self-consciousness that human uniqueness lies.[26] The Christian, while acknowledging the uniqueness of human self-consciousness, would say that the image of God in us cannot be reduced without remainder to self-consciousness; rather, self-consciousness is a precipitate or predicate of God's address to us.

Theistic and Atheistic Expressions of Existentialism

All theistic Existentialists insist on a distinction between religion and faith. Kierkegaard presses this point tirelessly. In the Bible, the prophet Elijah stands on Mount Carmel with the priests of Baal. He does not see the encounter as a contest of religions, the religion of Baal versus the religion of Yahweh, as if they were two things of the same order. Rather, he proclaims to the priests of Baal that Yahweh is going to act in such a way as to expose their deity for the utter non-entity that it is.[27] Religion, says Karl Barth, is humankind's attempt to justify itself before an arbitrary and capricious god; it is what people do to try to stay on the good side of a deity they are not too sure about. Faith, on the other hand, is our knowledge that God of his own free grace has already justified us.[28] This is a crucial distinction.

Jewish Existentialist thinker Martin Buber declared that modernity is open to religion but closed to faith.[29] There is no difference between these two in the eyes of most people, including most people in church; but for theistic Existentialists there is every difference. Regardless of the place given to great statements of theology, faith occurs only at the level of trust or commitment. At the time of the Reformation, faith

26. Readers of Existentialist literature should be aware that it regularly uses the term *consciousness* to refer to self-consciousness.

27. See 1 Kings 18.

28. Karl Barth, *Church Dogmatics* Vol. I, Part 2 (Edinburgh: T&T Clark, 1970), section 17, *passim*.

29. Martin Buber, *Eclipse of God* (New York: Harper & Row, 1957), chapter 5.

was understood as understanding, assent, and trust—in Latin, *notitia*, *assensus*, and *fiducia*. First we must understand something of the gospel, however minimally; then we must say "Yes" to it, acknowledging that it is true. But then we must commit ourselves to it, abandon ourselves to it, and this is where faith really begins for both the Reformer[30] and the Existentialist. Of this *fiducia*, or trust, the biblical archetype in both testaments is Abraham. Abraham abandons himself to the God who is his only future, and for this reason Kierkegaard spends an enormous amount of time and thought on the example of Abraham.

Another way of understanding this is to notice the difference between faith as an act on our part and faith as content, the things we believe. The former is *fides qua creditur*, or that *by which* we believe—the act of believing, expressed as commitment and action. *Fides quae creditur* is *that which* we believe. What we believe is of course necessary for the act of believing, but it is never sufficient.

Objectivisms of every sort ask, What is truth? But Existentialism asks, Am I truth? Kierkegaard says that truth is "an objective uncertainty held fast in the appropriation process of the most passionate inwardness."[31] The "objective uncertainty" is God: there is no proof of him. But a Christian holds fast to this objective uncertainty in the most passionate inwardness. She will stake her life on the truth that God is and loves, even though she cannot prove it. That is what Kierkegaard means by "an objective uncertainty held fast in the appropriation process of the most passionate inwardness." Kierkegaard also says that faith is precisely the contradiction between that passion of the individual's inwardness and the objective uncertainty; your inwardness, recall, is your relationship to yourself before God, and that is everything for you when you have no proof of God at all.

30. Luther maintained, "Faith resides in the personal pronouns," by which he meant that as long as I say, "Jesus Christ is the Saviour of the world," I remain remote from the Kingdom. When I can say from my heart, "Jesus Christ is *my* Saviour," then I am a person of genuine faith. See, for instance, "A Meditation on Christ's Passion" in Timothy F. Lull, ed., *Martin Luther's Basic Theological Writings*, 3rd ed. (Minneapolis: Fortress Press, 2012).

31. Kierkegaard, *Concluding Unscientific Postscript*, 203. For a statement that is virtually identical see p. 611.

This passion, and this recognition of objective uncertainty, are something we need to recover as Christians. What Kierkegaard deplores under the name *Christianity* is virtually the same as Nietzsche's "death of God": both men contend that Christianity has reduced God to a laughingstock. Kierkegaard, a Lutheran, remained a Christian nevertheless, whereas Nietzsche, whose father and grandfather were Lutheran ministers, did not—if he ever was one.

In addition to theistic Existentialism, there is *atheistic* Existentialism. This category includes people like Sartre, Camus, Beauvoir, and Nietzsche. Given Sartre's philosophical agenda, God's existence would be no more significant than his non-existence, for if authenticity arises solely through self-commitment, my self-commitment will make me authentic whether God exists or not. However, says Sartre, a God of the kind Christians apparently believe in—namely, One who is infinite transcendence, omniscience, and omnipotence—must be repudiated, because such a God, in his towering, overwhelming objectivity, would denature the human person; that is, he would reduce every human being to a *thing*. Such a God would leave no room for humans, making human authenticity impossible. Therefore, he must be denied. Christians have little patience for this kind of talk, but atheistic Existentialists must be heard; they hold up the mirror to Christian deficits. Perhaps God is not as Christians have traditionally described him.

Cautions and Commendations

Existentialism has reclaimed the orientation that, when combined with the logic of Scripture, characterizes the best of philosophy in the tradition of Socrates—namely, its insistence on courage and commitment, without which humans are mere wraiths. Existentialism also reminds us of life's complexities, contradictions, and absurdities.

Moreover, Existentialism prompts us to a healthy re-examination of traditional statements about God. Luther said at the Heidelberg Disputation of 1518 that the classical God—the God posited and espoused by those not informed by the gospel of God's self-definition as Israel's crucified One—is indistinguishable from the devil.[32] How many people have we met who uphold what can only be a satanic deity? Someone suffers from a severe physical or mental disability, or a community is wiped out by natural disaster, and people attribute it to the will of God. Such attribution only slanders God. Consider, rather, the incident in Luke's gospel where Jesus comes upon a woman who has been bent double for eighteen years. By that time many people have undoubtedly told her that her infirmity is the will of God and she must come to terms with it. Jesus, however, hisses, "Satan has done this," and straightens her.[33] Existentialists remind us that no relationship can be had with a putative God who is sheer power, sovereignty, transcendence, and impassivity. Only in Jesus Christ is the God of the gospel knowable.

At the same time, Existentialism must be embraced prudently. In rejecting conformity, bad faith, mediocrity, and so on, Existentialism can readily become a pose. Rebellion, protest, and resistance can become ends in themselves, and since they depend on having something to oppose, they tend to become parasitic. Some people who embrace popular Existentialism imagine, ridiculously, that it makes no difference what we commit ourselves to, as long as we are committed. The history and vocabulary of Existentialism easily lend themselves to mindless faddishness.

In addition, its concern for selfhood must not become the occasion or legitimization of aggressive egocentricity, as though in pursuing authentic selfhood I had the right to violate you.

Moreover, the whole notion of freedom in Existentialism is highly problematic. For Christians, freedom is the removal of every impediment to acting in accord with one's true nature as a child of God. In other words, to be *free* is always to have been *freed*—freed for the service of God and neighbour. Atheists, however, maintain that freedom is the capacity for self-determination. What precisely is the Existentialist notion of freedom, and how defensible is it? To what extent can it be reconciled with a Christian understanding of freedom?

Also problematic is the notion that human decision alone creates the human ethical good. Theistic Existentialists would ask whether the good is synonymous with the godly.

---

32. Lull, *Martin Luther's Basic Theological Writings*, chapter 5.
33. Luke 13:17.

Some forms of Existentialism, seemingly unaware that we become selves only in the context of human relations, are so preoccupied with self that they lose sight of the community. Self and community are polar correlates; that is, as Paul Tillich maintains, the self exists only in correlation with the world or community, and it is only in polar relation to a self that the world is world as opposed to a chaotic mass.[34] In other words, self and world are essential to each other. Some Existentialists fail to recognize this; among Christian Existentialists, that failure manifests as a weak ecclesiology.

Finally, Existentialism rightly recognizes the assorted determinations to which human reasoning is subject. There is no such thing as "pure" reason, and many Christians who naïvely vest their confidence in that mythical entity need to be reminded that our reasoning is affected by the Fall. However, atheistic Existentialism fails to understand that faith is a rational, albeit not a rationalistic, event; it is a reasonable human act and activity. Brought about by grace, it restores the integrity of reason that was collapsed by the Fall. In other words, so far from being irrational, the exercise of faith is consummately rational in that grace, owned in faith, delivers reason from the assorted rationalizations and social determinations to which it is subject in the wake of the Fall.[35] Freud, Marx, and the French sociologist Michel Foucault all made similar observations about reason and rationalization. Foucault in particular has shown conclusively that what passes for sound reasoning in any society—that is, what is deemed common sense—is the mindset of those who have access to social power. In short, what we call *reasoning* is highly socially configured. Only God's grace, owned in faith, heals reason of its bondage to rationalization and restores its integrity.

What can we take away from this overview of Existentialism? Earlier we discussed the impossibility of direct communication of reality.

---

34. Paul Tillich, *Systematic Theology,* Vol. 1 (Chicago: University of Chicago Press, 1965), 168–171.

35. In the wake of the Fall, the structure of reason survives—we remain rational creatures, otherwise we would no longer be human—but the integrity of reasoning is compromised, with the result that much of what we call reasoning is rationalization. More will be said about this in subsequent chapters.

In view of that impossibility, we might think we have detected no little irony in the fact that Existentialists have themselves written reams—direct communication—on the forging of the self and on the necessity of self-commitment for knowledge of reality. Why, in that case, should we pay any attention to them, or give them any credence? What more do we know for listening to them, and how can we tell whether what they say is true? What meaning can it have for us who are only reading verbal descriptions at second hand? It may seem, in the end, that they have in effect failed to say anything significant. They would readily admit, however, that they cannot deliver what they are writing about. They are describing it, commending it, pointing to it, urging it; but by definition their writing cannot deliver it.

In this regard we do well to recall the situation where Jesus is confronted with the demand, "How long will you keep us in suspense? If you are the Christ, tell us plainly."[36] He refuses, however, to reply directly—not because he wants to worsen their suspense, but because the reality he is *cannot* be communicated directly. Those who abandon themselves to him at incalculable risk (What if he turns out to be mistaken, or a charlatan?) will find both him and themselves "real," while those refusing such commitment will never know who he is or who they are. Jesus, we must remember, never directly said, "The kingdom *is*…" Instead he testified indirectly, "The kingdom is *like*…"—a fine pearl or a treasure hidden in a field, for which we give up everything to gain what can be possessed, cherished, and commended, but never conveyed.[37]

36. John 10:24.
37. Matthew 13:44–45.

2

Georg Wilhelm Friedrich Hegel: Dialectic

Introduction

Hegel is a philosopher many find extraordinarily difficult; for this reason he presents a particular challenge as the first one to be explored in this book. It is essential, however, to grasp the basic content of his thought in order to understand the Existentialists who subsequently reacted against him. To facilitate an elemental understanding of the philosophy of Hegel, this chapter will approach it from several vantage points, each of which will overlap with the others.

By way of introduction, it behooves us to examine the history and current use of the term *dialectic*, since it is probably the one that collocates most frequently with Hegel's name and is most often used to encapsulate his philosophy. Traditionally, dialectic referred to an argumentative exchange involving contradiction, or a method of discourse involving such exchanges. In Plato's era, dialectic meant beginning with one's opponent's premises only to derive conclusions that were contrary to one's opponent's; in other words, dialectic was the art of logical refutation. With Aristotle, the meaning of dialectic shifted slightly; while it was still a method of argumentation, it contrasted with demonstration in that it did not constitute an attempt to prove something scientifically or deductively. Dialectical argument nevertheless had to be sound, unlike sophistical arguments (deliberate attempts to bamboozle through specious reasoning) or eristic arguments (browbeating, or aiming at victory rather than truth).

Hegel's use of dialectic, on the other hand, was unique and referred to a specific formal structure involving the pattern of thesis, antithesis, and synthesis. It is a recurring pattern in which two contrary conditions or statements are taken up together into a higher one that both preserves and overcomes the contrast. Moreover, for Hegel this structure was not restricted to sets of ideas but was considered instead to characterize actual historical processes. In other words, the term *dialectic* moved from a *logical* notion of contradiction to a *metaphysical* notion of forces and counterforces, and from a method of *argument* to a theory of *history*: for Hegel, dialectic is the historical process of the development of "Spirit" or "Mind," or what he calls the "Absolute" or the "Idea."

The terms *Absolute*, *Idea*, and *Mind* are all synonyms in Hegel's vocabulary, and may be better terms to use than *Spirit* in view of the Christian tendency to associate that term with the Holy Spirit; Hegel uses it to mean something different from the third Person of the Trinity. He also uses the term *God* without ever quite meaning what Christian faith means by it, even though he was trained as a Lutheran clergyman. Later we will see, for example, that the radical transcendence of God, which Scripture everywhere attests, disappears in Hegel's dialectical philosophy—for the simple reason that a God who is utterly distinct from the creation is, by definition, limited by that from which he is distinct. To be truly infinite, argues Hegel, God must include both himself *and* the creation, infinite *and* finite—whereupon the notion of the radical transcendence of God (bedrock for biblical faith) is forfeited.

By the same token, Hegel uses the term *Idea* with a different meaning from the one it has in everyday usage. When we use the word *idea* (with a lower-case *i*), we normally have in mind an idea *of something*, presupposing a subject-object distinction: a person has in her head a specific idea about something on which she is reflecting. In Hegel's philosophy, however, by the time the dialectical process reaches the level of "Idea" (with upper-case *i*), the distinction between subject and object is overcome. "Idea" is not a subject's thought about an object; rather, it is thought thinking itself. At that point, "idea" in the usual sense disappears.

Other philosophers have offered a variety of responses to Hegel's dialectical system. Marx, for instance—as we saw in chapter 1—insisted that dialectic pertains to matter, not to Spirit, and that history is driven by the dialectical laws of materialism, not by the development or dialectic of absolute Mind "othering" itself in nature and returning to itself or realizing itself as Spirit. Kierkegaard, who is the progenitor of Existentialism, denied dialectic as understood by both Hegel and Marx, announcing instead, "Truth is subjectivity."[1] We must distinguish carefully here between subjectivity and subjectiv*ism*, a crucial distinction that will be explored thoroughly when we come to Kierkegaard; for now, let us say that subjectiv*ism* is the claim that each subject (or person) determines in her own mind what constitutes truth *for her*, without reference to anything outside herself. Subjectivism shades into sheer fantasy or wishful thinking. Subjectivity, on the other hand, in the context of Kierkegaard's claim, refers to an attitude or posture of self-investment or commitment on the part of the existing individual or subject, without which there can be no apprehension of truth.[2]

Hegel has two main concerns: the content of reality (that is, Spirit or Mind), and the method by which reality operates (dialectic). Note once again that dialectic is the operation of *reality*, not merely a mental process. It is the operation of mental process and historical process combined, in a concept that is unique to Hegel.

Ultimate reality, for Hegel, is Spirit, but not as an exclusive or monistic reality: Hegel never denies the reality of matter or material things. If he did, he would be leaving us with two one-sided assertions: one made by those who affirm the reality of matter and another made

---

1. See *Concluding Unscientific Postscript to Philosophical Fragments,* Vol. 1, ed. and trans. Howard V. Hong and Edna H. Hong (Princeton: Princeton University Press, 1992), chapter 2.

2. According to Kierkegaard, there is an apprehension of truth that we never gain as long as we are viewing truth with objective or scientific detachment. Theology as an academic discipline, for example, takes the stance of detachment (for the sake of reflection and assessment), putting forward propositions for intellectual analysis, comprehension, and evaluation. Faith, on the other hand, a radical commitment, has the posture or attitude of immediacy and is a living apprehension, on the part of our person, of the *Person* (not the idea or the doctrine) of Jesus Christ. Interestingly enough, despite the fact that Kierkegaard was a Christian, his notion that "Truth is subjectivity"—the notion that there is a being-in-truth on the part of those who truly *exist* as opposed to those who merely assess or evaluate or deliberate—had its greatest influence on atheist Existentialists in the twentieth century.

by those who affirm the reality of mind, or the affirmation of both by the same person with no relation or integration of the two. Rather, Hegel insists that "the truth is the whole"; therefore the truth must finally comprehend both mind *and* empirical reality. Moreover, he really does mean *both*—he is not thinking of a simplistic one-sidedness in which there is ultimately only mind, or only matter, and that one can be collapsed into the other so that they are understood as fundamentally the same thing and only *seem* different. He would disagree vehemently, for instance, with those today who would say that mind is reducible without remainder to brain, or that mind is no more than the off-scouring or exhaust fumes of electrical synaptic firings in our heads—a view known in philosophy as epiphenomenalism. On the other hand, he would disagree equally with those who would collapse all of nature into mind as the solipsists do, claiming that mind and ideas are the only reality there is. Both the solipsists and the epiphenomenalists, Hegel would say, are operating in a "night in which all cows are black," a way of seeing constituted by their own assumption that there is only one kind of thing, so that everything appears to them to be of that kind.[3] We must preserve both realities, Hegel insists, but without leaving them standing over against each other forever. We must preserve them both forever even as we transcend the mind-nature distinction (or the subject-object distinction), or else the truth is not the whole; as long as the alleged truth consists of two one-sided assertions, we are not at the truth yet. The truth is thesis, antithesis, *and* their synthesis.[4]

Within this truth-as-a-whole, Hegel claims, both Idealism and Realism are also preserved; here, however, he ultimately gives primacy to Idealism, insisting that true Idealism *entails* the truth of Realism. While Realism asserts that objects exist independently of our experience or knowledge of them and have properties independent of the concepts and language we use to understand and describe them, Idealism is the notion that reality is *not* independent of cognizing minds, but is mind-

3. Solipsism is, of course, logically defensible. When I see something in front of me, there is no proof that the image on the retina of my eye corresponds to an object in reality and is not a product of my imagination.

4. We will see below how this dialectic operates in Hegel's understanding of God's infinity.

correlative or mind-coordinated;[5] that is, one depends on the other in the way that right depends on left, or south on north. Ultimately, Hegel subscribes to Idealism in the sense that he posits the metaphysical *priority* of mind as opposed to the priority of nature; nevertheless, he will say that both mind and nature must be recognized and preserved—and their disjunction finally transcended in Absolute Mind or Idea.

There is a tendency among some Christians to make a quick translation from Hegel's metaphysics into the terms of biblical theology: Hegel's "Mind" is the Creator, they think, and his "nature," the creation. However, the God whom Scripture attests as Creator will always be radically, ontologically distinct from his creation, whereas for Hegel this distinctness is a penultimate position; the ultimate position must somehow eliminate or overcome all disjunctions in the universe, including that between Creator and creation. Despite this fundamental contrast between Hegel's philosophy and biblical theology, however, Hegel has had a significant influence on theology.[6]

Since Hegel insists that all one-sidedness must be opposed, meaning that nothing can simply be destroyed or left behind, his dialectic is not a simple linear progression from one thing to another. As the dialectic effects a higher unity (or synthesis) of a given thing and its contradiction (a thesis and its antithesis), that higher unity gathers up and *preserves* the contradictory elements it transcends. Given this understanding, we recognize that the contradictory elements, the "thesis" and "antithesis" of which Hegel speaks, are not contradictory in the sense of mutually exclusive; rather, the contradictory elements are essential "moments" of a process towards a higher unity.[7]

We can gain an understanding of Hegel here by reflecting on being. The concept of pure being, apart from any actual finite being, is

5. See Robert Audi, ed., *The Cambridge Dictionary of Philosophy,* 2nd ed. (Cambridge: Cambridge University Press, 1999), 412.

6. The ghost of Hegelianism lurks, for example, in the panentheistic theology of Wolfhart Pannenberg, one of Europe's most important theologians.

7. A logician might say that what Hegel calls "contradictory" things are actually subcontrary. In logic, two propositions are contradictory when the falsehood of one entails the truth of the other, and vice versa; two subcontrary propositions, on the other hand, can both be true, but they cannot both be false. Technically, Hegel's thesis and antithesis are in that relation.

wholly indeterminate; we cannot predicate anything of it. We can say or think things about specific beings, but if we try to think of pure being without any determination at all, we find that we are in fact thinking of nothing. In other words, the concept of wholly indeterminate being passes into the concept of non-being; the mind passes back and forth between being and non-being, as each disappears into its opposite. Now, the *truth* of being and non-being, Hegel maintains, is this *movement,* that is, this immediate disappearance of the one into the other. Thus the emergence of contradiction—in this case, the contradiction between being and non-being—is the power or force of the dialectical movement that drives it towards synthesis. And the synthesis of being and non-being is *becoming.* Becoming preserves the truth of being and non-being while moving beyond an otherwise endless alternation between being, negation of being, negation of the negation, and so on. In short, the concept of the Absolute as *being* is actually the concept of the Absolute as *becoming*, or the Absolute as a process of self-development.

Consider the implications of what Hegel is saying with respect to understanding and thinking. In his view, understanding is static and takes something as given, fixed, or limited. Thinking, on the other hand, is a moving activity that begins with this simple acceptance of the given, whereupon dialectic exposes the limited truth involved in that acceptance. Everything in the world, Hegel maintains, involves opposed and contradictory aspects, and this contradiction is not merely apparent or accidental, but real and necessary: contradiction is the motive force of the world. While the understanding that takes something as given is conservative, the dialectic of thought is a perpetual revolution that unfixes things by introducing or acknowledging contradiction.

Now, clearly we can agree with Hegel that nothing in our experience is stable; however, if there were just these two phases—understanding something as given, and recognizing its contradiction—philosophy would only be an endless revolutionary activity: there would only be something and its contradiction, in perpetuity. Instead, the dialectic points to a third thing beyond itself, which is *speculative thought.* By this Hegel does not mean guesswork, which is what we normally associate with the word *speculative*; rather, "speculation" names a metaphysical principle according to which philosophical thought gathers up and transcends the contradictions at lower levels of thought, preserving them and synthesizing them in a higher unity. The harmonies of speculative thought do not reject the disharmonies of dialectical thought; the overcoming of these disharmonies must entail their preservation, so that nothing is left out.

Consider another illustration: the progression in human apprehension from sense-certainty to perception to consciousness to self-consciousness, a progression Hegel covers in *The Phenomenology of Spirit*.[8] He begins with the lowest level, "sense-certainty," and then builds on it dialectically until he comes to what he calls the "absolute standpoint," which is Absolute Mind or Idea. Sense-certainty, the first stage, is the level at which an infant operates. It is the primary experience of something in our environment: raw, uninterpreted sense data. If, for instance, a rattle is dangled in front of a baby, the baby does not recognize it as a rattle, because that step already involves interpretation; rather, there is simply something that fills the baby's horizon of vision, and there is a sound that fills the baby's ears. Hegel calls this "sense-certainty." It can be described as a "blooming, buzzing confusion,"[9] and perhaps it is, for a baby. But then as the baby matures, and a thing persists in its experience long enough for language to be applicable, "perception" arises: the child sees an apple and thinks or says, "apple." Perception retains the immediacy of sense-certainty (bigness, redness) and adds the discovery of an opposition between the self and other things and people: once the baby can point to an apple and say "apple," she knows that the apple is external to herself. A distinction has arisen between the self and objects, and the ability to make that distinction is called "consciousness."

---

8. Hegel wrote in German, where the word *Geist* means both *spirit* and *mind*, like *esprit* in French; it has no exact translation in English. The title of the book in question is therefore sometimes rendered *The Phenomenology of Mind*, but neither rendering quite captures Hegel's intent. The word *mind* is too one-sidedly cerebral, and the word *spirit* too one-sidedly religious or pseudo-religious. I use both *mind* and *spirit* to refer to what Hegel meant by *Geist*.

9. The famous phrase, variously attributed to Immanuel Kant and William James, is sometimes cited as "booming, buzzing confusion."

Later still, the child distinguishes between herself as person and the person of a sibling or parent or friend, and "self-consciousness" arises. (There is a difference between the self as subject over against an object, and the self as subject over against another subject; only the recognition of the latter constitutes self-consciousness.) Finally, as the child grows up, she realizes that the self can reflect on itself, and indeed on its own reflecting; there is now a new and higher level of self-consciousness.

Note that the movement from consciousness to self-consciousness entails not only the distinction between self and other, but also the recognition of the self by another self: there must be a reciprocal recognition of self and other, because self-consciousness that is never acknowledged by another ultimately fails as self-consciousness. If this is the case, then we can say that self-consciousness always presupposes what is *distinct* and yet *not distinct*, in exactly the following sense: my self-consciousness presupposes recognition of another self distinct from me and recognizing me in turn, yet insofar as my self-consciousness cannot do without recognition from that other self, that other's self-consciousness is an aspect of my own. Here we see Hegel's dialectical thinking: one self-consciousness stands in opposition to another's self-consciousness, yet gathers that other self-consciousness up into itself even while preserving it.[10]

We will see later that self-consciousness in turn rises and rises until it reaches the standpoint of the Absolute (Mind, Idea, or Spirit). The Absolute is *a self-consciousness thinking only itself*, because at this level even the distinction between self-consciousness and the self whose consciousness it is has been transcended and the two are now one. In other words, the self-consciousness of the Absolute and an individual's finite self-consciousness are ultimately one: the Absolute gathers up the finite self-consciousness into itself, and yet preserves it. Hegel is claiming

10. Whether we agree or disagree with Hegel on this particular point depends on the meaning we give to the self, and the manner in which self-consciousness is required for selfhood. For Kierkegaard, as we will see, the self is ultimately a self-choosing; for other Existentialists, a self-making. For Marx, the self arises only as revolutionary activity is undertaken; apart from revolutionary commitment, "self" is mere projection. According to Marx, God, or divine selfhood, is always mere projection.

that it is possible for a human being, in her finite self-consciousness, to rise metaphysically so that her consciousness is fused with the Cosmic Mind knowing itself. More will be said about this below.

Lordship and Bondage

Introductory Comment: Hegel and Christianity

Hegel's *Phenomenology of Mind* contains a chapter entitled "Lordship and Bondage" in which he describes one phase of the rise of the self-consciousness towards the standpoint of the Absolute. It is one of the earlier phases of that ascent, and involves the complex interplay of consciousness and self-consciousness, of "master" and "slave." Hegel's account of this interplay is subtle and profound, and an excellent example both of his philosophical writing and of his dialectic. It also brings to light some important ways in which Hegel diverges from biblical Christianity.

Before examining it, however, I want to draw attention to an introductory summative statement by Allen and Springsted, the editors of one edition of "Lordship and Bondage"; it is a statement that encapsulates the logic inherent in Hegel's thought and so provides a context for detailed study.

"Hegel is best-known for his development of a dialectical method in which reality is understood as the historical manifestation of a realization of the Absolute,"[11] the editors assert. Here we are told in a few words what Hegel conceives reality to be. And that is, after all, the central question for any philosophy: What is reality? For Empiricists, reality is sticks and stones and asphalt—things we perceive with the senses. For the prophets and apostles, sticks and stones are *actual* in that they are not imaginary or mythological, but they are not *real*; reality, for the apostles and prophets, is the effectual presence and power of the Holy One of Israel. Hegel's understanding of reality differs from both of these views: reality, for Hegel, is a *process*.

There are three aspects of this process. First, the Absolute as Idea

---

11. Diogenes Allen and Eric O. Springsted, eds., *Primary Readings in Philosophy for Understanding Theology* (Louisville: Westminster John Knox Press, 1992), 210.

"others itself" in nature. This is how Hegel accounts for actualities such as apples and oranges and sticks and stones, which he recognizes are not Absolute Spirit: they are the result of the Absolute "othering itself." (We must avoid thinking of this process as the Absolute creating, because the word *create* presupposes a specific biblical logic that is foreign to Hegel.) This notion of the Absolute "othering itself" comes from pre-Socratic Greek philosophy, especially Parmenides, who was the first Greek philosopher to speak of Being-as-such, as opposed to particular beings—infinite Being as the ground of finite beings. However, whereas Parmenides distinguished between Being and beings, Hegel dissolves this distinction in the same way that he dissolves the radical distinction between God and the universe: by arguing that the infinite, if it is to be truly infinite and hence not limited by something it is not, must include the finite. Ultimately, Being is what *is*; therefore, argues Hegel, Absolute Being, infinite Being, must comprise *all* that is, *including* finite beings.

In the second aspect of the process, after the Absolute has "othered itself" in nature, humankind emerges out of nature. Humankind is distinct from the animals and the rest of nature by virtue of the fact that human beings have a history, while other creatures do not: they simply live and die. And it is this history that is the third aspect of the process: history is not merely a chance sequence of events, but the gathering up and overcoming of contradictions as the Absolute manifests itself on the way to its self-realization as Spirit. Recall that by "contradictions" Hegel means not logical contradictions or mutually exclusive propositions, but *entities* that are in opposition or contradistinction to one another; we will see, in "Lordship and Bondage," that among the contradictions gathered up and overcome in the Absolute's self-realization are the opposition between slave and master, the opposition between slave and master within the same individual, and the distinction between self-consciousness and Ultimate Mind.

"The relation between master and slave represents one stage in the growth of human consciousness from its most primitive state toward the realization of its affinity with the Absolute,"[12] assert the editors in the same introduction. Note, first of all, that what is meant by "human

12. Ibid.

consciousness [in] its most primitive state" is not yet self-consciousness; as we saw in our brief outline of how a baby comes to distinguish between itself and other things and people, self-consciousness is a higher stage. Second, according to Allen and Springsted in the above quotation, self-consciousness as conceived by Hegel eventually realizes its "affinity with the Absolute." But "affinity with the Absolute" seems a rather attenuated version of Hegel's thought on the subject; I maintain that what Hegel envisions is much more than mere affinity. His claim is that the self-consciousness (of the philosopher, at least) realizes a *union* with the Absolute. In other words, at the level of philosophical thought—a perspective higher even than that of religion—my self-consciousness *is* or at least is *one with* the self-consciousness of the Absolute. So it would seem that Allen and Springsted have weakened Hegel's claim considerably.

In a similar attenuation, they go on to describe Hegel as favourably disposed towards Christianity: "Unlike many of the writers of the Enlightenment, Hegel was highly sympathetic toward religion, and in particular Christianity. His immediate philosophic predecessors, for example Kant, reduced Christianity to moral teachings. Hegel however, treated the doctrine of the person of Christ as the God-man and the doctrine of the Trinity with a certain respect."[13] Leaving aside the imprecision of the expression "treat [a doctrine] with a certain respect," and the fact that it invokes a category outside philosophical discourse, it is more than a little misleading to say that Hegel treats those central Christian doctrines with "respect." What the editors mean is that Hegel had a place in his system of thought for the Christian doctrines of the Incarnation and Trinity, but only when reinterpreted as an aspect of the Absolute's knowing itself. When Hegel speaks of the Incarnation, he does not mean what Christians mean by it. For Hegel, who argues that (in order to be truly infinite) the infinite must include the finite while preserving the distinction between finite and infinite, the Incarnation is simply a pictorial representation of that philosophical truth: the togetherness of the infinite and the finite. Similarly, for Hegel the Trinity as affirmed by Christians is merely an illustration of the

13. Ibid.

simultaneous distinctness and yet interdependence of the self-consciousness of one self and another self; it is the pictorial representation of that philosophical truth.

This idea of pictorial representation is crucial, because it is Hegel's approach to the Christian faith in a nutshell: the things affirmed by the Christian faith are for him only an illustration or symbol of a truth that transcends them, a greater Truth which is the Absolute knowing itself as pure self—thought thinking itself. Hence the Incarnation and Trinity are always penultimate for Hegel, and in his system it is only people who lack philosophical ability who remain fixed at the stage of such pictorial representations. After all, he recognizes, not everybody is capable of metaphysical thought; some people need a "picture book." If they possessed greater philosophical ability, they would recognize the higher Truth lying behind the symbol or illustration, and the latter would become superfluous for them.

From a biblical perspective, however, there is nothing penultimate about the Incarnation, and no higher truth beyond it: it is the ultimate incursion of God into human history and human affairs. And the Trinity, from a biblical perspective, is not a pictorial representation of a philosophical truth lying behind it or above it; rather, the doctrine of the Trinity describes the eternal inner life of God himself. It does so imperfectly, because like any doctrine it is a human construct and can be improved on; but we affirm it as an adequate if imperfect description of the personal and relational nature of that God who is eternally self-existent. The point here is that Hegel's understanding of the Christian faith must never be confused with the apostles' understanding, and Hegel's God is not the same as the Holy One of Israel.

Like most metaphysics, Hegel's philosophy is not without vulnerabilities, a major one being the problem of evil. Hegel maintains that evil is rooted in finitude; evil is overcome, he claims, as finitude is gathered up into the infinite. There are serious problems, from a biblical perspective, with this way of thinking. To begin with, the identification of finitude with evil does not accord at all with Scripture, which affirms that the finite creation comes from the hand of the Creator as sheer good gift. Evil is a corruption of the finite; it is not synonymous with the finite. Moreover, if evil is an aspect of the good realizing itself, then it is good-on-the-way, good in embryonic form, or a condition of the good; it is a necessary element of the dialectical process of history, and in that case it is no longer evil. A latent good is itself good. Existentialist philosophers maintain that all metaphysical systems fail at this point, including Hegel's. Nevertheless, the notion that evil is an unpleasant but necessary aspect of the good has trickled down and embedded itself in popular thinking, and the result is a legitimation of evil and a failure to recognize radical evil for what it is.

Historically, the church has sometimes spoken of evil as a privation or absence of good; such a description, however, fails to capture the malignant power of evil. Here we return to the notion of a "nothing" that is something. A mere ontological privative or negative, the mere absence of good, is not the destructive cosmic power against which God has set his face and the defeat of which cost him his Son. While Scripture never informs us of the source of evil, it does face the existence of evil head-on, does not equivocate about it, and does not allow us to blame God for it.

Despite this problem in Hegel (found in any attempt to forge a metaphysically comprehensive system), there are nonetheless glorious profundities in his writing—among them his exploration, in "Lordship and Bondage," of consciousness and self-consciousness, and of the master–slave dialectic. To see the accuracy of Hegel's master–slave dialectic as it unfolds in the world we need only look at the history of African-Americans: how it came about that the white enslavers were themselves enslaved, while black people arrived at a self-consciousness and identity and dignity that the slave-owner had long since forfeited; how the slave-owner began by inculcating fear in the slave, but ended by fearing the slave's revolt.

The dialectical relationship between self and other

We are now ready to work our way from this background through the actual text of "Lordship and Bondage"—starting with a recapitulation, in Paragraph 178, of what we have observed about the dialectical relationship between self and other in self-consciousness: "Self-consciousness exists in and for itself only insofar as it exists in and for another; that is, it exists only in being acknowledged."[14] In order properly to be aware of myself, says Hegel, I need you to be aware of me. If you withhold your recognition from me, my own selfhood is threatened. In other words, self-consciousness presupposes what is distinct and yet not distinct: the other self is distinct from me, yet essential to my self and therefore in some sense an aspect of my self.

We can easily understand how this operates. If, for example, I were to come into a room with people in it and ask, "How are you folks today?" and no one looked in my direction or smiled or spoke, I would find it most disconcerting. If I continued to try to engage any of the people and got no response whatever, I would soon begin to suspect myself: I would wonder whether I were sane, or having a dream, or hallucinating. Every day, at every moment, the preservation of my selfhood depends on you as a self acknowledging me as a self.

In the subsequent paragraphs, Hegel develops this dialectic. "First, [the self] must supersede the *other* independent being in order thereby to become certain of *itself* as the essential being; secondly, in doing so it proceeds to supersede its *own* self, for this other is itself,"[15] he writes. But as he goes on to explain, by this act of superseding the other and hence also itself, the self is returned to itself; having seen itself in the other, it returns to itself and thereby lets the other go free.

In other words, I look to you to recognize me, since your recognition of me is essential to my self-awareness; but in so doing I reduce you to an instrument of my own self-awareness, an object, and thereby lose you again as a self who can recognize me, and hence lose myself; but at the same time, once you have recognized me, I am assured that I am a self after all, and can let you go free, at least for the time being. Meanwhile, the same is true of you: you become aware of your self through my recognition of you as a self. In fact, because your self-consciousness is essential to mine, I *must* recognize you as a self, meaning that your self is not a thing I can exploit. You cannot be to me as a stick or stone or other object, because an object lacks self-consciousness

14. Ibid.
15. Ibid., 181.

and therefore cannot affirm me in my selfhood. I need you to be a self who recognizes me, and in order for you to be that self, I must also recognize you. These two aspects of our interdependence—superseding each other so that we lose each other and each other's recognition, as well as recognizing and being recognized by each other so as to receive our self from each other—are happening at the same time, as a constant movement back and forth whose outcome, continually renewed, is our self-consciousness. This is the nature of Hegelian dialectic.

In Paragraph 184 we come across typical Hegelian vocabulary: "The self is at once aware that it is and that it is not another consciousness," he asserts. That is, I am aware that I am not you, and at the same time aware that as long as you are essential to me, there is a sense in which you *are* me. Hegel goes on to observe that the self can be *for itself*, existing in its own right, only when it supersedes itself as being for itself—that is, only when it transcends itself. Each self mediates itself through the other self; at the same time, insofar as the self by means of this process comes to exist *for itself*, the self is an immediate (that is, unmediated) being. Here is yet another dialectical conclusion typical of Hegel: he is describing the self as both mediated and immediate. My self is mediated by you in that I need your self-consciousness to acknowledge me in mine, and if you withhold this acknowledgment my sense of self will disappear; nonetheless, the self which is thus mediated to me by you is immediate in the sense that I am aware of myself not by means of deduction or inference, but immediately, here and now, as myself. And once again, the same is true in the other direction: your self is mediated to you by me and yet immediate to you in just the same way.

Then in Paragraph 187 we get to the first hint of the master–slave dialectic as it arises out of the dialectic of self and other. Hegel claims that although I need you to be a subject and not an object, so that you can be a self and recognize me, I am never satisfied with that. You are standing over against me, and I feel the need to assert myself as a self over against your self. In so doing, says Hegel, I objectify you; in some sense, if I am a subject, then you must be an object. I act on you, and in so doing I "slay" you—at the risk of my own self, I might add, since I need your selfhood to affirm my own. At the same time, you as a subject resist my objectification of you, and assert your self over against my self. At this point, says Hegel, we are engaged in what may be called a "prestige battle": who will blink first? "Thus the relation of the two self-conscious individuals is such that they prove themselves and each other through a life-and-death struggle," he explains. "They must engage in this struggle, for they must raise their certainty of being for themselves to truth, both in the case of the other and in their own case. And it is only through staking one's life that freedom is won."[16] I act on you; you act on me. I attempt to objectify you; you attempt to objectify me. The strange thing about it is that each of us needs the other to be a subject in order that the other may acknowledge him—because our self-consciousness depends on that acknowledgment—and yet here we are, attempting to slay one another in order to assert our independent self-consciousness. But until I risk myself in this struggle with another self, insists Hegel, I have not attained to my truth or reality as a self-consciousness. If I refuse to risk myself, what I have preserved is scarcely worth calling a self.

Out of this life-and-death struggle, continues Hegel in Paragraph 189, there emerges an inequality: there is now (1) a "pure self-consciousness" as well as (2) "a consciousness which is not purely for itself but for another." Each of these two is essential to the other. At this stage "they exist as two opposed shapes of consciousness; one is the independent consciousness whose essential nature is to be for itself, the other is the dependent consciousness whose essential nature is simply to live or to be for another. The former is lord, the other is bondsman."[17] In other words, as I emerge victorious from this struggle having "slain" you, your self-consciousness has been un-selfed, and now exists for *me* rather than for itself. *My* self-consciousness exists for me, and now *your* self-consciousness exists for me, too. In that sense, then, I have made you my slave or "bondsman," and I have become your master or "lord."

In such a master–slave relation, the master's independent consciousness is mediated through the dependent consciousness of the slave. As Hegel explains in Paragraph 190, the slave's whole existence

16. Ibid., 213.
17. Ibid., 214.

is to work on things—material objects such as stones and plants and so on—and therefore his self-consciousness is largely dependent on those things. To the extent that the slave's consciousness is dependent on *things*, it becomes itself a thing: the slave's consciousness is objectified. This objectification is what keeps him a slave. On the one hand, then, it is the master who has enslaved him, but now the slave comes to perceive himself as a slave, and to that extent is making himself a slave. The master's consciousness, meanwhile, is mediated through the consciousness of the slave, so that he relates to the slave as a thing and also relates to other things through the slave.

It may be easier to understand these complex relationships if we illustrate them by an example. Consider the African-American slave in the Deep South. His entire existence is picking cotton in the cotton fields all day long; he relates only to cotton. The master or plantation owner, on the other hand, does not go out and pick cotton. He has nothing to do with cotton itself, and has no use for it; he cares only about the wealth that the cotton brings him. Hence he never relates to the cotton directly, but only to the slave, and to the cotton only *through* the slave. The slave he regards as a thing also, a mere tool or instrument like the cotton, and in so doing "annihilates" the slave as a self-consciousness. The slave, however, cannot "annihilate" the cotton he works on; he cannot avoid working on it. His existence and consciousness are so wrapped up in the cotton that he himself becomes objectified, like the cotton, and therefore alienated from himself. He ceases to exist as a person.

Now, while the slave must work on the cotton as willed by the plantation owner, the plantation owner enjoys the wealth afforded him by the cotton. In other words, the plantation owner is master not only of the slave but of the cotton as well. He has "annihilated" the cotton as cotton, because its cotton-ness *per se* is nothing to him; it is nothing but a source of wealth to him. The slave, by contrast, is never lord over anything. The more he works on the cotton, the more he knows he will never be free of it and that it will never be anything but cotton to him. He cannot "annihilate" it; the cotton will always be something he must work on. And he himself will always exist only as an object for the master.

In this way, Hegel argues in Paragraph 191, the master achieves recognition through another consciousness—namely, the slave's. Moreover, in this process not only is the slave objectified by the master, but the slave comes to objectify himself as well. That is the worst feature of slavery: in being reduced to a thing by another person, you come to regard yourself as a thing.

However, at this point the dialectic we described earlier comes into play: *once the slave is a thing, he can no longer properly recognize the master*, with the result that the master lacks recognition by another self. Recall Hegel's observation that in order to be a self, one must be recognized by another self; in the master's case, recognition is now lacking, because in objectifying the slave the master has made it impossible for the slave freely to recognize him as master. The slave has become no different from a stick or stone or tool, and no recognition can come from an object.

Now, Hegel goes on to explain, if there is no other to acknowledge the master, he cannot look on himself as master either. The master is no longer quite certain that he exists *for himself*; he always thought that "being for self"—that is, existence in its own right, in his own regard—was the truth about him, but now he is uncertain. The essence of being the master is now the *opposite* of what the master wanted to be or thought himself to be. So we see how, in the movement of the dialectic, the tables have turned: (1) if I am going to be master, I need and want you to recognize me as master; hence (2) I act on you, compelling you to recognize me as master and so making you my slave; but (3) as soon as I act on you in this way, you become an object, and I have denied you as an independent self-consciousness; (4) once I have denied you as an independent self-consciousness, you can no longer recognize me as master; and (5) if you cannot acknowledge me as master, then am I master at all? Of whom am I master? I no longer exist as master.

Conversely, says Hegel, making a crucial turn in the argument, the slave's consciousness is "forced back into itself" and transformed into a truly independent consciousness.[18] That is, as the master deprived of recognition comes to question his own mastership, the slave in the meantime also comes to resist being objectified, and in so doing comes to have the consciousness of a non-slave. The slave says, "I don't have to take this! The master has always looked on me as a thing, and for the last four years I've looked on myself as a thing; but now [suddenly, inexplicably] I am finished with that. I'm an independent consciousness, too!"

At this point, since the master has been deprived of the master's consciousness, and the slave has rid himself of the slave's consciousness, who is master and who is slave? The master is now filled with dread at the prospect of the slave's revolt. In the Deep South a person could be hanged for teaching a slave to read, because a literate slave knew he was as good as his master. He could read about himself, and as soon as that happened, he was no longer content with slavery and no longer willing to look on himself as a slave. If he was no longer the slave, the master was no longer the master.

In Paragraphs 194 and 195 Hegel explains how this shift in consciousness alters the slave's relation to material things as well as to the master. Although the slave's consciousness was objectified by the master to the extent that he began to regard himself as a slave, it never *fully* ceased to be self-consciousness. His self-consciousness never really disappeared. At the same time, because the slave lived in dreadful fear for years, everything stable melted away for him so that he was left with pure being for itself, his own being. And pure being is the nature of self-consciousness, Hegel asserts. Moreover, although he seemed helpless under his circumstances, the slave was not entirely passive; he worked on things, and by the process of working on things he rid himself of his attachment to them.

In other words, while the slave in our Deep South illustration could not rid himself of the cotton, he eventually came to know by working on it that he was not cotton; he may have thought at first that his

18. This is crucial in Hegel's master–slave dialectic. Marx will contradict Hegel here, arguing that a slave's consciousness is not "forced back into itself" so as to become independent. The truly independent consciousness, according to Marx, arises only through revolutionary activity.

own being was wrapped up or embedded in the cotton's, but he came to recognize himself as distinct from the cotton even though he could not avoid working on it. Now, once the slave has rid himself of his attachment to things, his being is no longer dependent on or defined by them, and he is therefore no longer objectified; he has transcended objectification. He is a pure self-consciousness, and begins to live for the day when he never has to see or work with cotton again.

Meanwhile the master's relation to material things also undergoes a change. At first the master's desire for what the thing could bring him gave him a feeling of self; but once the thing had brought the master what he desired, his feeling of self disappeared. In the case of the owner of our cotton plantation, he was interested only in the wealth he could obtain by means of the cotton, but once he gained that wealth, he found that it diminished rather than enhanced his sense of self. Wealth is after all only a thing, an inanimate object, and can never recognize anyone as a self-consciousness. If accumulating and keeping track of wealth is all there is to your existence, your self-consciousness begins to disappear.

Whether or not we are persuaded of the likelihood of the slave's consciousness being "forced back into itself," or the ability of a slave to rise in this way after years of objectification, we can note the dialectic: the situation has turned into its opposite. The master acted on the slave and thereby objectified the slave; he related to cotton only through the slave and never directly, because he had no use for cotton but only for the wealth the cotton could bring him, and his desire for that wealth gave him a sense of self; now he has the wealth, but the wealth cannot recognize him as a self and only diminishes his self-consciousness. In the meantime, the slave became objectified and therefore equally unable to recognize the master as a self, with the result that the master's self-consciousness was threatened in a second way. Slightly further along in the process, the slave's consciousness was "forced back into itself," and he resisted being a slave. Moreover, his endless work on the cotton had the effect of ridding him of any attachment to it so that he was no longer defined by the cotton and no longer objectified by his direct relation to it. In fact, in the permanence of the cotton he saw its independence from him, and hence his own independence from the cotton. Now the slave is genuinely a self-consciousness and the master is not. In fact, while the master's selfhood has become fragile, the slave's is solidified: he continues to work on the cotton while desiring freedom from it, and that delay of gratification serves to strengthen, implicitly, his newly emergent sense of self.

This last point is one of the keys to Hegel's argument. In having to work on a thing that exists in itself, independently of him, the slave comes to see that *he* exists in himself, independently of *it*; and once the slave comes to exist *for himself*, he ceases to exist *for the master*. Now the slave sees pure being for self as his truth; he no longer regards being for another as his truth. Previously, if you had asked the slave who he was, he would say, "I am John Smith's slave; I exist to labour for the master." If you now ask the slave the same question, he says, "I am a self-consciousness in my own right." This is the crucial shift he has made in the course of the dialectic: whereas the slave thought previously that his relation to things objectified him, he now sees that his forced relationship to things yields in the end a free self-consciousness.

Now, however, the same dialectic operates in the other direction. The slave's free self-consciousness requires recognition by another—the master's self-consciousness—or it will fail. In other words, the slave now needs the master as thoroughly as the master formerly needed the slave. Having gone from A to B, we go from B to A, and then back to B, and the whole process is undertaken again.

At this point Hegel's argument moves to another level. So far we have been talking about the master's self-consciousness and the slave's self-consciousness as existing in two different persons. But what if both exist in the same individual? When the master–slave dialectic concerns not two individuals but two aspects of the same person—which it invariably does, eventually—it gives rise to the "unhappy consciousness." The contradiction or division in such an individual, the oscillation between master and slave within, is overcome only as he or she rises to *universal* self-consciousness: individual self-consciousness is always divided, whereas the universal self-consciousness is integrated.

Note that until we rise to the universal self-consciousness, the master–slave dialectic continues ceaselessly, moving back and forth both between and within individuals. It is never the case, for example, that having obtained recognition from another self, we can then let that other self go free *permanently*. Our self-consciousness is never fixed; it is always being lost and gained, always fading in and out, and needs constant renewal. We are always in search of recognition and dominance, always objectifying one another and being objectified, and always resisting objectification by one another.

This fluctuation is borne out by much of our experience. We all know people who seem to be in constant need of affirmation and recognition—or perhaps we are those people ourselves (and know how to be subtle about our insecurity). After preaching what he considers to be a good sermon, for instance, the preacher is anxious to hear from someone—especially from someone whose recognition is particularly important to him, such as his wife or friend or thoughtful congregant—that it was as good as the preacher thought it was; until he does, he is threatened with insecurity.

Let us take a more current example of the master–slave dialectic. Think of a couple who have been married for many years. The husband says to the wife, "Honey, I love you," and she makes no response; she does not even look up or smile, just goes on making supper. What does the husband do? Suppose he takes hold of her blouse and says, "I'm telling you I love you, sweetheart!" and she shrugs his hand off without replying. How much longer can that continue before the husband's self-consciousness is crippled? Or imagine a marriage in which the husband occupies the position of master, and his wife is the slave whom he has objectified by his insistence on recognition in order to bolster his own self-consciousness. Her life is wrapped up in the manual tasks of running the household, and in the stove, diapers, and vacuum cleaner, to which he relates only through her. One day her own self-consciousness is forced back into itself (to use Hegel's vocabulary), and she is tired of being the slave; she is tired of being no more than cook, cleaner, and diaper-changer, and it dawns on her that she is more than that and is distinct from all the things that occupy her. She has acquired a self-consciousness which is not that of a slave; but now she needs the recognition of her husband, and may need it so badly that she cannot escape her slave consciousness and assert her own self-consciousness over against her husband. What she has is a kind of latent or underdeveloped self-consciousness, and it will fail unless it is recognized. This is the stuff of life in many marriages and friendships.

People often ask, when they hear about women abused in relationships, why the woman does not simply walk out. They do not realize that she cannot take any initiative because her self-consciousness has been so thoroughly eroded. She is unable to leave, not because she is addicted to the relationship, but because her self-perception is so minimal that the inner resources required to take action are simply not there; it would take six months of intensive psychotherapy for her to regain them. The same is true of severely depressed people: at the absolute nadir of depression people do not commit suicide, because they do not have the self-consciousness—that is, the inner resources—to take that initiative. They cannot even bring themselves to get up and go down to the subway tracks, or to go out and buy the pills. It is when people are on their way down to or up from this point that they are likely to commit suicide and must be carefully supervised.

Concluding Reflections

In identifying our tendency to operate according to the master–slave dialectic, our need for recognition and our tendency to objectify other people, Hegel has put his finger on something we deal with regularly in the Christian community as anywhere else. This tendency and this need are implicitly addressed in Scripture, where Christians are urged to submit themselves to one another "out of reverence for Christ."[19] This instruction does not endorse mutual objectification or enslavement; neither does it counsel low self-esteem or self-victimization. Instead it radically transcends the "prestige battle" Hegel has described. *Mutual* submission means that nobody is trying to gain the upper hand. Mutual submission "out of reverence for Christ" means that the Lord who has humbled (and humiliated) himself in order to exalt his people has already

19. Ephesians 5:20.

elevated us as much as we can be or will ever need to be. It also means that the self-giving we see in Christ is the way to receive our self. For Christians, a profound spiritual reality and theological understanding eclipse Hegel's philosophical dynamic—although what that reality and that understanding entail practically in specific, sensitive situations is something we continue to struggle to work out in the body of Christ.

Hegel's master–slave dialectic is referenced in the work of Nietzsche, Kierkegaard, Simone de Beauvoir, and especially Sartre. In fact, it appears everywhere in philosophy after Hegel, and is therefore crucial for any understanding not only of Existentialist philosophy but also of other philosophies, including the social-economic philosophy of Marx. Marx understood Hegel's view of reality, but disagreed with him at key points; liberation theology also owes a great deal to Hegel, but disagrees with him at critical points. In any case, there is no denying the objectification of humans by other humans, and the relevance of that problem to all kinds of social contexts.

Consider, for example, the question of the legalization of prostitution: if prostitution is looked on as a legitimate industry, we can insist on medical supervision and provide medical care, collect income tax from prostitutes, and give them a pension when they retire. Prostitutes will be healthier, the people who use them will be healthier, and the income tax burden on other people will be reduced. On the other hand, can we legalize prostitution without objectifying women? After all, we do not legalize cock-fighting despite the obvious benefits, because that would be tantamount to legitimizing cruelty to animals. But suppose the prostitute comes to look on herself as a thing, a commodity like any other; then one day she becomes fed up, and her slave consciousness is forced back into itself. She decides she has had enough, and refuses to recognize the men who are buying her services. Yet she cannot quite write them off as selves, because she needs their recognition—unless she can get it from someone else.

The point is that the process Hegel examines in such detail is going on around us all the time. We see the master–slave dialectic even in churches, between pastors and their congregations or boards, and between members of the congregation. We see it within ourselves, too:

is not each of us internally divided to some extent? There are days when we think we know who we are and have confidence in our virtue and our significance, and other days when we seem to have no clue who we are and hang our heads in shame.

Hegel argues that we can escape from this internal contradiction by rising to universal self-consciousness. Kierkegaard strenuously disagrees; he maintains not only that universal self-consciousness is a myth, but that aspiring to it in order to resolve the problem of our own contradictory existence is *sin*. In fact, as we shall see in the next chapter, a good deal of what Kierkegaard says is a reaction to Hegel. Kierkegaard's philosophy, while more than sheer anti-Hegelianism, nonetheless always has Hegel's philosophy in mind and aims at setting forth an alternative to Hegel's understanding of human existence.

3

Søren Kierkegaard:
Subjectivity, Abraham, and
Other Key Themes

Introduction

The preceding chapter acquainted us with the rudiments of Hegel, whose philosophy is the immediate backdrop to Existentialism and the foil for all Existentialist protest. The first Existentialist, in the opinion of some, is Schelling. Others disagree, but in any case Schelling is significant if only because his disagreement with Hegel, according to Kierkegaard, was insufficiently rigorous.

As we saw earlier, Hegel maintained that philosophy is not a flight from reality, an exercise in building intellectual castles in the air, but neither is it merely an attempt to describe or articulate reality; rather, it is an aspect of reality realizing itself. It is an aspect of the Absolute coming to know itself through finite spirit as the finite spirit rises to the level of Absolute Spirit. This is a significant departure from traditional views of philosophy. Other thinkers—in the Aristotelian or Realist tradition, for example—would say that philosophy describes what is and how we relate to it. Hegel would agree that it does, but would insist that it goes beyond that; philosophy is an aspect of what is becoming itself in a higher manifestation or order—an aspect of the Absolute dialectically "othering itself" as nature and returning to itself as Spirit.

If Hegel's philosophy, or metaphysics, is an aspect of reality realizing itself, then, strictly speaking, philosophy should have terminated with Hegel. There should be nothing left to say, philosophically, after reality has realized itself and finite spirit has risen to the level of the Absolute and articulated it absolutely, that is, definitively. And in fact Hegel did consider himself to be the culmination or fulfillment, and therefore the terminus, of philosophy. There would be no philosophy after him. Not surprisingly, however, after Hegel left off writing it did not take long for philosophy to resume its relentless inquiry; in fact, it started up again while he was still alive. Philosophy never reaches its omega point, because it never arrives at a definitive answer to any of the important questions it pursues. Philosophers today discuss what philosophers have always discussed, without providing conclusive answers; nevertheless, philosophical inquiry is not for that reason to be discounted as a waste of time, since it is always refining those perennial questions.

Schelling was the first to criticize Hegel. He maintained that Hegel's philosophy moves in the direction of truth, but does not *yield* truth because it undervalues and even omits existence. No abstract thought or philosophical metaphysics can grasp the uniqueness, the reality, of human existence, insisted Schelling; the existing human being can never be reduced to thought or to mind. Think, for example, of the difference between understanding the notion of anxiety and actually being anxious: intellectual apprehension and lived reality are qualitatively distinct. The crucial place Schelling gives to existence, as evidenced by this critique, has led some to consider him the first Existentialist philosopher.

Kierkegaard, having read Hegel, went from Copenhagen to Berlin to hear Schelling lecture there; the rumour was that Schelling was going to overturn Hegel, and Kierkegaard was eager to hear him do so. After listening to the lectures, however, Kierkegaard decided that Schelling's criticisms did not go nearly far enough. Along with Marx and Nietzsche, Kierkegaard maintained that no matter how subtle the dialectic, and regardless of the finite spirit's rise to the Absolute (Infinite Spirit), Hegel's philosophy freezes the status quo because no profound change can ever be generated by mere philosophical reflection. The human existent must *act*, and in acting find herself transfigured into a profoundly different self.

Essentials of Kierkegaard's Thought as Contrasted with Hegel's

The nature of philosophy

The first point Kierkegaard made is that Hegel has confused *thinking* with *existing*, when they are in fact qualitatively distinct. Mental activity commits us to nothing, and no amount of deliberation is a substitute for decision: we can always defer making up our mind, but we cannot postpone making up our life. A bachelor may tell us that he cannot make up his mind whether to marry or stay single. While he has not yet made up his mind, however, he has obviously made up his life: he is not married.

Notice that Christian theology makes the same kind of claim: we recognize that however sound or refined a person's doctrinal understanding, understanding alone does not make that person a believer or commit him to discipleship. A theological or philosophical system can be superbly integrated at the level of thought, but armchair reflection of itself never finds us saying with Simon Peter, "We have left *everything* and followed you."[1] As Kierkegaard attested in one of his characteristically anti-Hegelian works, *Philosophical Fragments*, philosophical systems aim at comprehensiveness and may even claim (as Hegel did) to achieve it; life, however, is qualitatively different from thought and therefore can never be subsumed under a system. The reality of human existence is always fragmentary, Kierkegaard insisted; hence a philosophical system that aims at comprehensiveness never does justice to that reality. Philosophy can properly be done only in fragments.

Nietzsche, as we shall see later on, speaks in the same vein. If we were able to view the universe from a standpoint above it, we could philosophize comprehensively; nobody, however, has such a view. Each of us always has a view of the universe from our own perspective, and can therefore philosophize from that perspective only. We are not even standing above our own individual situation, let alone above the universe. In view of this limitation, Nietzsche advances a thesis known as *perspectivism*: there is no such thing as absolute philosophical truth, only

1. Mark 10:28.

philosophical perspectives, and as soon as someone claims absolute truth for his perspective, he has exposed himself as naïve.

As Christians we will want to examine Nietzsche's statement. Do we not also have a particular perspective on life—on God, on ourselves, on history, on the good? And is our perspective then as partial as anyone else's, and hence just as relative? If so, we are no better off than anyone else; if not, how is our Christian perspective different from naturalistic perspectives? What entitles our perspective to make a truth claim that Nietzsche says all perspectives must by definition relinquish? All claims based on a perspective are necessarily provisional and non-final, says Nietzsche, because our perspective may change. Now we might, as Kierkegaard did, dispute this when it comes to a Christian commitment to discipleship, because finality is in the nature of that commitment. A person does not experiment with Christian commitment, expecting later to try something else such as Buddhism, follow it with atheism and then Islam, and finally assess which is preferable. Christian commitment means pledging oneself to Jesus Christ *irrevocably* in the conviction that one has been apprehended by Truth. Are we simply being arbitrary and prejudiced in saying that? Or are we claiming that by God's grace, or the Holy Spirit's activity in us, we are given a perspective which is in fact the right one, the God-ordained one? If so, how do we make that claim, and why?

Kierkegaard agrees with Nietzsche that philosophy can only be done fragmentarily, because life consists of fragments. We do not have a God's-eye view, either of the world or of ourselves or of our own existence in the world. There is no reason to assume that my view of myself is superior to your view of me; in fact, your perception of me may be far more accurate than my perception of myself.[2] No philosopher, says Kierkegaard, has a God's-eye view of anything. However, he goes

2. There are undoubtedly situations where I have a better understanding of myself than others have of me. But it was only after much pain and public embarrassment that I realized there are other situations where almost anyone has a more accurate vision of me than I have of myself. Children are especially perceptive in this regard. They readily see through their parents, because by the time we adults reach parenthood, we have falsified ourselves so many times in so many situations that we have taken on the falsification ourselves—until a seven-year-old notices that the emperor has no clothes, and says so.

on to insist, any philosophy that has integrity ends up demanding a self-commitment, and self-commitment is by definition total. Any philosophy *that falls short of demanding a commitment which overcomes fragmentariness* ends by supporting decadence, whether knowingly or not. Philosophy is necessarily fragmentary and therefore penultimate, but it should call for a lived commitment that is total and final.

Existence

The foregoing points us to a second tenet of Kierkegaard's; namely, that existence cannot be thought. Thought can be thought, but existence can only be lived—a point gloriously illustrated in his extensive treatment of the story of Abraham and Isaac. In Genesis 22, Abraham is sitting at peace in his tent when he is summoned by God to offer up Isaac, the son born to him and Sarah in their old age when Sarah *knew* she was beyond conceiving. In light of God's promise to give Abraham descendants as numberless "as the sand which is on the seashore,"[3] the command is nothing less than absurd. It also creates an agonizing dilemma. If Abraham obeys God, the promise will be null and void, since he will have no descendant. If, on the other hand, he disobeys God, the promise will also be null and void, since he will have no descendant *in faith*. Either way, the command of God cancels the promise of God, plunging Abraham into a conundrum that can never be resolved by thought. What is Abraham to do? Should he cling to the promise of God and disobey the command of God? Or should he obey the command of God and nullify the promise of God? Abraham decides to obey God, trusting God to fulfill the promise in a way that Abraham, at this moment, cannot anticipate or foresee.

The conundrum that faced Abraham on Mount Moriah is found in assorted forms everywhere in life, says Kierkegaard. Such conundrums (*absurdities* is the word he prefers) can never be resolved by thought, regardless of how or how long one thinks about them. Human existence, Kierkegaard insists, is ultimately a matter of choosing; not choosing between this or that, or between doing this or that; rather, choosing *what sort of self one is going to be*. In other words, to exist is to make the

3. Genesis 22:17.

decisions that determine the kind of self we are going to become and own as our *self*.[4] The most important issues for humankind are resolved only by a commitment in which we become the self that can never be realized through any amount of detached reflection—let alone reflection that deceives by claiming to rise to a standpoint above existence.

Dialectic

Dialectic is another important feature of Kierkegaard's thought, but it is notably different from the dialectic employed by Hegel. Hegel's dialectic followed a process of resolution involving three steps: thesis, antithesis, and synthesis. Kierkegaard's dialectic involves three stages of life: the aesthetic stage, the ethical stage, and the religious stage, each transcending and taking up into itself the preceding. However, whereas Hegel's dialectic unfolds with respect to humanity generally as Spirit is actualized in individuals, Kierkegaard's is a movement whereby spirit (not Spirit) is actualized in the individual existent, not in a universal.[5] As we noted in chapter 1, only the individual existent is concrete; "humankind" is an abstraction and hence does not actually *exist*. Moreover, for Kierkegaard the transition from one stage to another occurs not by means of thought, as in Hegel's dialectic, but by means of decision. Again, this decision is a choice not of one option among others of the same order, as on a menu, but the choice of *what kind of self* we are going to be.

   Take, for example, the aesthetic stage, the first stage, which is self-gratification or the pursuit of pleasure. It makes no difference whether the meaning of our life is snorting cocaine or luxuriating in concerts of classical music performed by virtuosos. There may be a refinement and sophistication about the world of classical music that is missing from the cocaine party, but ultimately, insists Kierkegaard, there is no

4. Generally speaking, nontheistic Existentialists speak of decision—that is, commitment—as a self-making. The self you make is the sum total of your choices. Strictly speaking, for Kierkegaard, the self is not so much a self-making as a self-choosing, because the self that is forged in your obedience to God is not one you make yourself but one that your relationship to God effects.

5. For Kierkegaard, the notion of the individual being rendered *Spirit* is an inexcusable confusion between Creator and creature—and worse, between holy God and sinner.

difference: both are pursued for self-gratification. This is merely a choice of one aesthetic option from among many, whereas the choice he is talking about—the choice that moves us from one stage to the next—is a different order of decision altogether: a choosing of the kind of self we want to be. Do we want to be the self that arises through magnification of the pleasure principle, or the self that arises through our commitment to an ethical rigour requiring aesthetic self-renunciation? Ultimately, do we want to be the self that occurs only through Abrahamic faith? The choice of the self is the crux of the decision, and it is this *decision* (not thought) and resultant action that advance the dialectic and move the individual existent from one stage to the next.

In thinking about these stages of life in Kierkegaard's dialectic, it is important to remember that all theistic Existentialists distinguish carefully between what passes for religion, and religion as faith. By the "religious" stage of life—the final stage—Kierkegaard does not mean the aesthetic pursuit of religion for self-gratification, or religion as adherence to a moral code for its own sake, but religion as exemplified in Abrahamic faith. In his writings he ceaselessly criticized the Danish state church for its religious aestheticism, mere self-gratification in the form of culturally correct religious observance. The prosperity gospel of North America is a crude form of the same thing: "If I go to church, obey the rules, and believe in Jesus, I will prosper economically." An only slightly more sophisticated form of this is: "If I take part in all the religious observances, I will have a happier life and be less anxious." When religion is sold to people as promoting stable marriages and other goods that will improve their lives and make them more contented, it is mere aestheticism in religious guise, Kierkegaard would say. How contented was Jesus in Gethsemane? Was he not beside himself in inner agony, stumbling to his knees?[6] Kierkegaard maintained that Christendom had domesticated and prostituted the Christian faith so that "discipleship" was peddled as a convenient way of easing discomfort and ensuring success.

The third difference between Hegel's dialectic and Kierkegaard's is

6. In Luke 22:41, the imperfect iterative tense of the verb for "knelt" indicates Jesus collapsed repeatedly; he was incapable of remaining upright.

that for Kierkegaard there is no necessary progression from one stage to the next; it always requires a voluntary "leap" on the part of the individual, a commitment of the whole person.[7] Whereas Hegel said that a metaphysical dialectic unfolds continuously because it is driven by Spirit, and Marx would later say that a material dialectic unfolds necessarily because it is driven by the laws of history up to the point of revolution, Kierkegaard's dialectic never unfolds necessarily. A person can remain an aesthete for the rest of her life if she chooses; nothing will move her beyond that stage apart from her own commitment to a different kind of self. This is not just a commitment to a new philosophy, an intellectual choice made by way of assent to a certain idea, but a commitment of the whole person to concrete action. According to Kierkegaard, it is the *choice* we make that moves the dialectic forward, and choosing is *doing*, not thinking. Armchair philosophy, however intellectually profound, remains existentially shallow—merely another form of aesthetic existence or self-gratification.

Self

For Hegel, the self is finite but has an inherent dynamic towards the infinite as spirit rises via philosophical thought to the Absolute. While Kierkegaard does speak of existence in terms of "a synthesis of the finite and the infinite,"[8] he has something completely different in view: the encounter between the finite existent, who remains finite but forever transformed and reconstituted by the encounter, and the infinite God, who eternally transcends philosophical thought. Hegel believed that because every human being can rise to oneness with Absolute Spirit, there is something of the infinite *in* every human being. For Kierkegaard, however, Hegel's notion suggests pantheism (God is the

7. This "leap" has been caricatured as an arbitrary, irrational act; for example, a person standing on a diving board, being urged to become an authentic human being by leaping into the pool without knowing whether there is any water in it. As we proceed, it will become clear that such mindless risk is not the kind Kierkegaard means by *leap*. His leap is informed by the knowledge that arises from personal encounter.

8. Søren Kierkegaard, *The Sickness Unto Death*, trans. Howard V. Hong and Edna H. Hong (Princeton: Princeton University Press, 1980), 13.

essence of all that is). The infinite, insists Kierkegaard, is not an innate aspect of the human being; rather, an encounter with the ever-transcendent infinite is available to every finite human being. But while we may encounter the infinite (even "wrestle" as Jacob wrestled with God), it is never the case that we rise through philosophical thought to the standpoint of the infinite or Absolute. Even Abrahamic faith confirms that God is God, and we are not; God loves us more than we love ourselves (since God has spared us but did not spare his Son), yet remains Lord of the most intimate relationship with him. For Hegel, thought that has reached the Absolute standpoint no longer has an object independent of itself; thought is pure creativity developing itself by internal necessity, a divine self that unfolds in nature. Kierkegaard rejects all of the above. For him, the human self is acquired only in the course of a personal commitment, and human commitment is precisely what Absolute Spirit cannot do for anyone.

Truth

For Hegel, the truth is the whole, in the sense that the subject/object distinction is ultimately overcome. For Kierkegaard, there is objective truth—the kind arrived at in mathematics and natural science—but it is irrelevant to the existent's life of total self-commitment. Ultimate truth is subjectivity.

Subjectivity is a crucial matter for Kierkegaard, and we must be careful to understand it precisely. Subjectivity is not subjectivism. In his thesis that "truth is subjectivity," Kierkegaard is often mistakenly regarded as denying or rejecting objectivity and suggesting that we create our own reality. On the contrary, he recognizes and values the truths of objectivity, but maintains that they have only penultimate human significance in that they make no difference to the kind of self we become. No sophistication in mathematics or natural science or theology renders us a different person; it will certainly make us more learned, but it will not make us a qualitatively different person, nor forge the "self" that is always Kierkegaard's concern. That difference, that forging of the self, arises only through decision and commitment.

Why is mastery of objective truth never more than penultimate?

It is because objectivity is, by definition, characterized by detachment. The condition of detachment applies to all kinds of objective truth: to science, history, literary criticism, musicology, and also to theology or doctrine. Kierkegaard is never disdainful of objectivity anywhere in life, and is not opposed to doctrine; he is Lutheran, and his Lutheran articulation of doctrine is evident in much of his work.[9] However, he insists that no amount of doctrinal orthodoxy or theological sophistication of itself ever affects the human heart; for just as the physicist is personally detached from the experiment he is conducting, so the theologian is detached from the doctrinal issue he is working on. Theological inquiry must never be confused with the subjectivity of faith. At all times it must be remembered that radical detachment is essential to scholarship of any sort, while radical commitment is essential to faith.

For this reason Kierkegaard has little use for traditional apologetics. Apologetic argument belongs to the realm of objectivity, and as such can never lead to a self-renouncing encounter with the God of the gospel; rather, it establishes a deity that is not the God of the gospel, and a relationship to such a deity that is not faith. If you start with motion, and reason by regressive argument to the unmoved Mover, or start with cause and argue regressively to the uncaused Cause of all things, the deity up which the argument terminates is not the Holy One of Israel, who acts and speaks and requires everything from us only to lavish everything on us. Abraham never thought he was dealing from a position of detachment with an unmoved Mover and an uncaused Cause; he knew he was in anguished engagement with a living Person whose promised blessing he would gain only if, absurdly, he gave up everything on which the promise depended. Kierkegaard, following Hebrew logic, is aware that *the* characteristic of the living God is that he speaks, and speaks so as to require the consummately risky response from the human who hears. The singular absurdity of Jesus' proclamation is that only life in his company is worth calling "life," yet it is gained only by embracing a death that reflects his.

9. For example, in *Works of Love*, trans. Howard V. Hong and Edna H. Hong (Princeton: Princeton University Press, 1995).

No apologetic, doctrine, or philosophical theology, says Kierkegaard, ever arrives at the specificity and seeming paradox or inherent contradiction of the gospel. Objectivity (for example, apologetics) will yield a deity, but that deity is so far removed from the God of the gospel that the two have nothing in common. Natural theology (arguing, for example, from instances of limited power in the world to unlimited power and labelling it "God") will yield an all-powerful deity, but it will never yield the God who renounces coercion, humbling himself in a manger and humiliating himself on a cross to reconcile a wayward creation.[10]

Secondly, says Kierkegaard, Christian apologetics invariably attempts to argue for the superiority of the Christian religion over some other belief such as secularism, Empiricism, or Hinduism. The result is religious people who, in addition to being light years away from Abrahamic faith, are now also intellectual snobs, because they believe that their religion is superior to their neighbours'. It is a short step from a sense of superiority to contempt, and from contempt to hatred.[11]

Finally, says Kierkegaard, Christian apologetics diminishes the radical demand of faith, because it purports to make God believable by means of philosophy or logical argument. In other words, our apologetic becomes the condition of believing. Kierkegaard will say that God himself is the condition of believing in God: only God himself, in the Person of the Holy Spirit, brings people to faith. If we believe in God because an apologist renders him credible to us today, what happens if (or, more likely, when) a better philosopher comes along tomorrow and demolishes our Christian apologetic argument?[12] This kind of "belief" has nothing to do with faith; in fact, it is a contradiction of faith.

10. Roman Catholic tradition and some schools within the Protestant tradition have always seen a continuum between philosophy and theology; for them, the deity yielded by natural theology is one with the God of the Bible. Protestants whose theology is formed, informed, and normed by the Christology of the sixteenth-century Reformers emphasize a discontinuity.

11. Emil Fackenheim, Jewish philosopher and rabbi, once asked me why Christian apologetics always ends up trying to prove the superiority of the Christian faith to Judaism. This is a tendency that has often led to anti-Semitism, and it is a feature of patristic theology (along with misogyny and Platonism) that has always troubled me.

12. C.S. Lewis was depressed for many months after the apologetic set out in his little

Again, it is important to recognize that Kierkegaard does not denigrate theology. Theology is an instance of objectivity of the same order as chemistry. Chemistry benefits all of us—among other things, it has produced pharmaceuticals that relieve pain and cure illness—but no objectivity, however 'true,' should be confused with the truth of subjectivity. Ultimate truth for Kierkegaard is always an encounter—specifically, an encounter between us and God in which, in the manner of Abraham, we commit ourselves and our future to an unscripted relationship with God.

Since Kierkegaard is a Christian, his "Truth is subjectivity" amounts to faith: while subjectiv*ism* is simply wishful thinking, subjectivity always refers in the discourse of Kierkegaard to a *relationship* of subject with subject—and specifically, of the human subject with *the* Subject, God.

Religion

For Hegel, religion is a necessary but penultimate moment, always lower than philosophy, in the rise of finite spirit to the Absolute. It remains penultimate because religion is only the pictorial representation of a truth that transcends it.

Consider the Incarnation: for Hegel, as we saw earlier, the story of the Incarnation is a pictorial representation of a philosophical truth lying behind it—namely, that the philosophically astute human being can become one with cosmic Mind thinking itself. Not everyone has the philosophical acumen to apprehend this, however; those lacking such ability will always need the "picture book" of religious illustrations. For Kierkegaard, on the other hand, the Incarnation or the atonement is not an illustration depicting a truth that transcends it, but is itself the ultimate and paradoxical reality. Our passionate commitment to this reality in turn makes our existence real, though absurd in the eyes of the world.

Kierkegaard criticizes Hegel for blurring the distinction between God and human mind, insisting that he ends up with something that is neither. Not only is Hegel's deity not God, says Kierkegaard, but

book *Miracles* was roundly refuted by Elizabeth Anscombe, another Christian philosopher at Oxford.

his human being is also not authentically human, since no *human* can rise to the standpoint of the Absolute. Human existence is ultimately the relationship between God and us, and such relationship presupposes distinctness. To use a term favoured by Martin Buber, reality is *the between*; it is the encounter, either of one human being with another, or of a human being with God, the Holy One of Israel. If this God is given up, says Kierkegaard, then so is the possibility of being authentically human. Hegel's philosophy forfeits both. In fact, no philosophy will acquaint us with the God who forever transcends us; we encounter the unprovable God through a choice or decision (the celebrated "leap") fraught with objective risk and uncertainty—and *this*, according to Kierkegaard, is true religion. Not even an ethical life, superior as it is to an aesthetic existence, can substitute for this encounter—as we will see when we explore Kierkegaard's three stages in detail in another chapter.

Abraham as the Type of Faith

The story of Abraham offering Isaac is a central theme in Kierkegaard. It will be examined more fully in a subsequent chapter of this book, but must be introduced here as the narrative that informs and integrates his understanding of existence, truth, the self, and religion. Why has Kierkegaard fastened on Abraham rather than on Joseph or Miriam as the paradigmatic faithful human? It is not an arbitrary choice; as I mentioned earlier, Abraham is explicitly the archetype of faith in both Testaments of the Bible. In Jewish literature, more has been written about the story of Abraham and Isaac than about everything else in the book of Genesis put together. It preoccupies the Jewish people not only because they recognize Abraham as the prototypical believer but, more hauntingly, because their history is one in which they are always Isaac being offered up—with one terrible difference: in the story of Abraham and Isaac a ram was provided, sparing Isaac, while at Auschwitz no ram appeared. The Hebrew word by which the Jewish people know this story is the *akedah* (עקידה), or "binding": the Binding of Isaac.

The story, as told in Sunday schools, frequently depicts Isaac as a young boy no more than seven years old. Abraham and Isaac are going up the mountain, and Isaac is portrayed as asking naïvely, "Daddy, what's going on?" The story, however, informs us that Isaac is carrying wood sufficient to immolate his remains; a human body being largely water, it takes a great deal of wood to consume it, and Isaac is old enough to carry this quantity. In the Jewish tradition, he is thirty-seven years old: old enough not only to understand what is going on but also to consent to the proceedings. In other words, the Binding of Isaac is ultimately the father's sacrifice of his son and no less the son's self-sacrifice—in the same way that the sacrifice of Jesus, Christians maintain, is finally the self-willed sacrifice of Father and Son alike.

When Isaac asks, "Where is the ram?" his father says, "God will provide himself the lamb."[13] This does not mean that Abraham knows God will provide a substitute for Isaac. Abraham, rather, is deflecting Isaac's question. If Abraham is aware from the outset that at the last minute a substitute will show up to spare Isaac (and hence himself), then there is no trial of faith at all. When he says that God will provide, he means: "I cannot foresee at all how the contradiction between God's promise and God's command is going to be resolved, but at this moment I am going to obey God and slay Isaac, believing that he will be given to me *in this life*." The latter point is crucial: Abraham is not saying "Isaac will be resurrected in the life to come." For one thing, the notion of the life to come is not a feature of Israel's earliest understanding; for another, the text makes no mention of the life to come; and finally, any looking for the appearance of Isaac in the life to come undoes the contradiction between promise and command, trivializing the story.[14]

The truth of anyone's existence, says Kierkegaard, is the same as that of Abraham: self-renunciation at incalculable risk issues in the "self" of authentic existence *in this life*. To exercise Abrahamic faith is to slay Isaac now in the confidence that the God who provides will fulfill his promise *in this life*. For this reason Kierkegaard extends the story of Abraham and Isaac to human existence generally, reminding readers, "Only he who raises the knife gets Isaac."[15] According to Kierkegaard,

13. Genesis 22:7–8.

14. The significance of Abraham's trust that Isaac would somehow be given back *in this life* will be examined in greater detail in the next chapter under a discussion of Kierkegaard's concept of *infinite resignation*.

everybody is in this place at all times in the life of faith. The moment-by-moment exercise of such faith is Kierkegaard's celebrated "leap"; it is always informed by the story of Abraham's encounter with God.

In Gethsemane and at Calvary, the Son of God remains obedient to his Father even while aware of, and tormented by, the price of such obedience—with salvific significance for the entire world. It is to illuminate this truth that the apostle Paul picks up the story of Abraham and Isaac in the book of Romans, with one crucial difference between Abraham and Isaac on Moriah and the Father and Son at Calvary: while God spared Isaac, he "did not spare his own Son but gave him up for us all."[16]

Definitions of Key Terms According to Kierkegaard

Truth

Truth is "an objective uncertainty held fast in an appropriation-process of the most passionate inwardness,"[17] writes Kierkegaard. Every word here is pregnant with meaning. The "objective uncertainty," first of all, is God: God can never be proven. Philosophers have spent centuries developing teleological, cosmological, and ontological arguments for God's existence, but they have never managed to prove God. The arguments are challenged, seemingly refuted, and then refined many times over, but in all of it God remains an objective uncertainty. Kierkegaard is not saying that God is uncertain to the believer; Abraham knew it was Yahweh who was speaking to him. But God forever remains an *objective* uncertainty in that he is unprovable.

The "appropriation process" is the process of commitment of the whole person to that objective uncertainty, and "inwardness," as touched on before, is one's relationship to oneself before God—an ontological category, not a psychological one. This inwardness is "most passionate"

15. Kierkegaard, *Fear and Trembling*, trans. Howard V. Hong and Edna H. Hong (Princeton: Princeton University Press, 1983), 27.

16. Romans 8:32.

17. "Concluding Unscientific Postscript," in *Existentialism: Basic Writings*, ed. Charles Guignon and Derk Pereboom (Indianapolis: Hackett Publishing, 2001), 92.

because God requires *everything* of the person he summons. What greater passion can there be than a commitment of everything?

As defined by Kierkegaard, then, truth is not a quality predicated of a statement or assertion, such as "The sun is 93 million miles from the earth." If the scientist demonstrates this to be the case, we say the sentence is true. By contrast, the truth Kierkegaard is defining here is predicated of a *relationship*.

Paradox

Truth becomes a paradox when an objective uncertainty is asserted with passionate certitude. Objectively, the existence of God is uncertain, but the believer asserts this objective uncertainty with the utmost passionate certitude, declaring beyond doubt that God *is*. This is paradoxical. How can anyone assert with the utmost passion that which is objectively uncertain? Kierkegaard would answer that there *is* certainty, but it is located in the subject rather than the object.[18]

The absolute paradox is the Incarnation, as asserted by believers. God is already an objective uncertainty, but given that "there is an infinite qualitative difference between God and humankind," the notion that God, the Eternal, has entered time as an individual human being is an objective uncertainty of infinite proportions. Yet Christians assert it with passionate certitude.

Kierkegaard's use of the term *paradox* is often misunderstood. In his vocabulary, a paradox is not a logical or formal contradiction like a square circle, or God making a stone so heavy he cannot lift it; that is mere irrationality. The Incarnation is paradox of an entirely different order. Our bewilderment before this absolute paradox is not occasioned by an irrationality. Rather, it is occasioned by our perplexity regarding (1) human nature, and (2) the nature of God, and the fact that in the Incarnation, we apprehend the eternal perfectly realized in a temporal existence.[19] In other words, says Kierkegaard, from the perspective of detachment or objectivity we do not know who or what God is, nor do

18. This is known in some church traditions as "Christian assurance." Kierkegaard is borrowing from this notion.

19. For a helpful exposition of this point see C. Stephen Evans, *Passionate Reason: Making*

we know what it means to be a human being. Yet in the Incarnation, the God we do not know and the human we do not know are found together, and in faith we know both.

Those hostile to Jesus did not say of our Lord, "Look! There he is, God-with-us! Emmanuel, at last!" They said, "You are a phony and a blasphemer. You have a demon. You are illegitimate."[20] People do not look naturalistically at the Incarnate One and recognize God and the human united in one person; they see just one more ordinary human being, or perhaps a deranged one. It is only faith, according to Kierkegaard, that discerns in the Incarnation the simultaneity of the God we cannot know and the human being we cannot know, both now made knowable by God's action.

Faith

What is faith, then? Faith is precisely the contradiction between the infinite passion of the individual's inwardness, on the one hand, and the objective uncertainty on the other. The contradiction lies in the fact that faith clings passionately to a truth that can never be demonstrated. We cling passionately and with Abrahamic certitude to God and our relationship with him, knowing that this truth will always be an objective uncertainty.

Here again Kierkegaard points us to his understanding concerning the futility of apologetics. Christian apologists have developed arguments to support our passionate clinging to God and our relationship with him, but these arguments are no proof of anything; in fact, in attempting to render the Kingdom and faith more believable they denature them by removing the inherent contradiction. What philosophical argument could ever lead anyone to conclude that human authenticity is gained through being tried like Abraham and responding in self-abandonment to an absurdity?

Admittedly, an argument that is insufficient to kindle faith may yet be helpful or necessary in removing impediments to faith, especially

---

Sense of Kierkegaard's Philosophical Fragments (Indianapolis: Indianapolis University Press, 1992), 97–105.

20. For example, John 7:20.

where people's understanding of God or the gospel has been seriously distorted by various misconceptions or accretions. We might call such an argument a "negative" apologetic since it can serve to obviate unsubstantial barriers to faith. There is a place for argument that shows, for instance, that all one-sided, reductionist approaches such as those of Freud and Marx are self-refuting. We can expose their inadequacy, even their self-contradictory character, and hence remove them as obstacles to faith. But there is no positive apologetic, no philosophical argument that can move people *into* faith. We might think Christianity provides a better explanation of reality, but that depends on what is considered real by the person hearing the explanation. Or we might think we have a superior explanation of the human condition: we can speak of sin underlying the injustice in the world, but the secularist (for example) does not believe in sin and has his own explanation. In other words, apologetic arguments presuppose common ground, a shared universe of discourse, and such common ground is precisely what is lacking in the conversation between faith and unbelief. Faith remains a contradiction, insists Kierkegaard—specifically, the contradiction between an objective uncertainty and our passionate clinging to it—which can never be obviated through philosophical argument.

For this reason people of biblical orientation speak of divine revelation as the basis of faith: only God can render God believable and knowable. Admittedly people need *some* understanding of God if their faith in God is to be anything other than superstition; the Kierkegaardian leap is not made into a void. Yet even this understanding is not provided by a Christian apologetic or philosophical argument, but by proclamation of the gospel, whose content is vivified by the Holy Spirit.

The final position believers occupy, therefore, is not that of intellectual argument but of witness. Recall the discussion in chapter 1 of direct versus indirect communication: argument (or the attempt at proof) is direct communication. Jesus never adopts this approach or commends it to his followers. Witness, on the other hand, is always indirect communication, and Scripture's fondness for narrative attests the ability of indirect communication to reflect the logic of revelation.

A Taste of Kierkegaard's Discourse: *Concluding Unscientific Postscript to Philosophical Fragments*

Subjectivity and objectivity

Many regard *Concluding Unscientific Postscript* (*CUP*) as Kierkegaard's greatest work. While any such pronouncement is debatable, there is no denying that *CUP* is a seminal work. It is lengthy, about 700 pages long, but here we shall explore it selectively to see how Kierkegaard presents some of the key themes we have been discussing.

One of these is subjectivity versus objectivity. As we observed before, Kierkegaard never speaks slightingly of objective truth, or denies that it is truth. After all, if you need surgery, you want someone with expertise in objective truth. However, he makes the point that where objective truth is concerned, "the subject and his subjectivity becomes indifferent."[21] That is to say, the subject's existential concern, the matter of his authenticity, is suspended. A scientist working on the properties of rubber is concerned with rubber, not with himself; it is the object, and not himself, that is at issue. For this reason Kierkegaard declares that in all matters of objectivity or objective truth, the agent's subjectivity becomes indifferent. In other words, that which has scientific importance has no personal importance: the scientist at work on an object may manipulate it in any number of ways, but his person remains unchanged. "For all interest, like all decisiveness, is rooted in subjectivity," continues Kierkegaard. He is speaking of "interest" in terms of the self and of our choosing the kind of self we will become. This choosing arises only in subjectivity, and always issues in transformation. Objective truth, that is, information concerning an object, entails no such choice or decision; it leaves the self untransformed.

In the same vein Kierkegaard writes, "The subjective reflection turns its attention inwardly to the subject, and desires in this intensification of inwardness to realize the truth."[22] Recall that

---

21. "Concluding Unscientific Postscript," in *Existentialism: Basic Writings*, ed. Charles Guignon and Derk Pereboom (Indianapolis: Hackett Publishing, 2001), 86.
  22. Ibid.

inwardness is an ontological category rather than a psychological one; it has nothing to do with self-absorption, but rather denotes one's relationship to oneself before God. It has a twofold relational structure: first there is my relation to myself, and then there is that relation, in turn, in relation to God. It is in this layered relation of inwardness that we aspire to "realize the truth," by which Kierkegaard means owning the truth so as to transform the self, and in so doing to *exist*.

He then elaborates, in a very complex-sounding statement, on what truth is and what it is not: "[T]herefore the notion of the truth as identity of thought and being is a chimera of abstraction, in its truth only an expectation of the creature; not because the truth is not such an identity, but because the knower is an existing individual for whom the truth cannot be such an identity as long as he lives in time."[23] What does he mean? If we lived in eternity, Kierkegaard is saying, the notion of truth as the identity (that is, sameness or oneness) of thought and being would be possible; but we live in time, and our thought and our being are always relative to our standpoint in time. We never have an absolute or God's-eye view of thought and being. I can think about being; but being and my thought about it are not identical, because both change with my position in time: what I think about being today, I will have to revise tomorrow. Accordingly, although there is some relationship between being and my thought about it, they can never be identical. From God's perspective thought may correspond fully to being, but we do not have God's perspective.

For us who are in time, then, truth is never a statement or a concept, something that can be *thought*; rather, it is *who we are*. What is identical with my being is not my thought, but my existence. In other words, it is the self that I *am* in my everyday existence which is my being; I cannot claim to have a being that is deeper or better than that. If I lie, for example, I am a liar; I cannot claim that although I lie from time to time, I am not a liar "deep down." That may be my *thought* about my being, but that thought is not identical with my being; what is identical with my being is my existence. Hence, Kierkegaard would say, if I lie, that is

23. Ibid.

my being: a liar. In view of this, we should ask ourselves: What kind of self do I exist as? What is the nature of my existence?

Kierkegaard continues with a discussion of knowledge: "All knowledge which does not inwardly relate itself to existence, in the reflection of inwardness, is, essentially viewed, accidental knowledge; its degree and scope is essentially indifferent."[24] This statement is closely related to what he says about subjective and objective truth, self-choosing, and transformation. Once again, he is not dismissing objective knowledge; he is simply saying that it is "essentially indifferent"—that is, indifferent with respect to who we are. Only ethical and ethical-religious knowledge has an essential relationship to the existence of the knower, because it requires a choice or radical commitment in a way that aesthetic knowledge does not. Aesthetic knowledge—and all objective knowledge pertains to the aesthetic in that the pleasure of acquiring it keeps us pursuing it—simply drifts along in accord with the pleasure principle and is thereby never more than "accidental"; it is the human default position. Ethical or religious knowledge, on the other hand, since it characteristically entails a deliberate contradiction of our default position, has an *essential* relationship to the knower: it has to do with who we are—our being, the self we have chosen.

Kierkegaard brings all of this to a crescendo a few paragraphs later: "Inwardness in an existing subject culminates in passion; corresponding to passion in the subject, the truth becomes a paradox; and the fact that the truth becomes a paradox is rooted precisely in its having a relationship to an existing subject."[25] Note how inwardness is related to passion: inwardness being my relationship to myself before God, it is, appropriately, that which I take most seriously in life and about which I am most passionate. To relate myself to myself before God who is impassioned (according to Scripture, God is always impassioned) in turn renders me impassioned. The paradox is that I am maximally passionate—to the point of risking myself without reservation—about something that cannot be proved. The world understands people who are impassioned about a certainty (however penultimate, even trivial),

24. Ibid., 87.
25. Ibid., 88.

but it cannot understand people who are impassioned about an objective uncertainty such as God. The world looks on what is uncertain as vague, abstract, less than real: how could we stake our life on it? Seen from within the orbit of faith, however, God is the most concrete reality: weightier, denser, "thicker," more substantial than anyone could ever imagine. In our encounter with him, the vague, abstract, uncertain deity becomes for us the most concrete Reality.

Further to the notion of subjectivity, Kierkegaard expounds something for which he has been vehemently criticized by Christians who confuse it with subjectivism or pure relativism:

> When the question of truth is raised in an *objective* manner, reflection is directed objectively to the truth, as an object to which the knower is related. Reflection is not focused upon the relationship, however, but upon the question of whether it is the truth to which the knower is related. If only the object to which he is related is the truth, the subject is accounted to be in the truth. When the question of the truth is raised *subjectively*, reflection is directed subjectively to the nature of the individual's relationship; if only the mode of this relationship is in the truth, the individual is in the truth, even if he should happen to be thus related to what is not true.[26]

Recall that, for Existentialists, truth as subjectivity is whatever you are willing to stake your life on, with the result that you are "in the truth." Here Kierkegaard seems to be saying that this relationship of commitment is all that matters: as long as we are unreservedly committed, we are "in the truth" regardless of what it is we are committed to and how "true" it is in any objective sense. In other words, the person who commits himself irrevocably and self-forgetfully to Nazism, Marxism, or the American way of life is living in the truth just as much as the person who has staked her life on Jesus Christ. He illustrates this provocatively with the following example:

26. Ibid., 88 [italicization of "objective" mine].

> If one who lives in the midst of Christendom goes up to
> the house of God, the house of the true God, with the true
> conception of God in his knowledge, and prays, but prays in
> a false spirit; and one who lives in an idolatrous community
> prays with the entire passion of the infinite, although his eyes
> rest upon the image of an idol: where is there most truth? The
> one prays in truth to God though he worships an idol; the
> other prays falsely to the true God, and hence worships in fact
> an idol.[27]

It is easy to see why Christians have criticized Kierkegaard here. He appears to have reduced subjectivity to subjectivism; he appears to be saying that a whole-hearted commitment to idolatry means that the individual is "in the truth," even though the thing to which she is thus related is not real.

Before we vilify Kierkegaard on this point, however, let us look more closely at what he is saying and consider two things. First, see what he says about the so-called Christian worshipper. Despite having an idea of the true God, this person is in fact an idol worshipper because he prays in a false spirit: he relates to God as if God were an object at his disposal, turning God into an idol. Secondly, Kierkegaard has not said that the idol worshipper who has committed himself unconditionally to the idol has thereby turned the *idol* into anything true. His point is that the *person* is existing "in truth," because he does not exist in detachment, determined to manipulate without being transformed. Kierkegaard would readily admit that the idol remains an idol. He is drawing our attention to *how* rather than to *what*.[28]

Consider an example from history. Heidegger was deemed by many to be the most prominent philosopher of the twentieth century and an important figure in Existentialist thought. Rector of a German university, he joined the Nazi party, convinced that doing so was essential to his eschewing "bad faith."[29] Sartre, the most-written-about

---

27. Ibid., 89.

28. For an amplification of this point see Murray Rae, *Kierkegaard's Vision of the Incarnation* (Oxford: Clarendon Press, 1997), 217.

philosopher of the twentieth century and an icon of Existentialist thought, joined the French Resistance and risked his life to fight the Nazi party. Clearly, the fact that Heidegger's Existentialist philosophy led him to join the Nazi party does not make Nazism true, nor does Sartre's joining the Resistance to fight Nazism make Nazism false. The point, according to Kierkegaard, is that each man lives "in truth" insofar as each has risked everything in an unconditional commitment. People may be unconditionally committed to all kinds of things unworthy of their commitment, but at least they are not manipulators, schemers, or exploiters bent on shallow self-indulgence that costs them nothing.

It is the word *truth* that is problematic for many Christians here, because the only understanding of "truth" they countenance is the objective. In his illustration about the idolater and the person praying to the true God, Kierkegaard is making a statement *about the person who worships, not about the idol.* To live "in truth" is to live in authenticity—that is, to live for something on which we are willing to stake our entire life.

Zealous Christians too quickly overlook the wisdom here, for the person willing to risk everything on what may not be right will make an exemplary disciple when she encounters Jesus Christ: passionate sinners make passionate disciples. There is nothing commendable in tepidness. A lukewarm believer is scarcely different from a lukewarm unbeliever. Scripture warns the Christian community that those who are neither hot nor cold will find themselves rejected.[30] "The truth," writes Kierkegaard, "is precisely the venture which chooses an objective uncertainty with the passion of the infinite.... But the above definition of truth is an equivalent expression for faith. Without risk, there is no faith."[31]

Approximateness

What makes objective knowledge unfit for our ultimate commitment, what makes it unable to effect a transformation in anyone, is its *approximateness*. Kierkegaard writes:

---

29. This term, crucial in Sartre's thought, will be amplified in a later chapter.
30. Revelation 3:16.
31. Kierkegaard, "Concluding Unscientific Postscript," 92.

> When one man investigates objectively the problem of immortality, and another embraces an uncertainty with the passion of the infinite: where is there most truth, and who has the greater certainty? The one has entered upon a never-ending approximation, for the uncertainty of immortality lies precisely in the subjectivity of the individual; the other is immortal, and fights for his immortality by struggling with the uncertainty.[32]

All objective knowledge is an approximation, insists Kierkegaard. We tend to think the opposite: we think it is faith that is approximate because it is unprovable, and science that is definitive. But for Kierkegaard, the knowledge of faith is certitude. Abraham *knows* it is God who has spoken, and he *knows* what has been said; otherwise he would not be offering up Isaac. Scientific knowing, on the other hand, is always provisional, always open to revision and restatement.

Consider physics, for example. At one point Newtonian physics, with its particular view of space, time, and matter, was regarded as the last word. But it was superseded when Einstein came on the scene and exposed Newtonian physics as inadequate. Whereas Newton regarded time and space as absolute, Einstein showed us that space and time are relative: speed compresses time, and at the speed of light, time stands still. Einsteinean physics was then deemed to be the last word—until we arrived at particle physics. What will come next? All are approximations, because that is the nature of all scientific statement. To say that scientific statement is approximate or provisional is to say that a future generation will find more adequate articulation for the profounder insights concerning the nature of the universe. Needless to say, doctrine is similarly always provisional in that a future generation will find more adequate theological formulations.

Faith, however, is not provisional but final: unlike objectivity, subjectivity is never approximate. When the man born blind is healed by Jesus and harassed by detractors, he finally says, "One thing I know: I was blind, and now I can see."[33] Such knowledge is not going to give way to something better tomorrow. Moreover, the man has been transformed in a way that no objective knowledge ever transforms anyone. To know Jesus Christ is to be transformed by the encounter in a way that one can never be transformed by the intellectual apprehension of doctrine, a merely cerebral matter. The knowledge that pertains to subjectivity is the transformation of the knower, whereas the knowledge that pertains to objectivity is the acquisition of information that is necessarily approximate, hence devoid of "infinite decisiveness."[34] Objectivity does not require that I risk myself wholly in an irrevocable decision; it requires only that I give mental assent to one statement today, and then, when it is superseded by deeper insight and better articulation, to a different one. One's *self* is never at risk in the knowledge of objectivities.

The *nature* of the transformation, in subjectivity, accords with that to which we are committed. It is here that the issue of "Truth" as opposed to "truth" becomes salient—the issue of to whom or to what we commit, and whether that person or thing is itself true. The person who is wholly committed to an idol takes on the properties of the idol, while the person who is wholly committed to the God who identifies himself with the least, the last, the lowly, and the lost becomes conformed to God's nature. Whether we are committed to one or the other makes no difference at all to the thesis of subjectivity, but it makes all the difference in the world to the kind of self we become.

Kierkegaard finds that inferior professors of philosophy cannot understand the nature of subjectivity. He refers somewhat derisively to "[t]he entire objective truth of the System"—he means Hegel's system of thought—"which flirts with what the times demand and accommodates itself to *Privatdocents*..."[35] In Kierkegaard's era a *Privatdocent* was an academic lecturer of the lowest rank. His point is that inferior professors are unable to appreciate the difference between (philosophical) thought and (biblical) faith.[36] In their thick-headedness they espouse Hegel's

---

33. John 9:25.

34. Kierkegaard, "Concluding Unscientific Postscript," 91.

35. Ibid., 90.

36. When I began studying philosophy in 1962 and theology in 1967, the word in the air

system of thought, unaware that while thought can be thought, existence cannot be thought, only *lived*. Mesmerized by the certainty of objectivities (including metaphysics), they disqualify themselves for apprehending a certitude and passion like Abraham's. One is reminded of the occasions in Scripture when a voice is heard from heaven, and the person addressed by it knows that Someone has spoken, while bystanders think they have heard thunder.[37] They miss it.

Evil

There is yet another important point to note from the work under consideration. Kierkegaard, again targeting Hegel, maintains that all philosophical systems end up relativizing evil: "[A]nd hence it is objectively in order to annul the difference between good and evil."[38] Kierkegaard argues that all philosophical systems, by definition, aim at comprehensiveness, and this aspiration leads to a relativization of evil by assuming that evil is intelligible: in a comprehensive system of thought, a place must be found for it. Once a place has been found for evil, evil by that very fact has been denatured as evil. I have already mentioned the common platitude that if we only had the right perspective we would see that evil is a condition of the good, a latent or disguised good, a good on the way. "Everything happens for a purpose" is the popular version of this notion. All such pronouncements, however, render evil non-evil; anything that is a latent, potential, or disguised good is *ipso facto* good, since it necessarily fits into the proper order of things. Kierkegaard will not countenance this; to "annul the difference between good and evil" is to be evil yourself. As Emil Fackenheim once said to me in informal conversation, "Evil, especially radical evil, evil perpetrated for its own sake, negates the would-be comprehensiveness of metaphysical

was that the poorest theology student was the one who got a B in philosophy. The student who got an A was a good enough philosopher to know that philosophy can never yield knowledge of God, while the student who got a C in philosophy understood so little of it that it would never contradict what he was going to learn in theology. But a student who got a B knew just enough philosophy to get theology wrong.

37. For example, John 12:29.

38. Kierkegaard, "Concluding Unscientific Postscript," 91.

systems." Metaphysics, comprehensive by definition, can be so only if evil is regarded as non-evil.

Admittedly, as the apostle Peter teaches us, there is no situation, evil included, that God cannot use to refine his people and purify their faith.[39] While evil is a contradiction of God's will and his purpose, his purposes are not ultimately defeated by evil; he can use it. The book of Acts insists that Jesus was put to death by wicked men who will be judged for their wickedness; at the same time, the death of Jesus accomplished God's salvific purpose.[40] That God can use any situation, including evil, is true; but to say this is different from saying that there is no situation God has not caused. God is not the author of evil; otherwise, evil is indistinguishable from good, and God is indistinguishable from the devil. Evil is not part of the creation that came forth from God's hand; God is good, and can fashion only a good creation. It is not the case that God created both good and evil, suspended us between them, and said, "Now it is up to you to choose."

Then what is the provenance of evil? Scripture nowhere offers an explanation, even though it deals everywhere with the fact and nature of evil. Since God is good, and the creation is good, evil is ultimately and absolutely inexplicable. Paul speaks of "the mystery of iniquity."[41] There is a genuine mystery to evil that we tend to get over too quickly in our quest for an explanation, forgetting that to the extent it can be explained, evil is not evil. And although nontheistic Existentialists do not speak of sin, they relentlessly press the issue of evil, because any attempt to deny it plunges us into self-warping falsity. Since evil can be neither escaped nor explained, the only matter left to us is the *response* we are going to make to it.

What can we say in sum, so far, about Kierkegaard? Clearly, at least this: that for him it is ultimately only people of Abrahamic faith who truly *exist*, while everyone else lives in a ghostly pre-existent state. Paradoxically, we *live* only as we risk our entire life on an objective

---

39. 1 Peter 1.

40. E.g., Acts 2:22–31; Acts 7:51–60.

41. 2 Thessalonians 2:7.

uncertainty—and so find the passion and certitude of an existence that Jesus, using a slightly different vocabulary, named *abundant* and *eternal*.[42]

"Only he who raises the knife gets Isaac."[43]

---

42. John 4:14; 10:10; 16:22.

43. Kierkegaard, *Fear and Trembling*, trans. Howard V. Hong and Edna H. Hong (Princeton: Princeton University Press, 1983), 27.

4

Søren Kierkegaard:
What Is Faith? What Is a Christian?

The *Concluding Unscientific Postscript*

The final paragraphs of Kierkegaard's *Concluding Unscientific Postscript* gather together, concentrate, and illuminate the thesis of the preceding seven hundred pages. Understanding this conclusion is hence crucial to an understanding of Kierkegaard as a whole.

The first point he makes here is that *belief* is qualitatively distinct from *faith*. Belief is simply an aspect of one's mental furniture, an idea in the head, whereas faith is the attitude of the heart; it includes, but can never be reduced to, what is in one's head. Most people confuse faith with belief, declares Kierkegaard, and assume that a Christian is someone who assents to doctrines deemed essential to Christianity.

Two undesirable outcomes issue from this assumption. First, attention is diverted to the minutest detail of doctrine, tempting people to evade God's judgment, claim, and gift by hiding behind discussion of endless subtleties. Second, attention becomes focused on that which must be only approximate. In our earlier examination of the Kierkegaardian notions of subjectivity and objectivity, we noted a connection between approximateness and objectivity: whereas many people associate objectivity with accuracy, Kierkegaard maintains that all forms of objectivity, including doctrine, are only approximate. Doctrine approaches an endpoint asymptotically without ever reaching a definitive statement: that is, the doctrine that theologians articulate today will be refined and re-articulated in a superior way tomorrow, and will never be more than provisional. Although it describes Jesus

Christ adequately and truly, it never describes him exhaustively, and is therefore *always* approximate. We have already seen how, in the sciences (not to mention the humanities and the arts), there is never a last word; Newtonian physics gave way to Einsteinean physics, which in turn gave way to particle physics. Doctrine falls into the same category; like all forms of objective knowledge and all intellectual inquiries, it is approximate and provisional. Hence a confusion of *faith* with *belief in a body of doctrine* results in an undue focus of attention on that which is only approximate.[1]

Subjectivity, on the other hand, is never approximate. Jesus Christ is never approximate; he is definitive, and faith in Christ is final. The fact that we exercise faith in Jesus Christ means that we have recognized him as the finality of God and of human existence, and our self-abandonment to him as the finality of the truth of our own existence. There is nothing approximate about revelation, or about faith in it.

Not only is doctrine approximate, says Kierkegaard; it is abstract. *All* intellectual statements are abstract, whereas God is concrete; God is living Person. Each of us is also a concrete, living person, and most concrete in our encounter with God: there is nothing more solid and substantial—more *real*—than this.[2]

Being approximate and abstract, doctrine is also endlessly debatable, whereas the living person of God is not. According to Scripture (to recur to an oft-repeated refrain), *the* characteristic of the living God is that he speaks, and when he does, the person to whom he speaks knows three things beyond question. First, the person knows that a real event has occurred; someone has in fact spoken. Second, the person knows that the one who has spoken is God, for God identifies himself in his

1. What Kierkegaard says here is an echo of Calvin, who maintains that our knowledge of Jesus Christ—by which he means our participation in the life of Christ—is surer than our knowledge of natural science. This is contrary to what most people assume. See Victor Shepherd, *The Nature and Function of Faith in the Theology of John Calvin* (Vancouver: Regent College Publishing, 2004), 16–20.

2. We often fail to recognize that fact in the church today, with our left-handed legitimization of doubt. While congregants' doubts must be acknowledged, many sermons too readily end up confirming people in their doubt instead of moving them beyond it to faith—that is, to the concreteness of their lived engagement with the living God.

speech. Third, the person knows what God has said, since God's speech is never devoid of content. For the Hebrew prophet these matters are not debatable. Jeremiah has the word of the Lord in his mouth, and says that if he does not open his mouth and let this fiery word out, his mouth will burst into flames.[3] Moses comes down the mountain saying, "Yahweh spoke to me on your behalf, and it makes all the difference in the world."[4] Every Hebrew prophet knows that he lives under the enormous weight, pressure, and burden of the living voice of the living God.

The point here is that doctrine is of the same intellectual order as philosophy. It differs from philosophy in that doctrine begins with revelation, or human reflection on revelation, rather than with human speculation; nevertheless, the logic of doctrinal thinking and the logic of philosophical thinking are equally abstract, approximate, and endlessly debatable.

In view of all of the above, Kierkegaard insists that the proper question is not "What is Christianity?" but rather "Who or what is a Christian?" The former is a question of objectivity, the latter a question of subjectivity—not of subjectiv*ism*, but of subjectivity, and hence (as we saw in chapter 3) of *truth*. Since decision or commitment is suspended as long as the approximate remains approximate, a resort to doctrine as the definition of a Christian leaves no one a Christian, says Kierkegaard. It relegates to oblivion the *decision whereby one becomes a Christian*, because that decision is reduced to a matter of probability: what degree of confidence must obtain in order for us to commit to becoming Christ's follower? If we are 51% sure of the truth of doctrine, is that enough? Or would we have to be 78% sure, or 90% sure? The question makes no sense. Doctrine never requires from us the decision on which we stake our life; like any intellectual pursuit, it is always a matter of detachment, of suspension rather than decision.

Kierkegaard describes a variety of approaches to truth as objectivity, truth as matter for detached reflection. There is the learned approach, for example: an academic investigation. Two scholars may debate aspects

3. Jeremiah 20:9.
4. See, for example, Exodus 20 and Deuteronomy 6.

of Reformation theology, with one of them upholding Calvin's *extra calvinisticum* and the other arguing for Luther's *communicatio idiomatum*. They can hide behind that debate forever, and never live in the truth of subjectivity. A second approach is that of the anxious or timorous person who, refusing to commit without sufficient evidence, is never satisfied that she has it, hence never takes the risk of faith. This is the sort of person who was always asking Jesus for a sign, as if to say, "If you give us just a slightly better sign, then we will become disciples." Jesus refuses, saying, "If the Son of Man were raised from the dead, you still would not believe."[5] What these people mean by "sign" is some proof that Jesus is who he is, *irrespective of their commitment to him*; but there is no such sign, because it is only *in* our commitment that we know Jesus to be who he says he is. To the person who does not want to risk living in truth, no sign will ever be enough.

Of course there is always a place for reflection: God's address to the prophet is immediate and concrete, but in the wake of that address the prophet thinks about who has spoken to him, what he has heard, and what its ramifications are. Such reflection necessarily requires detachment, and is appropriate; we are commanded to love God with our minds, and ought therefore to be as theologically learned as we can be. Nevertheless, living faith—that is, subjectivity—is a matter of commitment, and can exist where there is little knowledge of doctrine or theology. When the hemorrhaging woman reaches out and touches the tassels of Jesus' prayer shawl, and he says, "Daughter, your faith has saved you, go in peace," is she saved? Yes: Christ has pronounced her that. How much does she know? She knows only this much: that Jesus is someone who can help her, and that life in his company is better than life not in his company. Is her understanding pure? No, it is tinged with superstition, or she would not be so intent on touching the tassels of Jesus' prayer shawl.[6] Similarly, to the penitent woman who washes his feet with her tears and wipes them with her hair, Jesus says, "Your faith has saved you."[7] The woman has reached out in faith to Jesus, but how

5. See Mark 8:12 and Luke 16:31.

6. Luke 18:44.

7. Luke 7:36–52.

pure or well-informed is her faith? Psychiatrists tell us that wiping Jesus' feet with her hair was a highly erotic act on the part of the woman; hence, in addition to her knowing relatively little doctrine, her faith is charged with an inappropriate erotic attachment to Jesus. Kierkegaard's point is that both these women are Christian despite minimal doctrinal apprehension, while, on the other hand, a person can have maximal doctrinal apprehension and still be light-years from the Kingdom. The question is, Do we live "in truth," or have we confused objectivity with living in truth?

Again, therefore, to define a Christian in terms of doctrine, Kierkegaard maintains, is to be left with a non-Christian. In the church we often do resort to such a definition: if a person can endorse the Apostles' Creed, that person must be a Christian. It is true that all Christians *should* endorse the Apostles' Creed, but doing so is no substitute for a living faith in the living Person of Jesus Christ. The heart includes the head, but can never be reduced to the head.

Since the attempt to define a Christian by what is necessarily approximate finds no one a Christian, continues Kierkegaard—speaking ironically—let us simply assume that *everyone* is a Christian. He calls this the "church theory," since the state Lutheran church in Denmark baptized everyone as a matter of course. The state promoted Christianity as a means of protecting Danish society against powerful foreign influence or invasion in the form of the Turk, the Russian, and the papist; that is, against Islamic threat, against national threat, and against a non-Protestant threat.[8] But such "Christianity" is purely utilitarian: people support it because it is *useful*, because it brings about a desirable state of affairs or advances their own safety and comfort. In other words, if evaluated in terms of Kierkegaard's understanding of the three stages of existence (touched on briefly in the previous chapter and to be revisited shortly), the church theory of Christianity is sheer aesthetics: like the first of his three stages, the aesthetic stage, it operates on the

---

8. It is interesting to note the perennial concern with protection against the Islamic threat. It characterized Christendom in Luther's day, was still a concern in Kierkegaard's day, and remains a concern today. To what degree is the American preoccupation with strengthening Christian religion and values related to fear of Islamic terrorism?

pleasure principle. Utilitarian Christianity, in essence, is no different from "Don Juanism." While it is not lurid or venereal, it is nevertheless the maximization of the principle of self-gratification.[9]

What is Christianity *really*, then? Kierkegaard goes on to say that Christianity is "an existence-communication." We have already probed what Kierkegaard means by "existence": to exist is to stand out, under God, in resistance to the conformity of society generally. We have also discussed his views on communication in its direct and indirect forms: indirect communication always pertains to existence, while direct communication pertains to thought. Kierkegaard points out that existence can be communicated, but never conveyed directly. We convey directly things such as nuclear physics or theology—but not faith, which can only be lived. In other words, I can tell you about faith, I can describe it, but my teaching cannot quicken faith in you; you must decide for yourself. Just as the most detailed description of marriage, however correct, will never render you married or give you an understanding of marriage from the inside, so no doctrinal discussion of faith will make you a self-abandoned follower of Jesus. By the same token, Kierkegaard maintains that we cannot invoke the tradition or sacraments of the church, especially infant baptism, and say, "I have been baptized, I have affirmed the Apostles' Creed; therefore I now exist as a Christian." Existence in faith cannot be conveyed directly by any such means.

Now some people, says Kierkegaard, "go further"—or *think* they

9. The real threat to genuine faith, says Kierkegaard, is not the Turk (a non-Christian religion), but our own unfaith, engendered and approved by Christendom under the church theory. So far from defending Christendom against the Turk, Kierkegaard insists that Christians should uphold genuine faith against the illusion that the Turk is the real enemy. Similarly, if he lived in North America today, Kierkegaard would say that the real threat to the church is not the rising tide of people of Muslim conviction; it is the unbelief found in all our churches. Confusion of faith with Christendom, or with shoring up Christendom, was for Kierkegaard the major problem in the Danish church of his time. Since then Christendom has more or less ceased to exist, and once Christendom has completely disappeared, it can no longer be mistaken for faith; but according to Kierkegaard, the trouble is that, having remained in the church with the misguided intention of supporting Christendom, people leave the church once the battle for Christendom is lost.

do: they claim that we are made Christians by appropriating doctrine "quite differently," that is, by an appropriation of doctrine so intense as to make us willing to die for it. Here Kierkegaard has in mind the wars of religion from 1618 to 1648, when so many lives were given and taken in the cause of religious belief. Of course doctrine itself will not save us, these people acknowledge, but if we believe it with utmost intensity and ardour, then our passionate affirmation of that doctrine will save us. No, replies Kierkegaard, it will not; it is far more likely to find you killing your neighbour. He is aware that from 1618 until 1648, Protestants and Catholics slew one another in Europe with unholy unrestraint; in fact, the devastation in Europe was so horrific that in many German and Austrian communities the death rate was 80%.[10] Do not imagine, says Kierkegaard, that intensity of passion around anything religious is the same as a commitment to living in truth. It is not subjectivity; it is merely one more form of objectivity turned fanatical. The "quite differently" proposed by such people is not a matter of qualitative distinction at all, he insists; it turns out to be only a matter of degree. It aims at subjectivity, but is only an amplification of objectivity. The church has never lacked people who are willing to go to the stake for doctrinal articulation; underneath their willingness there may or may not have been a genuine faith in Christ. The mere phenomenon of zeal has nothing to do with living in truth.

If faith is not assent to or comprehension of a body of doctrine, it is also not to be confused with simple ignorance, as many people use the word *faith* to mean. So-called faith in this sense is exercised as a poor substitute when what is really called for is understanding: after a while, when we attain to intellectual maturity and grasp what we could earlier affirm only as a matter of faith, faith will become superfluous and give way to understanding. People use the word *faith* in this way when they say such things as, "I don't know how car brakes work, but when I put my foot on the brake pedal, I have faith that the car will stop." What they are talking about bears no resemblance to faith as announced by the apostles and affirmed by Kierkegaard. A car mechanic knows how

10. If anyone wonders why the Enlightenment was so virulently antichristian, here is at least one answer.

brakes work, and once he explains it to you and you understand it, your so-called faith will be superfluous. In other words, this faith is the same as ignorance, whereas the faith of which Kierkegaard speaks is always *knowledge*: to live in truth is to *know* that you live in truth. Yet this knowing is different from intellectual apprehension, as we shall see.

We noted a few paragraphs ago that existence in faith cannot be conveyed directly by means such as baptism. For one thing, existence in faith cannot be conveyed directly at all, but only indirectly. For another, if we assume that the ritual of baptism has rendered us people of faith, we are concerning ourselves with outwardness and ignoring inwardness—which, you will recall, is our relation to our self before God. Even if we were to say, with a seeming concern for inwardness, "I must have been baptized, since I have the witness of the Spirit within me," that would still be to argue that the real mark of the Christian is baptism. Kierkegaard denies that it is, though many in the church continue to consider it so.

However, he continues, supposing we do argue in this left-handed way that the real mark of the Christian is the witness of the Spirit, that is, inwardness; in that case, we need an understanding of inwardness that distinguishes the witness of the Spirit (capital S) from all activities of spirit (lower-case s). Here Kierkegaard is setting himself apart from Hegel and from all forms of Romanticism that confuse spirit with Spirit. Romanticism of every kind confuses the human with the divine, and the mysterious depths of the human with the mystery of God. There are genuinely mysterious depths to the human, but they are not the mystery of God, and are not necessarily evidence of being moved by the Spirit.

We see this Romantic confusion in our own time. People like to talk about spirituality in nature—about the experience of standing on the dock at the cottage, for example, and hearing the loon warble over the lake as the sun sets, and feeling profoundly moved. They speak of it as if it were an experience of God, but it is not; it is an experience of God's creation. It is genuinely moving, because there is genuine mystery to the creation that is not an artifact of our own imagination, and it rightly elicits our wonder. Such apprehension of the mysterious dimension of the creation, however, is not to be confused with the mystery of God who transcends the creation. Similarly, any confusion of spirit with Spirit—Holy Spirit—is idolatry. Kierkegaard maintains that Hegel and Kant have made this confusion repeatedly; the whole Idealistic tradition has made it repeatedly in Germany, and all religious Romantics continue to make it.[11] In Pauline vocabulary, *spirit* is the whole embodied human being oriented *towards* God, and *flesh* is the whole human being oriented *away* from God. When Kierkegaard speaks of "spirit," he intends something similar to Paul's meaning; namely, the capacity of the whole human being to be oriented towards God or to exercise faith.

The existential pathos of faith

The appropriation that pertains to faith involves *pathos*, according to Kierkegaard, and it is of such a nature that it cannot be confused with any other kind of pathos. A person living in subjectivity or in truth undergoes an existential pathos that cannot be relieved.

This notion of existential pathos is crucial for Kierkegaard. There is a pathos or suffering related to objectivity, such as the suffering of physical injury or need, illness or psychosis, that we all endure and that we can and should try to eliminate. But the suffering that pertains to subjectivity or to living in truth cannot be alleviated. The suffering that pertains to discipleship is an inherent part of that discipleship and can never be eliminated except by renouncing the life of a disciple and living in untruth. Existential pathos must also be distinguished from the suffering of the person who is executed for voicing an opinion; even the suffering of martyrdom is not *per se* the existential pathos of faith, since a person can be martyred for holding a doctrine without being related to Jesus Christ at all. Even the most ardently zealous person can tragically miss subjectivity.

---

11. As will be explained in greater detail in chapters 6 and 7 on Nietzsche, Romanticism, in seeking to identify the "spirit" of a nation or people as something that transcends the individual, is closely allied with tribalism. The "spirit of the nation" is an elevation of the human spirit to the divine, or at least the numinous, and in that sense is very much like a tribal deity. As secularism sweeps away the public recognition of God or god, tribalism is reasserting itself in many parts of the world.

Loneliness is a part of this existential pathos. Any person who lives in truth lives an existence that is not understood, in isolation from the mainstream of society. She will not be understood by anyone in her college class, at her workplace, or on her street; her subjectivity, and the pathos it entails, can never be understood by those who do not live in truth. When Kierkegaard published his book *Either Or*, children (incited by their parents) taunted him in the streets, running after him and shouting, "Either or! Either or!" They had no idea what they were saying, but their parents had put them up to it to make a spectacle of him. To live in truth is to live in a loneliness where your only comfort is the assurance that you live in truth.

Another part of this existential pathos is the anguish of decision in the midst of uncertainty. To live in truth is to abandon security and live in a *venture*, with a *risk*. It is to live in a commitment that can never be objectively proved, and therefore involves the agony of life-shaping decision in the absence of objective knowledge of the outcome. This is the case even where the commitment is not specifically Christian: the member of the French Resistance who suspects (but cannot prove) that one of their number is going to betray twenty-five citizens to the Nazi Gestapo must decide how to act, and cannot avoid making a decision. Either he and his cohorts must deal conclusively with this Mr. X, or they must risk allowing the Gestapo to kill twenty-five innocent people as a direct result of Mr. X's betrayal. The decision is a risk; it must be made without objective proof, and is a decision that will make a life-or-death difference to many. Kierkegaard says that those who live in truth have committed themselves to a reality that they affirm but can never prove; such people must endure ongoing existential pathos.

I think that the church has frequently failed to come to terms with the pathos of discipleship, and the root of that distortion can be seen in most teaching on the Resurrection. Most Christians believe that Jesus is raised *healed*. It is commonly thought that Jesus' ministry was proceeding as might be expected, with good days and bad, until one Friday he had an extremely bad day—but then he got over it, and things have gone smoothly ever since. According to Scripture, however, Jesus is not raised whole and healed; *he is raised wounded*. He says to the doubters,

"Touch the nail prints in my hands. Put your hand in my side."[12] The wounds remain. Major strands of the church have typically affirmed that our Lord's Resurrection moved him beyond suffering, but when Paul is apprehended by Jesus on the road to Damascus after tormenting Christians, the voice says, "Why are you persecuting *me*?"[13] The risen Christ continues to suffer, and suffers particularly in the suffering of his people.

Or consider the scene in the book of Revelation where John looks for the Lion of the tribe of Judah. The church is being persecuted mercilessly by the regime of the Roman emperor Domitian, and the Lion of the tribe of Judah is the symbol of God's power. But when John's tear-blinded eyes dry enough for him to see, and he looks expectantly for the Lion of the tribe of Judah, there is only a bleeding Lamb.[14] Thereupon John apprehends that it is the still-bleeding Lamb who is the ruler of the cosmos. We all want the Lion of the tribe of Judah to come and fix everything in our lives; we have been looking for that Lion for two thousand years, but it has never shown up and never will. What we are given is the bleeding Lamb. The New Testament characteristically attests this truth, but we read past it because we do not want a discipleship that involves existential pathos. Kierkegaard admonishes us: If your Lord—victorious, risen, and ruling—is wounded and suffering still, do not expect to follow him and be spared existential pathos.

In this regard we should ponder the lyrics of a chorus sung frequently in church: "He bears my guilt, my shame, my cross." Unquestionably Jesus does bear my guilt and shame, but he does *not* bear my cross: he bears his own cross, and appoints me to mine. Worship lyrics such as these reflect the church theory of Christianity: pure utilitarianism. If Jesus bears my shame and guilt *and* my cross, my discipleship never entails cross-bearing and my life is rosy. In the gospels, by contrast, when people want to follow Jesus, he reminds them of the cost. He promises that in addition to the ordinary hardship that

12. John 20:27.
13. Acts 9:4.
14. Revelation 5:5–6.

is inevitably encountered in life, intimacy with him will entail its own characteristic suffering, since discipleship is necessarily cruciform.[15]

Faith as inward appropriation

What is it to be a Christian, then? The *how* of being a Christian is a paradoxical inwardness that corresponds to the absolute paradox, the Incarnation: no human thinking can comprehend the truth and reality of the Creator of the universe becoming a creature without ceasing to be Creator. No one can prove that God exists, and no one can explain the reality of God's becoming a human being. In short, all of this is an objective uncertainty, yet—in a corresponding paradox—the Christian stakes her life on it. Therefore, says Kierkegaard, faith—which can be communicated only indirectly—is *an objective uncertainty held fast by the utmost passion of inwardness*. By "utmost passion of inwardness" he means the willingness to risk everything, your very self, for the truth of your relationship to yourself before God. To invoke our oft-repeated example: just as there is no way of knowing the reality of being married apart from being married, there is no way to know the reality of life in the Kingdom without committing oneself to Jesus Christ; at some point, we must suspend our anxiety and doubt and take the leap of trust, the risk of making the commitment. We may decide that it is much safer simply to live in objectivity, to live according to what the social scientist, the life scientist, or the political scientist tells us; but to do that is ultimately to live a kind of shadow existence, to live in conformity to the herd, and never to find that self which arises only through radical, risky commitment.

Since the Incarnation as absolute paradox (the absurd) will never be resolved and hence never understood, Christian faith can never slide from the inwardly to the outwardly. This is not to suggest that the believer says, "Since the absurd is unintelligible, I will simply make my peace with it." Rather, it is as we remain repelled by the absurdity that faith remains impassioned.

Abraham was not explicitly faced with the absurdity of the Incarnation, but he was faced with the absurdity of the contradiction

15. Mark 8:34.

between God's promise and God's command, and the repulsion of that contradiction. We have already spoken of this: God's promise is that Abraham will have descendants as profuse as the sand on the seashore, but God's command is that Abraham slay Isaac, the one through whom this promise is to be fulfilled. To embrace both the promise and the command at the same time is to embrace an absurdity; human rationality cannot penetrate the paradoxical simultaneity of God's promise and God's command. Abraham risks everything for the absurdity, trusting God to resolve it in a manner he cannot foresee or anticipate. We, too, are called to embrace, by faith, contradictions of the same kind: Jesus says, "Do you want to be first? Then you have to be last. Do you want to save your life? Then you have to lose it."[16] It is the same absurdity, a contradiction we must trust God to resolve.

Moreover, continues Kierkegaard, the genuine faith of inwardness is unique in that reflection on it only increases passion, whereas reflection on a merely psychological matter diminishes passion. Suppose, for instance, that someone insults me. I am enraged—until I begin to reflect on what happened. I think to myself, "Perhaps she is having a bad day. Perhaps she grew up in a home without love, or perhaps she suffered an injury that affected her personality." The more I reflect on the incident, the more my passion is attenuated. By contrast, the more I reflect on the absurdity of living in truth, the more my passion is intensified: the more I reflect on the sheer absurdity of the Incarnation, the more I shake my head and fall on my knees in wonder. In other words, reflection on subjectivity *increases* passion. If we live in truth with respect to being a disciple of Jesus Christ, then to reflect on our discipleship ought to increase our ardour. It should not be the case that I was a more enthusiastic disciple twelve years ago than I am today, having become used to it.

There is no suggestion, in all of the above, that Kierkegaard is advocating intensity of just *any* passion as a measure of (or evidence for) subjectivity; after all, there is no shortage of religious fanatics. Nor does he ever advocate a mindlessness that eschews reflection. While reflection

---

16. See, for example, Mark 8:35 and 10:31.

is not faith, nor a substitute for faith, it ought nevertheless to engage us and magnify the passion of our faith.

Finally, the inward appropriation described by Kierkegaard is dialectical. Here he is intent on preserving a recognition of the dialectic between God the Subject and the subjectivity of our relatedness to God. In other words, God as Subject gives himself to us, but never gives himself up to us or over to us. While God allows us to know him truly and adequately, he never allows us to know him exhaustively, and in no situation allows himself to be reduced to an object of our knowledge. We never know God definitively. Neither do we know him in the same way that we know empirical matters. And although we can apprehend him (as we are apprehended by him), we can never comprehend him. Even in revealing himself to us, he hides himself: his self-communication is always indirect, so that his self-revelation can only be apprehended in faith. However, this dialectic does not entail the same sort of approximateness that characterizes the knowledge of the scientist, historian, or theologian; on the contrary, human subjectivity, the result of our relating dialectically to the God who relates dialectically to us, always issues in *truth*—that is, reality—and leaves us transformed in the way that objective knowledge never does.

The *bona fide* Christian is dismissed by others as an egoist, observes Kierkegaard, because she insists on the response of the solitary individual—on that inwardness which no one else can live for her. The Christian is also regarded as an enemy of others, since her concern with Christianity has nothing to do with protecting the community against the Turk or against any other threat. Moreover, the Christian's embrace of an absurdity makes her a laughingstock. In fact, remarks Kierkegaard with biting irony, society views us as a spectacle—entertainment for which the state ought to pay us!

Now, how can the Christian communicate this faith to the world? Only indirectly, insists Kierkegaard in a response that is now familiar to us; in other words, any direct medium to which we resort necessarily denatures the message. The message is the gospel; the medium is indirect communication. A story is indirect communication, a lecture is direct communication, and a sermon is usually a combination of both. Jesus characteristically uses indirect communication. When people come to him and profess to want to follow him, he does not list the qualifications and expectations of disciples. He says, "Once upon a time, a king decided to go to battle, but he made one mistake: he didn't reckon with how much it was going to cost. And he ended up looking like a fool, because he got halfway through the battle and had to quit. Now, you say you want to become a disciple? You'd better go home and think about it."[17]

Jesus uses a variety of methods of indirect communication, all of which invite or demand commitment. When Pilate asks, "Are you the Son of God?" in Mark's gospel, Jesus does not tell him the answer; he only says, "If you say so."[18] When detractors ask, "Is your authority human or divine?" he does not answer that question directly either. Instead he says, "Is the authority of John the Baptist human or divine?"—requiring them to come down on one side or the other. The questioners see that they are in trouble no matter which way they answer: if they say that John the Baptist's authority is divine, Jesus will demand why they did not listen to him, and if they say John the Baptist's authority is only human, the crowds will turn on them. So they reply, "We aren't going to tell you what we think." They refuse to commit themselves. Whereupon Jesus says, "In that case, I won't tell you the source of my authority."[19] In other words, you cannot know the nature of my authority until you commit yourself to me in faith. Jesus is always communicating indirectly, because existence, or subjectivity, cannot be thought; it can only be lived.

That is why, again, the ultimate stance for the Christian is never argument, but witness. No one has ever yet been argued into the Kingdom, no matter how gentle or polite the argument—a point that ought to give us pause concerning the supposed effectiveness of apologetics. Argument is always aimed at philosophical demonstration, and is direct communication, whereas witness is indirect communication. If our vocation is to be witnesses, all we can do is

17. Luke 14:28.
18. Mark 15:2.
19. Matt. 21:23–27.

witness to what it is to live *in truth*. We cannot *convey* that to someone else; we cannot deliver the reality of it. When Peter instructs us always to be ready to give an answer for the hope that is in us,[20] he is talking about witness, not philosophical demonstration; he is, after all, a Jew steeped in the logic of the Old Testament, not the logic of Aristotle. He is familiar with the category of witness, and he means that God's people ought to be able to articulate the truth vouchsafed to them; they ought to bear witness to the truth of Jesus Christ that now characterizes their existence. We are to bear witness to that truth, and leave the efficacy of our witness with the Holy Spirit. Apologetics attempts to generate its own efficacy by removing the paradox (what the Bible calls the scandal or offence) of the gospel. Two things are needed in bringing people to faith: human attestation of the gospel—that is, witness—and the work of the Holy Spirit.[21]

One more point should be noted regarding faith as the embrace of the paradox: for Kierkegaard, it is only this self-abandonment in faith that renders us a self, that allows us to *exist*, to stand out from the crowd. At the end of *Fear and Trembling*, Kierkegaard makes the following moving statement:

Either there is an absolute duty toward God—and if so it is the

20. 1 Peter 3:15.

21. As mentioned above, there remains a place for a kind of apologetics, not to argue for the superiority of the Christian faith, nor to ground its authority, but to show that many of the objections people have against the faith are not real objections at all. Philosophical argument for this purpose is legitimate. Even then, however, the point is never to belittle the other for his objections, or to justify oneself intellectually in the eyes of the unbeliever. It should be an expression of the ordinary courtesy that calls for respectful engagement with someone who addresses us. Notice that in Acts, the Greek word *logizomai* (λογιζομαι), meaning "to dialogue or discuss," is used twenty-five times; Paul is constantly engaging in dialogue and discussion. In one community, he is said to have done so for two years—evidence that he was respectful and not obnoxious, or he would not have lasted there for more than two days. As a student in residence at university, I found it especially easy to demolish reductionist objections to faith. I would always think that I had gained a triumph for the Kingdom, yet none of the people I browbeat into helpless silence ever appeared to become believers. For Kierkegaard, apologetics is the church's way of turning wine into water: a counter-miracle to the sign performed by Jesus at Cana, and a denaturing of the gospel.

paradox here described, that the individual as the individual is higher than the universal and as the individual stands in an absolute relation to the absolute—or else faith never existed, because it has always existed, or, to put it differently, Abraham is lost...[22]

This is a difficult statement to understand at first blush, so let us examine it. "The absolute" he mentions above (which I will henceforth capitalize in the interest of disambiguation) is God. If you live in truth, you stand in an absolute relationship—one that is unconditional, unreserved, and unhesitating—to the Absolute. That in itself is a wonderful paradox, says Kierkegaard: as an individual you are finite, merely one of many particulars, yet by virtue of your absolute relationship to the Absolute, the individual that you are is "higher," more real and more significant, than any universal. The question is, are you this individual, or are you a part of the crowd? Like all Existentialists, especially Nietzsche, Kierkegaard is concerned with avoiding being part of the nameless, faceless "herd." His answer to avoiding this is to stand in an absolute relationship of utter obedience, in faith, to the Absolute.

Kierkegaard is known as the philosopher of the individual. This does not mean that he turns his back on society, or that he has no ecclesiology; but he knows that God, while he loves the entire universe, speaks only to humans, and that God's address to us is a personalizing one, singling each of us out in an individuality not to be found anywhere else in life. God's address to you, summoning you to an obedience whose substance is an impenetrable paradox, *renders* you an individual, a person, a self, in the way that nothing else in the universe can. Only from the inside, as one who has abandoned herself unconditionally in response to this summons, can you grasp the paradox; and only in that absolute self-abandonment do you exist as a true self, living in truth.

Now, either all this is the case, concludes Kierkegaard in the quotation above, or Abraham is a fool. If God, the Absolute, did not

22. Søren Kierkegaard, "Fear and Trembling," in *Existentialism: Basic Writings*, ed. Charles Guignon and Derk Pereboom (Indianapolis: Hackett Publishing, 2001), 77.

summon Abraham to an absolute obedience that cannot be humanly understood, and in which he stands in absolute relation to that Absolute, then Abraham is a laughingstock, and you are *nothing*.

Even though Kierkegaard celebrated what it is to live in truth, he recognized his own deficiency of faith and was always aware that he lived under the judgment of what he wrote for others. Even his attack on the Danish national church, though relentless, was not arrogant; every criticism he advanced against the state church he also turned against himself. Whose faith is devoid of compromise? Kierkegaard holds up Abraham as the paradigm of faith, concentrating on the one incident between Abraham and Isaac that typifies real faith; but as we all know, even Abraham's faith was not uncompromised. He lied twice about his wife to save his own skin, and took the fulfillment of the promise into his own hands when he fathered Ishmael with Hagar. Nevertheless, Kierkegaard would say that even though Abraham's faith is as compromised by self-interest and sin as anyone's in any era, that faith as attested in Genesis 22 is real. Both Older and Newer Testaments declare nothing less. Abraham remains the prototype of all believers.

In Romans 4 Paul, too, refers to Abraham as a model of faith; and then in Romans 8, where Paul speaks of what God has done, he exclaims in utter amazement, "He spared not his own Son!" In other words, God did spare Abraham's son, and in so doing spared Abraham; but he did not spare his own Son—which means that God did not spare himself—for our sake. This, above everything else, is what moves Paul. As glorious as Abraham's willingness to sacrifice Isaac is, unspeakably more glorious is the fact that God was not only willing to sacrifice himself, but did so.

Kierkegaard's Spheres of Existence: Stages on Life's Way

In the previous chapter, by way of general introduction to Kierkegaard, mention was made of the importance in his thought of a dialectic involving three stages of life: the aesthetic, the ethical, and the *religious* (in a special sense of that word). We now return in greater detail to this aspect of Kierkegaard's Existentialism in order to make a connection with what has been said above about the nature of faith and what it means to be a Christian.[23]

Recall, first of all, that Kierkegaard's dialectic differs from Hegel's (and from Marx's) in that it is generated by human choice. Both Hegel and Marx posit a dialectic that is in some sense driven inexorably: Hegel's by Spirit, Mind, or Idea, and Marx's by the laws of Dialectical Materialism, which are the laws of history. For Kierkegaard, it is radical human decision that moves a person from one stage to the other. Second, while only one stage or sphere can be primary at any time, the three are not mutually exclusive. For example, we can move to the ethical without thereby forfeiting everything of the aesthetic, since even the person who lives with moral rigour and integrity rather than for self-gratification can still enjoy things for the sake of enjoying them. Third, the decision or choice that advances the dialectic is not the choice of a sphere or stage as such, but the choice of a *self* commensurate with that stage. In other words, if I move from the aesthetic to the ethical, it is not that I have chosen the principle of moral obligation over the pleasure principle; rather, I am choosing the kind of self I want to be. Do I want to be the kind of self that is exhausted in pleasure-seeking and self-fulfillment, or the kind of self that is constituted by a recognition of ethical duty and the sacrifice it requires? It is not so much a question of what you want to *do* as of the kind of self you want to *be*.

The aesthetic stage

The aesthetic stage is characterized by the pursuit of pleasure: whatever pleases me or satisfies me, whatever I find useful or profitable, I do. Such pleasure need not be lurid or vulgar; in fact, it characteristically is not, because people weary quickly of such pleasures. People tire much less quickly of more *refined* pleasures such as art, literature, music, or drama, and so can sustain the pursuit much longer. For that reason, observed Kierkegaard, refined pleasure is more dangerous with respect to living *in truth* than lurid or vulgar pleasure, since we do not despair as quickly through refined pleasure and hence do not come to our senses as quickly. Despair, in the sense of the undeniable hopelessness of our state, is what brings us to our senses. One reason the prodigal son came to his senses

23. I have been stimulated in my exposition here by Peter Vardy, *An Introduction to Kierkegaard* (Peabody, MA: Hendrickson Publishers, 2008).

as quickly as he did in the far country is that he was starving: not even pig food was available to him.

Any sort of profound satisfaction qualifies as *aesthetic*—for example, the pleasure that accompanies scientific success, or the pleasure to be found in solving a formidable mathematical problem. Paul Erdös, a Hungarian, was for years deemed to be the world's best mathematician, and went from university to university around the world holding seminars in mathematics. He went to one American institution where someone had written on the blackboard a problem that had remained unsolved for months. Paul Erdös looked at it for ten minutes, and wrote the solution. It is not difficult to imagine the pleasure not only that Erdös would find in solving the unsolvable problem but also that others would enjoy from watching him do so. Kierkegaard maintains that such a pleasure is legitimate, and can arise from many different sorts of objectivity—such as a scientific discovery, or a breakthrough in the exegesis of a difficult passage of Scripture. However, the pursuit of any pleasure for its own sake, no matter how legitimate, is the mark of life in the aesthetic stage.

For this reason Kierkegaard pronounced Kant and Hegel "philosophers of the aesthetic," in that they were preoccupied with achieving the intellectual satisfaction of metaphysical completeness or comprehensiveness. Kant wrote *The Critique of Pure Reason* for the sake of the work which followed it, *The Critique of Practical Reason*, in which he discusses moral obligation; at bottom, therefore, Kant is an ethical philosopher, or at least he was considered so by himself and others. According to Kierkegaard, however, he is an aesthete, since he appears to find his greatest pleasure in constructing a philosophical system. The system may support the ultimacy of ethical existence, but it is the construction of this system, in all its coherent and comprehensive glory, that affords its articulator the greatest pleasure. (Of course, as we saw earlier, Kierkegaard and other Existentialists would claim that this pleasure is based on an illusion anyway, since they deny there is such a thing as metaphysical or philosophical completeness or comprehensiveness. They insist that philosophy can only be done in fragments.)

Since the aesthetic stage is characterized by the pursuit of pleasure and self-gratification, it is also characterized by immediacy. The tendency is to seek peak experiences, those that satisfy in the short term and can be obtained most quickly. As a result, given the law of diminishing returns, an ever-greater stimulus is needed to achieve satisfaction, until finally the aesthete experiences satiety, boredom, and—eventually—despair.

Note, moreover, that the aesthete is dependent on fortune, in that satisfaction is frequently secured or denied by circumstances beyond our control. Did the orchestra play superbly or wretchedly? Were the paintings in the gallery exquisite, or were they mediocre? Whether the pleasure-seeker comes away satisfied or frustrated depends on circumstances over which she has no jurisdiction. For this reason, aesthetes feel themselves to be in the grip of fate, and seek to control circumstances.

This in turn leads to a preoccupation with self-protection. Just as the demons in the New Testament recognize that they are threatened by Jesus,[24] the aesthete is "demonic," says Kierkegaard, in that he finds God a threat to his control and independence. Kierkegaard is using *demonic* here in a way that is not customary in the church. When we say that someone is demonic, what is usually meant is that he is in the grip or under the influence of evil; Kierkegaard, however, uses the word to describe anyone who finds Jesus Christ a threat, just as the demons did in the gospels. The aesthete's self-sufficiency, her control and independence, are in fact threatened by God; for this reason she attempts to protect herself by means of "inclosing reserve" (a technical term in Kierkegaard):[25] she turns inward, builds a fort around herself, and lives inside it undisturbed by the claims of others, rejecting all obligations to God and to other people. She does not want to be upset by the suffering neighbour who makes a claim on her, so she fends off all such threats to her tranquillity by building a fort and hunkering down inside it. This is the principle of "inclosing reserve." Moreover, since the

24. For example, in Mark 5:7.

25. Kierkegaard, *The Sickness Unto Death,* trans. Howard V. Hong and Edna H. Hong (Princeton: Princeton University Press, 1980), 63–67, 72ff, 154.

aesthete is preoccupied with self-fulfillment, all love at this stage is need-love—that is, seeking to be loved, but not loving; craving love, but not giving it.

The aesthete cannot repent, declares Kierkegaard, since to repent is to surrender the identity she has worked out for herself. She has spent much time and energy in constructing the kind of self she cherishes, and is not about to give it up; in choosing and becoming that self she has foreclosed on the possibility of repentance. That being the case, says Kierkegaard, she can exercise repentance only as it is first given to her by God.

Seeing the ultimate futility of her aestheticism, the aesthete despairs, but her despair will not of itself precipitate the ethical stage; she must choose. She can live in despair indefinitely, or make a decision to move beyond the aesthetic stage. Again, the decision she makes is not ultimately a decision to *do* something different but to *be* someone different; it is the choice of a different self made for her by God.

The ethical stage

The second stage is the ethical stage. It is the attempt to realize a universal ethical obligation: the Golden Rule, or a similar recognized standard. It is the commitment never to lie, always to be fair, and so on. These are understood to be universal obligations—*everyone* ought to be truthful and fair—hence in this stage we are acknowledging and submitting to a claim or obligation laid on all humankind, rather than insisting on our autonomy like the aesthete. The essence of ethics is that the obligation is the same for everybody; hence the ethical stage pertains not to the individual but to the community. Moreover, whereas the aesthete is preoccupied with pleasure for *herself*, the ethical person is preoccupied with duty towards *others*, indicating a fundamental shift from self-orientation to other-orientation. If the love that characterizes the aesthetic stage is need-love, the love commensurate with the ethical stage is duty-love: "I love you" means "I am going to do the right thing by you." We are still, however, at a far remove from Christian love of neighbour, which will arise only at the religious stage.

The demands of ethical existence are rigorous. While they are simple, they are by no means easy; many of the simplest things in life are also the most difficult. Consider the obligation to tell the truth, for example: it is easy to understand, but difficult to fulfill, because there is no little cost attached. In fact, ethical existence is often fraught with tragedy related to this cost: in the classical Greek legend Agamemnon must kill his daughter, and in the Old Testament story Jephthah must kill his in order to keep his word. Brutus, a Roman leader, must kill his son, since duty to the state takes precedence over duty to one's family[26]—a claim we regularly recognize in extreme situations such as war.

One very significant point about the ethical stage, as conceived by Kierkegaard, is that God is irrelevant to our honouring any ethical code. The ethical code we recognize and to which we submit has no reference to God at all, even if it is the Ten Commandments.

This feature of moral uprightness in the ethical stage becomes clearer if we view it in sharp contrast to Luther's "First Commandment Righteousness." Kierkegaard was, after all, a Lutheran; his Lutheranism surfaces especially in his later work, when he moves away from philosophy into theology, but already here its influence can be discerned. For Luther, the first of the Ten Commandments includes not only the words, "You shall have no other gods before me," but also what some people regard as the preface: "You were slaves in Egypt, and I saved you with my outstretched arm." Understood in this way, the first commandment is pure gospel. "You were slaves, and I saved you of my own free will, out of my sheer mercy," God reminds his people; "therefore you will have no gods before me." The obligation expressed in the command is founded directly on the gracious act of God, and is the faithful response to it.[27] As Luther goes on to explain, the gospel both calls for faith and brings about faith, which is then expressed in obedience to the command.

Hence the first commandment, and all the rest that proceed from it, can be honoured *only in faith*. If we attempt to honour any of

---

26. Kierkegaard, *Fear and Trembling*, trans. Howard V. Hong and Edna H. Hong (Princeton: Princeton University Press, 1983), 57–58.

27. For an exposition of "First Commandment Righteousness" and the Decalogue, see Timothy J. Wengert, *Martin Luther's Catechisms* (Minneapolis: Fortress Press, 2009), chapter 2.

them merely as an ethical principle—saying, for example, "Stealing is wrong, therefore I will not steal"—Luther maintains we have *violated* the commandment because our action is not an expression of faith. No doubt Luther and Kierkegaard have in mind here Paul's pronouncement, "What does not proceed from faith is sin."[28]

The essence of the Ten Commandments is not an impersonal moral code to which we relate ourselves; rather, the Commandments are God's claim on his people's faithful obedience in response to his gracious, saving act. Apart from faith in him, there is no obedience; the unbeliever who refrains from stealing violates the commandment as surely as the unbeliever who steals, because the commandment not to steal can be kept only as our not-stealing is an expression of our faith in God. Where such faith is lacking, our not-stealing is merely an expression of our independence and hence *defiance* of God.[29] Sermons that reduce the Commandments to "Ten Moral Steps to Success" are sheer paganism. The Bible never deals in principles; it deals with the concrete Person of the living God, and our concrete person in relation to him.

To be sure, the ethical life requires dedication; but at the same time, its nature and goal can be understood by the world, publicly recognized and congratulated, and even publicly required—unlike Abrahamic faith. After all, do we not honour people who live morally exemplary lives? We may even award them the Order of Canada. Abraham would never have been nominated for the Order of Canada: he was going to kill his son. Only public contempt and a prison cell await the man who kills his son. The Order of Canada is for the person who lives a morally exemplary life, a life characterized by such virtue as we can all appreciate and endorse. By contrast, as Kierkegaard never wearies of reminding us, Abraham and Abrahamic faith we can never understand.

The reason we can all understand the ethical is that it is customarily grounded in philosophy; it is a construct of metaphysics.[30] As we have

---

28. Romans 14:23.

29. Nontheistic Existentialists regard a stance of defiance, in the face of the meaninglessness and contradictoriness of life, as essential to human authenticity. Such a position, however, must not be confused with defiance, disobedience, and disdain with respect to God, the primal sin of Genesis 3.

seen, however, the Existentialist maintains that all metaphysics and philosophical systems are eventually found to be empty—a fact which, for the person at the ethical stage of life, results in despair. This despair is multifaceted: in addition to the despair of realizing that ethics can ultimately never lend meaning to existence, there is the despair born of ethical failure ("Wretched man that I am, who shall deliver me from this body of death?"[31]). But there is also a despair born of ethical *success*, because the virtuous pagan remains unaware of herself before God as spirit and hence misses entirely the relation of inwardness. The despair of such a person is not the *feeling* of despair, the anguish of despair, but the actual *state* of being without hope whether one feels it or not.[32] Since we live in an era that psychologizes everything, we understand the notion of despair only as a feeling: clearly, if a person is profoundly depressed, he has despaired. But what if he feels happy and confident despite being in a genuinely hopeless predicament? Then he is unaware of his own despair.[33]

To *feel hopeless*, for whatever reason, is affective despair; to *be in a hopeless situation* is ontological despair—and this twofold nature of despair, maintains Kierkegaard, arises at the ethical stage just as it did at the aesthetic stage. Despair is, however, a heaven-sent provision that drives us to move beyond our present complacency, just as it drove the

30. This explains why we talk so much today about "values" rather than ethics. Ethics presuppose a philosophical or religious foundation and hence universal applicability, whereas values presuppose no foundation at all and are a matter of personal preference; one person can value this and another that, and no one need offer any argument for the claim of his own values or recognize the claim of anyone else's. Since most preferences are rooted in prejudice, there is no difference, in the end, between "values" and "prejudice." Traditionally, ethics is grounded either in philosophy or theology. Theology disappeared a long time ago in public life, leaving an aftermath of publicly-owned philosophy that would still support a universal ethic; but now this is also gone, since Postmodernism denies the legitimacy of all philosophy.

31. Romans 7:24.

32. *Desperare* is Latin for "to be without hope"; *sperare* means "to hope."

33. C.S. Lewis uses the illustration of passengers on two trains headed for collision. They cannot see the oncoming train as it snakes towards them through the hills; they do not know their predicament, and are therefore perfectly content. A person sitting on the hillside above the track, however, who can see both trains, sees that the situation of the passengers is hopeless, whether they feel hopeless or not. *The Great Divorce* (Glasgow: Fontana Books, 1972).

prodigal son to come to his senses in the far country; it is what keeps us from eddying at the aesthetic or ethical stage forever. For this reason, he says, far from trying to rid the world of such despair, we ought to magnify it.

The religious stage

The third stage is the religious stage. Before we proceed to describe what it involves, however, we need to acquaint ourselves with a particularly salient notion in Kierkegaard's understanding of what it means to be human. He maintains that human existence is "a synthesis of the temporal and the eternal." That is a peculiar phrase of his, because it seems to exude a scent of Hegelian philosophy—according to which, recall, the finite human creature can rise by means of philosophical reflection to the eternal standpoint, with the result that finite human thinking becomes one with Cosmic Mind thinking itself. However, Kierkegaard never intends any such notion; on the contrary, he is using Hegelian vocabulary to turn Hegel's philosophy on its head. By "a synthesis of the temporal and the eternal" he does not mean a hybrid of the human and divine. He is not suggesting that we become divinized or semi-divine, or that human speculation can ever give rise to consonance with God. He simply means that human existence at all times unfolds in relation to God. God can be fled, but God cannot be escaped, and therefore human existence always has to do with one's relationship to God, and to be truly human is to acknowledge, embrace, and dwell in that relationship.

This overarching unity of embraced relatedness, if you will, this synthesis of the temporal and the eternal, can only be brought about by means of a decisive, continuously renewed choice or commitment—a *leap*. To synthesize the eternal in time means to hear a divine summons and obey it; there is a *moment in time* when a person apprehends the eternal and responds to the summons it issues by acting on that summons in radical commitment. This moment is crucial. It is Abraham with knife in hand. It is Jesus in Gethsemane—not as he is pictured in Sunday School art, kneeling serenely at a conveniently flat rock with his hands folded and a shaft of light streaming down on him, but in anguish, staggering and falling repeatedly to his knees. Such a moment, when we discern God's summons to us and act on it, is the instant of synthesizing the eternal in time, and is what God mandates for every human being.

It is in this synthesis of the temporal and the eternal, this act of radical commitment, that we move from the ethical stage to the religious. Moreover, as mentioned above, the commitment must be continuously renewed. Here, as in many other instances, Kierkegaard echoes Lutheran theology: the first of Luther's *Ninety-Five Theses* is that the Christian life consists of daily, lifelong repentance. And as we saw before, repentance in the biblical sense does not mean tearful self-flagellation and remorse, but turning around: making a U-turn or aboutface, and heading back to God. Luther's point is that the Christian life requires a daily renewal of our commitment of faith in Christ.[34] Kierkegaard is making a similar point about the commitment that moves us from one stage of the dialectic to the next.

We can synthesize the eternal in time, then, only as we move to the religious stage—which can, in turn, be subdivided into Religion A and Religion B. The distinction is an important one for Kierkegaard. Religion A is religiosity, but not yet faith; it is the necessary precursor to faith. It is the attempt to relate oneself to God by means of a continuously repeated commitment exercised solely through one's own power. This is a commitment characterized first of all by *infinite resignation*, the surrender of all temporal aspirations; it is in this act of surrender that we gain an "eternal consciousness," an awareness of God. Note here the movement from *universal*, which pertains to the ethical stage, to *eternal*, which pertains to the religious stage.[35]

The concept of 'infinite resignation' requires amplification. It refers to the act of giving up, forever, that which is held most dear. Abraham's willingness to sacrifice Isaac is often misinterpreted as an instance of infinite resignation, as the act of relinquishing the thing he valued

34. The same is true of a marriage commitment, or any other sustained life commitment. For example, every day on waking I repeat my ordination vows. I have done this daily since May 13, 1970, when I first professed these vows in the service of ordination that publicly sealed my vocation.

35. Kierkegaard, *Fear and Trembling*, 48.

most: the son of promise, and thereby the promise itself. This is the misinterpretation expressed, for example, by a clergywoman who once talked to me about what she had given up to enter the ministry: "I'm just like Abraham," she said. "I gave up my dearest and best." She was mistaken, because Abraham's act was *not* one of infinite resignation, of giving up his dearest and best, but of faith: of giving it up *in the confidence that it would be given back to him.* Abraham believed that somehow, in a way he could not foresee, Isaac would be restored to him *in this life,* that he could obey God's command *and yet* possess God's promise even though the two were in blatant contradiction. He perceived the paradox, the absurdity, but entrusted its resolution to God.

This difference between faith and resignation is critical. Resignation is a preliminary movement presupposed by faith, but not identical with faith. Giving up everything out of devotion to God involves no paradox, and hence no faith. Faith is surrendering our dearest and best to God *in the confidence that it will somehow be restored to us.* Understood in this way, faith regards Jesus Christ as Saviour, while resignation regards him merely as a type of human perfection, as an exemplar or model to be imitated; Religion A, in other words, is not specifically Christian. In Religion A, Jesus exemplifies infinite resignation, and is the acme of God-consciousness; he was consummately aware of God, and can bestow on us the same God-consciousness if we imitate him in being willing to surrender everything.[36] But this is not faith.

If infinite resignation is the first expression of Religion A, the second is suffering, the suffering entailed directly by giving up, in a continuously renewed commitment, all attachment to finite aspirations. It is the pain of loss, even though it is loss we have voluntarily taken on ourselves. We suffer pain because that which we have given up is genuinely good. This suffering is of the kind that Abraham would have experienced if he had *not* held on to the paradox in faith: if he had obeyed the command in the belief that he would thereby surely lose the promise forever. It is not yet the existential pathos of faith,

---

36. Those familiar with the theology of Schleiermacher and of liberal theologians who followed him will notice the similarity.

described earlier in this chapter, but it is nonetheless intensely painful, and unrelievable except by a return to the aesthetic stage.

The third and highest expression of Religion A is "an eternal or perpetual recollection of guilt."[37] This is not yet the consciousness of sin, of having violated a Person. Rather, it is the form taken by despair in Religion A, "a constant awareness that one's own powers are insufficient to express infinitude."[38] In other words, it is an ongoing realization that our relationship to God, as we understand God to be, is defective—and that it must necessarily and eternally be so because of our finitude.

Religion B, by contrast, is Abrahamic faith. Unlike resignation, faith is an embrace of paradox, and cannot be understood. Abraham chooses to obey the command of God without reservation, all the while trusting the promise of God equally without reservation, when the promise and the command are contradictory. Therefore he cannot be understood, just as the Absolute Paradox (the Incarnation) cannot be understood. In Abrahamic faith the finite is given up—only, absurdly, to be received again in this life. That is to say, when Abraham raises the knife in order to plunge it into Isaac, he fully expects Isaac to die, yet he also continues to believe the promise that he will have descendants as vast as the sand on the seashore. Risking everything, he obeys the command that ensures the cancellation of the promise, while at the same time clinging to God's guarantee of the promise, trusting God to resolve the contradiction in some unforeseeable way.

When God spares Isaac, Abraham receives him back *with joy*. We might expect that, having genuinely given up Isaac in obedience to God's command, Abraham would subsequently be disappointed to find that he ends up keeping Isaac, as though he had done the wrong thing after all in surrendering him, or had misunderstood God's command. According to this scenario Abraham would feel better if Isaac had been taken away from him, because then he could be confident that he had done what God wanted. That would perhaps be true had Abraham's act been one of infinite resignation rather than faith, maintains Kierkegaard;

37. "Introduction" in *Existentialism: Basic Writings*, edited by Charles Guignon and Derk Pereboom (Indianapolis: Hackett Publishing, 2001), 13.

38. Ibid.

but in the surrender that is an expression of faith, the finite that is given up is received again *with joy*.

Kierkegaard's point is that we keep the finite, and keep it in its proper place, only as we surrender it in faithful obedience to God. We can see how this is true when it comes to parenting our children, for example. Some people live for their children, and the children in such cases invariably disappoint, because parents who live for their children always expect more than the children can deliver. If, on the other hand, we profoundly give up our children in trustful obedience to God, he gives them back to us to be enjoyed in proper proportion. The only person who properly rejoices in the finite, insists Kierkegaard, is the one who freely gives it up and joyfully receives it back.

The same point (echoing the declaration first made by Jesus in the gospels) is made nontheistically by other Existentialists, such as Jean-Paul Sartre: it is only when he is willing to give up his own life in the French Resistance that he receives his life back. Until he is willing to give himself up, he is (as we observed before) not a self at all; he is a shadow-self, a ghostly self. It is only once he is willing to give up his life that he possesses it and becomes an authentic self. To understand this point is to grasp one of the genuine profundities of Existentialist thought; we grasp it, however, only in the process of living it ourselves. No amount of description or argument will authenticate it for us.

A noteworthy feature of Religion B is awareness of sin (which is different from the "guilt" of Religion A) and acceptance of forgiveness. Note that forgiveness presupposes judgment: to say we have been forgiven is to say we have first been judged and condemned. This in turn raises the important distinction between forgiving and excusing: what is excusable we excuse, but what is utterly inexcusable can only be forgiven—or left unforgiven. When God forgives us, therefore, he has not excused us; he has first condemned us. In Religion B, the individual recognizes his sin against God and God's condemnation of it, but far from being plunged into despair, accepts God's forgiveness. In fact, it is in accepting God's forgiveness that the individual acknowledges his sin and the rightness of judgment.

In Religion B Christ is regarded not merely as exemplar but as

Saviour, and the individual is not merely an admirer of Christ but a follower. For Kierkegaard, being a follower of Christ is not a matter of imitating his good deeds moralistically (in a way typical of the ethical stage), nor of seeking to be like him in surrendering finite goods and aspirations (as one does in Religion A), but of existentially abandoning oneself to God in an act of faith, in the same way that the Son abandoned himself to the Father in complete and utter trust. Only those possessing Abrahamic faith are true followers of Christ. Love at this stage moves beyond need-love and duty-love to become, at last, free gift-love, love as the gift of oneself.

In the paradox of faith, as we have noted, the finite we have renounced is given back to us; in the same way, the choice to leave the aesthetic and ethical stages behind in order to embrace the religious stage finds us properly re-appropriating the aesthetic and ethical after all. At the religious stage we can descend to the aesthetic and properly enjoy what God has given us to enjoy. We can also descend to the ethical and love our neighbour, not in recognition of a philosophically-constructed duty or as dogged submission to a moral code, but as an expression of our relationship to God—that is, as First Commandment Righteousness.

5

Søren Kierkegaard:
Fear and Trembling

Introduction: "The Teleological Suspension of the Ethical" and Original Sin

One notion for which Kierkegaard has been particularly vilified is "the teleological suspension of the ethical,"[1] the laying aside of ethical considerations in order to fulfill a higher goal or end (*teleological* being derived from Greek *telos* [τέλος], meaning *end* or *goal*). Abraham, once again, is the illustration. He was willing to murder Isaac even though murder is forbidden, because he was subject to a higher claim: the will of God that he give up his son. Kierkegaard has been both congratulated and (not surprisingly) condemned for this controversial notion.

Obviously, caution must be exercised in interpreting and applying the "suspension." Martin Buber, a Jewish philosopher at the University of Frankfurt in the 1930s, was horrified when his students came to class wearing the swastika on their arms the day after Hitler came to power. When Buber remonstrated with them for wearing the Nazi armband, they replied, "It's the teleological suspension of the ethical: doesn't our duty to the Fatherland transcend all other ethical considerations? How is that different from Abraham's obedience to God transcending the prohibition to murder?"[2] Buber was aghast.

1. Søren Kierkegaard, *Fear and Trembling*, trans. Howard V. Hong and Edna H. Hong (Princeton: Princeton University Press, 1983), 54–67, 263.

2. Rabbi Dr. Lawrence Englander related this incident to me in a private conversation. For Buber's studied reflection on this topic see his *Eclipse of God* (New York: Harper, 1957), chapter 7, "On the Suspension of the Ethical."

Buber's students were missing a crucial fact about the Kierkegaard corpus. It is only in *Fear and Trembling* that he appears to advocate the teleological suspension of the ethical, and it is always to be remembered that the fictitious narrator of that work, Johannes Climacus, speaks from the standpoint of someone who is attracted to the Christian faith but has not yet made the radical commitment of the believer. Having discerned something of the nature of discipleship, Climacus does argue for an existential truth that is disclosed only to commitment and can never be apprehended apart from that commitment. However, as a non-Christian he does not endorse the doctrine of original sin, a doctrine that Kierkegaard considered to lie at the heart of the faith.

Kierkegaard compared the doctrine of original sin to the knot tied in thread when sewing in order to keep the garment from unravelling. Absent this "knot," the unbeliever perceives a bizarre suspension of the ethical in Abraham's case, failing to realize that original sin entails a sort of terrible "suspension of the ethical" for *everyone*: we are mandated to obey God, yet are utterly incapable of doing so, with the result that no ethical act can cure the condition of the human heart. In other words, the primary point of *Fear and Trembling* is to call into question the ultimacy of ethics; in so doing, it is laying the groundwork for pointing us to the ultimacy of faith.

It does not, however, purport to be a positive account of Christian discipleship with respect to the neighbour; that account is set out in *Works of Love*. There Kierkegaard makes clear that the story of Abraham and Isaac, while it illustrates perfectly the Abrahamic leap of faith each of us must make, cannot be taken as a paradigm for how we are to relate to the neighbour *after taking* that leap of faith. Having embraced the Absolute Paradox and abandoned ourselves without reservation to God, having accepted our condemnation and forgiveness and become followers of Christ as Saviour, having synthesized the eternal in time, we enter a qualitatively different stage of existence (in Kierkegaard's three-stage dialectic), and acquire a self whose conduct towards the neighbour is characterized by love rather than by moral obligation.

There is another, related point we should note here: because *the* Son was not spared on Golgotha, God will never ever ask any parent to sacrifice his child. Child sacrifice figured prominently in the religion of the Canaanite region surrounding Israel, and throughout the Old Testament the Hebrew prophets are categorically opposed to it. One major point of the Genesis 22 story (although not the main point), expressed in the appearance of the ram, is Israel's recognition that God *never* requires child sacrifice as a religious obligation. At Golgotha, on the other hand, no ram appeared; the Son *was* offered up by his Father on behalf of all, and for this reason no parent will ever be asked to offer up her child as an expression of Christian obedience. Admittedly, that is not the chief point of the story of the Cross, either, but certainly it is one of its implications. Meanwhile, forms of child sacrifice continue in our world today, such as in the sex trade, or in the abortion industry; in fact, in some of the rhetoric of the pro-choice movement we hear arguments for the teleological suspension of the ethical. Kierkegaard, however, does not use the expression, from within either the ethical or the religious stage, to legitimize unethical behaviour. He uses it only as a description of the pivotal moment when, by an unconditional commitment, Abraham embraced the irresolvable paradox and moved to a life-stage that transcends the ethical (without being indifferent to it, as will be seen below).

After writing *Concluding Unscientific Postscript*, and following two years of silence, Kierkegaard again takes up his pen and resumes writing—not as Climacus but unambiguously as a Christian, in his own voice and from within the orbit of faith. It is in these later writings that he upholds the doctrine of original sin which governs a correct understanding of "the teleological suspension of the ethical."

There are several crucial matters to keep in mind with regard to the church's understanding of the doctrine of original sin. First, it means that every dimension or aspect of the human is corrupted by sin. It is therefore not possible for us to *will* ourselves out of our own depravity; intensified effort merely confirms the will's captivity to sin. Neither can we *think* our way out of our depravity as the Rationalists maintain, because (as we have already seen) reasoning is as much corrupted by the Fall as our will. Equally corrupted are our affections, and we therefore cannot love our way out of depravity either. To be sure, we are capable of love, but our love is as "bent" as our thinking and our will, with the result that we love what we ought to hate and hate what we ought to love. In other words, there is no way that any one aspect of the human can save the rest, and hence no way we can overturn the arrears of the Fall ourselves. That is the first point to be made about original sin.

Kierkegaard upholds this everywhere. He echoes the emphatic conclusion to the story in Genesis 3, in which an angel with a flaming sword guards the entrance to Eden after the expulsion of Adam and Eve so that they cannot re-enter it on their own resources. We should note that Adam and Eve did not stride out of Eden defiantly or wander out of it ignorantly; they were expelled by a judicial act of God. That being the case, they can be re-admitted to Eden only if God's judgment is rescinded. It is after all not our sin, but God's judgment on our sin, that alienates us from God. Therefore we can be reconciled only if that judgment is dealt with from God's side. We are not reconciled by feeling remorse about what we have done and deciding of our own volition to return to God.[3] The flaming sword held by the angel at the entrance to Eden turns "this way and that," or every which way, meaning that all human attempts to go back to Eden are foreclosed by God. There being no way back, there is only the way ahead; that is, through the provision God has made in the Cross.[4]

Kierkegaard accordingly rejects the Platonic notion of *mimesis*, or recollection—the notion that deep down in the unconscious or semiconscious psyche we already have within us all that we need to know, and it is the role of the midwife-philosopher (such as Socrates), by asking leading questions, to help us give birth to it—to help us become aware of what we already know. Kierkegaard insists that the sword-wielding angel at the conclusion to Genesis 3 puts an end to any such hope with respect to both our being and our knowing.[5] We cannot

3. Some treatments of the parable of the Prodigal Son would suggest this sort of unilateral action on our part: no matter what we have done, we can always go back to God and be welcome. But the parable presupposes the Cross, which overturns God's judgment on our sin; absent the provision of God, we can never go back.

4. Only in the wake of the Cross, it should be noted, is it even possible for us to repent.

5. See Søren Kierkegaard, *Concluding Unscientific Postscript to Philosophical Fragments*, Vol. 1, ed. and trans. Howard V. Hong and Edna H. Hong (Princeton: Princeton University Press,

recollect anything of Eden salvifically and hence cannot gain re-entry by that means; the only way we can recover is through the provision made for us in the Cross. Only in the wake of that provision, where God's judgment is rescinded, can the "Welcome Home" sign be posted and the sinner invited to repent.

Second, on account of the devastation of original sin, we become aware of this truth only through the gift and revelation of God. In *Philosophical Fragments*, Kierkegaard has Johannes Climacus admit that the condition of our gaining authentic selfhood is one that must be provided by "the Teacher."[6] In other words, the condition of knowing or gaining truth is not something we have in ourselves; it must be given.

Existentialists after Kierkegaard disagree with him: Sartre and Camus maintain that we do have the condition for gaining truth within us. Kierkegaard, however, insists otherwise because his whole Existentialist understanding of the Christian faith presupposes original sin, total depravity, or human corruption—call it what you will—as the knot that keeps the garment from unravelling. The human predicament is rooted not in something we possess naturalistically but in our situation under God, the just Judge. Kierkegaard's Existentialist philosophy unfolds from that assumption, and everything he writes must be read in light of it.[7] Just as there is no self-willed restoration or reconciliation

---

1992), 205–206; see also his *The Sickness Unto Death*, ed. and trans. Howard V. Hong and Edna H. Hong (Princeton: Princeton University Press, 1983), 195–196. Additional support is to be found in Kierkegaard's *Upbuilding Discourses in Various Spirits*, ed. and trans. Howard V. Hong and Edna H. Hong (Princeton: Princeton University Press, 2009), 259.

6. Kierkegaard, *Philosophical Fragments,* trans. Howard V. Hong and Edna H. Hong (Princeton: Princeton University Press, 1985), chapter 2, "The God as Teacher and Savior."

7. John Wesley took a similar position long before. He said that there was an irreducible core of the Christian faith, surrounded by concentric circles of decreasingly important aspects of faith and practice, the outermost consisting of the unimportant. At the irreducible core he posited three things: original sin, justification by faith, and holiness. If original sin is dropped, he insisted, the whole Christian theological scheme collapses. Jesus came and took the Cross on himself not because we were at risk before God but because we were already condemned. See Victor Shepherd, "John Wesley: A Gift to the Universal Church," *Canadian Theological Review* (Winter, 2012): 54.

with God, there is no self-willed knowledge of God, for original sin cuts off all epistemic effectiveness with respect to the knowledge of God.

Paradox and the Theology of the Cross

"Abraham," says Kierkegaard, "was greater than all, great by reason of his power whose strength is impotence, great by reason of his wisdom whose secret is foolishness, great by reason of his hope whose form is madness, great by reason of the love which is hatred of oneself."[8] Note the plethora of paradoxes in this description: power whose strength is impotence, wisdom whose secret is foolishness, hope whose form is madness, love which is hatred of oneself. Kierkegaard is bringing forward paradox after paradox to express the truth of faith that the world can never grasp. The world can easily grasp a strength whose form is strength, or a weakness whose form is weakness, but a strength whose form is weakness is beyond the world's understanding. We see this kind of statement elsewhere in Kierkegaard, too, with reference to the self-revelation of God: even in revealing himself to us God remains hidden, says Kierkegaard—by which he means that the revealed God (in Jesus Christ) remains hidden to the world at large because he is accessible and knowable only through faith.

Where does Kierkegaard get this penchant for seeing paradox in the truth of faith? It is in accord with his reading of biblical logic generally, and that reading is informed by Luther. It is yet another evidence of the Lutheranism we have detected elsewhere in Kierkegaard. Specifically, in this case, he is echoing Luther's *theologia crucis*, or theology of the Cross, which we will explore shortly.

Faith, Kierkegaard maintains, is absurd in the eyes of the world. From within faith, faith makes perfect sense, but to the person standing outside faith, to the person not yet "Kingdom-sighted," it is an absurdity. No one can investigate the faith without confronting its inescapable absurdity. The inquirer approaches faith until she is standing at its very edge, where the absurdity seems to her unbearable; at this point she must either retreat from it back into a non-paradoxical ethical existence, or

---

8. Søren Kierkegaard, "Fear and Trembling," in *Existentialism: Basic Writings*, 2nd ed., ed. Charles Guignon and Derk Pereboom (Indianapolis: Hackett Publishing, 2001), 30.

embrace faith *with* its absurdity by making a decision. As we saw before, the decision is necessarily a *leap* because it is the radical commitment to an objective uncertainty that no intellectual understanding of the issues can ever obviate.

The absolute paradox of the Incarnation is, of course, at the heart of the Christian faith: the Creator who renounces divine prerogatives and privileges to become one of his own creatures. The paradox of the Cross—the crucified Messiah—is also at the heart of the Christian faith; it is celebrated in the gospels, and should always be front and centre in the proclamation of the gospel. The tragedy of the church, according to Kierkegaard, is that it persists in "de-paradoxing" the paradox: instead of holding people to the radical commitment of the crucified Messiah—itself a contradiction—the church mutes the contradiction and tries to make faith "reasonable" in the eyes of the world. Instead of declaring to people that it is only in laying down our life that we find it, the church promotes easy belief-ism.

This distortion results in a shallowness that not only stunts individual believers but also robs the world of blessing. Recall that at the end of the story in Genesis 22, Abraham is told three times in succession that *because* he did not withhold his son, *because* he offered him up, *because* he obeyed God, all the Gentile nations of the world will be blessed. There is no suggestion that if Abraham had failed there would have been a Plan B for blessing the Gentiles; we who hear the story listen breathlessly to see what Abraham will do, knowing that the blessing of all nations hangs in the balance. Twelve hundred years after Abraham there is in Gethsemane another Jew who embraces the call to radical obedience, and this time the salvation of the entire cosmos hangs on his choice. There is no Plan B then either, and there can be none: God has only one Son. Everywhere in Scripture, what is at stake in any one person's obedience is everyone else's blessing. Too few Christians appear to be aware of this point; part of the reason we are cavalier about our discipleship is our failure to recognize that our disobedience entails forfeiture of our neighbour's good. A rereading of Genesis 22, the gospel accounts of the trial in Gethsemane, and *Fear and Trembling* would do much to restore Abrahamic rigour to casual discipleship.

Luther's *theologia crucis* captures the paradoxical character of the gospel, and it is this theology that informs Kierkegaard. Throughout his work after 1518, but especially in his *Heidelberg Disputation*, Luther eloquently sets forth in a series of contrasts the diametric opposition between the way the world perceives the Cross and the reality of the Cross as perceived by the eyes of faith.[9] The world, he observes, perceives only shame at the Cross; yet according to John's gospel, the Cross is our Lord's moment of glory.[10] The world sees the Cross as an instance of weakness, whereas in fact the Cross is God's manifestation of strength: does not God reconcile a wayward world to himself at the Cross? What is a mightier act of God than such a reconciliation? The Cross is sheer folly in the eyes of the world, for Jesus submits seemingly gratuitously to its horror when he could have spared himself merely by saying the right words; yet Paul tells us that the Cross is the consummate wisdom of God.[11] The world (especially the religious world) perceives the Cross as condemnation, for in Deuteronomy we read that anyone who dies on a cross is accursed.[12] Yet everywhere in Scripture, the Cross is our acquittal. And finally, concludes Luther, the world perceives only sin and death at the Cross, while the New Testament tells us that the Cross is our righteousness and our life.[13]

Luther glories in these paradoxes. Kierkegaard, in his turn, loves the category of paradox because its contradictory character illustrates again and again how the truth that makes perfect sense to the believer is sheer

9. See Harold Grimm, trans., *Luther's Works,* Vol. 31 (Philadelphia: Fortress Press, 1979), 39–58.

10. Note his declaration—in contrast to what is typically heard from the pulpit—that it is the *Cross* that is Jesus' moment of glory, not the Resurrection. The Resurrection is the revelation or unveiling of the glory of the Cross.

11. 1 Corinthians 1:18–20

12. Deuteronomy 21:23.

13. Here one might protest that it is the Resurrection of Jesus, not the Cross, that is our life. However, it is because our condemnation and death are absorbed at the Cross that we have life. As Athanasius points out, when the Father cursed the Son at the Cross, he cursed himself, and thereby fully absorbed the curse; there is no curse left for us, because the Father has absorbed his own just judgment on human sin. In the Cross, our death was absorbed by the Son and his Father, leaving only life for you and me. For this reason, says Athanasius, our resurrection is stored up in the Cross.

absurdity from the world's perspective. Crucially, paradox bears out the difference between knowledge as subjectivity and as objectivity, and it bears out the need for a "leap," a radical choice to embrace what one cannot prove or make objectively intelligible.

Consider, as an example, just the first paradox in Luther's litany: the shame and glory of the Cross. Jesus says, beginning in John 12, that the Cross is his hour of glory.[14] Then in John 17, in the high-priestly prayer as he prepares for death, he says, "Father, glorify thy name; as I have glorified you, now glorify me"—and he means, *at the Cross*.[15] Yet the Cross is an instance of shame for many reasons, not the least of which is that the Romans always crucified people naked, thereby heightening shame for Jewish malefactors. Unlike the Greeks, the Jews had an earthy but modest view of sexuality and deplored public nudity. All of our pictures in Christian art show the crucified Jesus wearing a loincloth, but in fact he would have been crucified naked as a sign of enforced humiliation at the hands of Roman executioners. The Cross is the acme of shame in the world's eyes, yet Jesus insists it is the hour of consummate glory for himself and his Father.

All of these paradoxical truths about the Cross, intelligible only to faith, are part of Luther's *theologia crucis*, or theology of the Cross. He maintained that the *theologia crucis* must always be distinguished from a *theologia gloriae*, a theology of glory, the latter being an anti-gospel that is unfortunately often touted by the church. A theology of glory, Luther observes, is found whenever God is identified with the endpoint of metaphysical speculation, as was largely the case in the tradition of medieval theology and its incorporation of ancient Greek philosophy. The deity supposedly proven by philosophical argument has little (if anything) to do with the living God who humbles himself for our sake in the manger and humiliates himself at the Cross. It is for this reason that Kierkegaard rejected the metaphysics of Hegel.

A theology of glory is also found whenever the church confuses Christ's victory with that of the institution and therefore engages in strong-arm triumphalism, strutting menacingly and acting coercively.

14. John 12:23, 27–28.
15. John 17:1–5.

When contemporary Christians deplore the alleged marginalization of the church, and lament the passing of a day when the church enjoyed a position of power in society, they forget that a church with social clout invariably persecutes. We are mandated to uphold the triumph of Jesus Christ, but we do so always remembering that his triumph is in the Cross, not the Resurrection. It is at the Cross that Jesus exclaims, "It is finished,"[16] not at the Resurrection; the resurrection of Jesus *reveals* the victory of the Cross. When the church loses sight of this truth, it portrays the Resurrection triumphalistically. It is a short step from such triumphalism to the victimization of those outside the church.

A theology of glory, finally, is found whenever it is thought that the truth and nature of God can be read off nature, or off human history. This is the claim of natural theology, but its trajectory always terminates in a projection of human features onto a divine screen. Human power, for example, is something we all recognize. Natural theology simply magnifies this power to infinity and attributes it to God: God is the one who has unlimited power of the same kind that humans have. (Calvin maintained that a god of sheer power could never be worshipped;[17] Luther stated that apart from Jesus Christ, God is indistinguishable from Satan.) Such unqualified almightiness is clearly a contradiction of the gospel, for the gospel acquaints us with a God who acts most effectively and most characteristically (in accord with his nature, which is love) precisely where from a human perspective he is utterly powerless: the Cross.

Similarly, a *theologia gloriae* results from an attempt to read the character of God off the face of history. In 1759 the English defeated the French on the Plains of Abraham at Québec. Are we to conclude from

16. John 19:30.

17. See Calvin, *Commentary on John*, Part One, trans. T. H. L. Parker (Grand Rapids: Eerdmans, 1974), 126, where Calvin insists that *all* of God's power is found in Christ [crucified] alone, and 67, where he avers that apart from Christ all so-called knowledge of God is "nothing but a dreadful fountain of idolatry and superstitions." See also Calvin, *Commentary on John*, Part Two, trans. T. H. L. Parker (Grand Rapids: Eerdmans, 1994), 68, where Calvin maintains, "...on the cross He triumphed over Satan, sin and death." See, too, Timothy F. Lull and William R. Russell, eds., *Martin Luther's Basic Theological Writings*, 3rd ed. (Minneapolis: Fortress Press, 2012), chapter 3, "Heidelberg Disputation," *passim*.

this that God prefers Anglophones to Francophones? What if tomorrow somewhere there is a French victory somewhere in the world? The notion that God can be read off the face of history is something we are inclined to embrace if only because history is written by victors, and we assume that our victories are God's victories and that our vanquished foes are *ipso facto* God's enemies. Such a theology is merely one more human projection, however, and one more contradiction of the gospel.

In making our peace with Christendom, Luther maintained, we have sold the gospel for a theology of glory; what we ought to do is recover the gospel and cling to a theology of the Cross. Kierkegaard had the same to say about the Danish Lutheran church. He insisted that it had domesticated the gospel, exchanging a theology of the Cross for a theology of glory.

One of the implicates of a *theologia crucis*—and we have already touched on this in our discussion of Christian discipleship as cross-bearing—is that any Christian whose discipleship is not invisible can expect to incur the hostility of the world. Kierkegaard was certainly acquainted with that hostility. Wherever he went in Copenhagen, people mocked him, and on one occasion in the country some hooligans beat him up. The Christian can also expect trial, the trial that tests and strengthens our faith and keeps it alive and vibrant. As our faith is tried and tested day by day, it is refined; impurities are driven out of it, and what remains is stronger, more useful, and more attractive.

But in a Christendom that has given up on a theology of the Cross, and in which religion is viewed as a means to enhance one's life and increase national security, Christians do not anticipate trial or hardship as a concomitant of their discipleship; in fact, they regard it as essentially alien to faith, and hence are not equipped for it. Both Luther and Kierkegaard, however, would insist that trial and suffering are a necessary concomitant of faith.[18] "Abraham was God's elect, and it was the Lord who imposed the trial," writes Kierkegaard.[19] God tempts no one in the sense of seducing people into sin, but God *does* try or test the

18. Trial, or *Anfechtung*, is a major theme in Luther. In that trial, Luther declares, the Christian must cling to the Word, who is Christ.

19. Kierkegaard, *Fear and Trembling*, 32.

faith of his people; he tried even Abraham, his "elect" or chosen one. In fact, Kierkegaard is pointing out, trial is intrinsic to discipleship: to be summoned to faith is to know that one's faith must be tried.

All people experience suffering and conflict, of course, simply on account of their finitude and frailty. The suffering peculiar to discipleship, however, the cross-bearing of which Scripture speaks, is different. Pain of the former sort should be reduced wherever possible, and for this reason the church serves the neighbour through its ministry of healing. Pain of the latter sort, as we have already noted, can be reduced only if the Christian renounces faith. The *theologia crucis* understands that "existential pathos" (Kierkegaard's term for the suffering that is part of faith's radical commitment) can never be remedied in this life.

Moreover, aware of the paradox inherent in the *theologia crucis*, the Christian has an orientation to affliction that is met with sheer incomprehension by the power-fixated world. Such incomprehension forever renders the Christian an alien in the world (and no less in the church), and this alienation is yet one more form of cross-bearing.

A Survey of Passages on Faith in *Fear and Trembling*

In *Fear and Trembling* Kierkegaard makes a similar point about the incomprehension of the world: "Abraham became old, Sarah became a laughingstock in the land, and yet he was God's elect and inheritor of the promise...."[20] Sarah became a laughingstock in the land simply by virtue of her patient hope in the promise, before Isaac was ever born; how much more did Abraham become a laughingstock, and even the object of hostility, when he laid Isaac on the altar and embraced the contradiction of God's promise and God's command? Kierkegaard's point is that the obedience of faith always courts the world's ridicule. If, when asked to slay Isaac, Abraham had simply given up the promise, he would have been understood and remembered as a hero but would not have been the prototype of faith: "If [Abraham] had said to God, 'Then perhaps it is not after all Thy will that it should come to pass,

20. Ibid, 31.

so I will give up the wish'...he would not be the father of faith. For it is great to give up one's wish, but it is greater to hold it fast after having given it up."[21] The contrast here is the one we examined earlier in Kierkegaard's three stages of existence, the contrast between faith and infinite resignation. Faith, which is the greater of the two, means holding fast to the promise after having given it up. Faith is greater than infinite resignation, but it is incomprehensible to the world and elicits only ridicule and hostility.

Because our faith must be renewed every day, especially in the face of trial, it is always fresh. "He who believes," writes Kierkegaard, "preserves an eternal youth."[22] Abraham was an old man when Isaac was born, and even older when Isaac was offered up—especially if, as in the Jewish tradition we referenced earlier, Isaac was thirty-seven years old when he accompanied his father up the mountain. "If Abraham had not believed," Kierkegaard amplifies, "...[he] would not have understood the fulfillment but would have smiled at it as a dream of youth. But Abraham believed, therefore he was young." In other words, if he had given up on the promise, Abraham would have become "old": he would have looked at clinging to the promise as a youthful self-indulgence, a form of naïveté, and abandoned it in favour of the sober realism of maturity. It is his passionate and unwavering embrace of the promise, even while obeying the contradictory command, that keeps him young. Kierkegaard is telling us that regardless of our chronological age, faith is never old; our engagement with God renews us constantly. In fact, faith is the *only* way to preserve the youthfulness of the spiritual newborn.

Abrahamic faith also keeps us engaged in this present earthly life:

> Yet Abraham believed, and believed *for this life*. Yea, if his faith had been only for a future life, he surely would have cast everything away in order to hasten out of this world to which he did not belong. But Abraham's faith was not of this sort, if there be such a faith; for really this is not faith.... But Abraham believed precisely *for this life*, that he was to grow old

21. Ibid.
22. Ibid.

in the land, honored by the people, blessed in his generation, remembered forever in Isaac, his dearest thing in life....[23]

Kierkegaard here maintains that so-called faith is not really faith if it is "only for a future life"; it is mere infinite resignation. If Abraham had exercised infinite resignation instead of faith, he would have said, "I'm giving up Isaac in this life, but I shall see him in heaven." But then he would have been eager to leave this world and go to heaven, as though not really belonging here; this world would have been of no consequence to him anymore. While it is true in one sense that believers do not entirely belong in this world, Kierkegaard insists that we must not hasten out of it, because it is only in this world that existence can be gained. Our faith, like Abraham's, should be *for this life.*

Kierkegaard envisions yet another option for Abraham if he had lacked faith—namely, to take his own life instead of Isaac's. Even if Abraham were dead, the promise could still be fulfilled as long as Isaac were spared, for there could still be descendants. However, "Abraham believed and did not doubt, he believed the preposterous," writes Kierkegaard. "If Abraham had doubted.... [h]e would have plunged the knife into his own breast. He would have been admired in the world, and his name would not have been forgotten; but it is one thing to be admired, and another to be the guiding star which saves the anguished."[24] In other words, says Kierkegaard, Abraham could have gained the world's admiration through self-sacrifice; he would have been a hero. Yet he did not plunge the knife into his own breast, because he believed "the preposterous": that somehow the promise of God would be fulfilled even as he obeyed the command of God that contradicted it. The result, for Abraham, is something far better than the world's admiration: he became "the guiding star which saves the anguished." As the prototype of any Christian whose faith is on trial, Abraham is a model and an encouragement to all who follow.

In fact, writes Kierkegaard, "Let us then either consign Abraham to oblivion or let us learn to be dismayed by the tremendous paradox which

23. Ibid, 32 [italics mine].
24. Ibid, 33.

constitutes the significance of faith."[25] To put it another way, let us not merely admire Abraham; if we are only going to admire him we might as well forget him, as mere admiration for Abraham misses the point altogether. Instead we must allow ourselves to be overcome, appalled, by the "tremendous paradox," the utter preposterousness of what Abraham believed.

What Abraham believed was so preposterous, continues Kierkegaard, that "[h]e said nothing to Sarah, nothing to Eliezer [his servant]. Indeed, who could understand him?"[26] Everyone understands the ethical hero, but no one understands the knight of faith. When Abraham contemplated undertaking something as monstrous as the slaying of Isaac, why did he not talk to Sarah about it? He kept silent because it was to *him*, and not to Sarah, that God had spoken. Sarah would have said, "You're insane, and moreover you're a murderer." The person who is addressed by God and brought to the trial of faith cannot be understood by anyone else. Not only is he a laughingstock in the world; worse, he is regarded as insane.

It is important not to pass over this statement, because it brings us again to the crucial issue of subjectivity and objectivity. Abraham does not tell Sarah or Eleazar what he is resolved to do because they will think him deranged. Since it is not to them that the command of God has come, they are unable to evaluate Abraham's response for what it is. The same situation arises today whenever someone claims to have heard a direct word from God: how can any of us evaluate the veracity of such a claim advanced by someone else? Suppose someone says, "I have heard from God, and he has told me that at the height of rush hour I should go out and dance in the middle of the busiest intersection downtown, and he will save my life." We would say this person needs help. On the other hand, if someone says, "God has told me to go to Papua New Guinea and announce the gospel to a Stone Age tribe there," this person may be just as psychotic as the first—or he could really have received a divine summons. How would anyone else know? No one else *could* know. I maintain that I had a vivid vocation to the ministry at the age of

25. Ibid., 55.
26. Ibid., 32.

fourteen; I have also met numerous other people who have heard voices and whom I take to be instances of *homo religiosus,* a psychosis whose expression is religious. Is my vocation any different from their hearing voices in their delusion and paranoia?

The point is this: there is, by definition, no test that can be applied in advance to prove the authenticity of a divine summons; *it is known only in the course of carrying out the summons.* My vocation to the ministry is confirmed only in the exercise of it. Here we have the essence of the Existentialist claim: truth can only be lived. Truth is subjectivity. And there are, by definition, no objective criteria for subjectivity.

While that fact does not excuse madness or folly, we should remember that Jesus' family, according to Mark 3:31, came looking for him in order to take him home because they thought he was out of his mind and considered him a public embarrassment. We deem Jesus to have been sane; however, as the one human being who was completely faithful to his Father, he sometimes behaved like those who *are* out of their mind—which is why his family wanted to bring him home so as to avoid public embarrassment. From without, faith appears indistinguishable from *subjectivism*; from within, faith is *subjectivity* and authenticates itself as truth.

The "Problemata"

Under the heading "Problemata" in *Fear and Trembling,* Kierkegaard addresses some philosophical approaches to the story of Abraham that highlight a failure to understand the point of it. Philosophy has no grasp, for example, of the absurdity or paradox of giving something up to God believing that he will give it back to us. Yet that is exactly the conviction of the person of faith: "Only he who draws the knife gets Isaac," maintains Kierkegaard. Merely to give something up presents no paradox; but in the paradox of faith Abraham's willingness to give up Isaac, all the while believing that God's promise would yet be fulfilled, means that Isaac is in fact given to him. Philosophers think they understand the story of Abraham, but they miss this central point, says Kierkegaard. "They exalt Abraham—but how? They express the whole thing in perfectly general terms: 'The great thing was that he loved God so much that he was willing to sacrifice to him the best.'"[27] No, insists Kierkegaard: the point is not that Abraham loved God so much that he was willing to give up Isaac. Innumerable people have given up their dearest and best out of love for God. The point of the story, rather, is that hope is the reconciliation of God's contradictory promise and command.

Neither can philosophers appreciate the anguish of Abraham, which is directly related to that contradiction of promise and command. "What they leave out of Abraham's history is dread," continues Kierkegaard; "for…to the son the father has the highest and most sacred obligation."[28] In other words, when Abraham set off for Mount Moriah, knife and fire in hand and accompanied by Isaac, he was tormented in spirit. He dreaded what he was about to do: slay his son, distress his wife, and cancel the promise. Still, he trusted God, and therefore trusted a resolution of the contradiction without being able to see how that resolution could occur. This is the existential pathos suffered by Abraham; it is a pathos that can never be eliminated for those who live in truth, and it is not accessible to philosophy.

According to Kierkegaard, not even theologians understand or properly appreciate the story of Abraham, though they think they do. He writes, with biting irony:

> After all, in the poets love has its priests, and sometimes one hears a voice which knows how to defend it; but of faith, one hears never a word. Who speaks in honour of this passion?… Theology sits rouged at the window and courts its favour, offering to sell her charms to philosophy. It is supposed to be difficult to understand Hegel, but to understand Abraham is a trifle. To go beyond Hegel is a miracle, but to get beyond Abraham is the easiest thing of all. I for my part have devoted a good deal of time to the understanding of the Hegelian philosophy, I believe also that I understand it tolerably well, but when in spite of the trouble I have taken there are certain passages I cannot understand, I am foolhardy enough to think

27. Ibid., 36.
28. Ibid.

that he himself has not been quite clear.... But on the other hand when I have to think of Abraham, I am as though annihilated. I catch sight every moment of that enormous paradox which is the substance of Abraham's life, and every moment I am repelled.... I strain every muscle to get a view of it—that very instant I am paralyzed.[29]

Kierkegaard is lamenting the fact that, in his day, theology has prostituted itself to philosophy. Theologians and philosophers alike are impressed by the profundity and impenetrability of metaphysical thinkers like Hegel—while Abraham, they claim, can be understood by any fool. Kierkegaard disagrees: Hegel, however challenging his ideas, *can* be understood (and where he cannot, it is probably because of his own opacity), but Abraham can *never* be understood. Part of Kierkegaard's sarcasm here has to do with the fact that Hegel, believing his philosophical system to be the endpoint of philosophy, supposed there was no "getting beyond" it. Nonsense, insists Kierkegaard; there is nothing miraculous in getting beyond Hegel. His philosophy is not ultimate. By contrast, there is no getting beyond Abraham, because faith *is* ultimate. We can never finally understand Abraham, because faith can never be rationalistically comprehended. Who can understand anyone who offers up his son at God's command, and yet expects to have him? Kierkegaard declares that no matter how often he revisits the story of Abraham, his mind cannot get past the paradox nor his heart past the anguish he finds there; he is overwhelmed to the point of paralysis. "I am as though annihilated," he says. Not only is he "as though annihilated" by the story of Abraham, he is "repelled" by it. Here again he is contrasting Abraham's story and the life of faith with Hegel's philosophy. Anyone who probes Hegel's philosophy is attracted by its cumulative force: first it gathers up inanimate nature, then animate nature; next it gathers up human existence, and finally it even manages to comprehend divine existence. Imagine a philosophy that can comprehend the divine! Meanwhile, anyone who looks at Abraham is appalled by the story.

29. Ibid., 39–40.

This incomprehensibility of Abraham is a theme to which Kierkegaard returns constantly: "Abraham I cannot understand," he writes a few pages later; "in a certain sense there is nothing I can learn from him but astonishment."[30]

Still reflecting on the fact that reason can never access Abrahamic faith, Kierkegaard offers his own paradox: "I am convinced that God is love," he writes; and then, three lines later, in a seeming contradiction, he says, "But I do not believe it."[31] How are we to understand this? Luther said that if we want to grasp the gospel, we must close our eyes and open our ears. He meant that all we see around us in the world contradicts the message of the gospel that we hear with our ears and our heart. The gospel we hear tells us that God has gone to hell and back for us, that he loves us more than he loves himself (since he has spared sinners but not his own Son). Yet when we look out on the world and observe what unfolds every day, what we see offers no support for that gospel. Kierkegaard is making the same point: he is convinced that God is love, while acknowledging that world occurrence belies that belief.[32] He finds nothing in world occurrence to support the abstract belief that God is love, yet he knows in his heart, having staked his life on it, that it is true.

---

30. Ibid., 43.

31. Ibid., 40.

32. If we are inclined to deny the point that Luther and his Lutheran descendants uphold, it is because we fail to appreciate the horror of evil. In forty years as a pastor, I have found that many Christians have an all too naïve, benign, innocuous understanding of evil—despite the fact that the Christian faith acknowledges human depravity and the existence of the satanic. I remain puzzled that so many Christians have a less vivid apprehension of evil than the non-believing world has, and am convinced that it is because many Christians fear the only way they can preserve faith in the goodness of God is to render evil somehow less evil: if evil is only slightly evil, they think, we can continue to believe that God is good; but if we were to own how hideously evil evil really is, we would have to give up the goodness of God. My mind moves in the opposite direction: the longer I live, the more I find that evil hideously manifests itself as sheer evil, and thereupon the more convinced I am of the goodness of God. As a pastor I have seen evil perpetrated, and human suffering born of it, that is so shocking as to defy the imagination of most church people. It is precisely my recognition of horrific evil that magnifies for me the goodness of God. Kierkegaard's point is the same, expressed in terms that are provocatively paradoxical: "I am convinced that God is love, but I do not believe it."

The distinction Kierkegaard makes here between abstract belief and staking one's life on something is related to one of the most crucial points for all Existentialists: the difference between thought and existence. It also distinguishes Religion A from Religion B, or infinite resignation from faith, in Kierkegaard's three-stage dialectic. "The infinite resignation is the last stage prior to faith," he writes, "so that one who has not made this movement has not faith; for only in infinite resignation do I become clear to myself with respect to my eternal validity, and only then can there be any question of grasping existence by virtue of faith."[33] In other words, in infinite resignation we become conscious of who we are from an eternal perspective, and only then can we move *beyond* that stage to "grasp" existence itself in faith.

Elsewhere Kierkegaard says that infinite resignation gives rise to an "eternal consciousness," by which he means one's consciousness of God. Of itself, however, consciousness of God—or consciousness of anything—is not existence, and never becomes existence. Infinite resignation, then, while it may engender a consciousness of God and hence be a necessary *condition* for faith, is still not the same as grasping existence, for the simple reason that consciousness is by definition not existence. Consciousness is *thought*, and existence can never be *thought*; it can only be *lived*, says Kierkegaard (and every other Existentialist). Existence can be reflected on after the fact, but while you are reflecting on it existence is suspended. Even thought that is engaged in prior to existence cannot of itself yield existence. Thought is abstract; existence, staking one's life on something, is concrete.

This distinction has direct bearing on the life of a Christian. Consider the number of people who assume that if they think theologically, if they reflect on matters of faith, they are living in faith. Many people, similarly, flatter themselves that in thinking about ethics they are living ethically, or that if they contemplate sacrifice they have gone a step further than someone who has made no sacrifice. They fail to realize that thinking about sacrifice is qualitatively different from making it. Thought (that is, ideas) can be thought, but existence cannot

---

33. Ibid., 50.

be thought; existence is born of radical commitment, and can only be lived.

In the same vein, Kierkegaard declares in the last line of this section on the "Problemata" that "faith begins precisely there where thinking leaves off."[34] By this he does not mean, as some people have wrongly supposed, that we can rely on rational thought up to a certain point, after which we must exercise faith because intellect is useless—as though faith were a substitute for thinking. What he means is that thinking is no substitute for faith. He means that as long as a person is only thinking and not acting, he is still an armchair philosopher, has risked nothing, and has made no commitment. Faith begins with the commitment that follows thinking and issues in living.

If it is crucial to distinguish between thinking and existing, we must also distinguish between the paradox of our life arising from our vocation under God, on the one hand, and the contradiction of our life arising from our own sin. Everyone's life is complex; to the natural complexity of life we add the complication of sin, sinning so pervasively that our life becomes increasingly complicated until it devolves into sheer self-contradiction. We must never confuse that contradiction, however, with the paradox of our life arising from God's summons to obedience and trust. Many people mistakenly think they are living authentically because they are so keenly aware of life's complexity and contradictions, when the most poignant contradiction they experience is merely the product of sin. Abraham knew the difference between the self-contradiction of sin and the paradox of faith, says Kierkegaard.

"[T]hese three and a half days were infinitely longer than the few thousand years which separate me from Abraham,"[35] he writes at the conclusion of this section, in another paradox. The "three and a half days" to which he refers here is the time between God's speaking to Abraham and his arrival on Moriah. The time between Abraham and us, by contrast, is a "few thousand years," yet (Kierkegaard implies) he is our contemporary. How so? Twelve hundred years after Abraham, Paul writes a letter to the Romans in which he describes Abraham as

34. Ibid., 55.
35. Ibid.

the prototype of the person of faith; yet those twelve hundred years are nothing, because everyone who exercises faith in Jesus Christ exercises by definition the same faith as Abraham's. And two thousand years after that letter of Paul's, everyone who exercises faith in Jesus Christ today still exercises the same Abrahamic faith. Hence the 3200-year span between Abraham and ourselves is nothing: in all eras the believer stands in the same position as Abraham. At the same time, the three and a half days of Abraham's anguish are everything; they are indescribably long for us, because they are the story of our own life. We suffer the same anguish he did, which is the pathos inherent in living in truth.

It breaks Abraham's heart to put Isaac to death. Part of his anguish is that he is giving up his son, unable to imagine how the promise will be fulfilled but doggedly believing that it will; and part of his anguish is that *God* is the one putting him to this trial. He is anguished with respect to both Isaac and God.

Some people have suggested that Abraham was confident God would raise Isaac from the dead; but if he assumes that Isaac will be raised from the dead, is he making any sacrifice at all? Kierkegaard would say that this is a much weaker trial of faith, for while it entails no little suffering, it involves no paradox: death followed by resurrection is not a paradox. Moreover, to say that Abraham expected Isaac to be resurrected is to read a Christian category into a Jewish story. Resurrection is a Christian phenomenon. The Older Testament, however, does not characteristically speak of resurrection; it knows only life and death. Abraham, it must be understood, is not expecting Isaac to be raised; he is trusting that the promise and the command can be fulfilled simultaneously, even though he cannot imagine how.

Do we have the courage to be subjected to such a test? Do we have the courage to live in Abrahamic faith, embracing the irresolvable paradox and enduring the anguish of it? This is the challenge Kierkegaard makes to all who read him.

6

Friedrich Nietzsche:
Superman and the Last Man

Introduction

Although Sartre is the philosopher most voluminously written about in the twentieth century, Nietzsche is the one most widely read. While it might appear he lacks the philosophical rigour of Kierkegaard or even of Marx,[1] his formative place in the history of Western philosophy cannot be denied; the shift from Modernism to Postmodernism is indisputable, and Nietzsche is considered by many to be the thinker who underlies Postmodernism. Anyone wanting to understand Postmodernism and its roots in Existentialism, therefore, must grasp him. His famous pronouncement, "God is dead, and we have killed him," is familiar to many who are unaware that this "death" was not something over which Nietzsche rejoiced: he realized that the consequences of our having slain God were momentous, and that many of these consequences would prove destructive.

Nietzsche was born in 1844 and died in 1900 at the age of fifty-six. A brilliant scholar, he was trained first in philology, the science of language, and was gifted in ancient as well as in modern languages. At the astonishingly early age of twenty-four he was appointed to a chair of Classical Philology at the University of Basel, the youngest person in the history of the university ever to have held that position. Ill health forced him to resign only eleven years later, and by age forty-five he had become insane. In his short career, however, he wrote brilliantly

---

1. In a private conversation Emil Fackenheim remarked that of the three major anti-Hegelian thinkers, Kierkegaard was the most rigorous philosopher, followed by Marx.

on many different subjects, including religion, morality, culture, philosophy, and science, and his influence in philosophy remains formidable. He had a remarkable ability to express himself in German, making deft use of literary devices such as metaphor and irony that require alertness on the part of the reader to avoid misinterpreting. His writing is highly aphoristic—replete with pithy, quotable, memorable one-liners that communicate profound insight with simple elegance.

Nietzsche's father and grandfather were both ministers in the Lutheran state church; he was familiar with Christian tradition and was an astute critic of what he perceived to be its failings. He had a special affinity for the Greek philosophers—not Plato and Aristotle, whom he regarded as relatively modern Greeks, but those who preceded them. He repudiated the body-soul dualism of Plato because, like every version of body-soul dualism including that espoused by much of what passes for Christian theology, it exalted the soul and devalued the body: in Plato, the body is considered an impediment to the soul, an encumbrance from which we will one day be gloriously freed to live as pure intellect. Nietzsche valued earthliness and earthiness; he recognized the legitimacy of human psycho-physical "instincts," or what present-day psychology calls "drives."[2] Christianity, on the other hand, he despised, because it characteristically denied and suppressed natural human drives. The long tradition of celibacy and asceticism in Christendom, for example, he adduced as evidence to support his case.

Nevertheless, we might question whether the dualism rejected by Nietzsche is in fact upheld by Christian faith, or is instead a feature of an ersatz Christianity infected and distorted by Platonism. There is no doubt that many Christians today embrace a body-soul dualism that is at odds with a Hebrew understanding of Scripture. In the creation sagas in Genesis, when Adam and Eve are created, they are formed from the dust of the ground and God breathes life into them; in other words, we humans are animated bodies.[3] We are not the confluence of two

2. Today, instinct is attributed only to animals; it is distinguished from biological urges in humans, such as hunger or sex, which are subject to our control and whose gratification can be delayed. The latter are known as "drives."

3. Soul, *nephesh* [נֶפֶשׁ] in Hebrew, is animated body.

distinct entities, soul and body, with the soul superior to the body; that is Greek metaphysics. Yet to many Christians, any denial of a discrete soul is heretical. In repudiating body-soul dualism, was Nietzsche despising the Christian faith correctly understood, or a misguided version of Christianity that has traditionally appropriated an alien Platonism as if it were the gospel?

Nietzsche objected to Platonism not only because it was body-denying but also because he could not accept Plato's predication of a pure intellect which grasps the eternal world of "forms"—the transcendent archetypes of all that is, but especially of the good, the true, and the beautiful. For one thing, Nietzsche considered this putative eternal world of forms to be mere invention. Moreover, he insisted, the pure intellect posited by Plato does not exist either, because all our reasoning is highly determined. As has already been observed in this book, sociologists have repeatedly demonstrated that what we call reasoning is socially determined to an extent few people appear to appreciate until they are shown how it operates and then can no longer deny it. Reasoning is significantly determined by economic position, social situation, historical particularity, and (not least) by gender. While people readily appeal to "common sense," observation of any committee meeting will show that there is no such thing; there is no consensus on what is sensible. Michel Foucault, a French philosopher and sociologist, has demonstrated conclusively that what passes for common sense in Western societies is identical with the mindset of those who enjoy access to social power.[4]

As discussed in the context of Kierkegaard, the notion that human intellect is not "pure" and is subject to multiple determinations is upheld by Christian theology. Christian theology maintains that our reasoning[5] is fallen: the structure of reason survives the Fall (or else we would not be human), but the integrity of reasoning has been compromised by

4. See especially Michel Foucault, *Power/Knowledge*, ed. Colin Gordon, trans. Colin Gordon, Leo Marshall, John Mepham, Kate Soper (New York: Pantheon, 1988), chapter 6, "Truth and Power."

5. I am using the term *reasoning* rather than *reason* advisedly, to avoid the suggestion of a *faculty* or *compartment* of the human being. Reasoning is an activity in which humans engage.

the Fall (and devastated concerning knowledge of God and knowledge of ourselves with respect to God), so that what we call reasoning is largely rationalization. Only grace, owned in faith, restores reasoning's integrity. When Paul declares in Ephesians 4 and Romans 1, "Their senseless minds became darkened, and they became futile in their thinking," he is not denying that unbelievers can perform logical operations or do algebra. What has become futile is not our ability to acquire knowledge about the creation, but our capacity to access or glimpse the Kingdom of God by means of that knowledge. As we saw before, failure to recognize this distortion is part of what underlies the evangelical concern with apologetics: most apologetics erroneously assumes that reasoning (unlike willing and feeling) is unaffected by the Fall, and therefore conduces to apprehension of the Kingdom.

Key Concepts and Terms in the Nietzschean Vocabulary[6]

Nietzsche has often been misinterpreted and misappropriated in the century following his death. One reason for this is a failure to recognize when he is speaking ironically, saying the opposite of what he means. Another is a poor understanding of some of his most characteristic vocabulary. The remainder of this chapter will familiarize readers with the primary concepts and terms encountered in the writings of Nietzsche; from that foundation, the next chapter will explore selected passages from his works.

Resentment and irony

One major feature of Nietzsche's philosophy, and one we have already touched on briefly in our general introduction to Existentialism, is the notion of resentment, for which many English translations of his writings retain the French term: *le ressentiment.* Nietzsche maintains that resentment is the basis of slave morality. Slaves are frustrated at being slaves; they resent their masters and their lot in life. According to Nietzsche, such resentment characterizes Christianity and the church,

6. In this section I have been assisted by Robert C. Solomon and Kathleen M. Higgins, *What Nietzsche Really Said* (New York: Schocken Books, 2000).

because (as he never tires of pointing out) the earliest Christians came from the submerged classes of society; many, in fact, were slaves. Slaves are typically and understandably riddled with resentment, a bitter emotion based on a sense of inferiority and frustrated vindictiveness.[7] Resentment is obsessive, says Nietzsche; it festers relentlessly, never exhausting itself. Unlike spite, which may lash out on the spot, resentment is calculating; it nurses the grudge and strategizes a way to even the score. It is ultimately concerned with self-preservation and rises in the face of threat. And its ultimate weapon is irony.

Irony—saying one thing while meaning the exact opposite—is a tactic regularly employed by people who are speaking from a position of weakness. Ironic speech is a form of passive aggression, a strategy almost impossible to deal with by those against whom it is directed because it *is* aggressive while appearing to be passive. This subterfuge conveniently allows the user to affect innocence, so that when the other person reacts in anger to the irony, the passive-aggressive person can reply, "What is your problem? I merely said such-and-such." In Nietzsche's view it is an impotent ploy, and therefore pathetic; it is also characteristic of Christians.

By his account, then, Christians are not only characteristically resentful, but disingenuous and pathetic in expressing their resentment. According to Nietzsche, much of what Christians angrily decry as sin in others is actually behaviour in which they would also like to engage but are afraid to, because it violates rules they feel constrained to follow. They resent seeing other people do what they would like to do themselves but lack the courage to do. As a pastor I have observed numerous instances that bear out Nietzsche's assessment: people making a Christian profession regularly express bitter resentment at what they find non-Christians doing and denounce them for doing it, because deep down there is an unresolved desire to do the same thing themselves.

---

7. Vindictiveness must be distinguished from vindication. Many Old Testament passages appear to be vindictive when in fact they are pleading for God to vindicate his own name and his people. More will be said later in this chapter about this important distinction.

Superman and the Last Man

Perhaps one of the best-known terms used by Nietzsche—even though he barely used it outside his work *Thus Spake Zarathustra*—is *Übermensch*, variously left untranslated or rendered in English as *Overman* or, more popularly, *Superman*. It is a term that has been famously claimed by the Nazis as well as by other tyrants. Nietzsche did not invent it,[8] but used it to refer to his own concept of the superior human being. Superman stands in contrast to Nietzsche's "Last Man," a pathetic creature who is risk-averse and seeks only his own comfort. In Christian parlance, the Last Man would be called a man of sloth—sloth being one of the seven deadly sins in the Middle Ages (and one rarely discussed in the church today). To be slothful is not so much to be lazy as to be inert, indifferent, culpably unaware of one's God-appointed glory; to be so thoroughly spineless, apathetic, and timid as to do nothing but protect oneself. The slothful Christian has no capacity to risk anything for Christ or his Kingdom. Nietzsche has this kind of character in mind when he speaks of the Last Man,[9] and it, too, is a phenomenon I have had no little opportunity to observe as a pastor: the professing Christian who will not make the slightest investment of time, money, or energy in a Kingdom endeavour without an ironclad assurance of "success" of some sort.

Superman, on the other hand, is devoid of timidity and embraces risk; he aspires to human enhancement through the mastery of fear and lives life as a creative endeavour, forging a self in the process. Note that Superman's self as conceived by Nietzsche is a self-*making*, in contrast to Kierkegaard's *authentic* self which comes ultimately from God and is therefore a self-*choosing*. The two terms point to a subtle but important difference between the theistic and the nontheistic Existentialist.

The will to power

Another concept Nietzsche writes about, especially in *Thus Spake Zarathustra*, is the will to power. Most people, including the Nazis

8. The term probably originates with Lucian, a fabulist in the second century who wrote about the *hyperanthropos*, and it had already been used before Nietzsche by German poets such as Heine and Goethe.

9. Here the Christian would note the contrast with the *last Adam* of Romans 5.

who co-opted the term, misunderstand it as the will to dominate or coerce, when in fact Nietzsche ridiculed any "will to power" in that sense, regarding it as ignoble and even subhuman. The will to power as understood by Nietzsche is a characteristic of the Superman, and is not a will to brutalize others but rather a self-overcoming that enhances the self. Jewish philosopher Emil Fackenheim declared that the Superman would be recognizable by his ability to manifest authority without exercising force; Nazism, which operated above all by force, is therefore completely wide of the mark in its appropriation of the will to power.[10] Force is what is exercised by a person who *lacks* genuine authority; the person of genuine authority has no need to manifest force, because his authority is recognized. A clear distinction can be made here between authoritarianism and authority: authoritarianism says, "You will do as I say or I will hammer you into the ground," whereas authority is an influence that others recognize and honour because of its superior wisdom and inherent capacity to advance individual or corporate good. The difference between authority and authoritarianism is the difference between Superman and tyranny.

The will to power as understood by Nietzsche is exemplified in many artists who have overcome enormous difficulties in order to channel their creative energy productively. In Nietzsche's view it is almost impossible to be an artist and not to suffer. While his statement is no doubt hyperbolic, there does seem to be a disproportionate occurrence of bipolar disorder and other forms of psychiatric suffering among highly creative people. Robert Schumann, for instance, wrote all of his glorious piano compositions in two hypomanic periods of his life and then committed suicide. It seems that Charles Wesley, the best hymn writer in the English language (and a poet more prolific than Wordsworth), suffered from cyclothymia, a psychiatric condition in which one's mood swings are much more pronounced than normal.[11]

10. Fackenheim made this remark in response to a student's question. I am not aware that he has published it anywhere.

11. Some historians have even suggested he was bipolar. He was not, in view of the fact that there is no record he was ever psychotic, and he could always manage to function as preacher and spiritual counsellor.

There are many other examples of poets, novelists, painters, or composers whose genius not only appeared in the midst of unrelieved suffering, but seems to have been testimony to their overcoming a burden they could not shed. Thus, while Nietzsche overstates the case when he observes that it is *impossible* to be an artist and not to be sick, there may be more truth to his assessment than we sometimes like to admit. He was careful to elaborate, however, that health is not the *absence* of disease; it is the ability to *overcome* disease—a key point for Nietzsche, because one characteristic of Superman is that his self is birthed and maintained through self-overcoming. Fear and sloth are the chief impediments to the realization of this self.

We should consider, as Christians, whether Nietzsche might be at least partly right on this score. In the gospels, the most frequent commandment on the lips of Jesus is "Do not be afraid"—evidently because fear is the single greatest impediment to human thriving.[12] We humans are steeped in fear; it is our innermost "default setting," with the result that any perceived threat paralyzes us. As for sloth, it was one of the cardinal sins in the Middle Ages, yet the church says little about it today. Always quick to condemn pride (unrealistically thinking too highly of ourselves) we readily accommodate sloth (no less unrealistically thinking too little of ourselves), while both are equally deadly.

"The herd" and the state

One of the many things we fear, says Nietzsche, is retaliation by the state, a fear that frightens us into conformity and thereby into mediocrity. For Nietzsche, the government is merely a more complex version of "the herd": the undifferentiated, unremarkable mass of humanity that contents itself with mediocrity. Every Existentialist philosopher has a version of this; Heidegger calls it "the *they*,"[13] while

---

12. Some would insist that sin is the impediment. According to Jesus, fear that persistently deflects us from entering the Kingdom and living as its citizens is sin.

13. Something of what is meant by "the they" can be understood from the words stencilled into the brick over the archway of the University of Aberdeen, a saying I liked to read as a graduate student there: "They say. What do they say? Let them say." "The they" has nothing to say to me, declares Nietzsche.

Sartre speaks of the non-reflective and non-courageous as those living in "bad faith." People sunk in the mentality of the Last Man, declares Nietzsche, are always afraid of the government; Superman, on the other hand, recognizing the herd, is unintimidated by it or by its manifestation as the state; he overcomes its seduction and intimidation, and stands out from it.

Before we disdain this attitude as a glorification of arrogance, we must recognize that Nietzsche, in disdaining the herd, is not expressing contempt for ordinariness. Mediocrity is not the same as ordinariness. Much of the world's trouble is caused by people who resent being ordinary, who cannot live with their own ordinariness. The word *humility* comes from the Latin *humus*, meaning "earth" or "soil"; genuinely humble people are "down-to-earth"—they own their earthiness and earthliness, and are content to be ordinary. Excellence readily coexists with ordinariness. The people I know who have excelled in any area of life are highly ordinary; they need not strut or boast or otherwise pretend they are extraordinary. In fact, humility is an accompaniment of excellence. Mediocrity, on the other hand, appears when someone fears lack of recognition in the eyes of the "herd" and strives to gain it, unaware that excellence is always a self–overcoming.

Moreover, Nietzsche insists, when it comes to intimidation the church is the chief accomplice of the state; in fact, Christianity provides a legitimization of the state. He is thinking, of course, of the place the church occupied in Germany in his era, and its relationship to the German government. Yet even where the church is not formally affiliated with the government, we should always be aware of what the church's role is with respect to the state, and what it ought to be. Scripture, we should note, speaks of the state as both blessing and bane: the epistle to the Romans describes the state as ordained by God to restrain evildoers, while the book of Revelation depicts it as the beast from the abyss, slaying the people of God. In neither case, however, should the church uncritically regard itself as a God-appointed legitimization of whatever kind of power the state wishes to exercise.

Freedom

Like all Existentialists, Nietzsche has much to say about freedom. To become free is to overcome one's animal nature—not to extirpate it, but to overcome it. By "animal nature" he means not vulgarity or promiscuity but our legitimate human drives or passions. To overcome our animal nature is to control our drives and passions, but never to eliminate them; the person who has eliminated her drives or leads a passionless existence has shut herself down. Such a person is pathetic. Freedom, by contrast, is the ability to organize the chaos of one's passions and sublimate one's impulses. One feature of passion, conventionally understood, is passivity; we claim not to be responsible for our behaviour when swept away or controlled by our passions. But the Superman is never passive. The Superman is always an active, self-overcoming self, mastering his passions and sublimating his impulses.[14]

Freud helps us understand what is meant by the sublimation of an impulse—the channelling of an unacceptable drive or desire into an acceptable activity. Have you ever thought about what makes some people become surgeons? If a person from a prescientific society were to enter an operating theatre in one of our hospitals, her first instinct would be to restrain the surgeon. Surgery would look murderous to her, whereas in fact the surgeon is promoting life and health. The surgeon, in all probability, is a person who has sublimated the impulse to cut people, channelling it into a beneficial activity. And that is exactly the kind of person we want at the operating table. We do not want the surgeon to be hesitant and squeamish about cutting people; we want someone practised and skillful in it, who does so with confidence and efficiency, undeterred by emotional considerations and social opinion. Vocation, Freud reminds us, has much to do with the sublimation of impulses.[15]

To become free, according to Nietzsche, is also to give style and beauty to one's character. The Jewish philosopher A. J. Heschel

---

14. The Christian, of course, will consider here what the apostle says in Galatians 5 about the Holy Spirit, Christian freedom, and self-control as a fruit of the Spirit.

15. For a discussion of psychopathic traits found in surgeons, politicians, and company presidents, see Kevin Dutton, *The Wisdom of Psychopaths: What Saints, Spies and Serial Killers Can Teach Us about Success* (Toronto: Doubleday, 2012).

ceaselessly urged people to live so as to render their life a work of art.[16] This is precisely Nietzsche's point: we fashion art, or beauty, by what we do with what life brings us. His characteristic remark is, "Whatever does not destroy me makes me stronger,"[17] because it is in the course of overcoming adversity in life that the self is forged. Life brings us adversities every day, and horror invades everyone's life at some point; but in the face of these, only the Last Man, only someone who has settled for the herd, gives up and negates life. The Superman affirms life and in the midst of horror even fashions something beautiful. Furthermore, we are to make not only our own personal history into a work of art; by overcoming, we also contribute to the beauty of humanity as a whole. The goal of humanity, insisted Nietzsche in contrast to Darwin and Hegel, does not lie in its end but in its highest specimens.

Romanticism

That which comes later in time, then, is not necessarily more valuable. Nor is that which comes earlier in time: Nietzsche's Superman was no embodiment of the nostalgic ideals of Romanticism. Romanticism was an artistic and intellectual movement of the late eighteenth century and the first half of the nineteenth; it was heartily despised by Nietzsche because Romantics are always pining for a bygone era, whereas Nietzsche maintained that the way ahead is always forward, never back.[18] Among Christians, too, there are those who sigh about how much better things used to be in the church of the 1800s, or the 1700s, or the 1500s, but they are romanticizing the past. In Geneva, where Calvin lived, the registers of the town council have recently come to light,

16. See especially Abraham J. Heschel, *A Passion for Truth* (Woodstock, Vermont: Jewish Lights Publishing, 1995), and *I Asked for Wonder*, ed. Samuel H. Dresser (New York: Crossroad Publishing, 1991).

17. Quoted in Walter Kaufmann, *Nietzsche: Philosopher, Psychologist, Antichrist* (New York: Meridian Books, 1965), 111.

18. My grandfather, who spent all his life labouring in an automobile factory before there was any union protection for workers, used to say, "Never let anybody talk to you about 'the good old days'; the old days may have been old, but they were never good." He was right: anyone aware of economic and social history knows "the good old days" to be no more than a figment of romantic ignorance and naïveté.

and they confirm that the Christian community in Geneva was as badly behaved as any congregation today. The registers show, for instance, how frequently discipline was exercised against sexual offenders (including Calvin's own sister-in-law).[19] It is sheer Romanticism to think that the church was less sinful five hundred years ago than it is today. It is also defective theology, because the church at any time consists exclusively of sinners. And when we mourn the "good old days" of decency in public life, we might take note that in eighteenth-century England, Parliament had to be suspended many times because members were so drunk they could not vote.[20]

There are worse things about Romanticism, however, than a deluded hankering for the past; Nietzsche despises it primarily because cruelty lurks beneath its sentimentalism. Romanticism is always allied with nature, and nature everywhere exemplifies the principle of survival of the fittest: the only creatures who manage to survive are those rapacious enough to dominate the less fit. It is but a short step to maintain, as Hitler did, that the only ones *entitled* to live are those who eliminate their rivals without compunction.

Romanticism is also related to tribalism, and tribalism in turn invariably leads to a pursuit of ethnic purity culminating in ethnic cleansing. Nazism was highly Romantic: it romanticized the Black Forest, the Fatherland, the Teutonic people in direct descent from their illustrious ancestors, and the historical superiority of German culture. Under this view non-Aryans were fit only to be gassed. Nietzsche was German, but he despised the German mentality of his time as tribalistic and cruel, a sign of anything but the appearance of Superman. The Romantics make much use of lofty and poetic vocabulary, but it conceals a superstitious sentimentality and heartlessness.

Moreover, the Romantic exalts primal drives without qualification, whereas the Superman, without suppressing or denying them, overcomes them. Superman knows the subtle difference between the

19. See William Naphy, *Calvin and the Consolidation of the Genevan Reformation* (Lousiville: Westminster John Knox Press, 2003), esp. chapters 3 and 4.

20. See J. W. Bready, *England Before and After Wesley* (London: Hodder & Stoughton, 1939), chapter 8.

Romantic and the Dionysian. The Dionysian—about which more will be said later—exemplifies exuberance for life, but without brutishness. Romanticism, on the other hand, being allied to nature, indulges unrestrained frenzy.

Liberal Protestantism is highly Romantic in its tendency towards pantheism or panentheism. Wordsworth speaks of "that immortal sea," the immortal sea of Being, which is purportedly God. We humans are supposedly taken up into that immortal sea of Being. Wordsworth's sea of Being, however, is not the God of the Bible who is unalterably personal, the Creator who is active among his creatures yet distinct from them, intimate with human beings yet always transcending them. Liberal Protestantism imagines itself to be inclusive, generous, humane, and large-hearted, yet it illiberally writes off all kinds of faithful people who recognize its non-Kingdom agenda and resist its accommodation to the world.

Eternal recurrence and amor fati

Nietzsche's emphasis on self-overcoming and the overcoming of adversity is related to his concept of "eternal recurrence." The term sounds as though it denotes a theory of the basic structure of time or the cyclical character of history; Nietzsche's notion of eternal recurrence, rather, is a test of our willingness to affirm life, to embrace *amor fati*. *Amor fati* literally means "the love of fate," but Nietzsche does not believe in any deity that has decreed fate or even in the concept of fate advanced by ancient Stoic philosophy; by *amor fati* he means the unreserved affirmation of one's own life as it unfolds with all of its good days and bad, its delights and disasters. As the test of eternal recurrence, *amor fati* means embracing the entirety of one's life so thoroughly as to be able to will its repetition. Those who are able to do so thrive as human beings, says Nietzsche; anyone who cannot do so is life-denying, cowering, and self-shrivelling. That is because each time we reject a portion of our life, wishing that we could be without this or that negative experience, we have rejected the opportunity it offers us to become stronger through self-overcoming, and so by that fact are made weaker. Anything less than *amor fati* means we have impoverished ourselves.

While Christian theology might express the concept differently, this issue of being life-affirming or life-negating is a profoundly significant one. Are we able to accept and even embrace every part of our lives? The apostle Paul never instructs us to give thanks *for* everything, but he does say that we should give thanks *in* everything.[21] Can we give thanks in the most hideous days of our life? Nietzsche, when he looked around at the Christians of his time, saw too many who were not life-affirming at all; they were life-negating, bitter about their own failures and hardships, exuding resentment over their assorted victimizations. To fail the test of eternal recurrence, to refuse *amor fati*, is to be fixed in resentment. If we are to thrive, Nietzsche insists, we must embrace the whole of life without qualification or reservation. In other words, the more we insist on a safe and painless existence, the smaller the universe we come to inhabit: the most risk-averse person lives as safely as possible in a universe she has reduced to the size of a thimble. Nietzsche considers such a person pathetic.

We can think of it this way: our life is like a baseball that is hit hard many times over, with the result that the cover comes off and the tightly wound threads inside begin to come loose. Some people cannot live with their loose threads; ashamed of the supposed unsightliness, they cut the threads off. The baseball then retains the appearance of a perfect sphere and seems elegant, but it has become a little smaller. Soon there is another loose thread, and then another, and these, too, have to be excised because the person cannot endure appearing imperfect and unsightly. Before long the baseball, still retaining its socially-expected shape, has shrunk to the size of a pea. The question Nietzsche asks us is: Can we own our "loose threads," our seemingly embarrassing, unacceptable features? Can we own our whole self, and even take delight in it, recognizing the "loose threads" as precisely what saves us from the clutches of the herd, and therefore as the measure of our richness? Or do we make ourselves pathetic by reducing our own existence in an effort to make it more acceptable and attractive, more manageable, safer for us and for others?

According to Nietzsche, the aesthetic task—exemplified by the early

---

21. 1 Thessalonians 5:18.

Greeks but denied by Christianity—is to find or create beauty *in the midst of* suffering and tragedy. Nietzsche exalts the Golden Age of Pericles, when people were distinguished by style and refinement. Subsequently, he argues, under the body-soul dualism developed by Socrates and Plato, the Greeks denigrated the body, adopted an other-worldly stance, and sought the human good in an escape from all that is concrete, earthly, and historical. Christians, Nietzsche claims, have followed suit: denying their bodiliness in favour of the realm of spirit (so-called), they are preoccupied with getting to heaven, always looking beyond this life for a life to come. They undervalue *this* life and the task of self-overcoming, and so neglect to fashion beauty in the execution of that task. Nietzsche finds them pathetic.

Perspectivism

Perspectivism is another important concept in Nietzsche, and in Existentialism in general: you may recognize it from chapter 1 and from our study of Kierkegaard, who thought of it in terms of *fragmentariness*. Perspectivism is the insistence that there is no such thing as a neutral, "God's-eye view" of the world. Each of us, unavoidably, has a perspective from which we see everything, and we cannot get out from behind it. We can never have a comprehensive view of life, the world, history, and art, because we are immersed in it; there is no one who stands above it all so as to have a God's-eye view of it. Only God could have a God's-eye view of the world, and as far as Nietzsche is concerned, God does not exist. Given the inescapability of our perspective, Nietzsche maintains, systematic philosophy or metaphysics is impossible; philosophy can only be done in fragments. The same claim was made by Kierkegaard, who died in 1855, the year after Nietzsche was born. Nietzsche, opposing so much of what Kierkegaard had to say, nevertheless agreed with him in at least one crucial matter: metaphysical comprehensiveness is impossible.

Here, too, Nietzsche offers more than a grain of truth. Systematic thinkers tend not to question their primary assumptions, since these assumptions are the foundation on which their entire system rests; once these are questioned, the system collapses. In fact, the internal coherence of a system determines every part of it integrally, with the result that to remove any one part is to collapse the whole. The outcome is an artificial narrowing of thought that gives rise to shallow thinking, because every time a challenge is voiced, one's protective reflex is to hear it only in terms of one's system. Such a system is a closed structure; it is certainly coherent, but since it is the product of a finite perspective, its coherence is contrived and no guarantee of its truth. Hence one can philosophize only fragmentarily.

This does not mean, however, that any perspective is as good as any other, or that perspective is a matter of arbitrary preference. Concerning his perspectivism Nietzsche has notoriously said, "There are no facts, only interpretations."[22] That is not an endorsement of subjectivism, of "reality" being the product of the individual's imagination based on sheer arbitrary preference, but rather something akin to what Kierkegaard also claimed: a perspective is always *occupied*—by a person engaged with other persons and entities in a given context, hence it is by definition never a detached angle of vision. It always entails a specific commitment. Our occupying a perspective means that our perspective *on* something determines the nature *of* that thing in our engagement with it: the human body, for instance, palpated by an examining physician, dissected by a forensic pathologist, or caressed by a passionate lover, is scarcely the same entity in each context.[23] Recognition of this obviates a criticism of Nietzsche that is equally applicable to *any* thinker, Existentialist or not, theist or not.

The Christian also has a perspective—on God, the world, the self—that presupposes her particular commitment; hence her perspective is not universally compelling. Nonetheless the Christian would never agree that this fact by itself means her truth claim is insupportable and should be abandoned. After all, what world view is any different in that regard? If charged with arbitrariness concerning his own perspective, Nietzsche could easily turn the tables on the critic: "Your criticism

22. Friedrich Nietzsche, *Will to Power*, trans. W. Kaufmann and R. J. Hollingdale (New York: Vintage, 1967), paragraph 481.

23. See Robert Solomon, *Living with Nietzsche* (London: Oxford University Press, 2003), 38.

attests that you, too, have a perspective, which you are advancing in the conviction that it has validity."

Perspectives are not arbitrary, but embraced on account of their experienced adequacy and cogency in making some kind of sense of life's complexities, complications, and contradictions. This is fully consistent with Nietzsche's Existentialist understanding that philosophy is finally not an argument but an engagement with life.

Christianity

Finally, Christianity is one of Nietzsche's major preoccupations. We have already encountered several of his criticisms of the Christian faith in relation to other themes in his writing; now we come to the heart of his anti-Christian polemic. Nietzsche insists, first of all, that the Christian tradition is nihilistic: it is a nay-saying aspiration after nothing. In Christianity, he argues, the highest values devalue themselves.

Consider, for instance, the Christian virtue of self-control. According to Nietzsche the self is to be self-overcoming, but Christians understand self-control as a fruit of the Holy Spirit. If it is produced by the Holy Spirit and not by one's own self, then any aspiration to so-called "self-control" is in fact an exercise in self-repudiation and self-alienation: it is an aspiration to be controlled by another (namely, the Holy Spirit). Hence the self that should be a self-forging through self-overcoming turns out to be a rejection of the self. In a similar way, argues Nietzsche, all Christian values are ultimately a form of self-hatred. The Christian tradition elevates the least, the last, the lowest; it elevates everything negative and parades it as a virtue. It disdains this world and denies the value of this earthly life, perceiving humankind through the lens of a life-denying ideal. In short, Nietzsche concludes, Christianity is nihilistic.

Once more we must ask ourselves whether Nietzsche is legitimately criticizing Christianity, or denouncing a caricature. (To say the latter is not to deny that the caricature is seen often enough to exonerate the critic.) The history of the primitive church has no lack of people who withdrew from the world, took a vow of celibacy or poverty, hived off into the desert, ceased to bathe, renounced every good they could find to renounce, and thought it all virtuous. But is this what Jesus Christ exemplified, the party-goer whose convivial exuberance earned him the charge of overdoing food and drink? Despite his contempt for a (church-distorted) Christianity, Nietzsche esteemed Jesus, finding him earthy and life-affirming amidst the depressives whose asceticism contradicted the goodness of the creation. Nietzsche admires Jesus but despises Paul, viewing the latter as body-denying and life-negating. The teachings of Paul skewed Christianity, says Nietzsche, and nothing good has unfolded in Christendom ever since.

There is considerable truth to the charge that some Christians have refused to honour their God-appointed earthiness. The appetitive nature is deeply rooted in us; clearly, it must be disciplined—sublimated or overcome, Nietzsche would say—but there is a difference between disciplining it and denying it. While we apprehend the world through mind and spirit, we also apprehend it through our bodiliness,[24] and this bodiliness is a gift of God in which we ought to delight. Yet there is no doubt that an anti-body tendency has manifested itself in some Christian traditions.

Christian charity, according to Nietzsche, is another example of the devaluation of values. He regards the Christian virtue of charity as little more than contempt for one's neighbour, since people typically look with compassion or pity only upon those whom they regard as inferior. "Charity," from the Latin caritas, is simply another word for love, but what we refer to as charity is often not so much loving as demeaning. It is exceedingly difficult to help people, especially financially, without demeaning them, because we naturally interpret the ability to help as superiority and the need for assistance as inferiority. We are all familiar with situations in which someone rejects a gift and insists on paying her own way lest she be made to feel inferior or indebted by being the object of someone else's charity. We pity those we regard as inferior, and always like to be able to find someone inferior in order to feed our sense

---

24. People sometimes assume that because I am a philosopher and a theologian, I live in my head. I do live in my head, but no less in my body. I relish cycling long distances as fast as I can, at high noon in the height of summer. I played hockey for twelve seasons. I continue to find immense pleasure in sheer physicality.

of superiority.[25] Even compassion for "the lost" can be a mask for self-congratulation by believers. Moreover, declares Nietzsche, Christian charity or pity perpetuates the status quo by confirming the pitied in their present state rather than encouraging them to be self-overcomers. In short, the Christian preoccupation with love of neighbour is merely a subtle form of contempt for the neighbour, an attempt to establish and maintain one's superiority at the expense of someone else. To what extent is this a just criticism of much Christian practice?

Nietzsche also took issue with what he understood to be the Christian interpretation of suffering as punishment. Suffering is inescapable in life, and is bad enough to begin with; but to regard it as punishment simply adds one crushing burden to another. If, in contradiction to Nietzsche, we want to argue that suffering *is* a kind of punishment in some situations, we must ask ourselves two questions: (1) What are those situations, and why is it appropriate to think of suffering as punishment in them? (2) Even if we venture to conclude that at least some of our own suffering is punishment, do we ever have the right to say the same about anyone else's? Is it not the case, rather, that a vast amount of suffering is not punishment of any sort but the inevitable concomitant of living in a fallen created order, a creation that "groans" as it awaits restoration?[26] The identification of suffering with punishment, according to Nietzsche, is simply another manifestation of Christian self-hatred.

Nietzsche regards Christianity as dross compared to Judaism. He admires the Older Testament and has a high regard for the Jewish people, acknowledging that they have been self-overcomers, enduring, achieving, and even triumphing amidst a history of unparalleled torment. Christianity, on the other hand, is a negation of the glories of the Older Testament. In the writings of Paul, Augustine, and Luther, Nietzsche claims, faith is merely a cover-up for fanatical hatred,

25. I suspect that, for example, one reason we feel the way we do about criminal deviants and mentally ill people is that their existence reassures us of our superiority. We all have days when our character is compromised or we feel our sanity to be at risk; but when we see the criminal in prison or the psychotic shouting on the street-corner we know we are not that bad, and immediately we feel better.

26. Romans 8:19–23.

specifically of Judaism and the Jewish people. Descended from generations of Lutheran pastors, he is piercingly aware of Luther's remarks with respect to the Jewish people, and the catastrophic developments in which those remarks were a factor.[27] The eloquent commendation of love in 1 Corinthians 13 Nietzsche considers to be an accidental flare-up of the eternal flame of Judaism, an exception to Paul's cloaked hate-mongering.

As for the doctrine of justification by faith (according to which those in the wrong with God are set right with him by trusting in the guilt-bearing Crucified), Nietzsche regards it as disgusting self-excuse on the part of those who fail to practise what they claim to uphold. Before commenting on this pronouncement, we should note the crucial difference between excusing and forgiving. If a behaviour we find offensive can be excused, then it is only reasonable to excuse it: no forgiveness is needed. What is excusable we excuse; what is not and never will be excusable we can only forgive. In other words, we excuse the excusable and *forgive the inexcusable.* To be forgiven by anyone, human or divine, can only mean we have been judged utterly inexcusable. We must acknowledge, then, that Nietzsche would be correct if justification by faith pertained to the merely excusable. Then it would mean that faith is sufficient to excuse us. If, on the other hand, justification by faith pertains to what God can never tolerate or excuse, Nietzsche's understanding is defective. To say that God forgives us is then to say that God has already judged us and condemned us as intolerable, and yet visits us with mercy.

At the same time that Christians cavalierly excuse themselves through the doctrine of justification by faith, Nietzsche charges, their doctrine of a resurrection at the end of time supports a notion of retribution: Christians, cherishing the notion of hell, relish the prospect

---

27. There is no denying that Luther's writings have provided a pretext for horrific anti-Semitism. When the notorious Nazi Rudolph Streicher was tried for war crimes at the end of World War II, he quoted Luther in his defence. He was only repeating what many before him had adduced as justification for their anti-Semitism. For an exploration of Luther's attitude to all matters Jewish see Eric W. Gritsch, *Martin Luther's Anti-Semitism* (Grand Rapids: Eerdmans, 2012).

of ultimate eternal torment for their enemies and detractors. Here, too, we must acknowledge the legitimacy of Nietzsche's criticism; undeniably, several thinkers in the church's history have declared that one of the pleasures of God's people in heaven will be hearing and beholding the sufferings of the damned in hell. Are there are not also Christians today who, while distancing themselves from such crudeness, seem nonetheless to find satisfaction in the endless suffering of those who are finally impenitent?

According to Nietzsche, faith is the refuge of those whose pathetically weak self-image finds them unable to posit themselves as their own end—those who are fundamentally self-rejecting, self-belittling, and self-negating. We have already noted the unwholesome tendency in some Christian circles to equate self-rejection with humility. Moreover, declares Nietzsche, faith is exercised by those deficient in thinking in order to compensate for their intellectual deficits. While Nietzsche might be dismissed as ridiculous here since the church has never lacked intellectual giants, it has also never lacked those who discouraged scientific or intellectual inquiry, zealously claiming, "What we cannot understand we shall simply have to believe. Thinking will only confuse us." The frequently proposed illustration referred to in an earlier chapter, "I don't understand how car brakes work, but I have faith that the car will stop every time I press the pedal," is not only unhelpful but also a contradiction of what is meant by faith. Faith is not the position we assume when reason falls short or fails, let alone something we exercise as an alternative to thinking or to acquiring ordinary knowledge of the created order.[28] As we found from our study of Kierkegaard, faith is a leap or commitment born of decision rather than mere thought, but not an irrational one and certainly not a cowardly one.

Earlier we noted Nietzsche's disgust at the Christian tendency to deny our animality and suppress legitimate human appetites. One device employed by Christianity in enjoining people to repudiate instinct, he claims, is its assumption of "free will." Nietzsche despises the notion of

28. One is reminded of Mark Twain's famous dictum, "Faith is believing what you know ain't so."

free will, because it always suggests to people that they should somehow be able to divest themselves of their appetitive nature by simple choice. Nietzsche maintains that we can indeed exercise the will so as to achieve a kind of "victory" over our appetitive nature, but it is not the victory of *Übermensch* or Superman, a victory of self-overcoming; it is the so-called victory of self-hatred. According to Nietzsche, Christians defend the notion of free will because they want to regard the repudiation of bodily appetites as virtuous. A concomitant Christian notion, he would add, is that those who manage to suppress bodily appetite (through their free will) are superior to those who do not.

Let us return, in connection with Christianity, to one of the concepts for which Nietzsche is most famous, and one which is most often misunderstood: the *will to power*. As noted briefly earlier, the will to power is not the will to coerce, dominate, or control; will to power in that sense is merely the desire to brutalize, and Nietzsche declares it to be evil. Positively, the will to power is the foundation of Greek culture, reconciling Apollo and Dionysius.[29] It is the basic drive found in all human efforts, and its finest expression is the enlargement of the self in rendering one's life a work of art: in other words, the will to power is consummately expressed in the self-overcoming that results in human excellence. After all, if the self is a self-making, why make something ugly? The will to power is expressed in genuinely creative acts, and every such act contains its own new norms. When Mozart wrote his music, he created new norms for music; when Brahms or Beethoven created their own music, different from Mozart's, they in turn created new norms for music. The creative expression of the will to power, exemplified in cultural achievements such as these, is seen most tellingly in *the* achievement: the self-overcoming that forges new norms for a particular self.

Improperly understood, however, the will to power is the barbaric torture of others and the ascetic torture of oneself—twin aspects, for Nietzsche, of one and the same mindset. The ascetic torture of oneself can be highly gratifying as an exercise of will, but it remains a negative

---

29. For a brief amplification of this point see the subsection "Apollo and Dionysius" in this chapter.

undertaking and perverse achievement, the antithesis of self-overcoming.

We saw how Nietzsche relates this self-overcoming to *amor fati*, the will to own one's whole existence, complete with its adverse aspects, and to rejoice in all of it even to the point of being willing to repeat it indefinitely. The notion of *amor fati* raises an issue that will always be a matter for discussion in formal Existentialist philosophy; it is one also raised in the context of Kierkegaard's thought, using other terms such as self-commitment and self-choosing. If the self is a self-making, who is to say that the self-made torturer is any worse than the self-made humanitarian? By what set of criteria is one a work of art and the other a work of ugliness?

Nietzsche's reply would be that humankind *recognizes* the inherent triumph in the self-overcoming, a triumph that makes its own case when juxtaposed with the accomplishment of what is humanly destructive. Whether that is a satisfactory response on the part of Existentialists will be discussed later. Certainly there has been no lack of those who claimed Nietzsche as the authority for their version of the will to power while contradicting his intent.

The Nazis, again, are a case in point. Nietzsche repeatedly used the phrase "the blond beast" to refer to the lion as a symbol of what he regarded as manifestly noble. The Nazis, however, misreading him here as they characteristically did elsewhere, assumed he was exalting the lion as unmodified or unrestrained power and rapacity. They failed to see that Nietzsche despised such power since there was no self-overcoming in its exercise: it simply exacerbated suffering and destruction. Not understanding how he was using the phrase, the Nazis claimed it for themselves in allusion to their fair hair and skin and their ascendancy over other peoples: "We are the blond beast of the world, the lions of the world," they exulted. Attempting to co-opt Nietzsche at this point, Nazism exposed itself as a ludicrous falsification of him.

Now, for Nietzsche, one sign of true power is to be above resentment or desire for revenge. Jesus, unlike his followers, exhibits no vengefulness: when reviled he does not revile back, and when he is nailed to the wood he calls down forgiveness on his tormentors. But while there is no evidence of resentment or desire for revenge in Jesus, it is pervasive in his followers, insists Nietzsche: Christians are eager to see God wreak judgment on evildoers, and they rejoice in the suffering of their enemies.

Is he correct? Some people cite the Psalms to justify such vindictiveness on the part of God's people. We have all read passages in which the psalmist seems to delight in seeing his enemies suffer. But everywhere in the Bible, vindictiveness is expressly forbidden. The book of Leviticus commands that if anyone sees the animal of his worst enemy going astray, he is to bring it back to its owner, and whoever sees the donkey of his worst enemy collapsed under its load is to go to its aid. Job tells his accusers that regardless of what other sin he may or may not have committed in his life, he has never once taken delight in the misfortune of an enemy.[30] The Bible repudiates vindictiveness as sin.

At the same time, the Bible everywhere pleads for the vindication of God's name and his people, *for the sake of God's honour*. When God's name is dragged through the mud and his people are ridiculed by every nation in the world, they cry, "Will you not act, God, to uphold your reputation, and to vindicate your people as the apple of your eye?" It is for God's sake, and for the sake of his agenda in the world, that they utter this cry, not to satisfy their own thirst for revenge. The psalmist says to God, "Your enemies are my enemies; I hate them with perfect hatred."[31] But notice he does not say, "My enemies are your enemies." God's enemies are our enemies because we want the honour, truth, and way of God and the people of God upheld and vindicated.[32]

The Hebrew mind is always earthy and concrete. We tend to abstract evil from its human perpetrators, praying "Thy Kingdom come" without any concrete sense of what is entailed by the process of God's Kingdom coming and the kingdom of evil departing. The Hebrew

---

30. Leviticus 19:18; Proverbs 24:17 and 25:21; Job 31:29.

31. Psalm 139:22.

32. In his discussion of the Psalms, C.S. Lewis deplores the sheer hatred, vehemence, and hostility he claims to find there, while admitting that it was understandable in view of the torment visited upon God's people. Lewis was not often wrong, but he was wrong in reading the text as promoting vindictiveness rather than pleading for God's vindication. See Lewis, *Reflections on the Psalms* (London: Fontana Books, 1965), chapter 3, "The Cursings."

believer, on the other hand, insists on the concrete outworking of God's self-vindication. He knows that cocaine dealing contradicts the Kingdom of God; he also knows that cocaine dealing can be traced directly to cocaine dealers. Unashamedly, therefore, he prays for God to deal effectively with the cocaine dealer—"May the cocaine dealer drop dead"—so that God's Kingdom may become manifest: he is pleading for the vindication of God's name and cause, not for the settling of his own scores against his own enemy. This is the difference between vindictiveness, or a desire for revenge, and a cry for vindication. Failing to grasp this difference, or acquainted with Christians who failed to grasp it, Nietzsche insists that what Christians seek is the suffering and destruction of their own enemies for their own satisfaction.

Describing as weak those who attempt to exert power and control over others, Nietzsche argues that the weak seek to master other people because they cannot master themselves. That which we understand, we can control; if we understand the physical properties of water we can generate hydroelectric power, and if we understand peanuts we can generate suntan oil, cooking oil, and fertilizer.

How often, when we complain of not understanding another person, are we in fact frustrated by our inability to control that person? We would rather manipulate that other person than adjust our own attitude and behaviour so as to foster human intimacy and cooperation; we would sooner control someone else than overcome our self, the latter task being unspeakably more challenging.

Understandable, then, is Nietzsche's claim that the weak, unable to master themselves, seek to master others. Christians are quick to declare that we are called to love others; in the wake of the Fall we should be the first to admit we find it easier and preferable to control others. Are not virtually all dysfunctional human relationships rooted in the desire to control others?

Nietzsche goes on to observe that self-mastery is the condition for happiness, and that happiness in turn gives rise to virtue—the inverse of the claim that is made by many, including some Christians, who see virtue as the source of happiness: virtue is its own reward and generates happiness, according to many a traditional moral philosopher. Nietzsche, on the contrary, insists that the only person who behaves well is the person who is already profoundly happy; people who are profoundly unhappy are resentful, and like all resentful people they behave cruelly.[33]

There is more than a little truth here. We all know people who are simply nasty; but the trouble they cause is nothing compared to that caused by the fundamentally unhappy person—the one who is deep-down wounded, in pain, and chronically discontented. One learns to work around a nasty person, realizing that his nastiness is simply a characteristic that colours his behaviour equally in all relationships; but the wounded, unhappy person lashes out without warning, without any sense of proportion, without self-understanding, and without restraint. Only the pervasively happy, maintains Nietzsche, are devoid of resentment and therefore finally virtuous.

Any moral philosopher who cannot agree with him concerning the causal sequence just delineated can nevertheless agree that happiness and virtue are companions. Nietzsche has his own expression of this notion: ultimately, he declares, happiness is the inextricable togetherness of power and joy. If power is the exercise of self-overcoming and the capacity to sublimate passion without extirpating it, and if this is married to joy, which is the ability to rejoice in the whole of one's existence, that combination adds up to happiness. Moreover, he maintained, this happiness cannot coexist with fear. It was observed earlier in this chapter that the most frequent command on the lips of Jesus is "Fear not." Another frequent command in the New Testament is to rejoice, and in the gospels, those whom Jesus heals are said to "go on their way rejoicing." They do so because joy and fear are incompatible. The person who is always fearful, therefore, is never happy. In recognizing that fear and unhappiness are dangerous obstructions to virtue, Nietzsche is not without insight.

---

33. Compare Wesley's insistence that only the holy are finally happy with Nietzsche's seemingly antithetical dictum. Wesley reiterated his "holy/happy" aphorism not fewer than thirty times, evidently considering it normative for the Methodists. See "Justification by Faith," in *The Works of John Wesley*, Bicentennial Ed., Vol. 1, ed. Albert C. Outler (Nashville: Abingdon, 1984), 185.

Apollo and Dionysius

Apollo and Dionysius, finally, are frequently referenced by Nietzsche, and are important symbols for him. These are ancient Greek figures, pre-Socratic and pre-Plato. Apollo represents the capacity to create harmonies and measured beauty, the beauty of proper proportion and structure. The strength to shape one's own character, and the form-giving force exemplified in Greek sculpture, are one and the same attribute of Apollo. Dionysius, in Nietzsche's earlier writings, is sheer undisciplined, mindless indulgence—Apollo's opposite. Dionysius represents the force akin to drunken frenzy that threatens to destroy all forms, the ceaseless unrestraint that defies all limitations. It is, for example, the ultimate abandonment that is sometimes sensed in music: music is universally recognized as having tremendous capacity to move people, and some music suspends self-control and precipitates suggestibility.[34]

In *The Birth of Tragedy*, Nietzsche appears to favour Apollo, although he upholds both Apollo and Dionysius as complements: without the Dionysian, he maintains, the Apollonian genius of the Greeks cannot be understood. In other words, an exuberant creative surge must be present in order for it to be shaped and given form as art; culture is born of the interplay and conflict of Apollo and Dionysius. The later Nietzsche, however, favours the Dionysian and redefines it as fundamentally positive, speaking of himself as Dionysian in *Dionysius Versus the Crucified*. Dionysius in that context has come to mean passion mastered, in the manner characteristic of Superman—in contrast to passion eliminated, which is Christianity. The later Dionysian, then, is a synthesis of the earlier Dionysian and the Apollonian.

Some Concluding Thoughts and Questions

Many Christians have tended to dismiss Nietzsche because of his hostility to Christianity. Yet we have seen that this reaction on the part of Christians results from an incomplete understanding of what he is

---

34. For this reason totalitarian displays of power are often accompanied by music that breaks down the people's resistance, and by the outlawing of other music likely to encourage the people to throw off control.

about. We cannot deny that Nietzsche accurately perceives much of what is unhealthy in modern society, nor that he identifies a number of distortions that have come to characterize the life and message of those in the church. If he is that insightful with respect to the diagnosis, why does he seemingly fail to perceive the cure? This is a question we could ask equally of many other thinkers. Discerning what is wrong is not nearly as challenging as proposing an effective remedy.

It is also the case that every thinker with profound things to say falls prey to equally profound misunderstandings by those who receive his or her work. Nietzsche was co-opted by the Nazis because they read one part of *Thus Spake Zarathustra*; if they had read the next part, they would have wept for themselves. They read about the will to power, but misunderstood it as glorying in the rapacity of the blond beast; they missed the fact that the will to power is a mastery of oneself, not the barbaric domination of others. Admittedly, even the most thoughtful students of Nietzsche arrive at differing understandings of his work. Such disagreement does not mean, however, that he is opaque and therefore discardable.

We do not know what influence Nietzsche's father and grandfathers had upon him, or how much of his thinking was an outcome of his upbringing in a pastor's home; but any church historian or social historian can reconstruct the mindset of mid-nineteenth-century German Lutheranism, and we can therefore attempt to ascertain where he legitimately criticized it and where he did not. We can identify where he diverges from the gospel or misinterprets it; I hope we can also have the humility to recognize where he correctly criticizes the church and the distortions engendered by its misreading of the gospel.

Nietzsche philosophizes in fragments, the only way possible in light of his observation that even the wisest human being has only a limited perspective. He is insightful, admittedly; but lacking an understanding of revelation, his philosophical wisdom lacks the penetration of prophet and apostle. As Christians, we are not about to say that Nietzsche has pronounced the last word, but we must say that he has pronounced a word we cannot afford to ignore.

7

Friedrich Nietzsche:
The Gay Science and *Twilight of the Idols*

Nietzsche's *The Gay Science*

"*What does your conscience say?* 'You shall become who you are,'" writes Nietzsche.[1] This brief, pithy statement, made with no amplification, is crucial to an understanding not only of Nietzsche specifically but of Existentialism generally: the self, for all Existentialists, is not a given but occurs as it is forged through radical commitment born of decision. It is a self-*making* for nontheistic Existentialists; for Kierkegaard a self-*choosing*, since the self is forged most profoundly through an encounter with God that elicits the radical decision of faith. For all Existentialists, theistic and nontheistic alike, if our self is anything other than a self-making or -choosing, it lacks authenticity; it has been surrendered to the world at large, and the world is therefore telling us—and making us—who we are. Such a self is other-directed, other-formed, other-informed, and other-normed. Moreover, since it has been fashioned by the world, such a self has also been reduced to a mere object or thing that images the world. The only self that remains *self* is the one that is self-made.

Who tells us who we are? As Christians we often reply glibly that God tells us who we are, and quote Colossians 3:3, "Your life is hid

---

1. Friedrich Nietzsche, "The Gay Science," in *Existentialism: Basic Writings*, ed. Charles Guignon and Derk Pereboom, 2nd ed. (Indianapolis: Hackett Publishing, 2001), 142:270. Unless indicated otherwise, all italicized emphases occur in Nietzsche's text.

with Christ in God." It is easy to repeat these words when, meanwhile, another actuality is underway deep in our hearts: our social position is telling us who we are, or our job is telling us who we are, and when we lose our job or our social privilege we no longer know who we are. Nietzsche's question, "*What does your conscience say?*" and his answer, "You shall become who you are," are intended to warn us against surrendering our self to the world to be determined by it and made in its image.

"You shall become who you are" is an admonition taken up in a theistic context by the apostle Paul. The burden of so much of Pauline vocabulary is, "You *are* a new creature in Christ: now *be* one." In other words, *live* as that new creature. In faith we have put on Christ; now we are to live out that reality. When Paul urges his readers, "Work out your salvation in fear and trembling,"[2] he does not mean we are to work *up* our salvation, or work *at* it; that would be a form of self-righteousness and therefore no more than unbelief. He means that we are to live out the reality of who we are in Christ: "Become who you are," he is urging us. The difference between Paul and Nietzsche is that, for Paul, who we are is ultimately who or what we are in Christ, whereas for Nietzsche, who we are is whom we make ourselves.

In the previous chapter we explored the Nietzschean concept of the *Übermensch* or Superman, a better kind of human to come. Paving the way for Superman are "preparatory, brave human beings," whom Nietzsche describes as follows:

> human beings who have an inner penchant for seeking in all things what is *to be overcome* in them; human beings to whom cheerfulness, patience, simplicity, and contempt for the great vanities belong as much as do magnanimity in victory and indulgence for the small vanities of all the defeated; human beings with a sharp and free judgment about all victors, and about the role played by chance in all victory and fame.[3]

2. Philippians 2:12.
3. Nietzsche, "The Gay Science," 143.

Noting first of all his insistence that these human beings have an inner penchant for seeking *in all things* what is to be overcome in them, we are reminded of the importance for Nietzsche of the related concept of *amor fati*, or eternal recurrence. Recall that by "eternal recurrence" he means such a wholehearted affirmation of life as to be able to wish the re-occurrence of *all parts* of our own life, not regretting or rejecting any. We all have aspects in our lives that we wish we could do without; however, as we saw earlier, the condition of the negative we want to avoid is very often the condition of the positive to which we aspire, and vice versa: if we want the joy of playing hockey, we must accept the risk of being hurt. Nietzsche's point above is that the "preparatory, brave human being," the truly cheerful and life-affirming human being, accepts *all things* in life as occasions for self-overcoming.

In my four decades as a pastor I came to recognize how crucial it is to be life-affirming. I found people who, in the midst of numerous misfortunes and intense stress, were nonetheless always moving ahead, always positive. They had "down" days, of course, days when they staggered under the burden of what they had to endure, but overall they exuded a life-affirming attitude even though they seemed to have the least grounds for it. I found others who were just the opposite: always finding something to be negative about, always complaining, even though they faced relatively little real hardship in life.

Nietzsche's brave humans, precursors to Superman, "seek in all things what is to be overcome *in them*"—that is, in themselves. In our first encounter with the concept, we observed that Nietzsche's Superman never seeks to overcome or dominate others, and is never characterized by brutality or coerciveness—despite the Nazis' unfortunate misunderstanding. Brutality, insisted Nietzsche, is always a sign of weakness. The overcoming referred to by Nietzsche is invariably a *self-overcoming*, and as such the true manifestation of strength.[4] If my self-formation is a self-overcoming, I will in all things seek that *in me* which I am to overcome, never that *in you*. As soon as I think it is my task

---

4. According to Hannah Arendt, violence is the opposite of power. People and institutions resort to violence when it becomes apparent to them that they lack power. See her *On Violence* (New York: Harcourt Brace & Company, 1970), 35–56.

to overcome something in *you*, I am on my way to coercing you. The world is full of people who want to overcome the supposed weaknesses in others, and all they do is wreak havoc. It is challenge enough for us to overcome what needs to be overcome in our own self.

Nietzsche goes on, in the above quotation, to speak of human beings in whom cheerfulness, patience, and simplicity are redolent. Cheerfulness is mentioned with great frequency in Nietzsche's work, particularly in *The Gay Science*. Significantly, it also figures largely in the New Testament. "Be of good cheer," Jesus commands his disciples, "for I have overcome the world."[5] And when blind Bartimaeus is brought to him, friends say, "Be of good cheer; Jesus is calling you."[6] If we look at the place occupied by cheerfulness in the gospels and epistles, we must conclude that there is no authentic Christian faith that is not cheerful. Being cheerful does not mean wearing an artificial grin when we are in the grip of suffering, but it does mean that there ought to be a confident hope to our discipleship at all times, expressing itself in a lightness of heart that forestalls teeth-gritting grimness. Nietzsche has transferred this feature of elemental cheerfulness, largely absent (he maintains) in people who make a Christian profession, to his understanding of self-overcoming and the Superman.

It cannot be denied that cheerfulness is frequently scarce among professing Christians, if only because the Christian tradition has one-sidedly magnified and exalted miserableness. While the Bible speaks of repentance as simply making an aboutface in our life, all too often the church's understanding of repentance is that we should feel "devoutly" miserable about ourselves: we ought to be filled with regret and remorse about the sordid mess we have made of our lives, and should punish ourselves through emotional (if no longer physical) self-flagellation. The more tearful we are, the more profound we consider our repentance to be. But that is not the biblical understanding of repentance. For Nietzsche, such self-induced misery and gloominess over our failures is mere unproductive self-indulgence. It has been aided and abetted in the church by a preference for depictions of Jesus that overemphasize

5. John 16:33.
6. Mark 10:49.

the title "Man of Sorrows," making him out to be mostly miserable and overlooking the fact that he partied so ardently as to be called "a glutton and a drunkard."[7]

The "brave" human being described by Nietzsche is also characterized by "contempt for the great vanities." Nietzsche is aware that a great deal of which the world boasts is in fact vain, even worthless. As for "a sharp and free judgment about all victors, and about the role played by chance in all victory and fame," Nietzsche is here insisting on a recognition that many of the people we adulate have attained their status through sheer fortune: they inherited above-average intelligence, were born into a more privileged social class, or happened to enjoy better opportunities, and hence can take little credit for their achievement. We mistakenly assume that the starting point in life is the same for everybody, whereas the child born into social or financial disadvantage, for example, or born with fetal alcohol syndrome, is born with biological equipment and immersed in a social and cultural setting light years removed from what most people enjoy. While it remains incumbent on each of us to do our best with what we have, and while some do more with what they have than others, there is no denying that much of the success for which we admire and congratulate people is simply the result of chance. To exercise "a sharp and free judgment about all victors" is to appreciate this fact in all cases.

Nietzsche goes on to urge us to embrace risk, adding: "For, believe me, the secret to reaping the greatest fruitfulness and the greatest enjoyment from existence is *to live dangerously*! Build your cities by Vesuvius! Send your ships into unexplored seas!...The time is nearly

---

7. Part of our tendency to depict Jesus in this sombre way stems from our difficulty in coming to terms with his humanity, a ghost of the first heresy to afflict the church. Docetism was the notion that Jesus was certainly divine, but only seemingly human. Another part may come from our difficulty in coming to terms with our own humanity, our lack of understanding of what it means to be human. When Jesus was attacked for partaking exuberantly at a celebration, he said (and I paraphrase), "What can I say about you people? John the Baptist came neither eating nor drinking, and you said he was insane; I come both eating and drinking, and you say I am immoral. You were unhappy with John the Baptist because he was abstemious; you are just as unhappy with me because I am the opposite—life-embracing and life-affirming." (Cf. Luke 7:31–35, Matthew 11:17–19.)

gone when it could be enough for you to live hidden in the woods like shy deer!"[8] As we saw earlier, the risk-averse person lives a shrivelled life in a shrunken world. To be risk-averse is to "live hidden in the woods like shy deer," to be life-negating rather than life-affirming; nevertheless, many people prefer this kind of existence because it is safe.

The apostle John assures us, in his first epistle, that "perfect love casts out fear."[9] I maintain that the converse is equally true: perfect fear casts out love, as evidenced by a surprising number of Christians who live withdrawn into themselves because they are fearful. In one congregation I pastored, we started a "neighbouring" program in which designated "Good Neighbour" families would each look out for four or five other families in the congregation who lived in the same neighbourhood. The idea was to relieve the elders of some of the burden of visitation. There was no little resistance to the program, for now the "Good Neighbours" were expected to invite people into their own homes instead of calling on other people in the latter's homes. Several were afraid the visitors would look down on them for not having elegant furniture, or might even be tempted to steal something valuable; they were afraid to talk to people they did not know, fearing, too, that conversation might wither if a common topic could not be found. In short, their fear prevented them from reaching out to and welcoming others in their own neighbourhood and in their own congregation. Evidently many people in the church would rather live "in the woods like shy deer," their love cast out by fear, than assume the slightest risk. So pathetically shrivelled, vulnerable, and fragile is our sense of who we are that we fear exposure to one other human being lest our identity, exceedingly tenuous and therefore readily threatened, be seen through and dismissed.

In the same vein, Nietzsche writes towards the end of *The Gay Science*, under the heading "The great health": "[F]or a new end, we also need a new means, namely a new health, a stronger, shrewder, tougher, bolder, gladder health than any health has been up till now."[10] Here again, by "tougher," Nietzsche does not mean rougher, more brutal,

---

8. Nietzsche, "The Gay Science," 143.

9. 1 John 4:18.

10. Nietzsche, "The Gay Science," 169:382.

less considerate, or more inclined to bully others. He means tougher in the sense of more resilient: capable of overcoming disease and hardship, impervious to the ridicule or disapproval of others. In addition to being stronger, the resilient person is on the whole bolder because less risk-averse, and gladder because less inclined to self-pity. Of course, when it comes to natural resilience to disease, certain individuals may have an accidental advantage on account of gender, genetic predisposition, environment, history, and so on; nevertheless, regardless of our natural endowment, each of us can develop greater resilience of *character*. Resilience is something that the self acquires in the process of self-making and self-overcoming: "Whatever does not kill me makes me stronger."[11]

Sheila Cassidy, an Englishwoman trained in medicine, went to Santiago, Chile to practise orthopedic surgery while that country was suffering under the Pinochet regime. One day a man was brought to her with a broken leg, and without hesitation she set it for him, treating him as any physician is expected to do. This man, however, was a revolutionary, an opponent of the Pinochet regime. Cassidy was immediately arrested and soon punished by the Pinochet forces for helping him. In addition to the torture applied to her directly, she was made to hear the cries of others who were undergoing torture, and in the course of this experience made a sobering discovery: she found that the Marxists who were imprisoned and tortured by Pinochet's forces held out far longer than the Christians. Cassidy was a nominal Roman Catholic when she went to Chile, and never recanted this profession, but as a result of her experience she became an ardent believer and a nun.[12] She has written an excellent book on suffering,[13] and is herself an

---

11. Some might contend that Nietzsche is being naïve about the residual effects of human distress and the limits of human resilience. There are people, such as those who suffer from Post-Traumatic Stress Disorder, who are so horrifically wounded by their experiences as to have no inner resources left to enable them to cope, let alone *overcome*. Nietzsche is addressing the great majority who are not so deeply wounded, but tragically live as if they were.

12. Cassidy subsequently became medical director of a small hospice and was a visitor to the L'Arche community in Richmond Hill, Ontario.

13. *Sharing the Darkness* (London: Darton, Longman and Todd, Ltd., 1988).

illustration of the resilience Nietzsche is envisioning when he writes of the "tougher, bolder, gladder" health of Superman.

"The great health" to which Nietzsche refers is "a health such as one does not simply have, but also constantly acquires and must acquire, because one is giving it up again and again, and must do so."[14] It is a crucial point in Existentialist philosophy that the self which arises through self-making is never our possession. We do not *have* it; we must constantly acquire it and reacquire it, because it is tested and assaulted every day and is remade and re-owned in the face of each new threat.

We can think about the above-mentioned point in connection with the temptations of Jesus. We read in the gospels that Jesus was led by the Spirit into the wilderness at the beginning of his public ministry, was tempted for forty days, and emerged from the ordeal ready for his ministry to unfold. The implication of our conventional retelling of this narrative is that Jesus was tempted *once*, at the onset of his public ministry, and put temptation behind him once and for all in that single encounter with the enemy, never to be assaulted again. This can hardly have been the case. Rather, the story typifies the resistance Jesus made to temptation as often as he was tempted throughout his earthly life. When he is in the Garden of Gethsemane, sweating blood and staggering under the prospect of what he is about to endure, is he not also undergoing temptation? The letter to the Hebrews tells us that Jesus Christ was tempted "at all points, just as we are."[15] If this is the case, it cannot be that he was tempted once at the onset of his public ministry and then never again; he must have been tempted repeatedly in a variety of contexts.[16] And if not, he is of no help to

14. Nietzsche, "The Gay Science," 170.

15. Hebrews 4:15.

16. When the fictional movie *The Last Temptation of Christ* (based on the novel by Nikos Kazantzakis) was screened in Toronto in the late 1980s, many Christians picketed the theatres on the grounds that the film defamed Jesus. They were particularly enraged by the suggestion that Jesus might have faced sexual temptation. While the movie's depiction of Mary Magdalene as a seductress is completely unsupported by Scripture, we should not imagine that Jesus never encountered sexual temptation; if he was tempted in all points as we are, he did. Jesus was fully divine, and at the same time fully human, living as an obedient human; this was a *novum* for the Lord of the universe, who had no experience of being human before the Incarnation. He knew

us, since we face temptation of every kind in a variety of contexts, again and again, and must resist it and overcome it afresh each time. To state the same idea positively, we must each day and hour reorient ourselves towards God and reaffirm our intention to live as his child. The first of Luther's *Ninety-Five Theses* is, "The Christian life consists of daily, lifelong repentance." Every morning we must again turn from our distrust and return to God.

When Nietzsche insists that we never possess our self, then, he is recognizing a truth of human existence closely related to what we have just said about temptation, and to Luther's statement about repentance. Given that Nietzsche's father and grandfather were Lutheran pastors, it is not surprising to find a number of Christian and specifically Lutheran themes resonating in his secular philosophy. He has retained much of the content of the faith in which he was raised, even while secularizing it throughout.

He continues:

> And now, after having been on our way like this for a long time, we Argonauts of the ideal, braver perhaps than is prudent, and having been shipwrecked often enough and brought to grief, but healthier, as I said, than one would like to let us be, dangerously healthy, healthy ever again—now it would seem to us as if, as a reward for this, we have a yet-undiscovered land before us, whose boundaries no one has yet discerned....[17]

We are still healthy, declares Nietzsche, still life-affirming despite frequent shipwrecks and griefs, and eager for the next challenge. "How could we,...with such a burning hunger in our conscience and our science, still be content *with the human beings of the present?*"[18] In other

what it is to be human in the sense that he designed and created human beings, but only in the wake of the Incarnation does he know what it is to be human from the inside, including the full strength of human temptation. Only the human who obediently resists it knows the full strength of temptation.

17. Nietzsche, "The Gay Science," 170.
18. Ibid.

words, How could we settle for so little? Or, in Kierkegaardian terms, Why settle for the lowest stage of human existence, the aesthetic stage, which ends in boredom and despair? People settle for it because, while it may be boring and end in despair, at least it is safe. Only if we are thoroughly risk-averse, says Nietzsche, can we "still be content with the human beings of the present."

The Gay Science concludes with an Epilogue whose last two lines are: "You will be able to hear his [i.e., Superman's] music and melody all the more clearly, and also *dance* to his pipes all the better. Do you *will* that?"[19] The first point to note here is that Nietzsche chooses a bodily activity, dancing, as the image that best expresses the exuberance and abandon of the new kind of human he envisions. We cannot dance and be body-denying; we cannot live exclusively in our heads and dance. Dancing suggests delight in our bodiliness, a finding of our self in self-forgetfulness: surely the person who dances most exuberantly is (as the saying goes) the one who dances as if no one were watching her. It is in that self-abandonment, insists Nietzsche, that the self is forged.

The second crucial point in these concluding lines by Nietzsche is that life-affirming boldness must be *willed*. We cannot come on it fortuitously. This claim of Nietzsche's speaks tellingly to me partly because, in all my life as a pastor, I have seen the opposite: I have seen people who are not life-affirming, who do not dance in any sense of the term, who are not exuberant. They are waiting for this life to end so they can go to heaven. Admittedly there is such a thing as a godly aspiration for heaven, but there is also an escapist kind of longing for heaven that is a denial of the gospel; after all, if God so loves the world, why should we be so eager to flee it?

I have also come to realize the level of fear that characterizes many people's lives, the preoccupation with self-protection. In the church, too, people are afraid to make contact with newcomers or strangers, and if the newcomer is psychiatrically or intellectually troubled or has a criminal record, the fear is compounded many times.[20] In my ministry to

19. Ibid., 171.

20. Our relationship to "the other," and the way the other functions in terms of arousing fear in us, is a frequent theme in Sartre, as we shall see.

psychiatric patients, ex-psychiatric patients, convicts, and ex-convicts, I have found less to frighten me than in my interaction with many typical church people. Jesus tells us he has overcome the world, and promises us his presence and power. Why do we choose, or will, fear instead of life-affirming boldness?

Reason in Existentialism

Before proceeding with Nietzsche's *Twilight of the Idols*, in which he criticizes the pursuit of philosophy, it is worth revisiting and examining more closely the place and status of reason in Existentialism. The Existentialist understanding of reason is, not surprisingly, a prominent theme in *Twilight of the Idols*, and constitutes a major stumbling block preventing many Christians from appreciating the contribution of Existentialism generally.

First of all, it is crucial to distinguish between reason or rationality, on the one hand, and rational*ism* on the other. It is a mistake to maintain that Existentialism denigrates reason or rationality; what it opposes is rational*ism*, a rival philosophy advancing reason as that which grants access to ultimate reality. Second, reason or rationality as a capacity, ability, or characteristic of human beings must be distinguished in turn from the process or activity of reason*ing*, the exercise of reason. All Existentialists recognize the manifold determinations of reasoning—including, among others, countless social determinations thoroughly documented by sociologists—and Christians ought to recognize that reasoning is skewed at least by sin; yet many Christians appear to embrace a form of rationalism, as if sin compromises only our loving and our willing, and leaves the integrity of our reasoning intact.

One of the social determinations of reasoning, for example, is poverty. An acquaintance of mine, a social worker who lives in an affluent suburb and enjoys the dividends of a large stock portfolio, has as his clients some of the most materially disadvantaged residents of the inner city. He wonders why he has virtually no credibility among the needy people he is trying to relate to. "When I talk to them they don't get the point," he laments, not realizing that there is no such thing as "*the* point": when he is attempting to communicate with people from impoverished backgrounds, there is *his* point and *their* point, and the two seem not to overlap. None of us gets *the* point, because *the* point does not exist; there is no sphere of pure, undetermined rationality. How we think is governed in large part by our situation.

More to the point, as a Christian I would argue that, at its deepest level, our thinking is governed by the most profound aspect of our "situation"; namely, what we love. The reason we are commanded to love God rather than to understand him is that love determines both our thinking and our doing. Our thinking is corrupted to the extent that, deep down, we are in love with sin: as a result of the Fall, we love what we ought to hate, and hate what we ought to love. We have no access to a standpoint of pure rationality above that corruption. While nontheistic Existentialists do not acknowledge sin, Existentialism has always recognized that our reasoning is determined by what we love, and that it is skewed by the inescapable limitedness of our perspective or vantage point.

Rationalism, a rival philosophy to Existentialism, makes at least four affirmations. First, it affirms that reason has access to ultimate reality; second, that ultimate reality is what is naturally intelligible; third, that reason is the essence of humankind; and fourth, that reasoning—not its activity but its integrity or the end it serves—is unimpaired; or, at least, so slightly impaired as to be naturally correctible.

The Christian faith challenges every one of these assumptions. Christians affirm that only faith, a predicate of grace, has access to ultimate reality: it is faith that knows God. To claim that faith knows God, or that faith *is* knowledge of God, is to say that there is an access to reality that cannot be had except by faith; hence there is *no* natural access to ultimate reality. There is a natural access to empirical actuality—such as nuclear physics, or organic and inorganic chemistry, for example—but not to things that are ultimately *real*. There is no natural access to God; nor is there any natural access to the human self, because from a Christian perspective knowledge of self is always a predicate of knowledge of God. Apart from faith we know neither God nor ourselves, although we may be under the illusion that we do.

Moreover, ultimate reality is Spirit, or the effectual presence of

Jesus Christ. According to Roman Catholic theologian Hans Urs von Balthasar, "the Word of God is not of this world, and hence can never be discovered in the categories and accepted patterns of human reason."[21] He adds, "I was appointed by God from all eternity to be the recipient of this...eternal word of love, a word which, pure grace though it be, is...more rational than my reason, with the result that this act of obedience and faith is in truth *the most reasonable of acts*."[22] According to the unbelieving world, faith is an instance of irrationality; but the Christian maintains that if we are appointed by God to exist in faith and intimacy with him, then faith is ultimately rational, because that is where we find our human authenticity.

Third, Christians affirm that "spirit" (with a lower-case s), which is a name for our having been created for relationship with God, is the essence of humankind. Whereas the Rationalist maintains that *reason* is the essence of humankind, the Christian maintains that spirit is the essence of humankind—but far from being in opposition to reason, spirit *includes* reason: we are appointed to love God with our minds.

Aristotle defined human beings in terms of reason. A human being, he claimed, is a rational animal. That is, we are distinguished from the apes by our capacity for abstract thought: we can do algebra. From a biblical perspective, on the other hand, the human being is distinguished as the one creature to whom God speaks. Humans are related to the other animals—in the creation story in Genesis 1, God made the human on the same day that he made the animals—but human beings are the only creatures whom God addresses. A biblical understanding of spirit affirms, in turn, that we are the creature who is (1) able to *hear* God speaking to us, and (2) obliged to *respond* to God. In other words, because we are response-*able*, able to respond to God, we are also response-*ible*, obliged to respond to him.

Again, for Christians, spirit—our orientation to God—includes reason; however, reason as a *source* of the knowledge of God or of God's Kingdom, or of the highest wisdom, has been devastated in the Fall. Many Christians erroneously assume that reason has been spared the

---

21. Hans Urs von Balthasar, *Prayer* (San Francisco: Ignatius Press, 1986), 61.

22. Ibid., 62. Emphasis added.

effects of the Fall, when in fact it is only the structure of reasoning that survives, while its integrity is devastated with respect to knowledge of God and knowledge of the human *qua* human. Even many secular thinkers recognize that reasoning cannot be relied on for access to ultimate truth in light of its malleability due to social determination and a proclivity to rationalization. In the thought of Freud, this bent towards rationalization is laid at the door of unresolved psychosexual conflict, whereas Marx attributed it to our place in the socio-economic hierarchy and our aspiration to move higher in it. Both agree, however, that our reasoning is largely rationalization, and that our conclusions about reality are determined by our situation and history. Recall the statement of Foucault, borne out by empirical observation, that there is no agreement even about common sense; what passes for common sense in any society is simply the mindset of those who have access to social power. Modernism, beginning with the Enlightenment, had enormous confidence in reasoning, believing that it was value-neutral, that it was simply a tool or instrument; the Postmodernists, however, have shown beyond dispute that reasoning is *never* value-neutral.

Even as "new creatures in Christ," Christians have theological grounds for distrusting their reasoning as a source of the highest wisdom, because we are aware of living under two determinations: we are indeed new creatures in Christ, but the old creature still clings to us, with the result that we are determined both by the restored integrity of our reasoning in Christ and by the corrupt rationalization of the creature of sin, the old thinking that still haunts us and is (according to Scripture) utterly "futile" even though perfectly logical. It is not that sin has made us *irrational*; as pointed out earlier, when Paul speaks of "the futility of their thinking"[23] he does not mean an inability to use logic or to think coherently about matters mathematical or empirical. He is talking about futility in thinking about life, about ourselves, about the good, about God. Our rationalization is consistently logical (which is part of its seduction), but it is used in the service of sin rather than in the service of God and God's Kingdom. *All* rationalization, in fact, is logical thinking used in the service of an unconscious end—often, multiple unconscious

23. Romans 1:21.

ends. God says to Jeremiah, "The heart is deceitful, and desperately corrupt; who can understand it?"[24] In other words, the activity of human reason is so thoroughly subverted by the welter of unconscious motives as to defy understanding even by humans themselves.

Christians recognize that in the wake of the Fall there is still an earthly wisdom of which humankind is capable and which we ought not to disdain. We continue to be rational creatures—otherwise we would not be human—and we can use that rationality for earthly good (though we inevitably also use it for evil: from our understanding of biochemistry comes pharmacy, but also the drug trade). Even the psychotic person remains a rational creature; he thinks rationally, but has a diminished capacity for reality-testing.[25] Similarly, apart from grace and faith we have a diminished ability for spiritual reality-testing.

Existentialist philosophers are right, then, in recognizing that while the rationality of reasoning is never diminished, such rationality serves corrupt ends until corrected. They attempt to point us in the direction of what they consider to be the corrective. The Christian faith affirms that the only corrective is grace alone, owned in faith: that is what restores reason's integrity. Recall from our discussion of Kierkegaard that one of the themes in his work is the angel with the flaming sword who stands at the east end of the Garden of Eden, preventing re-entry by natural means: Adam and Eve, having been expelled from Eden by a judicial act of God, are prevented from regaining the Garden on their own. We cannot ourselves generate or apply any corrective to restore the integrity of our thinking; we can think correctly about God only in the wake of God's revelation, and the substance of that revelation is redemption: it is transformative. Only as the beneficiaries of God's transforming, restoring revelation can we think adequately about God, and hence about ourselves. Given such restoration, God's command that we love him with our minds is not impossible; in fact, not to love God as *rational* creatures is both disobedience and idolatry. Faith is not a species of irrationality.[26]

---

24. Jeremiah 17:9.

25. As G. K. Chesterton famously observed, the deranged person is not the person who has lost his reason, but the person who has lost everything but his reason.

The point of the foregoing is to address a resistance to Existentialism, including on the part of Christians, on the grounds that reason can provide the corrective for what ails humankind. The Christian, above all, should recognize that we cannot think our way to God or to human authenticity. There is no such thing as pure, uncorrupted reason. If we do not listen when the Existentialist tells us so, we shall do well to listen when the gospel tells us.

Nietzsche's *Twilight of the Idols*

Nietzsche subtitled this work *How to Philosophize with the Hammer*, another expression of his that has been thoroughly misunderstood. Since he is opposed to brutality or coercion in any form, when he speaks of philosophizing "with the hammer," Nietzsche is not suggesting that philosophy ought to assert itself forcibly or aggressively or that it should be expressed in the domination of others. In fact, he is not thinking at all of the kind of hammer used to drive in a nail by pounding on it. Rather, he has in mind the hammer that strikes the string on a piano, even *pianissimo*, and causes it to play the note; or the hammer used to strike a fine bell ever so delicately, so that it rings with a true, clear tone. It is a very subtle hammer he has in mind, one for tuning instruments. In other words, to "philosophize with the hammer" is to pursue philosophy with a sensitivity and subtlety that elicits a fitting resonance in humans.

The book opens with these words, under the heading "The Problem of Socrates":

> The wisest sages of all times have come to the same judgment about life: *it is good for nothing.* Always and everywhere we have heard the same sound escape their mouths—a sound full of diffidence, full of melancholy, full of fatigue with life, full of hostility to life. Even Socrates said, as he died, "Living—that means being sick a long time. I owe a rooster to the savior Asclepius." Even Socrates had had enough.[27]

26. Historically, Christians have made a notable contribution to the field of logic. Isaac Watts wrote a textbook on logic that was used for forty years at Oxford, Cambridge, Harvard, and Yale. Wesley, too, wrote a textbook on logic.

Recall that when Nietzsche adulates the Greeks, he is thinking of the pre-Homeric or Homeric Greeks rather than Socrates, Plato, or Aristotle, all of whom came later. Nietzsche repudiates the Platonic tradition inasmuch as it longs for an eternality that disdains earthly life; in its contemplation of the world of eternal forms, the Platonic tradition disdains materiality, history, and earthiness. Nietzsche finds this a life-denying, timid, cheerless, and generally effete position. In fact, he considers the Platonist position decadent in its devaluation of life: "Does wisdom perhaps appear on earth as a scavenger-bird, excited by the scent of rotting meat?"[28] he asks at the end of this same opening section, and declares in the next section, "I recognized Socrates and Plato as symptoms of *decay*, as instruments of the Greek disillusion, as pseudo-Greek, as anti-Greek."[29] Socrates and Plato he regards as "anti-Greek" or "pseudo-Greek" because they are a declension from the Homeric Greek epitomized by Dionysius. According to Nietzsche, much of what passes for wisdom in the Christianized West is characterized by decay and disillusion, one aspect of which is anti-earthiness and anti-bodiliness.[30]

Further on, Nietzsche comments on the one-sided exaltation of reason in philosophy:

> When one finds it necessary to make a tyrant out of *reason*, as Socrates did, then there must be no small danger that

27. Nietzsche, "Twilight of the Idols," in *Existentialism: Basic Writings*, ed. Guignon and Pereboom, 2nd ed., 172.

28. Ibid.

29. Ibid [italics mine].

30. As we have already seen, there is a Platonized form of Christianity that exhibits the same anti-body tendency. Positing a body-soul dualism in which the soul inhabits a body, this kind of Christianity always ends up magnifying the soul and demeaning the body: salvation is for the soul, which is the *real* person, while the body is merely an encumbrance to be left behind. In fact, however, a genuinely Hebraic, biblical concept of salvation speaks of the redemption of our bodies, and honours human bodiliness by referring to the church as Christ's "body." The Greek word *zoë* [ζωη], which means "life," is misleadingly rendered "soul" in some English translations of the New Testament, so that in the parable of the rich fool (Luke 12:20), Jesus says, "This night thy soul shall be required of thee"—as though the rich fool's soul only, and not his body, were being claimed by God. A more accurate translation is "This night your life is required of you."

something else should play the tyrant. Rationality was at that time surmised to be a savior. Neither Socrates nor his "sick patients" were rational by free choice—it was *de rigueur*, it was their final means. The fanaticism with which all Greek speculation throws itself at rationality betrays a situation of emergency—they were in danger, they had to make this choice: either to be destroyed, or to be *absurdly rational*.[31]

The philosophy of Rationalism did not arise until the seventeenth century, but Nietzsche obviously finds an anticipation of it in the ancient Greek world. He maintains that reason should be a servant, not a tyrant; once again, it is not rationality that he and other Existentialists oppose (or they would never have written any books), but rational*ism*, what Nietzsche calls the tyranny of reason. Socrates and the rest of the post-Homeric Greeks, according to Nietzsche, chose an absurd rationalism as an alternative to destruction. Why "absurd"? Rationalism is absurd for all the reasons we have discussed above; yet the ancient Greeks chose that absurdity deliberately, fearing that otherwise they would succumb to chaotic passion and its concomitant destruction of civilization. They regarded rationalism as a preferable alternative, but failed to recognize its inherent absurdity.

Clearly, what we want is neither absurd rationalism nor impassioned, destructive chaos. We want to uphold rationality while also embracing life-affirming passion—as found, for example, in the form of love and joy. Each of us must decide for herself whether the Existentialist has found a way to do both.

Nietzsche finds that the absurd rationalism chosen by the Greeks has in turn led to an insane moralism:

The moralism of the Greek philosophers from Plato on is pathologically conditioned; likewise their assessment of dialectic. Reason = virtue = happiness simply means: one must imitate Socrates and produce a permanent *daylight* against the dark desires—the daylight of reason. One must be cunning,

31. Nietzsche, "Twilight of the Idols," 175.

sharp, clear at all costs; every acquiescence to the instincts, to the unconscious, leads downward.[32]

Moralism from Plato on is "pathologically conditioned" because it is rooted in an equally pathological rationalism. Here again Nietzsche makes a statement that resonates with biblical understanding. There is a fundamental difference between moral*ism*, grounded in "the daylight of reason" or anywhere else, and the commanding claim of God. Biblically, what people imagine to be morality or ethics is not morality or ethics at all but the claim and command of the living God on our obedience. Luther's notion of First Commandment Righteousness is the understanding that the Ten Commandments can be fulfilled only in faith, as our response to the gracious, saving promise of God uttered in the First Commandment. And this faith is our living engagement with the living God. Therefore, what appears to be a moral code—the Ten Commandments—is nothing of the sort: it is the "conduit" or occasion of the claim of the living, speaking God on our heartfelt obedience.

Nietzsche's answer to moralism grounded in reason does not, of course, appeal to First Commandment Righteousness. He appeals instead to a recognition of the value of the unconscious, and an acceptance of what he calls "instinct"—normal human drives. He disagrees with the Platonic notion that "every acquiescence to the instincts, to the unconscious, leads downward." Rather, he insists that there is a great deal in our unconscious existence to which we have no rational access but which nonetheless nourishes and sustains us and is essential to our well-being.

Because Freud spoke of the unconscious largely in terms of psychosexual conflict, many Christians dismiss him out-of-hand, denying altogether the existence of the unconscious or disregarding its importance. However, we need not assume that psychosexual conflict is the sole content of our unconscious. Our unconscious life, including our dreams, "slips of the tongue," and even our hunches, is a wellspring of richness that we should not ignore. As a theology student I took a course under Dr. James Wilkes, at that time a psychiatrist on the staff

32. Ibid., 176.

of Toronto's Centre for Addiction and Mental Health. In the course of casual comment one day in class, he told us we should always trust our hunches. By definition, hunches are judgments that we cannot explain rationally, the "subterranean" distillate of a wisdom acquired unknowingly for years and now stored deep in our unconscious. Our hunches are not always right, Wilkes insisted, but they will be right far more often than they are wrong. Nietzsche recognizes as much, and for this reason cherishes the unconscious as a repository of wisdom, earthiness, and psychic energy. As for instincts, or drives, we have already discussed the need to own and honour them. Certainly we are often obliged to delay their gratification—as human beings we are able to do so—but to deny or repress them is to reject an essential part of our humanity.

I was raised in the city and had never hunted growing up; in fact, I could not understand people who hunted. How could anyone enjoy sitting in a duck blind with cold water running down the back of his neck, or tramping for miles through the bush in order to shoot an animal? Then I became a rural pastor in northern New Brunswick, where everyone hunts, and I recognized something in my parishioners that I lacked abysmally. Not only are hunters far more sensitive than non-hunters to animal suffering and the destruction of the natural environment; they also have a kind of sixth sense about when and where an animal will show up. Where I could see nothing but trees, the hunter who allowed me to accompany him on one trip intuited the absence or the presence of deer, and knew exactly when and where to stop and wait. A few minutes later he had venison for the winter. I discovered a similar "sixth sense" among the fisherfolk in New Brunswick, who could steer across miles of heaving, seemingly uniform seascape without a compass, out of sight of land, and yet know exactly and inexplicably when they had reached the spot where their lobsterpots were. I realized that my foreparents had spent thousands of years doing these things, developing these "senses" and intuitions, in order to stay alive. They had also spent thousands of years sitting around fires, singing, dancing, and celebrating. I came to understand why these things are so very deep in us. While there is no rational explanation for dancing or singing, or for poetry, human life would be impoverished without them.

Owning this extra-rational aspect of our humanity, Nietzsche maintains that the Platonic tradition in philosophy submerged it, while metaphysics purports to have transcended it. Kierkegaard said that metaphysics consisted merely of thought experiments that never touch life; Nietzsche, of a similar mind, insists on a recognition of the totality of human existence—including passion, instinct, and the unconscious.

His critique of classical philosophy then turns to its standard argument for what is ultimately real:

> The *other* idiosyncrasy of philosophers, which is no less dangerous, consists in confusing what is first with what is last. They posit what comes at the end—unfortunately, for it should never come at all!—the "highest concepts," that is, the most universal and emptiest concepts, the final wisp of evaporating reality—these they posit at the beginning *as* the beginning. This, again, just expresses their way of honouring something: the higher is not *permitted* to grow out of the lower, it is not *permitted* to have grown at all.[33]

The point of this somewhat obscure passage is that philosophical abstraction as practised by Plato, Aristotle, and others of their ilk is ultimately *unreal*. This anti-metaphysical streak in Nietzsche is shared by most Existentialists. By "what comes at the end" but "should never come at all" he means that which philosophers consider to be the ultimate reality, the *ens realissimum*; for example, Kant's categorical imperative or Hegel's Absolute Mind or cosmic intelligence—none of which, Nietzsche insists, is real at all, let alone ultimate. He continues, "All the supreme values are [according to classical abstract philosophy] of the first rank; all of the highest concepts—that which *is*, the unconditional, the good, the true, the perfect—all this cannot have become, and *must* consequently be *causa sui*. But all this cannot be at odds with itself either, cannot contradict itself. That's where they get their stupendous concept

33. Ibid., 178.

'God.'"[34] In other words, Nietzsche is saying that in the history of metaphysics, what is supposed to be ultimately real is what is self-caused: God, Spirit, Cosmic Mind, Aristotle's Unmoved Mover. Ultimate reality is the god posited as the end-term of classical philosophical argument—all of which Nietzsche dismisses as sheer mythology.

Recall the question raised in our discussion of apologetics: Does the true and living God attested in Scripture have anything to do with the god posited by philosophy? Is the unmoved Mover an aspect of or on a continuum with the Holy One of Israel who is Father, Son, and Spirit? Or is there a categorical distinction between the deity who is the outcome of philosophical argument and the God who defines himself in the powerlessness of manger and cross? Theistic Existentialists would say that these two are categorically distinct—and, moreover, that only the God of Scripture is real; but Nietzsche, being an atheist, does not believe in either one.

Nietzsche finishes the section with a crescendo: "The last, the thinnest, the emptiest concept is posited as the first, as a cause in itself, as *ens realissimum* [the most real being]. To think that humanity has had to take seriously the mental distortions of sickly web-spinners! And it has paid dearly for having done so!"[35] What the metaphysical philosophers and scholastic theologians—the "sickly web-spinners"—call the most real being, Nietzsche calls "the thinnest, the emptiest concept." It is anything but concrete; it is an abstraction, and humanity's preoccupation with it has had deleterious consequences. Metaphysics leads to a disastrous end, Nietzsche maintains, because it presupposes a so-called "absolute standpoint" which in fact is never realized by any human being; we really have only finite, partial standpoints. Philosophy can never be done systematically but only in fragments, he insists, agreeing with Kierkegaard. Moreover, the claim of metaphysics to have grasped wholeness has merely fostered sickliness.

It may seem that Nietzsche is contradicting himself by engaging in meta-reflection about whether we have or do not have a God's-eye view. What he is doing, in fact, is using metaphysical vocabulary in

34. Ibid.
35. Ibid.

the service of an anti-metaphysical agenda because there is no other vocabulary available. Theologians do something similar: even those who deny a continuum between the substance of philosophy and the substance of theology are still obliged to use a philosophical vocabulary to talk about theology. Theology thinks conceptually; it is a form of what Kierkegaard called "direct communication," and cannot confine itself to the vocabulary of the Bible as some people misguidedly suggest, since the Bible thinks perceptually and stands far closer to literature and "indirect communication." For instance, in theology we correctly say that God infinitely transcends the universe, meaning that God made the universe out of nothing and is its author, ruler and judge. We go on to say that because he infinitely transcends the creation, God's being is necessary and infinite, while the being of creation is finite and contingent. The words *transcend* and *contingent* are philosophical terms and are not in the Bible, but they are the best words for the theological concepts under discussion.

Nietzsche is not the only one to make use of metaphysical vocabulary in the service of an anti-metaphysical agenda. There is another example at the conclusion of Kierkegaard's *Fear and Trembling*. He has just done his utmost to demolish Hegel's notion of the Absolute, insisting that Abrahamic faith, as attested in Genesis 22, renders impossible Hegel's philosophy of the Absolute "othering" itself in nature and returning to itself as Spirit. Then, in the last line, Kierkegaard writes, "Thus, either there is a paradox, that the single individual as the single individual stands in an absolute relation to the absolute, or Abraham is lost."[36] He has just redeployed Hegelian vocabulary to make his most profound anti-Hegelian point.[37]

Having criticized rationalism and abstract philosophy, Nietzsche comments on the notion of "the will"as an invention of both:

36. Søren Kierkegaard, *Fear and Trembling,* ed. and trans. Howard V. Hong and Edna H. Hong (Princeton: Princeton University Press, 1983), 120.

37. In Exodus 12:36 we are told that the departing Israelites plundered the Egyptians; that is, they adopted cultural artifacts of Egyptian life without embracing pagan Egyptian religion. John Wesley said that one task of the church and of theology is to learn how to "plunder the Egyptians." Kierkegaard does just that when he redeploys Hegelian vocabulary to oppose Hegelian substance with a trenchant articulation of biblical truth.

> *Reason* sees actors and actions everywhere; it believes in the
> will as an absolute cause; it believes in the "I," in the I as being,
> in the I as a substance and *projects* its belief in the I-substance
> onto all things—that is how it first *creates* the concept "thing."
> Being is thought into things everywhere as a cause, is *imputed*
> to things; from the conception "I" there follows the derivative
> concept "being." At the beginning there stands the great and
> fatal error of thinking that the will is something that *acts*—that
> will is an *ability*. Today we know that it is merely a word.[38]

For Nietzsche, in other words, the will as a discrete entity or faculty
is mere fancy, an invention. Before protesting that it is more than this,
Christians should remember that Jonathan Edwards, one of the greatest
Christian minds, also denied the existence of the will; according to
Edwards, what we call will is mere inclination. What is the source of
inclination, and how is inclination modified?

The traditional "faculty psychology" posited three faculties: reason,
will, and affect.[39] Reason thinks; will wills; affect feels. However, this
taxonomy is now passé. Once the non-integrity of reasoning was
brought to light, little was left for *reason*, because it became clear that
what we call reasoning is in fact rationalization governed by an
unconscious motive. Similarly, what we call *will* is simply the expression
of an unconscious inclination. All that remains of the three faculties is
affect: we do as we feel, and we think as we feel. More to the point, what
(or whom) we *love* governs what we *do* and how we *think*.

It is tempting for Christians to dismiss this seeming reduction
as shallow, until we recall that the Great Commandment is to *love*
the Lord our God and our neighbour. We are never commanded to
understand God or our neighbour, nor in the first place to *will* something
with regard to God or our neighbour; the command is to *love* God and
our neighbour. It is true that we cannot genuinely love either God or
our neighbour unless we understand something of God, and then of
our neighbour; but what we understand, we understand for the sake

38. Friedrich Nietzsche, "Twilight of the Idols," 179.

39. I have used all of those terms in this book as well, as a sort of shorthand.

of loving. If you genuinely love me, I can trust the understanding you come to have of me; but if you try to understand me without loving me, I know that all you want to do is manipulate me.

For Nietzsche, if one of the laughable features of metaphysics is that it claims a God's-eye view and can rely on reason to access ultimate reality, the other is its pretension to an independent will. The will is no more than a word, insists Nietzsche. He has grasped more than a little truth here. An alcoholic, in the short run, can will himself not to drink even though he craves alcohol. He is then what is called "chemically sober" but "dry drunk"; that is, he is sober—there is no alcohol in his bloodstream—but he is not yet contentedly sober. Eventually (and sooner rather than later), he will re-offend, since affect ultimately controls volition. In the long run, we *will* what we *love*. If we love God, we come to understand him truly and adequately (without, of course, understanding him exhaustively), for love apprehends and understands what unlove cannot. And if we love God, we will choose to live the expression of that love. But if we do not love God, we can neither think nor act rightly. It is our *affections* that must be converted, insists Jonathan Edwards, for it is only when we love God and his Kingdom that we will think what is true and do what is good.[40]

Is there will (volition), then, or is there only affect? In denying will as a distinct faculty or ability, Nietzsche perhaps discerns what Scripture captures even more profoundly when it commands us above all to love. He does not go so far as to declare that love is ultimate; while he speaks of the love of self in the context of self-overcoming (stating that the profoundest love of self is self-overcoming), he does not commend love of one's neighbour, nor love of God. For that we must look to a theistic Existentialist such as Buber.

40. Edwards' *affection* must not be confused with emotion. His definition of *affection* is precise: a *felt* response to an object, grounded in an understanding (however rudimentary) of the nature of that object. Plainly something must be understood of God before God can be loved. At the same time, the understanding required in order to love God is slight compared to the understanding of God that is granted to those who love him. Edwards acknowledges that much emotion attends religious revivals; it must always be distinguished from emotion that, by definition, is devoid of understanding. See *The Works of Jonathan Edwards*, Vol. 2, ed. John E. Smith (New Haven: Yale University Press, 2009), *passim*.

If Nietzsche grants no reality to the will, what of *passion* or *instinct*, to which he refers relentlessly? What of thinking? He would ground all of these in a unified selfhood that cannot be compartmentalized nor reduced to any of them. The self includes passion, but cannot be reduced to passion; it includes instincts, but cannot be reduced to instincts. Self-overcoming clearly requires thoughtfulness and deliberation; nonetheless it cannot be reduced to thought. The entire self thinks, chooses, desires, and feels, but is not divisible into faculties.

Towards the close of *Twilight of the Idols*, Nietzsche condenses his criticism of classical Greek philosophy into four main propositions, the second of which reads as follows:

> The distinguishing marks which one [that is, Plato] has given to the "true being" of things are the distinguishing marks of non-being, of *nothing*. The "true world" has been constructed by contradicting the actual world—this "true world" is in fact an apparent world, insofar as it is merely a *moral-optical* illusion.[41]

Here he is exposing Plato's work as ridiculous. Plato spoke of ultimate reality as the eternal world of the forms, but the "marks" of this eternal world of the forms are the same as the marks of nothing, since no one has ever apprehended them: the so-called "true world" is neither visible, nor touchable, nor sniffable, nor audible. In other words, it is simply an anti-world, a contradiction of the actual world. The good, the true, and the beautiful, as abstractions or ideals posited by Plato, do not exist; they are pure mythology, mere illusion. Since the true and the beautiful are illusions that relate to perception, Nietzsche calls them an *optical* illusion; and since they are bound up with the good, a moral entity, the optical illusion entails a *moral* illusion.

Of course, Nietzsche would make the same argument about Christianity. We can talk about the Christian life as discerning and honouring the gift, claim, and command of God only if there *is* a God

---

41. Nietzsche, "Twilight of the Idols," 180.

who gives, claims, and commands. If this God is an optical illusion, then by definition the Christian life is a moral illusion.

Nietzsche's criticism of Plato is that he called the actual world illusory for the sake of constructing a transcendent real world, when in fact the transcendent world is the illusory one. What is illusory, and what is real? That is the question each of us must decide.

8

Martin Buber:
I–Thou and the Primordium of the Person

Introduction

Martin Buber is a giant in Jewish philosophy and biblical studies. Here we are concerned primarily with his work as a philosopher, and specifically as an Existentialist philosopher; however, he acquired his reputation first as an exegete and always maintained that his work in Scripture was his chief task. It is therefore not surprising that even a cursory study of his philosophy discloses a reliance on the logic of the encounter between God and humans in the Jewish Bible. According to Emil Fackenheim,[1] Buber used to say with a twinkle in his eye, "I'm only as much of a philosopher as I need to be, when I need to be." When he needed to be a philosopher, however, he was an astute one, as may clearly be seen in his insights and criticisms concerning Heidegger, Sartre, and others.

Buber was born in 1878 in Vienna, Austria but spent most of his early years in Germany. He immersed himself in its post-Enlightenment liberal Judaism, the latter marked by an undeniable wealth of scholarship but also, in Buber's assessment, by a diminution of biblical substance. Buber himself, in his younger years, was no less a product of the Enlightenment, and his specifically Jewish intellectual orientation was not apparent at first.

However, by 1933 the Nazis had come to power, and Buber was

---

1. I had the privilege of studying philosophy under Emil Fackenheim, an acclaimed Buber scholar, at the University of Toronto. I refer to Fackenheim several times in this chapter and the next.

targeted along with all other Jewish intellectuals; startled and disappointed by the Enlightenment's hostility to all matters Jewish, he began thinking seriously about Zionism, and never departed thereafter from his insistence on a Jewish homeland (albeit not a Jewish state) for the Jewish people.[2]

From 1896 to 1904 Buber studied philosophy, religion, and art history at a variety of European universities, including those at Vienna, Berlin, Leipzig, and Zurich. It was common in those days, especially for students in the humanities, to spend a year or two in each of several universities in order to gain exposure to several different scholars representing different schools of thought. Originally he was attracted to mysticism, and eventually it became the subject of his doctoral dissertation. Subsequently, however, he came to distance himself from mysticism; in fact, the later Buber would have agreed with Karl Barth, who spoke of mysticism as esoteric atheism.[3] As this position is jarringly contrary to that held by many thoughtful Jewish and Christian believers over the centuries, we must ask whether there is a specifically *biblical* mysticism such as that exemplified by Daniel's trance, Peter's vision of the descending sheet filled with clean and unclean animals, Paul's experience on the road to Damascus, his visitation from the man from Macedonia, his being taken up to heaven to see and hear what may not be uttered, and so on. Perhaps there is a legitimate mysticism that is biblically normed and informed, even if much of what passes for religious mysticism is indeed a form of atheism.[4]

Buber was also heavily influenced by Existentialist thinkers, specifically the writings of Kierkegaard, Nietzsche, and Dostoevsky. In addition, when he realized how severely attenuated his Jewishness was, he looked to Hasidism. The Hasidim (*hasid* [חסיד] is the Hebrew word for "pious") come out of eastern Europe and to this day have never been

---

2. For a thorough exploration of Buber's reservations about a Jewish state see Maurice S. Friedman, *Encounter on the Narrow Ridge: A Life of Martin Buber* (New York: Paragon House, 1993), Section 3.

3. See Karl Barth, *Church Dogmatics* I:2, ed. G. W. Bromiley and T. F. Torrance, trans. G. T. Thomson and Harold Knight (Edinburgh: T&T Clark, 1956), Paragraph 17.

4. For amplification of the logic of Buber's opposition to mysticism see the next chapter.

affected by the Enlightenment.[5] As a post-Enlightenment, liberal Jew in Germany, Buber was not tempted to don the fur hat and long black coat, but he recognized the spiritual vitality in Hasidism and felt that Jewishness as a whole could be enriched by it. Hasidism had revitalized eastern European Jewry in the eighteenth century, but by Buber's time large sections of post-Enlightenment Jewry had come to regard it as fossilized, and it was confined chiefly to communities in eastern Europe. Nevertheless, Buber was persuaded there was a substance to Hasidic thought and literature that could revitalize contemporary Judaism. Hasidic belief and practice hang on the primacy and immediacy of an encounter with God—and, as a derivative of that, the immediacy and importance of one's encounter with the neighbour. While encounter with the neighbour is not the same as encounter with God, the Hasidim maintain that all genuine encounter with God necessarily includes encounter with the neighbour. There are obvious affinities here with the Great Commandment, which we rehearse regularly in the Christian church—we are to love the Lord our God, and we are also to love our neighbour as ourself. But whereas these are often regarded as two parallel tracks or two separate issues, the Hasidim insist that there is but one commandment with two aspects: we genuinely love God only as we simultaneously love the neighbour.

Buber developed a personalist philosophy out of the theme of encounter. The recurrent theme of Buber's work could be said to be: "All real living is meeting."[6] In other words, reality is an encounter, the "between" of an "I" and a "Thou." Reality is not God, but our encounter with God. We do not know God-in-himself, because we do not have access to God-in-himself; we know God only in his relationship with us. What is ultimately real, then, at least for human beings, is the lived encounter or engagement with God. The Kierkegaardian theme of

---

5. In this respect they are like the Eastern Orthodox tradition of Christianity, which until recently also escaped the influence of the Enlightenment. Both Catholic and Protestant thought—especially Protestant—were significantly affected by the Enlightenment.

6. See Maurice S. Friedman, *Martin Buber: The Life of Dialogue* (London: Routledge, 2002), chapter 10, "All Real Living is Meeting."

engagement is easily recognized here; Kierkegaard, in turn, took it from the Hebrew Bible.

A crucial element of Buber's philosophy of encounter is his philosophy of dialogue, by which he means not simply conversation but profound mutual self-giving. This mutual self-giving is accompanied by speech because, as speaking beings, it is by the word spoken to our neighbour that we give ourselves. If I say "I love you," and am sincere, I am not offering mere words; my speech is a vehicle of my self-bestowal. Therefore dialogue is an encounter between two whole persons (human or divine) accompanied by speech.

This is true both from God's side and from ours. Central to biblical Jewish logic is that the Person of God is present in all the acts of God; therefore, when God speaks to us, God gives himself to us. If it is true that *the* characteristic of the living God in Scripture is that he speaks, and if reality is encounter with God, and if the nature of that encounter is a mutual self-giving, then the characteristic feature of God's relationship with us is that he gives himself to us in speaking to us.[7] Correspondingly, *the* characteristic of the human is that in giving ourself to God, we also speak to him—which is to say that prayer is the quintessential human act. We are never more fully or authentically human, Buber would say, than when we pray—not in the sense of merely uttering words but in the sense of committing ourself to God, speaking to him in response to his having spoken to us.

This view of reality is markedly different from other contemporary views. The Empiricist understanding of reality is *things*: that which can be investigated scientifically, measured, seen under a microscope, and so on. For Idealist philosophers it is something else: mind, ideas, forms, universals. For Existentialists reality is closer to what Buber says it is, although for the nontheists among them reality cannot be the mutual self-giving of oneself and God; it might be the mutual self-giving of oneself and another human. We live in a predominantly empiricist world, where physical objects are regarded as real, solid, and substantial,

---

7. *Davar* [דבר], the Hebrew word for *word*, also means *event*. According to Hebrew logic a word is always an event; when someone speaks, invariably something happens.

while relationships are deemed to be vague and insubstantial. Buber insists we have it backwards.

In 1923 Buber wrote his famous book *I and Thou*, about which more will be said below. In it he developed the twofold notion of relationship: I–It, or person to thing, and I–Thou, or person to person. Of these two relationships the fundamental one is I–Thou, because the encounter of one person with another (again, whether human or divine) is the concrete reality that underlies everything else. Our relationship to a thing, on the other hand, is qualitatively different; it is derived rather than foundational, and abstract rather than concrete. In other words, however wonderful the work of the scientist in investigating things and developing or using technology, it pales before the concreteness, reality, and immediacy of *person*, and of personal encounter and engagement. This is difficult to understand for people in the empiricist age; to the Hebrew prophet, however, it makes perfect sense, since nothing is more real or vivid than his encounter with God—his being called, spoken to, and sent by God. Informed by biblical logic, Buber maintains that personal relationship, and above all the relationship of the human person with the divine Person, is the most substantial reality of all. It is a mistake to think that material objects and our relation to them are more real or substantial.

The opposite mistake, also common, is to assume that if the I–Thou relation is the most real and substantial, then the I–It relationship is inherently evil. On the contrary, maintains Buber, the I–It relationship is a necessary part of life. If we want to live, we must eat food, which means treating wheat or fruit as a thing and using it for our own nourishment. We may even have to kill an animal and eat it, which entails objectifying the animal. In fact, whenever we do business even with another person—when we go to the barber, for example—there is an element of I–It in the interaction. We are using the barber to get a haircut, and the barber is not only entirely aware of that intent, but also cooperating with it in order to be paid. When we submit to surgery, the surgeon regards our body as a thing for the purpose of correcting a malfunction, and that is precisely what we expect and hope for; in fact, we also relate to the surgeon as a thing, as a sort of animated tool. There is no evil in that, as far as it goes.

Nevertheless, we do not relate to any person *only* in terms of I–It; we also relate in terms of I–Thou. Thus while the I–It relation is not of itself evil, it has its limits, and *becomes* evil if it is exploitative, destructive, or coercive, or if it is the primary way of relating to another person. Moreover, if we have collapsed our total existence into I–It relations, our humanness will be a shrivelled one. In fact, Buber would maintain, we will spiral down into evil, for that is what evil is: a self-willed reduction of human relationship to I–It. When we visit cruelty on another person, it is because we are relating to that person only as an It.

Until he wrote *I and Thou*, Buber had been known as a biblical scholar; this book brought him recognition as a philosopher. Subsequently he wrote another philosophical work, *Between Man and Man* (1947), and then *Eclipse of God* in 1952. Note that the latter was written seven years after the conclusion of World War II. In it Buber argues that God did not disappear at the Holocaust, because he cannot disappear; rather, God was eclipsed. When a celestial body such as the sun or moon undergoes an eclipse, it is not removed, nor does it vanish; rather, something else comes between us and the sun or moon and obscures it so that its light is blotted out. Afterwards, of course, whatever obscured it passes on in its trajectory, and the light shines forth again. Using this metaphor, Buber maintains that the Holocaust does not mean the disappearance or death of God, but the eclipse of God.

God may be eclipsed for any of us at a given point in our life; we can feel that God has been blotted out, that we cannot apprehend him or that we have no access to him.[8] In Scripture, the suffering Job endures such an eclipse of God, and so does the psalmist on numerous occasions. In Psalm 10 the psalmist cries out, "Why are you so far from helping me? Just when I need you most, I cannot find you. Just when

---

8. The medieval Christians called our rejoicing in God's presence *consolation*, and a sense of God's absence they called *desolation*. An important pastoral question involves the relation between desolation, a spiritual category, and depression, a psychological category; a pastor who is unable to discern between the two may offer only spiritual assistance to someone who also needs psychiatric help.

I want a word from you, you fall silent." The silence of God can be a form of the eclipse of God, or the anticipation of such an eclipse. And from a Christian perspective, of course, God *was* eclipsed monumentally, historically, truly, and with cosmic effect at Calvary.[9] Buber would maintain, without owning the Christian significance of Good Friday, that no human being is ever forsaken by God, though many experience the eclipse of God. Be that as it may, *Eclipse of God* is thought by many Jewish scholars to be Buber's best work.

In 1938 Buber left Germany; by that time the Nazi menace was undeniable and irreversible, and he foresaw what would befall European Jewry. He immigrated to Palestine, where he was appointed professor of social philosophy at the Hebrew University in Jerusalem. He died June 13, 1965.

A study of Buber's work is endlessly fruitful because his thought is so profound. Several years ago, a dozen students from Tyndale Seminary who were majoring in counselling had *I and Thou* assigned to them; they eagerly began reading it, only to find they had considerable difficulty understanding it. They came to me for help, and as we were talking about the text one student said, "Aha! I get it! Buber is talking about the Incarnation!"—to which I replied, "No, he isn't; Buber doesn't even believe in the Incarnation." In other words, she had altogether missed what he was trying to say. My point is that while Buber's vocabulary and sentence structure are simple, his thought is profound. In this respect

---

9. I maintain that when Jesus cried, "My God, my God, why have you forsaken me?" he not only *felt* godforsaken, he *was* Godforsaken. Some Christians hold that Jesus could never have been forsaken by the Father, because if he had, the Trinity would have collapsed; he merely *felt* forsaken, and it was a horrific experience because the meaning of his life was unbroken unity with his Father. While I grant there are difficulties with my understanding of the Dereliction, I remain convinced that on Good Friday, Jesus was forsaken by God for our sakes. I would go one step further and say that because Jesus was profoundly Godforsaken on Good Friday, there is no human being anywhere in the world at any time who is forsaken by God, no matter how much she may feel that she is. This does not mean that everyone is a believer, wants to be a believer, or is going to be a believer; nor does it mean that it makes no difference whether someone is a believer. It means only that no human being in the world at any time is abandoned by God—because in his vicarious humanity Jesus endured and absorbed that abandonment for us all.

he resembles the apostle John, whose Greek is the simplest of all the New Testament writers, but whose thought is everywhere profound. Buber characteristically uses simple words to express remarkably rich apprehension of God, the world, humans, and God's engagement with humans for the sake of the world.

Not surprisingly, Buber has had a significant influence on educational theory, because ultimately education is less about the transfer of information than about the formation of persons through relationship. What is it that we do when we attempt to educate children? What is the relationship of information to the person? What part does speaking and self-bestowal play in human formation? As mentioned above, the understanding of Hebrew logic is that the Person of God is found in all the acts of God, so that whenever God speaks to us he is present in person, and we are dealing not simply with an utterance but with God himself. What about our own speech, including when we are teaching another? When we speak, is our speaking at the same time a self-bestowal, or are we merely imparting information, all the while withholding ourselves?

Primordium of the Person

When Buber came to Princeton University in 1958, Emil Fackenheim and his wife Rose drove from Toronto to see him. In the course of their conversation Buber pointed out that although he had written and published dozens of articles and books on different topics, he had not started to *think* until the age of forty-five, when he published *I and Thou*. He then wheeled on Rose Fackenheim, who by this time was twenty-four years old, and said penetratingly, "Have *you* started to think?" For Buber, thinking had moved beyond shuffling and reshuffling the clichés that society regards as profound; thinking that was worthy of the name now had to conform to God's engagement with those uniquely made in his likeness and image, because thinking was an aspect of that engagement. We do not start to think, according to Buber, until we have had a "heart seizure" at the hands of the Holy One of Israel, and have been drawn into that bedrock relationship which underlies all others. Until then, we are mere triflers spinning our intellectual wheels, regardless of the reputation we may have established. It is our lived engagement with the living God that facilitates thinking.

To appreciate why Buber attaches thinking to our engagement with God, we must understand what might be called his "*primordium* of the person*.*" Buber posited two kinds of knowing: scientific knowing, which is secondary, and personal knowing, which is primary. The two are qualitatively different.

Scientific knowing arises, first of all, as a *subject* investigates an *object*—a statement in which we immediately recognize an overlap with Kierkegaard. In scientific knowing, some *person*—self-conscious, intelligent, and higher in the order of being—investigates some *thing* of a lower order, such as a peanut.

The second characteristic of scientific knowing is that it is acquired for the sake of using the object: controlling it, manipulating it, and ultimately mastering it. All technology is a mastery of things, a mastery of nature for the sake of controlling it. Water flowing over Niagara Falls, for instance, is useless to us apart from being beautiful to look at, unless we can control and master it; then we can generate hydroelectric power. Similarly, of itself a peanut growing in the soil is of no use to anybody. If we exploit it, however, we have food, suntan oil, cosmetics, cooking oil, lubricants, cattle feed, and fertilizer. In this process we are the superior being, visiting our expertise and domestication on what is inferior in the order of being.

A third feature of scientific knowing is that it presupposes a natural intelligibility of the creaturely order, corresponding to the structures of empirical knowing in the human mind. The properties of natural things fit the human capacity to apprehend and categorize them, and the behaviour of natural things follows consistent, regular patterns that are observable by humans and are amenable to analysis by the human intellect. Otherwise, not only would scientific knowing be impossible; life would be impossible. Both are possible only because the intelligibility inherent in natural things corresponds to the structure of knowing of the human intellect.

The knowing that is peculiar to science also presupposes objectivity or detachment on the part of the knower or subject (echoes of

Kierkegaard once again), which in turn facilitates and enhances manipulation of the object for the sake of exploiting or using it. Note that the exploitation or use of an object is not necessarily destructive and is not inherently evil. We exploit natural resources all the time, and very often for good purposes. We extract minerals from the ground, for example, and turn them into various products that benefit everyone. But in all such endeavour it is only through our detachment from the object—a condition of our mastery of it—that we can profit from our activity.

Personal knowing, which lies at the heart of Buber's thought and which he regards as primary, is categorically different. First of all, personal knowing arises only through the intimacy of one person with another. Whereas the condition of knowing a *thing* is detachment, the condition of knowing a *person* is intimacy born of commitment—a fundamental contrast. When we know another person, we do not stand over against them as subject to object; we engage them as another subject.

Secondly, personal knowing is never acquired for the sake of using another person. To use another person is to objectify that person, to treat the person as a *thing* and therefore not to know the *person* at all. To manipulate another person is always evil.[10] Each of us has a visceral and vehement objection to being manipulated, because we know, even if we cannot articulate it, that we are being looked on as a thing. To *master* another person is to enslave. That the slave is humanely treated, fed, and watered makes no difference; he is still a slave, and therefore dehumanized.

Furthermore, personal knowing is gained not in order to acquire information about a person, but in order to be changed by that person. Here is the point that so many people find difficult to understand because

10. It is evil, that is, when people are regarded as things as a matter of principle. It is true that the police officer who arrests at gunpoint someone suspected of a criminal offence is coercing that person, and thereby treating him as a non-person, temporarily for the sake of protecting the personhood of others. It should be noted, however, that the society that permits the use of force in unusual circumstances simultaneously insists on the humane treatment of suspects and even the humane treatment of those who must be incarcerated. The law guarantees that even the most reprehensible convict not be treated as less than a person.

of our immersion in a culture of Empiricism. In empiricist knowing, to know is to acquire information: to know peanuts is to acquire information about the properties of peanuts. Personal knowing, however, is not a matter of acquiring information about a person but of being transformed through an intimate relationship with that person.

In the course of living with my wife I have gathered a great deal of information about her. She is a retired schoolteacher, speaks French fluently, and plays the piano. At five feet tall, she is petite. I have reliable knowledge of a lot of facts about her, her likes and dislikes and so on, and am acquiring more every day. In terms of personal knowing, however, I know my wife only to the extent that living with her for forty-five years has made me a different person. The measure of my knowledge of my wife is the *difference* that living with her has effected in *me*: if after those forty-five years I am unchanged, then I do not know her at all, regardless of how much information I have acquired about her. Personal knowing, then, is the transformation of the *knower*, whereas scientific knowing is acquisition of information about the *thing*. If all real living is meeting, says Buber, then all real knowing transforms the knower.

Of course, we do also acquire information about people in the course of coming to know them. The acquisition of information about someone, we must caution ourselves at all times, inherently gives us the capacity to manipulate them; and the more skillful we are at manipulating others the more easily we can do so without their realizing it. However, to manipulate persons is to objectify and abuse them, and in so doing to perpetrate evil. As soon as the manipulated person becomes aware of such mistreatment, she is invariably and justifiably incensed at the violation.

Buber's insistence that personal knowing is transformative comes from the Bible. In the Bible, to know God means to be altered by having encountered God. When the prophet complains that Israel does not know the Lord, he does not mean they are unable to recite information about God; after all, the Israelites knew more about God than any other nation in the world. Rather, the prophet means that regardless of their acquisition of information about God, the people's hearts remain untransformed; what they know makes no *difference* to the sort of people they are. In that sense they do not know God. The prophet who yearns for the day when knowledge of God "will cover the earth as the waters cover the sea"[11] is referring not to people's theological subtlety but to their profound transformation through an encounter with the living God.

Moreover, personal knowing, at least with respect to God, does not presuppose a natural intelligibility. God cannot be known naturally, for two reasons: the creature has no inherent capacity for apprehending the Creator, and the sinner has no ability to apprehend the Righteous One. God can be known only by grace; that is, we can know God only as he permits and facilitates our knowing him, as he gives himself to us in the word that empowers us to understand and respond to what he has done. Even with respect to our fellow humans, a creaturely parallel to grace is essential to knowing: we can know other humans only to the extent that they give themselves, open themselves, and disclose themselves to us.

The foregoing has a direct bearing on the stance we take as would-be knowers. In order to know something scientifically, we act on an object so as to control or dominate it; knowledge depends on domination, and yields further domination. Knowing another person, on the other hand, requires that we expose ourselves defencelessly to that person and surrender all attempts to dominate. In other words, in the realm of personal knowing, knowledge depends on vulnerability.

We retain a vestigial symbol of this in the custom of shaking hands with our right hand: it originated in the Middle Ages as proof that a person carried no weapon and would not attack the neighbour he was greeting. Boy Scouts and Girl Guides go further; they customarily shake hands with their *left* hand, the shield-carrying hand in medieval times, signifying that they have "cast aside their shield" and are therefore not planning to defend themselves. And whenever we embrace someone we extend *both* hands, indicating that we intend neither attack nor self-defence: to hug someone is a gesture of utter vulnerability and trust.

With consummate self-exposure, in utter defencelessness and vulnerability, God meets us at the Cross, where Jesus' arms are extended to embrace the world. But contrary to what some people imagine, the

11. Isaiah 11:9.

vulnerability of God was not a brand-new thing in the New Testament, confined to the Incarnation; nor is it in any way at odds with the picture of God revealed in the Older Testament. Buber and other Jewish thinkers would maintain that the vulnerability of God is writ large in the Older Testament, because God is always being ignored, rejected, defied, betrayed, and generally mistreated by his people. The suffering of God as he grieves and weeps for Israel is a key theme of the Older Testament, and to speak of God's suffering is to imply God's vulnerability. There is a strand in Christianity that insists on God's invulnerability on the grounds that he is sovereign. God *is* sovereign, or he is not God; nevertheless, the God who exposes himself to our mistreatment at the Cross is the same God who exposes himself to mistreatment at the hands of the world and of his people in the Older Testament.[12] He achieves his purpose—to obtain a people who love him and live for the praise of his glory—with complete effectiveness, yet does so precisely at the point of his utter powerlessness, on the Cross. In other words, the sovereignty of God is the unimpeded efficacy of God's defenceless vulnerability.

Like vulnerability, grace characterizes God in the Older Testament just as much as in the New; we must reject any suggestion that the Older Testament is all about law and wrath, while the New Testament is all about God's love and grace. In fact, the Older Testament says far more about God's love and patience than the New Testament does, and both testaments speak repeatedly about the grace of God. Biblically, God's grace is his faithfulness to his covenant: "I will be your God." Nothing can deflect God from his faithfulness to his promise, his endlessly re-enacted self-giving. That is God's grace. In a contract, if either party reneges on its obligation, the other party is released; but God's relationship with Israel is covenantal, not contractual. No matter how often Israel violates the covenant, God in his grace remains faithful to the

12. Interestingly, though it is in the Calvinist tradition that the sovereignty of God is characteristically emphasized, Calvin never once uses the expression "sovereignty of God" in the 2000 pages of his *Institutes*. He speaks of the majesty, grandeur, and beauty of God, but not of the sovereignty of God. Many people understand sovereignty to mean unlimited, unqualified power, or the capacity to coerce and control. However, this kind of power is more typical of evil. God is sovereign, but he is not all-controlling; the problem with the world is that, while God is sovereign, *we* are in control.

covenant and to his promises, and continues to be Israel's God despite the heartbreak this entails. It is because of this self-giving grace and vulnerability that we can know God at all. In a similar way, all human I–Thou encounters are tacitly covenantal, embodying a parallel grace and vulnerability—grace and vulnerability without which no personal knowing is possible.

If knowing another person is transformative, and if God knows us, then what transformation has there been in *God*? Have we affected him at all? Since God knows us who are sinners, the difference we have made to him is at least this: we have broken his heart, provoked his anger, aroused his disgust, and mobilized his judgment; we have seen him delay the day of condemnation and protract the day of grace. And what about God's knowing his people who are obedient and faithful? The prophets and apostles attest that we have brought him pleasure and caused him to rejoice.[13] Certainly God is affected by knowing us, according to Scripture. And God knows us so very thoroughly not because he is an exceptional investigator, nor even because he made us, but because he has committed himself to us and has come among us defencelessly.

With respect to our transformative knowledge of God, consider the following text: "If you continue in my Word, you will know the truth."[14] Truth here is not information; truth in John's gospel is *aletheia* [ἀλήθεια], reality, and reality is Jesus Christ. If we continue in his Word, we will know him, and so be transformed by him. When Paul speaks of wanting to "know him and the power of his resurrection,"[15] he does not mean gaining theological insight but having his life altered through his engagement with the resurrected Christ. Similarly, when he says, "Now I know in part, but then I shall understand fully, even as I am fully understood,"[16] Paul is anticipating not the acquisition of a comprehensive theology but the thorough transformation of his whole being. We get a glimpse of this also in Jesus' encounter with Mary Magdalene, about whom it is said that seven demons were cast out of her

13. See, e.g., Isaiah 62:5.
14. John 8:32.
15. Philippians 3:10.
16. 1 Corinthians 13:12.

through her encounter with Jesus Christ.[17] Seven is the biblical number for completeness or wholeness; to say that seven demons were cast out of Mary Magdalene is to say that her life was wholly transformed through her encounter with Jesus.

Interestingly, Buber's understanding of the I–Thou relationship, especially with God, is diametrically opposed to Sartre's. Sartre maintains that since God infinitely transcends any creature, the human who encounters God is necessarily objectified to the same degree as a stick or a stone. That is, since God is said to tower so massively above us, we are reduced to utter insignificance in his shadow. Even a *look* from God, declares Sartre, would be enough to "un-person" us and render us subhuman; hence, if humankind is to exist, God must be rejected (or *slain*, in Sartre's vocabulary). Indeed, an encounter with *any* other, whether human or divine, diminishes us—and God, says Sartre, is the quintessence of the other.

Buber counters that God is not the *quintessence* of the other, but rather the *absolute* Other. By this he means that God is indeed other than we, but he is not "otherness" quantitatively raised to the nth degree; rather, God is *uniquely* other. God is the unique instantiation of Thou, the one and only Thou who is the condition of our becoming most profoundly a self; far from shrivelling us, our relation to God as Thou, and his address to us as Thou, is precisely what makes us persons. In other words, the absoluteness of God's otherness gives rise not to the antithetical relation of Subject over against object, but to the reciprocal relationship of Subject to subject—of I and Thou. To be sure, God never permits himself to become an object for us, but neither does he ever permit us to become objects to him.

In the introduction to this chapter it was noted that, according to Buber, since (1) the primary relation in the universe is I and Thou, and since (2) it is our I–Thou relation with God that renders us truly human, and since (3) I–Thou relationships are characterized by self-giving speech, therefore (4) the most authentically human act is our response to God in prayer. This being the case, Emil Fackenheim always maintained that the one thing that could ever invalidate Judaism would

17. Mark 16:9.

be the failure of prayer to be heard. Catastrophic disaster coming upon Israel does not invalidate Judaism; Israel's history is replete with catastrophic disaster, none more catastrophic than the Holocaust. Job exclaims, "Though he slay me, yet will I trust in him."[18] Job may be slain, and Judaism not falsified; however, if Job prays and is not heard, Jewish faith *is* falsified. Unless prayer is heard, said Fackenheim, Judaism will come to an end.[19] Buber implies nothing less.

A Survey of Excerpts from *I and Thou*

Since *I and Thou*[20] is the book through which Buber gained his reputation, and since it is his most frequently read work, it is the best one to probe in order to acquire a basic understanding of his form of theistic Existentialism. Anyone interested in studying Buber more closely should read the entire book, but even a brief examination of representative passages is worthwhile.

I–Thou and I–It

At the outset Buber writes, "The world is twofold for man in accordance with his twofold attitude. The attitude of man is twofold in accordance with the two basic words he can speak."[21] By now we understand

---

18. Job 13:15.

19. Emil Fackenheim, *What Is Judaism?* (New York: Summit Books, 1987), 183.

20. Buber wrote in German, which has two pronouns for the second person singular: *du*, which is familiar, and *Sie*, which is formal. Modern English no longer has this distinction, but the archaic *thou* is still sometimes used poetically to convey intimacy, and Ronald Gregor Smith, the first translator of Buber's *Ich und Du*, presumably chose it advisedly in 1937. Because his translation was for a long time the only one, the pronoun *Thou* became a fixed part of the discourse surrounding Buber's philosophy. For these reasons I have used *Thou* in all my general discussion of Buber in this book. However, Kaufmann's 1970 translation of *Ich und Du* is somewhat easier to understand for today's lay readers, and is the source of the excerpts I have selected for study here. Since he translates *du* by the modern *You* (except in the title, the original *I and Thou* having become iconic), I have followed that usage when referring directly to passages quoted from Buber. It is a good idea for any serious student of Buber to read both translations side by side, as each has its advantages.

21. Martin Buber, *I and Thou*, excerpted in *The Martin Buber Reader: Essential Writings,* ed. Asher D. Biemann (New York: Palgrave MacMillan, 2002), 181.

that the "twofold attitude" consists of the attitude towards things and the attitude towards persons. These are the two ways of relating, but note that they are also two ways of *being*; in other words, to be is to be-in-relation.[22] The "two basic words" are likewise I–Thou and I–It, or what we might call *reality* and *actuality*, using the same distinction we encountered in Kierkegaard. Physical objects and our relationship to them are "actual" in the sense that they are not mythological or imaginary. The word *reality* Buber reserves for I–Thou, our way of relating or being with persons human or divine. Reality is I–Thou; actuality is I–It. He concludes that first short section by stating that "the I of the basic word I–You is different from that in the basic word I–It."[23] This difference is something we have already looked at; we saw that in I–It, the I dominates, whereas in I–Thou, the I surrenders and commits.

In the next section he elaborates: "Basic words are spoken with one's being.... The basic word I–You can only be spoken with one's whole being. The basic word I–It can never be spoken with one's whole being."[24] When he declares that basic words are "spoken with one's being," it is another way of saying that the ways of *relating* expressed by these basic words are ways of *being*: they involve certain attitudes or stances on the part of the subject. One therefore "speaks" the basic words not merely with one's lips but with one's being. However, only the I–You relation—that is, the person-to-person or subject–subject relation—involves one's *whole* self or being, because in it there is no element of detachment and therefore no holding back, only complete surrender. When I am sawing lumber or harnessing nuclear power, only part of me is involved; another part is observing, planning, reflecting, analyzing, strategizing, making judgments. When I am encountering my wife, on the other hand, or encountering God, the whole of me is involved in a self-giving. This is why Buber asserts that the basic word *I–Thou* must be spoken with one's whole being, whereas the word *I–It* cannot.

22. At some point every Existentialist philosopher reflects a concern with being, and for Buber, the two ways of relating are equivalent to two ways of being.

23. Ibid.

24. Ibid.

Buber adds in the next section: "Being I and saying I are the same."[25] In other words, the person is present in his speaking. Recall the note made earlier with respect to the Hebrew logic of the Older Testament, that the Person of God is present in all the acts and utterances of God, and that in speaking to us God gives himself to us. If as human beings we speak and are not present as persons in our speaking, we merely manipulate or deceive; we are misrepresenting ourselves. God never acts in this manner: the Person of God is always present in the speech of God.

"Whoever speaks one of the basic words enters into the word and stands in it," continues Buber. That is, we may stand in either an I–It world or an I–Thou world, depending on which of these "words" we are "speaking":

> The life of a human being...does not consist merely of activities that have something for their object. I perceive something. I feel something. I imagine something. I want something. I sense something. I think something.... All this and its like is the basis of the realm of It. But the realm of You has another basis. Whoever says You does not have something for his object.... Whoever says You does not have something; he has nothing. But he stands in relation.[26]

The basis of the I–It world is my domination, manipulation, possession, or experience of an object; I am the centre of perception and action, and the It is by definition objectified and reduced to my experience of it. The You, however, we can never objectify or reduce to our experience or possession, because the You is another subject. To exist in an I–Thou relationship is never to *have* another person, as if she were our tool or toy; rather, we *stand in relation to* that person, and live in the immediacy of the relation. In other words, I do not *have* a wife; I *am* married to her.

Buber goes on to expound the limitations of our experience of things, the limitations of I–It. "Man goes over the surfaces of things

25. Ibid., 182.
26. Ibid.

and experiences them," he writes. "He brings back from them some knowledge of their condition—an experience.... But experiences alone do not bring the world to man. For what they bring to him is only a world that consists of It and It and It, of He and He and She and She and It."[27] Buber's point is that in the It world, we speak only in the third person, *about* things (or people perceived as things): He, She, It. We do not address things or give ourself to them. But when we say "You," we speak in the second person, and our speaking is the vehicle of our giving ourself to another.

Psalm 23, like many of the psalms, begins in the third person—"The Lord is my Shepherd, I shall not want"—and then, halfway through, shifts to the second person: "Thou preparest a table before me in the presence of mine enemies." Why is there a sudden shift from third person to second? It is because the psalmist begins by speaking *about* God, but as he does so he is so overtaken and overwhelmed by God himself, so drawn up into God's own life, that he finds himself *addressing* God instead. He cannot avoid standing in the immediacy of the relationship.

We find these different postures in the lyrics of hymns as well. Most of the hymns we sing in church are of two kinds: subjective and objective. Subjective hymns sing about ourselves, even about ourselves in the light of God: "Oh that will be glory for me." Objective hymns sing about God: "Glory be to the Father; glory be to the Son." Neither of these kinds of hymns is in the second person, however, because God is not addressed in them. Our best hymns are those that address God, and hence use the second person: "Be thou my vision, O Lord of my heart"; "More love to thee, O Christ."

Incidentally, consideration of second versus third person brings us back to our earlier reflection on Luther's "First Commandment Righteousness." When we regard the Ten Commandments abstractly as a code of ethics or a pattern for moral living, we stand in the I–It world, the world of the third person: "Stealing is wrong." When we understand the commandments as the personal address of the living God to us, flowing from his giving himself to us as Saviour, and understand

27. Ibid.

our obedience to them as a response that expresses our trust in him and love for him, then we are standing in the world of I–You. I–It rules are promulgated in the third person: "Trespassers will be prosecuted." The Ten Commandments, however, are expressed in the second person: "Thou shalt not..." They are a vehicle of the personal address of the living God. "I'm talking to you," he says to us, and we render obedience to God-in-person rather than behavioural conformity to a code. When we take this truth to heart, Luther's point that the commandments of God can only be fulfilled in faith becomes transparent.

"I experience something," writes Buber in that same paragraph, and goes on to press the point that this experience, however profound, is itself an It. "All this is not changed by adding 'inner' experiences to the 'external' ones.... Inner things, like external things—things among things!" When we encounter the You, whether God or another person, we do experience the encounter, of course. How could we not? But our experience—even our "inner" experience, Buber is telling us—must not be equated with the encounter itself. The reality is the *encounter*, not the *experience of the encounter*, because the experience is that which we then turn over in our mind and frequently try to intensify; we massage it and seek to replicate it or at least to preserve it. We try to live off it. In other words, the experience becomes a thing, and at that point the You, the other subject, disappears along with the "between" of our encounter.

Buber is suspicious of the vocabulary of experience because it is self-referential; *we* are the point of reference of our experience, whether it be the experience of a person or a thing. In much of the church today there is a misguided emphasis on our experience of God. If we are serious about *God*, our experience with God will in fact overtake us; but if we are serious first of all about an *experience* of God, that is qualitatively no different from a seriousness about our experience of anything. "God" becomes no more than the intrapsychic event of our experience, and the reality of the personal encounter escapes us. In fact, in a later section Buber suggests an outright opposition between experiencing and standing in relation, treating them as mutually exclusive states of being: "The human being to whom I say 'You' I do not experience. But I stand in relation to him, in the sacred basic word.

Only when I step out of this do I experience him again. Experience is remoteness from You."[28] According to Buber, I do not experience my wife; I stand in relation to her in the sacred basic word *I–You,* and experience her only when I step out of that relation. In other words, experience is a manifestation of It: something we can talk about, analyze, and assess. Experience is a matter of what someone else can do for us, so that the *someone* becomes our tool or toy.

"After all," Buber writes elsewhere, "producing the sound 'You' with one's vocal cords does not by any means entail speaking the uncanny basic word. Even whispering an amorous 'You' with one's soul is hardly dangerous as long as in all seriousness one means nothing but experiencing and using."[29] What he means is that we can always utter the word *You* without meaning it, when what we really have in mind is acquiring an experience of some sort. And if we are preoccupied with acquiring an experience even in saying "You" to God, how does it differ in principle from injecting heroin in order to experience a high?

Romanticizing the experience does nothing to alter its status as a thing, Buber reminds us. He closes this section by exclaiming, "Oh, mysteriousness without mystery! Oh, piling up of information! It, it it!"[30] We may romanticize our experience, either of other humans or of God, by attaching a mysterious quality to it, but that does not keep us from objectifying the experience and becoming preoccupied with it. Moreover, such spurious *mysteriousness* is liable to be confused with the genuine mystery of the encounter. There *is* a genuine mystery to any personal encounter, either with a human Thou or the divine, in the sense that words can never do justice to the profundity of the encounter itself. But merely adding an aura of mysteriousness to a preoccupation with our experience does not move it from the third person to the second, and may obscure the genuine mystery of the encounter.

Further on, Buber expands on the twofold taxonomy of relation by subdividing the personal or I–Thou encounter into two kinds:

28. Ibid., 184.
29. Ibid., 186.
30. Ibid., 182.

There are three spheres in which the world of relation arises. The first is life with nature. Here, the relation vibrates in the dark and remains below language. The creatures stir across from us, but they are unable to come to us, and the You we say to them sticks to the threshold of language. The second is life with men [and women]. Here, the relation is manifest and enters language. We can give and receive the You. The third is life with spiritual beings. Here the relation is wrapped in a cloud but reveals itself; it lacks but creates language. We hear no You and yet feel addressed; we answer, creating, thinking, acting.... In every sphere, through everything that becomes present to us, we gaze toward the train of the eternal You; in each, we perceive a breath of it; in every You, we address the eternal You, in every sphere according to its manner.[31]

The surprising notion expressed at the outset of this quotation, of the possibility of an I–Thou relation with natural things, will be picked up in the next chapter in a discussion of an article by Emil Fackenheim. About the relation with other humans we have already said much; that is the second sphere. The "spiritual beings" and "eternal You" of the third sphere refer to God, with whom we have a qualitatively unique and paradoxical relation. We do not hear God's address with our ears in the way we hear other persons speak to us, says Buber, yet we are aware of being addressed. God reveals himself, yet remains hidden: the relation is "wrapped in a cloud." Language is inadequate to express the relation, yet the relation gives rise to language and shapes it: it is because we are spoken to by God that we can speak in response. In fact we respond to him with our whole being, "creating, thinking, acting."

But there is more here, and it is crucial. Buber declares that *we address God in every one of our other I–Thou relations*. On the one hand, the I–Thou relation with God is absolute and unique; on the other hand, it is the ground of every I–Thou relationship anywhere in life. In other

31. Ibid., 183 (addition mine). The *train* Buber mentions is the same *train* Isaiah saw filling the Temple when he saw the Lord "in the year that King Uzziah died": the skirt or gown of Yahweh, billowing throughout the Temple. See Isaiah 6:1.

words, if the I–Thou relationship is primary with respect to I–It, then our I–Thou relationship to God is the primary one with respect to *all other* I–Thou relationships. The reality of that encounter underlies the reality of all others.

The You we encounter in any other person is a unity. "Even as a melody is not composed of tones, nor a verse of words, nor a statue of lines—one must pull and tear to pull a unity into a multiplicity—so it is with the human being to whom I say You," continues Buber. "I can abstract from him the color of his hair, or the color of his speech, or the color of his graciousness; I have to do this again and again; but immediately he is no longer You."[32] A melody is indeed made up of tones, but the melody is not the concatenation of the tones; it is the unity of the sound, and only by denaturing the melody can we attend to the individual tones in the sequence. In the same way, Buber is insisting, the You we encounter in another person is a concrete, singular unity. As we have already noted, anyone who says "You" speaks with his whole being, and addresses the whole being of the You. We turn a unity into a composite only by analyzing it, by tearing it apart; it is possible and even unavoidable at times to attend to and identify the various aspects of another person—psychological, biological, sociological, and so on—but as soon as we do so we have rendered the concrete You abstract, and have lost the You.

I–Thou with God and I–Thou with other humans

Then Buber says something readers may find bewildering: "And even as prayer is not in time but time in prayer, the sacrifice not in space but space in the sacrifice…. I do not find the human being to whom I say 'You' in any Sometime and Somewhere. I can place him there and have to do this again and again, but immediately he becomes a He or a She, an It, and no longer remains my You."[33]

What Buber means is that time and space do not exist independently as a sort of backdrop for our I–Thou relations; rather, time and space are constituted by those relations—and sanctified by

32. Ibid.
33. Ibid.

them. The sacrifice, biblically, is the vehicle of our encounter with God. Time occurs in the sacrifice, says Buber; that is, time is constituted and sanctified by our I–Thou relationship with God.

In still simpler words: time is made what it is, and is made to serve its peculiar purpose, in our encounter with God. History—time and space—is the sphere of God's activity, not in the sense that time and space are the scene or setting of that activity, but in the sense that God's self-giving to us in speech and action is what *constitutes* time and space. And in the same way, time and space are the sphere of our self-giving to God (our sacrifice and prayer, or our obedience), not as an independent setting or backdrop for our self-giving, but as that which is *sanctified* by our self-giving.

In other words, the I–Thou relationship between God and us is what gives time and space meaning; it is what makes time and space what they are for the purpose of that reciprocal relationship. And in the last part of the above quotation, Buber extends this same point to our human I–Thou relationships, which have their foundation in the primary I–Thou relationship with God. If we identify the human Thou merely as an element populating or occasioned by a certain space in a certain time, that person is no longer "You" but becomes a "He or a She, an It": nothing more than part of the scenery.

What makes history significant? What makes history *history* instead of a string of events? Each philosophy has its own answer to this question. A Marxist, for instance, would answer that history is significant because it is the vehicle of a dialectic that precipitates the revolution and brings about the classless society. A capitalist would proffer another answer, and a psychoanalyst yet another. Buber's answer is coherent with his personalist philosophy: history is made, and made significant, by God's presence with us and his incursion among us, and by our response to him; in a word, by the I–Thou relationship of God to us and of us to God.

"As long as the firmament of the You is spread over me, the tempests of causality cower at my heels, and the whirl of doom congeals,"[34] continues Buber poetically in the same section. He is

---

34. Ibid., 184.

making a powerful claim here; namely, that the reality of the "between," the encounter with Thou, dethrones the nexus of cause-and-effect and frees us from fate. As a You, my wife does not *cause* something in me the way an It (such as medicine) does, or the way I do in an It. The I–Thou relation defies determinism. This is particularly important for us, because Christianity has been heavily influenced by Stoic philosophy without our knowing it; most Christian doctrines of Providence, including Calvin's, are borrowed wholesale from Stoicism, and as such are indistinguishable from philosophical determinism.[35] Buber, rightly apprehending biblical logic, maintains that when we exist in the I–Thou relationship with God, fate is dethroned and the nexus of causality is broken—which is another way of saying that *miracle occurs*. Miracle is more than mere bizarre happening; miracle arises when an encounter with God brings causality to heel, to use Buber's metaphor.

In the next paragraph Buber returns to grace as the bedrock of all I–Thou relations. "The You encounters me by grace—it cannot be found by seeking,"[36] he writes. To seek is to objectify, because not only do we have a preconceived notion of what or who it is we are seeking, but we are expecting to bring about the encounter ourselves by finding. Thus we control the encounter and make the other person our instrument. Even to seek an experience of God is to seek some *thing* and hope to engineer the encounter in some way. We never encounter the You by seeking and finding, insists Buber; we encounter the You only in the free self-giving of the You. The You of God comes upon us by grace, and a parallel grace enables any encounter with another human.

We, in turn, give our self to the You. "The You encounters me," Buber continues. "But I enter into a direct relationship.... Thus, the relationship is election and electing, passive and active at once."[37] We

---

35. Ironically, Calvin insists we have no knowledge of God apart from Jesus Christ, yet when he comes to write two whole chapters on the doctrine of Providence in his *Institutes* he barely mentions Christ at all. See John Calvin, *Institutes of the Christian Religion*, ed. John T. McNeill, trans. Ford Lewis Battles (Philadelphia: Westminster Press, 1960), Book One, chapters 16 and 17. Once our understanding of Providence is no longer informed by the reality of Jesus Christ, we are left with Stoic determinism.

36. Buber, *I and Thou*, excerpted in *The Martin Buber Reader*, ed. Biemann, 184.

37. Ibid.

can see how this is true in our relationship with God. When we are elected by God, we are passive: he comes upon us and chooses us, as it were, and we are chosen. But when we respond to him in obedience, we actively elect God, and he is elected by us; hence the relationship is both election—by which Buber means "being elected"—and electing. It is both passive and active. This fact, too, has a parallel in any I–Thou relationship with another human: we are chosen by another person, and we choose that person in response.

Buber then makes an important point about the inevitable fluctuation between You and It. We have heard him talk about how, "again and again," he identifies separate aspects of the You, sees the You as the occupant of a certain time and place, or reflects on the experience of encounter, so that the You becomes an It. There is no avoiding this, he insists. "Even love cannot persist in direct relation," he writes; "[i]t endures, but only in the alternation of actuality and latency.... Every You in the world is doomed by its nature to become a thing or at least to enter into thinghood again and again."[38] In other words, all I–You relationships constantly alternate with an I–It relationship to the same person.

To see how this is the case, consider again the example of the barber: I go to get my hair cut by the barber, and I give him money in a contractual exchange of commodities. My relation to him concerning the service he renders is an I–It relation. Still, I do not relate to him as It *only*—if so, I have dehumanized him. Similarly, I may say to my wife, "I don't have time to take my broken car to the mechanic today; would you please take it for me?" To which she may answer, "Yes." At that point, no matter how polite our exchange, she is existing for me as a car-ferrying errand woman. That is an I–It relation. If that is the sum total of my relationship with her—"Would you mend this for me? Will you cook my dinner? Will you wash the car, please?"—if such exchanges exhaust my relationship with her, then the Thou has disappeared entirely. Without I–It, says Buber, we cannot survive; but if I–It is all there is, we have died without knowing we are dead, and so have not survived at all.

38. Ibid., 184–185.

His point is that all personal relationships constantly move back and forth between I–Thou and I–It, and they do so not arbitrarily but necessarily and even normatively: not only do we have practical needs that can only be met by others, but we are by nature beings who reflect and analyze. As he affirms at the end of that paragraph, "The It is the chrysalis; the You, the butterfly. Only not always do these states take turns so neatly; often it is an intricately entangled series of events that is tortuously dual...." The alternation between It and You in our relation with other persons is not wrong; but It can no more be confused with You than a chrysalis with a butterfly.

A chrysalis that never gives way to a butterfly is, of course, anti-normative. We can bury ourselves entirely in the It relation and renounce authentic human existence. Speaking of the world that is all around us, the world of things and objects and processes and so on, Buber writes:

> [I]t permits itself to be taken by you, but does not give itself to you. It is only about it that you can come to an understanding with others; although it takes a somewhat different form for everybody, it is prepared to be a common object for you, but you cannot encounter others in it. Without it you cannot remain alive; its reliability preserves you. But if you were to die into it, then you would be buried into nothingness.[39]

It is *about* things in the world—peanuts, auto mechanics, or preparation of tonight's meal—that I come to an understanding with other persons, and I must do so in order to go on living; but it is not *in* those things that I encounter the other person, the You. As necessary as objects are to our survival, and as much as they enter into our relations with others for that purpose, we will be suffocated by things if we give ourselves over to them without remainder. In a society as materialistically preoccupied as ours, is that what has happened? Have we become so enamoured with the It that we have surrendered ourselves uncritically to it, and as a result suffocated ourselves in it and reduced ourselves to nothing (as it

39. Ibid., 185.

were, since in the economy of God such reduction may be ultimately impossible)? I–It is necessary, but it will not sustain real human living. Recall Buber's insistence that "All actual life is encounter"[40]—or, in an alternative and perhaps preferable translation, "All real living is meeting."[41]

Unlike any other person, God, on the other hand, is always and only Thou, *never* It. When Buber says that God is the absolute or unique other rather than the quintessence of the other, he means that unlike human persons God can never be objectified. We can extrapolate and project the human other cosmically, and call that extrapolation or projection "God," and think we can use God the way we can use other people; but that extrapolation and projection is *not* God, and God cannot be used. Israel liked to think God could be used: the temptation of idolatry was not to give up Yahweh for Baal, but rather to combine what Israel regarded as the advantages of both. Yahweh's mercy had brought them out of slavery in Egypt, and subsequently his long-suffering non-abandonment had preserved them through the wilderness; Baal, on the other hand, would allow them endless self-indulgence. Why not have both? But as soon as we combine Yahweh and any other person or thing, say the Hebrew prophets with one voice, we are attempting to denature and use Yahweh. Any such attempt incurs God's judgment.[42]

At the same time—this bears repeating—Buber reminds us that there is nothing inherently evil about the I–It relation; in fact it is a necessary aspect of the creaturely order. "The basic word I–It does not come from evil, any more than matter comes from evil,"[43] he writes. There is no trace in Buber of a Platonic or gnostic disdain for the material. The problem is only that when the It world is allowed to take over, the I of a human being "loses its actuality, until the incubus over him and the phantom inside him exchange the whispered confession of their need for

40. Ibid., 184.

41. From the translation by R. Gregor Smith.

42. The prosperity gospel, once again—in all its subtle manifestations—is nothing short of an attempted objectification of God, which (Buber maintains) God forever resists.

43. Buber, *I and Thou*, excerpted in *The Martin Buber Reader*, ed. Asher Biemann, 187.

redemption." Redemption is precisely the restoration and freeing of our I to be once again in relation to the Thou.

All I–Thou relations, finally, occur within the I–Thou relation of our self with God; that is where they originate, that is where they are rendered significant, and that is where they are redeemed. "Extended, the lines of relationships intersect in the eternal You. Every single You is a glimpse of that. Through every single You the basic word addresses the Eternal You. The mediatorship of the You of all beings accounts for the fullness of our relationships to them—and for the lack of fulfillment."[44] In other words, the living God is the source and end of *all* I–Thou encounters, the atmosphere in which they occur; and that is why our other relationships are as rich and full as they are. Yet because they are not direct encounters with God, these relationships also *lack* ultimate fulfillment, and we will burden them intolerably if we expect them to yield what only an encounter with God can yield.

Moreover, the primacy of the I–Thou relationship with God means that we can live in the "between" even if we have relatively little objective knowledge (that is, doctrinal information) about God; after all, such information is always short of the truth as *reality* anyway. We saw the same point made by Kierkegaard. "Some would deny any legitimate use of the word 'God' because it has been misused so much," reflects Buber. "Certainly it is the most burdened of all human words."[45] But he then goes on to say,

> And how much weight has all erroneous talk about God's nature and works (although there never has been nor can be any such talk that is not erroneous) compared with the one truth that all men who have addressed God really meant Him? For whoever pronounces the word "God" and really means "You," addresses, no matter what his delusion, the true You of his life that cannot be restricted by any other and to whom he stands in a relationship that includes all others.[46]

44. Ibid.
45. Ibid.
46. Ibid.

This point is crucial. Despite misunderstanding, despite theological confusion and the inevitable inadequacy of our statements *about* God, to be encountered by God and cry inarticulately "You!" is to live in "the between." If a person, however inchoately, knows herself addressed by God and responds, then the I–Thou relationship is forged there regardless of deficiencies in understanding. As we have already observed, the Bible bears witness to many genuine encounters with God where the human understanding of God or of the encounter is clearly defective. In the church, therefore, we must resist the temptation to cast aspersions on another person's relationship with God because of a deficiency in her theological understanding or articulation.

The word *God* is overlaid with all kinds of superstition, distortion, and misapprehension, Buber acknowledges, but we cannot jettison it; and even where the word is not used, there are people who are addressed by God and respond as person to Person. We must remember that the saving encounter with "the Eternal You" is a matter of grace, not the correctness of our theology. And this all-important encounter, the encounter with "the true You of our life," is one that cannot be restricted by any other, for it includes all others.

9

Martin Buber: Two Papers by Emil Fackenheim

Fackenheim's "Martin Buber: Universal and Jewish Aspects of the I–Thou Philosophy"

Martin Buber remains as significant for the church as he does for the synagogue.[1] He appears, in fact, to be owned less critically by the church, and more critically by Jewish people, many of whom are offended by his seemingly cavalier attitude to *Halakah*, or Jewish rabbinic law. Even when he moved to Israel, for instance, Buber did not consider it necessary to abide by the Sabbath prohibition against turning on a light switch or pressing an elevator button, both of which are forbidden by rabbinic law as a form of lighting a fire. He also felt free to use a telephone on the Sabbath, not hesitating to call up Jewish friends.[2] His non-observance of every detail of Halakah certainly rendered him less than popular with the Orthodox community. Nonetheless Buber was ardently committed to, knew, and spoke movingly of the God who speaks, imparts himself in his speaking, and summons our obedience. Christians neglect him at their peril.

In the preamble to the first article by Emil Fackenheim to be examined in this chapter, Fackenheim draws a contrast between Kierkegaard and Buber on the point of interhuman encounter, referring somewhat questionably, I believe, to "Kierkegaard's Christian Existentialism (which opposes divine–human encounters to interhuman

---

1. For a discussion of Buber's influence on Christian thinkers see Maurice S. Friedman, *Martin Buber: The Life of Dialogue* (New York: Harper and Row, 1960), chapter 27.

2. Dr. Lawrence Englander, rabbi of Solel Congregation in Mississauga, Ontario, informed me in a private conversation of this trait of Buber's.

ones)."[3] This may have been true of Kierkegaard up to his writing of *Concluding Unscientific Postscript*, but in later writings such as *Works of Love* he suggests no such opposition. Nevertheless, Fackenheim is correct in asserting that "Buber's existentialism shows its Jewishness when it makes divine–human encounters exclusive of interhuman ones quite impossible." This point has been made already in our treatment of Buber—that a genuine encounter with God, while it can never be reduced without remainder to an encounter with humans, always *includes* encounter with humans.

Fackenheim's agenda in this article is "to reconnect the universal or philosophical elements in Buber's thought with its particularistic or Jewish elements, at the same time showing that perhaps the first, far from being abstractable from the second, depend on and derive from them."[4] The distinction Buber makes between I–Thou and I–It is a universal in that it pertains to everybody in any society, but it is derived from the particularity of Judaism: "*I and Thou* may seem to be a purely philosophical and universal work," writes Fackenheim, adding that "considered as such it raises many problems which may resolve themselves only in terms of Buber's lifelong commitment to the Bible."[5] In other words, his philosophy raises problems that cannot be answered by philosophy, but only by the Old Testament.[6] Thus, Fackenheim probes only Buber's *I and Thou* and *Moses* for the purposes of this article.

Fackenheim contrasts I–Thou and I–It

Beginning with a short summary of the differences between I–Thou and I–It relationships, Fackenheim acknowledges first of all a crucial point we have already noted in this book: that the *I* is different in these two

3. Emil Fackenheim, "Martin Buber: Universal and Jewish Aspects of the I–Thou Philosophy," *Jewish Philosophers and Jewish Philosophy* (Indianapolis: Indiana University Press, 1996), 75.

4. Ibid., 76.

5. Ibid., 77.

6. Buber produced (in collaboration with Franz Rosenzweig) a German translation of the Old Testament which he deemed superior to that of Martin Luther. Buber considered Luther's translation idiosyncratic at several places and therefore questionable.

types of relationship. Everyone recognizes that Thou and It are different, since persons and things are incommensurable, but Fackenheim's point is that the *I* is also different in each kind of relationship. The I in I–It is the I that dominates; the I in I–Thou is the I that surrenders and commits.

Secondly, an I–It relationship is unilateral, while the I–Thou relationship is bilateral. One aspect of this contrast is that in an I–It relationship, both I and It are replaceable, whereas in an I–Thou relationship neither party is replaceable. In all scientific research, the viewing subject and the viewed object are, and must be, replaceable by any subject and object of a similar kind. If I am doing scientific work on atomic fission, my experimentation must be replicable by any scientist; water is found to consist of hydrogen and oxygen not only for me but for any scientific investigator and any sample of water. What the scientist discovers about the amoeba, likewise, can be confirmed by any scientist with respect to any amoeba, or science is not being done. The situation is quite otherwise in an I–Thou relationship, whose essence is the engagement between one unique subject and another, each committed rather than detached, and each involved with their *whole being* rather than merely their scientific or historical mental apparatus. Moreover, in an I–Thou relationship both participants address, are addressed, and respond: it is a two-way encounter, mutual and dialogical. Therefore the I and Thou are correlates: if either is replaced, the other is no longer the same, and it becomes a different relationship altogether.

Finally, explains Fackenheim in this summary, while an I–It relationship does not alter us in any profound way (merely increasing our store of information), we never emerge from an I–Thou encounter unchanged. All genuine meeting is transformative. Buber's logic on this point is simply the logic of the Hebrew Bible, where the transformation born of genuine encounter is exactly what is meant by *knowing*. If our life has not been transformed by our engagement with God, for example, we have not really encountered him as Thou, and we do not know him.

"Buber tells us quite unequivocally that an I–Thou relationship does not consist of feeling,"[7] Fackenheim points out, although feeling is a concomitant of the relationship. Each person's feeling is that person's feeling only, and there is no guarantee that the two participants in the relationship have the same feeling. Love is neither one person's feeling nor the other's, nor their sum; love is "the between." In another context, Buber says that love is the commitment of one person to another; specifically, "love is responsibility of an I for a Thou."[8] If you love someone, the question is not how you *feel* about that person; there are many days when God is utterly exasperated with us, if the Bible speaks truly about God's anger and disgust. Yet he does not give up on us, because he has committed himself to us irrevocably and assumed responsibility for us in his covenant. This point about commitment is crucial in Buber—although, as Fackenheim notes, Kierkegaard made it first; recall Kierkegaard's thesis that "truth is subjectivity" (and by now there should be no need to point out the distinction between Kierkegaard's *subjectivity* and the notion of *subjectivism*).

As with Kierkegaard, however, one can put to Buber the question that Fackenheim proceeds to ask: "How can I be sure that an I–Thou relation is *ever* actual? How can one ever be certain that a supposed dialogue is not a disguised monologue?"[9] Perhaps it is really the case that in an I–Thou relationship I am merely relating to myself and projecting that self onto another person. Buber's answer is very much along the lines of Kierkegaard's: there is no objective test or external criterion by which to prove the actuality of the relationship. In other words, an I–Thou relationship is self-authenticating, and to seek external authentication of it is to reduce it to I–It. We can only *stand in* the relationship, insists Buber—which is a risky matter, because we might just discover that what we thought was an I–Thou relationship is a monologue after all. Nevertheless, it is only when we stand in the relationship and endure its risk that we can know it to be a relationship.

Here we are reminded of Kierkegaard's discussion of objectivity and approximation: the objectivities of science (or of history or

7. Fackenheim, "Aspects of I–Thou," 79.

8. Buber, *I and Thou*, trans. Ronald Gregor Smith (New York: Charles Scribner's Sons, 1958), 15.

9. Fackenheim, "Aspects of I–Thou," 79.

theology) seek verification, and they are always approximate because today's conclusions are overturned by tomorrow's. Subjectivities, on the other hand, are not amenable to independent verification, and are not approximate. Nothing supersedes or transcends our heart's seizure at the hand of God; this is real and immediate. Certainly the quality of our engagement with God can always be improved on, but the truth and substance of it cannot, because there is no improvement on God. Later in this paper Fackenheim, echoing Buber, will raise the question of the person who is obviously insane but claims her relationship with God is self-authenticating. There is no way to be certain of any I–Thou relationship from the outside, Buber maintains; we can only stand in it and endure its risk, letting the relationship bear fruit and authenticate itself in the transformation of our life.

Fackenheim then discusses the various types of I–Thou relationship in terms of the various types of Thou. First he mentions Buber's "puzzling assertion" that there can be I–Thou relationships with nature, including inanimate objects such as trees and haystacks. Without dwelling unduly long on this point, because it is not the heart of Buber's thinking, we ought to recognize its force in an era of environmental concern. We tend to look on nature purely as an It, ours to do with as we wish, and are discovering the terrible cost associated with this attitude. We have been appointed creation's stewards, not its rapists. Moreover, there is a kind of "two-way" character to the relationship: when we abandon our relation of stewardship and assume the right to dominate nature, we find that (in a manner of speaking) nature retaliates. If we persist in polluting the air, for example, the day will come when the polluted air kills us.

In any case, Fackenheim points out, Buber *must* assert the possibility of an I–Thou relationship with nature, since he maintains that ultimately there are not two realities but only one, and that I–Thou is the basic or primary way of relating to *all* of that reality. Buber considers the I–Thou relationship to be foundational and concrete, while the I–It relationship is derivative and abstract: "[T]he I–Thou relation is deeper and richer….[U]ltimate reality becomes accessible to us only when it is confronted as a Thou and not when it is observed as an It."[10] And if the

I–Thou relation is basic, then it must be possible with God, with our fellow humans, *and* with nature.

The second type of I–Thou relation, says Fackenheim, is with other human persons. Virtually no one doubts the existence of such relationships. Some Empiricists, however, deny their immediacy; that is to say, some Empiricists insist that the I–Thou relationship is *mediated* through other people's facial expressions, body language, exclamations, and so on, which we perceive through the senses. In other words, we can only *infer* a human–human relation. This point is crucial when it comes to human–divine relationship, because if it is true that I–Thou relationships can never be immediate and are only inferred, then such a relationship with God is impossible given that he is inaccessible to the senses: he has no facial expression, no body language, and no physically audible voice.

Fackenheim deals with the Empiricist denial of immediacy by invoking the example of a baby. A baby *can* feel its mother's pain, Fackenheim points out, and this is not because he is involved in inferential reasoning from the mother's groans or movements to the conclusion that she is likely in pain, since the baby is not yet able to organize his experience in this way.[11] "The baby is born," observes Fackenheim, "with a primal experience which is communal, and out of which gradually emerges the separation of self from other…. [P]rior to this separation of self from other, there exists a more primitive bond."[12]

10. Ibid., 80.

11. To the potential objection that this fact itself makes the baby not an I and therefore incapable of an I–Thou relation, Buber would say that the baby and mother exist in that I–Thou relationship even though the baby may not be aware of it and cannot articulate it. We exist in all kinds of relationships, including intimate ones, whose nature we cannot articulate (or articulate adequately) and may or may not be fully aware of. I am aware of my relationship to my wife, but I am not conscious of all its dimensions and aspects and cannot articulate them. To say that our relationships, anywhere in life, are immeasurably deeper than any description or analysis we can bring to them is simply to say that genuine mystery surrounds all relationships at all times. To that extent we are all in the position of the infant.

12. Fackenheim, "Aspects of I–Thou," 81. Note Fackenheim's preference for the Idealist tradition over the Empiricist tradition. Recall that Idealism is the notion that reality is mind-correlated; real objects, according to Idealists, are not independent of cognizing minds, but exist

In other words, it is not the case that we are primordially alone, and only subsequently relate to others; rather, we are *primordially with others*, and subsequently detach from them. This point is bedrock for Buber's argument that I–Thou is primary and I–It secondary.

An analogous point may be made with respect to our relatedness to God. Christians have characteristically maintained that, as creatures of the Fall, we are born alienated from God, and subsequently come to know God through faith in Christ; it is at that point, they would say, that the I–Thou relationship with God is forged. In one sense this is true, of course; more profoundly true, however, is the fact that because we are made in the image and likeness of God, one aspect of which is God's addressing us and imparting himself to us, even the unregenerate sinner who is alienated from God nevertheless exists in relationship with him. The relationship may be a highly distorted one—what else is sin, but a distorted relationship?—but it is a relationship nonetheless. In other words, there is no human being at any time in the world to whom God does not relate as I to Thou, regardless of how that human being relates to God.[13] Thus Fackenheim and Buber maintain that I–Thou is always primordial. Fackenheim uses the instance of the baby and its mother to show that we are born primordially relating to others, but theologically we could say as much about ourselves and God.

Immediacy, I–Thou, and "the other" generally

In sum, then, while Buber's affirmation that humans are not primarily alone finds agreement in the Idealist school of philosophy, both the Idealist and the Empiricist disagree with his assertion that the I–Thou

only as in some way correlated to mental operations. Realism is the notion that objects exist independently of our experience or our knowledge of them, and have properties independent of the concepts with which we understand them or the language with which we describe them. For the briefest discussion of Idealism and Realism I am indebted to *The Cambridge Dictionary of Philosophy*, 2nd ed. (Cambridge: Cambridge University Press, 1999), 412, 562-3.

13. We preach the gospel, then, to people with whom God has always had an I–Thou relationship. There exists no human being in the world whom God does not love, and therefore no human being who does not exist in a relationship with God, even though she may not know it, may even contradict it, and may never come to faith. This is a crucial point to remember in evangelism.

relationship is immediate. Christians who hear Buber insist on the immediacy of I–Thou relationships might protest, on theological grounds, "But isn't Jesus Christ the Mediator? Therefore, isn't any relationship with God mediated?" It is, and yet it is not, and therein lies no contradiction. On the one hand, Christ is the Mediator who mediates God to us and us to God. On the other hand, however, our relationship with God, forged *in* the Mediator, is not inferred or deduced but immediate. Christ is a *mediator*, not an *intermediary*; an intermediary is neither the first party nor the second but a third party distinct from both, and would therefore have to be neither God nor human; as Mediator, on the other hand, Jesus Christ is both. In the Christian understanding, then, we can speak of a "mediated immediacy" whereby God gives his very self to us *in Christ*, and *in Christ* we respond in turn with our whole self. Indeed, if our relationship with God is not immediate, it makes no sense to say that God speaks to us, because the speaking of an I to a Thou is not mere locution but self-giving. In particular, as we noted before, if I say with sincerity, "I love you," it is obvious that my speech is the vehicle of my self-bestowal. And you do not infer it; you know it. So it is between God and us, *in* Christ the Mediator.

Consider another example of immediate versus inferred relationship: suppose I said that because my wife cooks good meals for me, cleans the house, washes the car, cuts the grass, and warms my bed, I infer that she loves me. If I were to say this, people would consider our relationship impoverished: after all, what if her cooking is mediocre, or she cannot start the lawn-mower? Can I still be certain that she loves me? That is not how an I–Thou relationship functions. Rather, I can rightly claim to *know* in my heart, with an immediacy that needs no shoring up by mere inference, that my wife loves me. Similarly Job cannot say of God, "Though he slay me, yet will I trust him,"[14] unless the I–Thou relationship with God is immediate. If Job had to rely on inference, he would say instead, "There is no earthly reason for me to trust God; he has let me down so many times." But Job has undergone a heart-seizure

---

14. Job 13:15 (KJV).

at God's hand, which means that all earthly evidence to the contrary cannot dull the piercing immediacy of the relationship for him.

The Existentialist school of philosophy, meanwhile, agrees with Buber on both counts: that *we are not alone*, and that *solitude is not overcome only by inference*. Nevertheless, Fackenheim notes, there remains a diametric opposition between Buber's understanding of relationship and that of the Existentialist Jean-Paul Sartre. Sartre's early philosophy also acknowledges an "I–Other" relationship, but there the relationship is not the occasion of a richer, deeper existence of I; rather, it is the occasion of a threat to the I, a threat that must be eliminated in order for the I to flourish. If I am to realize my freedom, Sartre insists, I must negate the other, because the other calls into question my integrity as a person, my self-sufficiency, my status as a subject rather than an object; as soon as the other looks at me, I am objectified, and once objectified I have been "un-personed." Nor can Sartre be dismissed as arbitrarily hostile, admonishes Fackenheim, because there is undeniably an evil aspect to interhuman relations. Who knows this better than the Jewish people with their anguished history? At the same time, the early Sartre is forced by this position to conclude that sadomasochistic relationships are the norm: another person elementally threatens me, and I live with that threat.[15]

A propos of the above: it is worth noting that one of the distinguishing features of any philosophy is how it regards the other person. Recall Nietzsche's attitude to "the they," for example, which differs both from Buber's view of the other and from Sartre's. For Nietzsche, although the mentality of the herd can flatten human existence into a kind of mindlessness, the herd as such is not a threat in quite the same way that the other is in Sartre's philosophy. Meanwhile Buber's understanding of the other is essentially *positive* no matter how much the relationship is disfigured by sin, because he considers the I–Thou relationship fundamental to our existence.

This question of the other is not an academic one; each of us must come to terms with it in our own existence. Sooner or later there not

---

15. The later Sartre, who absorbed more from Marxism, moved away from this assertion, but it does arise in Sartre's early writings; see chapter 11 of this book.

only will be others in our life who threaten us but others whom we find to be downright destructive to our well-being.

The possibility of I–Thou with God: Buber's antinomy

Following his summary, Fackenheim presses the question as to how Buber justifies this understanding of I–Thou: Has Buber done no more than assert it arbitrarily? Here Fackenheim compares and contrasts Buber's thought with that of Ludwig Feuerbach, another Jewish thinker who, long before Buber, also asserted an I–Thou relationship culminating in love. Feuerbach, however, maintained that human I–Thou relationships are possible only as humans become independent of God; that is, God must be sidelined (if not *slain*, as Sartre would say) in order for me to relate to you. Buber maintains the exact opposite: divine–human relationship is the necessary sphere within which *all* I–Thou relationships occur. Only if God exists do we have any significance at all, and apart from God's relationship to us we do not relate as Thou to anyone else. According to Buber, the human I–Thou relationship is possible not through an act of human freedom, "but rather a given mystery of mysteries—that, though finite, an 'I' can go outside himself and relate himself to a 'Thou'"; and the grounds of this mystery are that "the I–Thou relation among men points to an I–Thou relation…between men and God."[16]

This relation, Fackenheim points out, has a dialectical dimension: not only must I and Thou be open to each other, but the difference between them means also that the relationship cannot be forced. The more we seek the Thou, the less likely we are to find her, because our seeking tends to objectify her. We see this in interhuman relations all the time: the more we try to engineer an I–Thou relationship, the more the other person recedes from our advances, because engineering is something properly done to things rather than persons. The Thou must "come upon" us; yet if the Thou comes upon us and we do not respond, says Fackenheim, "nothing happens." We must also be present to the Thou as an I.

Buber was aware, of course, that secularists considered the human

---

16. Fackenheim, "Aspects of I–Thou," 82.

world closed to the incursion of a divine Thou. They still do. He maintained, in the teeth of this claim, that the world *is* open to the incursion of the divine; God *can* come to us, speak to us, give himself to us. However, says Fackenheim, Buber insisted that "it is only as one turns *radically* and becomes *wholly* open that the divine–human I–Thou relationship becomes a possibility."[17] The key words here are *radically* and *wholly*, and this is where the Existentialist commitment comes to the fore. Turning to God in a way that is not radical and whole is like trying to swim with one foot on the bottom, the Existentialist would maintain.[18]

The problem is that as soon as Buber makes the possibility of divine–human relationship dependent on our openness to it, he exposes himself to the objection of subjectivist reductionism: as Freud and Marx (and other such luminaries) argued, the affirmation of a divine–human I–Thou relationship is sheer projection or wish-fulfillment. And there is no doubt that many devout people have sincerely believed themselves to have been addressed by God when in fact they were suffering from an illusion. But since Freud begins with the *a priori* assumption that God is not real, that only conclusion open to him is that any putative relationship with God is illusory. Buber boldly maintains that God *is* real, and that the subjectivist reductionist simply fails to take that reality seriously enough to bother distinguishing between genuine dialogues with God on the one hand and disguised monologues on the other. Buber admits that any particular supposed divine–human dialogue *may* be no more than a disguised monologue—we cannot prove otherwise—but to insist that every such dialogue is *necessarily* a disguised monologue "is not to *experience* that the world is closed to a divine incursion, but rather to *presuppose* it."[19]

Note that Buber begins with the assumption that God is real because he proceeds on the logic of the Hebrew Bible. The Hebrew

17. Ibid., 83.

18. Are we *ever* radically and wholly open to God, we might ask? How can we know if we are? What counts here, I am convinced, is the *aspiration* to a relationship with God that is radical and wholly open.

19. Fackenheim, "Aspects of I–Thou," 83 (emphasis Fackenheim's).

Bible nowhere argues for the existence of God; it simply assumes God as that looming, overwhelming, dense Presence that only a fool (Psalm 53:1) would deny. The burden of the Old Testament prophet is not his inability to find God but his inability to escape God. For the Old Testament prophet, the person who claims to doubt the presence and power of God is spiritually psychotic and not to be reasoned with. From this starting point, observes Fackenheim, "Buber maintains...that subjectivist reductionism in all its forms is not a discovery of objective truth, but rather a flight from God."[20] Again, this is Hebrew logic: the person who denies God is in fact fleeing him, whether she is aware of it or not.

So far, however, we have not come across any justification for Buber's assertion *per se*, continues Fackenheim; we have only seen Buber disarm the objection of the subjectivist reductionist. But we may arrive at the crux of Buber's argument, suggests Fackenheim, if we take his notion that the subjectivist reductionist does not take the divine seriously enough, and juxtapose it with his notion that the mystic takes the divine too one-sidedly seriously. Mysticism, according to Buber, is not an I–Thou relationship between the divine and human at all, but rather "an ecstatic conflux in which the human I dissolves into the divine ocean."[21] Mysticism cannot be an I–Thou relationship, because in order for an I–Thou relationship to obtain there must be an I and a Thou who are (and remain) distinct from one another, whereas in mysticism God absorbs the human I into himself, negating the being of the human person and leaving no I to relate to the divine Thou. If subjectivist reductionism is a flight from God, mysticism is actually a flight from the world, argues Buber; and we have already heard him insist that there is no relationship to God which does not include a relationship to the world.

Note that Buber is not opposed to anyone's having a glorious experience of God that is beyond description; on the contrary, he relishes that.[22] As someone formed and informed by the Hebrew Bible,

20. Ibid.

21. Ibid., 84.

22. Similarly, as Christians we glory in the richness of our experience of the Holy Spirit, apart

what Buber finds objectionable is a mysticism that dissolves the human partner. In the Bible, God's self-bestowing speaking does not "un-person" the one to whom he speaks, but rather identifies and guarantees that one as an individual. In this connection recall our earlier observation that Jewish people stand rather than kneel to pray, understanding themselves to be dignified and not abased by God's address.

How does Buber counter Sartre's objection—and Schelling's even earlier one—that it is logically impossible for a finite I to exist over against an infinite Thou *without* being swallowed up? Schelling maintains that since we know the I exists, therefore "God [so-called] can only be an eternal process of self-realization, the infinite end of which is the merging of God and man."[23] Disagreeing with both the mystic on one hand, and Sartre and Schelling on the other, Buber upholds the antinomy or paradox that the infinite God exists *and yet* the finite exists "over against" God; in a similar paradox, God is absolute *and yet* personal. "To speak of an absolute person is the paradox of paradoxes,"[24] he acknowledges. After all, a person is by definition relative, in that her relation to other persons is what constitutes her a person. God, however, is absolute in his personhood and needs no other person.[25]

Buber does not attempt to obviate this paradox, but simply accommodates himself to it. "I am given over for disposal," he says, since God's infinitude must dissolve our being—and yet "It depends on me,"

from which we are engaged merely in reshuffling theology. At the same time, that experience of the Holy Spirit always confirms us as God's partner; it does not absorb us into God.

23. Schelling, quoted in Fackenheim, "Aspects of I–Thou," 84 (my qualification).

24. Buber, quoted in Fackenheim, "Aspects of I–Thou," 84.

25. The Christian would obviously have something to say here about the Trinity. While the Jewish tradition does not have a doctrine of the Trinity, neither does it understand God as an undifferentiated being. Jewish thought speaks of the *shekhinah* [שכינה], the presence or manifest glory of God, in such a way that God is not static and inert-in-himself, but self-differentiated so as to be able to give himself to his human creation without thereby diminishing himself in any way. It has also often been noted that *Elohim* [אלהים], the Hebrew word for "God," is plural, and that in the Genesis story of creation God says, "Let us make man in our image." Buber does not appeal to this differentiation in God's being, however, maintaining simply that while our personhood is relative, God's is absolute: he can be Person without a finite person to relate to.

since the I nevertheless remains distinct and capable of free response. Nor does he probe philosophically any further; instead, he maintains that we must *live* the antinomy; that is, we must live the unity of both sides of the paradox.[26] Fackenheim quotes Buber as observing, "That event whose worldly side is turning [in other words, something *I* do] has at its divine side what is called redemption [in other words, something done by God]."[27] Buber references a single event with two "sides." Fackenheim himself, in his article "Elijah and the Empiricists" (one of the finest pieces of writing he ever produced), speaks of repentance as both a turning and a being turned.[28] On the one hand, when we are summoned to repent (that is, turn), *we* must do the repenting; on the other hand, we are unable to do it, and therefore must be turned by God. The Bible reflects this dialectical pattern repeatedly.

Fackenheim maintains that Buber's *I and Thou* is a philosophical work, and as such "requires justifications for its central assertions."[29] Yet the unavoidable upshot of all this probing of Buber's arguments is that both his rejection of reductionism and his rejection of mysticism appear to rest on what are essentially arbitrary commitments. Here, says Fackenheim, Buber advances a key tenet of Existential philosophy; namely, that "every existentialist structure of philosophical thought must ultimately have roots in existence itself" or in "an existential decision." This statement is crucial to our understanding of Buber as an Existentialist philosopher. As we have seen so far, every Existentialist has his own existential commitment; Buber's is his self-exposure to, and encounter with, the Hebrew Bible and the God of the Hebrew Bible.

In the Bible, says Fackenheim, the heart of the divine–Jewish encounter is the establishment of the covenant at Sinai.[30] The Bible's

26. Cardinal Cushing of Boston, in a related paradox, used to say that we should pray as if it all depended on God, and work as if it all depended on us. I agree, but I would eliminate the "as if": We should pray because it all does depend on God, and we should work because it all does depend on us. That is an irresolvable antinomy; our job, Buber would declare, is to live the antinomy.

27. Fackenheim, "Aspects of I–Thou," 85 (Fackenheim's insertions).

28. Fackenheim, "Elijah and the Empiricists," in *Encounters Between Judaism and Modern Philosophy* (London: Jason Aronson, Inc., 1994), 29.

29. Fackenheim, "Aspects of I–Thou," 85.

account of the I–Thou relationship of God with his people "makes its case" against both the mystics and the reductionists by insisting that God is God, the human is human, and "a veritable gulf separates the two: yet they are immediately related."[31] God is not a projection of the human, nor is the human collapsed into God; God and the human are at the same time separated by an infinite gulf, and yet in immediate relationship. This relationship is Buber's root commitment and "the ultimate foundation of his dialogical philosophy,"[32] explains Fackenheim. In short, Buber's philosophy comes out of his reading of the Hebrew Bible.

To illuminate Buber's understanding of the paradoxical character of the covenantal I–Thou relationship between God and Israel, Fackenheim then adduces Buber's commentary on Exodus 19:4–6, a text made much of in Jewish tradition:

> You have seen what I did unto the Egyptians, and how I bore you on eagles' wings and brought you unto Myself. Now, therefore, if you will hearken unto My voice and keep My covenant, then you shall be Mine own treasure from among all the peoples, for all the earth is Mine; and you shall be unto Me a kingdom of priests and a holy nation.

In his commentary on this passage Buber speaks of election, deliverance, and education all in one. Fackenheim summarizes:

Without *deliverance,* the people would be dead, and even God cannot have a covenant with a dead people. Without *election,* the human partner would be an abstraction such as mankind-in-general but no one in particular. And without *education,* everything would remain the doing of God, and nothing would be the doing of man. Mutuality—the covenant—would vanish.[33]

The covenant assumes and requires the participation of both the

30. Ibid., 86.

31. Ibid.

32. Ibid.

33. Ibid.

finite human people, in all its earthy embodiedness and particularity, and the infinite, absolute-yet-personal God. So far from God's infinitude being a threat to humans, then, God's infinitude is seen to be essential to his covenant with us. (Here Buber inverts Sartre.) Moreover, observes Buber in his commentary, the biblical phrase referring to Israel as "a peculiar treasure among all the nations" is immediately followed by "for the whole earth is mine," indicating both the *particularity* and the *universal significance* of the covenant that forms the existential root of Buber's philosophy. That is, the passage that highlights God's covenant with one people also describes that covenant as being forged for the sake of the whole world (hence the title of Fackenheim's article). No one can accuse Buber of Jewish narrowness or exclusivism.

We are left, says Fackenheim, to ask about the nature of Buber's determinative encounter with the Bible. Since he is a biblical *scholar*, Buber must uphold the detachment required of all scholarship. At the same time Buber insists that, just as there can be a reductionist accusation with respect to one's encounter with God, so there can be a reductionist kind of scholarship. To be sure, "the scholar, *qua* scholar, has no access to the biblical Presence of God. He does have access, however, to the biblical *experience* of the Presence of God,"[34] Fackenheim points out. This biblical experience is the historical fact with which the scholar works.[35] And the experience of the biblical person is this: to be addressed by God in a way that startles with its "radical surprise." "Radical surprise" is a favourite expression of Fackenheim's. He speaks of "surprise," because there is no way we can anticipate divine incursion or know in advance what it will be like; it defies our expectation. And the surprise is "radical," in that our experience cannot be reduced to a naturalistic phenomenon; if it could, it would be an experience of the world that we are only imagining to be an experience of God.

Buber's openness to the Bible, its logic, and the experience it attests does not of itself justify his own commitment to the possibility of divine–human dialogue, concludes Fackenheim; this commitment can

34. Ibid., 87.

35. To say this is not to suggest that, as *participants* in an I–Thou relationship, we focus on the experience; as we have seen, to focus on the experience is to objectify it and miss the Thou.

be accounted for only in faith. In this regard, Buber testifies concerning any person today: "If he is really serious he, too, can open himself to this book, and let its rays strike him where they will."[36] In other words, declares Buber, whenever any of us engages the Bible with openness, God may speak to him.

"Martin Buber's Concept of Revelation" [37]

Fackenheim begins this article by pointing out the core of both the Jewish and Christian faiths: the confession that *revelation has occurred*. Such revelation presupposes on the one hand, he says, a radical ontic distinction between God and the creation; that is, it presupposes that the being of God and the being of the world are utterly distinct. It presupposes on the other hand God's involvement with the world; that is, although distinct from the world, God is proximate to it. Moreover, Fackenheim observes, this revelation presupposes that God's involvement with the world occurs for the sake of his involvement with humans; that is to say, God relates to the world as a whole because we human beings are the apple of his eye. To put it yet another way, nature subserves history, and the significance of all history is determined by the history of God's engagement with his covenanted people.

Both Jews and Christians would agree, continues Fackenheim, that God has revealed himself at least once, in the Exodus; that is, at the Red Sea and at Sinai. (Christians would add that God has revealed himself definitively in Incarnation, Cross, and Resurrection.) This revelation does not preclude subsequent revelations, since Elijah, Elisha, and many other biblical figures received revelations after Moses. (For Christians, in a similar way, Paul exists after *the* revelation in Jesus Christ but was visited with an abundance of revelations. See, for instance, 2 Corinthians 12:1 and 12:7.) In other words, anyone has the right to claim to have been visited with a revelation, but such claims are always measured by the "root" revelation. The root revelation, if you are a Jew, is Red Sea

---

36. Fackenheim, "Aspects of I–Thou," 88.

37. Fackenheim, "Martin Buber's Concept of Revelation," in *Jewish Philosophers and Jewish Philosophy* (Indianapolis: University of Indiana Press, 1966), 57–74.

and Sinai; if you are a Christian, the root revelation is Red Sea, Sinai, Incarnation, Cross, and Resurrection.

Fackenheim's aim is to counter scientific and philosophical objections to the claim that revelation has occurred; he acknowledges that such a claim has been rendered problematic by the historians, biblical critics, and psychologists of the nineteenth century. Historians charge that Scripture makes historical claims without being written by impartial historians; biblical critics, in tracing the development and transmission of the biblical text, have made untenable the earlier "bolt-from-the-blue" notion of divine inspiration; and psychologists (not to mention social philosophers such as Marx, Foucault, and others) have shown the degree to which so-called religious experience is rooted in the unconscious mind.

Fackenheim also points out that the very possibility of revelation is at odds with modern thinking, because modern thinking pursues the discovery of uniformities (or general laws), while revelation is necessarily an instance of singularity—specifically, the singularity of divine incursion. Divine incursion does not conform to known laws and causes, and is impossible if we accept naturalistic presuppositions. Moderns tend to regard God as either a power beyond the universe and therefore inaccessible and unknowable (as in Deism), or a power within the universe and therefore indistinguishable from it. The biblical God, of course, is neither of those; the biblical God is beyond the universe, but enters into it and is therefore accessible to us.

Alternatively, says Fackenheim, moderns explain God as an aspect or projection of the human—which is the same subjectivist reductionist view described in the first article by Fackenheim which we discussed above. According to this view, when we talk about God we are really talking about ourselves without knowing it.[38] And if God is merely a dimension of the human with no independent existence, then he cannot be that Other who acts on and addresses the human; hence there is no such thing as divine revelation.

This and all other forms of reductionism Fackenheim once again opposes. Acknowledging the possibility that any person at any given

38. This is a notion not far from the Hegelian Idealism we examined in chapter 2.

time *may* mistakenly think she is involved in a dialogue with God when she is not, he points out that this does not rule out divine–human dialogue in principle. His question is: Does Buber offer an account of revelation that meets modern critiques?

Fackenheim devotes Section three of the paper to answering his own question. He lays the groundwork by explaining Buber's understanding of revelation in terms of the now familiar distinction between I–It and I–Thou. The I–It relation is abstract and never embodies the unique individuality of the other; it is substitutable "from both ends," as it were. To illustrate, Fackenheim adduces the example of a carpenter building a house: the carpenter's relation to the house is I–It, in that *any* carpenter can substitute for him functionally, and *any* house can substitute for the house that he is building. The I–Thou relationship, on the other hand, is concrete, personal, mutual, and hence (says Fackenheim) unsubstitutable.

The I and Thou address each other and respond to each other; we could say they are correlates rather than correspondents, in the sense that the removal of one eliminates the other. Both the I and the Thou are unique and irreplaceable, or else they are depersonalized and no longer Thou to one another.

Given the uniqueness of the Thou, argues Fackenheim, *revelation*—which is an instance of an I–Thou relation—*can be understood only from the standpoint of revelation itself.* This is the crucial point. Only the person standing within the economy of revelation understands the truth or veridicality of revelation, while the spectator outside revelation finds it unintelligible.

We see this in the New Testament: the people who were intimately related to Jesus recognized him and confessed him to be the Son of God, while those who may have been physically close to him at times but were not intimately related to him remained indifferent, perplexed as to why others were so transfixed by him, or (at worst) hostile to him. Since reality is "the between," no one standing outside the immediacy of encounter with God can understand the reality of revelation—in consequence of which (to repeat a point we have now visited from the perspective of more than one philosopher), any argument or rational defence for the claim to revelation is unconvincing to the unbeliever and entirely superfluous to the believer.[39]

Modernists tend to deny that Buber's "I–Thou knowledge" is *knowledge* at all, though in the judgment of Fackenheim this non-recognition is sheer bias. In our empiricist world no one disputes scientific knowing, but many regard personal knowing as a form of mythology or romanticism. Even if they grant that a knowing of persons is possible, Empiricists would deny the knowing of God, specifically, as genuine knowledge. (There are, of course, many in our postmodern age who would also deny that knowledge of human persons is possible, but Fackenheim is addressing the objection of the Modernists and Empiricists.) In this regard, maintains Fackenheim, modernity commits two errors: one is to assume that empirical knowing is the only kind of knowing, and the other is to reduce the self-disclosing person to the status of an object.

All epistemologies that restrict knowledge to the realm of It (and that includes all metaphysics) are at odds with Buber's concept of revelation, because they proceed on the assumption that reality can be apprehended rationalistically. The self-disclosure of persons, meanwhile, is categorically distinct from rationalistic inquiry. Paul, in 2 Corinthians 5:16, speaks of how he once regarded Jesus only according to the flesh, but does so no longer; he means that before coming to faith he apprehended Jesus in terms of naturalistic categories, and as long as he did so the reality of Jesus Christ escaped him. It is only as he sees Jesus Christ in the light of revelation that he understands Christ's self-

---

39. At the risk of repetition, however, it is important to note that while Buber's concept of revelation transcends rationalism, it never endorses irrationality. Recall the distinction made earlier between rationalism and rationality, and the contrast between rationalism and faith: rationalism maintains that reason has access to ultimate reality, while faith maintains it is spirit (that is, the human enabled to hear and respond to the address of Spirit) that has access to ultimate reality. Faith always includes rationality; far from contradicting reason, faith corrects reason distorted by the Fall. If God *is*, then faith in him is the most rational human act. Buber's understanding is similar, in that his concept of revelation transcends rationalism without ever endorsing irrationality. Because revelation occurs only in "the between"—that is, only to those who have abandoned detachment in favour of commitment—it is impossible to demonstrate revelation to the non-committed.

disclosure—and, Paul says in the same passage, it is only in the light of this revelation that he understands the self-disclosure of other persons as well.

As in the previous article, here, too, Fackenheim insists on the qualitative distinction between the I–Thou encounter with God, on the one hand, and either subjectivism or mysticism on the other. We cannot infer God from religious feeling or experience; to do so is sheer idolatry. In biblical Israel the idols can be apprehended, but they do not speak, whereas *the* characteristic of the living God is that he speaks. God addresses us, and in that address we are given our personhood and constituted as Thou for him, and we *know* that he has addressed us. Nor can we summon God at our will, conjure him, as it were, or force him to speak, for God ever remains Lord of his self-disclosure; yet he neither consumes us nor absorbs us.

Since revelation is the encounter of Person with person, it is also qualitatively distinct from dogmas and laws and Torah, explains Fackenheim. As we have noted before, there is a difference between the detachment and abstractness of theology and the radical commitment and concreteness of faith. Dogmas and laws, while appropriate and even necessary, belong to the realm of I–It; even our relationship to the Bible, however necessary and devout, is always I–It, since the Bible is a thing. Our relationship to the Lord of the Bible, on the other hand, is I–Thou. In the moment of the encounter, the Person himself is found in the word he speaks; hence we relate not to an utterance, which is a mere It, but to the Person of God present in his speaking to us. And hence also we honour the commandment of God *only* as we honour the Person who commands. It is the same point Luther made in his First-Commandment Righteousness.

The particularity of revelation

"All this is true," says Fackenheim, "because the Giver who is present in the given is not a timeless Presence. The God of dialogue, like any Thou of any dialogue, speaks to a unique partner in a unique situation, disclosing himself according to the unique exigencies of each situation."[40] In the words of Buber, this God who speaks "is always the God of a moment, a moment God." This means not only that God's address cannot be anticipated (because he remains Lord of his self-disclosure), but also that God addresses himself uniquely to unique situations. In Exodus 3:14, when Moses asks for God's name, God declares, "I shall be there." In Scripture, *name* means person, presence, nature, deserved reputation; hence to ask God's *name* is to ask God to disclose his nature. And God's answer to Moses is, *Ehyeh asher Ehyeh* [אֶהְיֶה אֲשֶׁר אֶהְיֶה], "I am who (what) I am"—or, since Hebrew grammar equally permits a reading of the future tense, "I shall be who I shall be." Martin Buber translates this expression as "I shall be there." In other words, "You will know me in that moment in which you encounter me." Regardless of where life takes us, it will never take us past the self-disclosure of God; God will be there.[41]

Buber's point is that God addresses himself not generically to generic situations (that would put his address in the realm of It, the realm of abstractions), but uniquely to unique situations—and to unique persons who can respond only out of their unique situation. Unless God's address is particular, he is not addressing a Thou; while God loves the whole world, in the Bible he characteristically addresses individuals. Each individual is unique in her situation, and because she is unique, her situation is duplicated nowhere else.

If this is the case, however, what is it that enables us to identify and recognize the revelation of the God *of this moment* as a revelation of the same one Lord, the infinite and eternal? In answer to his own question, Fackenheim points out that a concept of revelation can never presuppose a pre-revelation category or criterion to which revelation must conform, or else revelation would not be revelatory at all.[42] This is a caution against natural theology, in which we approach revelation from pre-revelational categories and impose those categories on it. Genuine

40. Fackenheim, "Martin Buber's Concept of Revelation," 66.

41. For the Christian, Moses' question is answered on Easter morning: "I am the One who raised Jesus from the dead." God is revealed in his acts; if we discern what he does, we come to know who he is.

42. We notice, in this denial of an appeal to a category above revelation in order to identify revelation, a direct connection to the earlier assertion that it is only from within revelation that revelation can be recognized and understood.

revelation supersedes and overturns all anticipatory or pre-revelational categories. Fackenheim pointedly concludes, "Thus if God is known as eternal and infinite, it is not by thought which rises above the encounter to speculate on his essence; it is known *in* the encounter. God is infinite, because in the moment of encounter there is no It which can limit him; he is eternal, because it is known in the here and now that he cannot turn into an It in any here and now."[43] In other words, in the moment of encounter, in the moment of the divine incursion into the world, God is known by the fact that every It is at his disposal as the instrument of his self-disclosure. God uses a cross made of wood; God uses the storm of the Red Sea; and God uses a bush, a donkey, a lamb, bread and wine, and the Roman means of state execution, to reveal himself.

As God speaks into a specific situation, we must respond out of that situation; otherwise, a conceptual anticipation would domesticate God. Faith is always a matter of responding to God—not, for instance, of understanding or endorsing doctrine. The form of the particular response varies with each situation—we respond concretely, "in real time," as it were—but every response to the divine Thou must be characterized by complete commitment. Faith must be all or nothing. "[C]ommitment cannot here admit of degrees," writes Fackenheim. "This relation is the absolute relation, that is, the relation which exists either absolutely or not at all."[44] His declaration is reminiscent of the epigrammatic closing sentence of Kierkegaard's *Fear and Trembling*: "Thus, either there is a paradox, that the single individual stands in an absolute relation to the Absolute, or Abraham is lost."[45]

Another antinomy

The above in turn raises another question: Does this mean that revelation is revelation only as there is a response? Or is revelation independent of the response? At times, says Fackenheim, Buber appears to lean toward both conclusions, but he ends up rejecting both, finding

43. Fackenheim, "Martin Buber's Concept of Revelation," 67.

44. Ibid., 68.

45. Kierkegaard, *Fear and Trembling/Repetition*, ed. and trans. Howard V. Hong and Edna H. Hong (Princeton: Princeton University Press, 1983), 120.

himself compelled to approach this question, too, in terms of an antinomy or paradox. There remains in a faith-encounter an impenetrable mystery that must be *given* ("I am given over to disposal"), and yet remains a *human* affirmation and activity. On the one hand, explains Fackenheim, by the very act of addressing us God makes us into his Thou, capable of listening and responding; yet on the other hand, unless we actively choose to listen, we cannot be his Thou, nor can he be ours. Since our *listenership* must be given to us by God, has he really given it to us if we do not listen? At the same time, can we listen if God does not make us listeners? A Christian would say that on the one hand, only by the Holy Spirit can we say "Jesus is Lord,"[46] yet on the other hand, *we* have to say it. We are confronted once again by a paradox or antinomy, and just as we saw in our study of Fackenheim's previous article, Buber accepts that the antinomy cannot be resolved by thinking about it; he simply embraces and *lives* both parts of it.

What does living the antinomy involve? Revelation, being unique, is fraught with different content in different situations and therefore calls forth different actions in response. Consider, for example, God's revelations to Hosea and to Paul: to Hosea God says, "Marry a prostitute,"[47] while to Paul he appears to say, "Do not marry anyone." God does not say the same thing to every human being. If the content of revelation could be specified beforehand, then revelation would be an It.[48] Since the content is not specified beforehand, only the person irretrievably committed to God can know what is from God; we must take the risk of letting the revelation bear fruit in our lives.

Moreover, just as there is a divine side and a human side to the encounter, in which God's address constitutes us a listening Thou and yet we ourselves choose to listen, so there is a divine side and a human side *to the revelation itself*: all revelation is God's self-disclosure, and yet all

---

46. 1 Corinthians 12:3.

47. Hosea 1:2.

48. I am persuaded it is God's providence that Jesus never wrote a book; if he had, we would all be preoccupied with the book instead of embracing Jesus. While the Bible has a unique role in God's economy, we must never confuse our I–It relationship to the Book with our I–Thou relationship to the Lord of the Book.

revelation in the course of being received is *translation*, a human product. We see evidence of this human translation in the fact that we have four written gospels in our canonical collection. They all agree that Jesus is Saviour, Lord, Son of God and Son of Man, and Messiah of Israel; nevertheless each gospel writer has a different angle of vision on Jesus and the economy of faith. In his book on Moses, Buber maintains that while God speaks precisely and clearly at Sinai, Moses stammers.[49] Yet Buber remains confident concerning the economy of revelation: "It is laid upon the stammering to bring the voice of Heaven to Earth."[50] Every preacher stammers, metaphorically speaking, yet the preacher's stammering testimony to Jesus Christ is just what God will use to acquaint hearers with him.

In the "moment" of revelation we cannot demarcate between grace, on the one hand, and our human appropriation or reception on the other. In other words, we cannot say that up to this or that point it is a matter of God's activity, after which the rest is ours; rather, all of it is simultaneously God and us. A certain kind of predestinarian might say that it is *all* of the Holy Spirit and nothing of us, but that would negate the personhood of the human, reducing us to It.

Fackenheim's "third thing"

In the final section of his article, Fackenheim makes an important point that diverges from Buber's own thought and attempts to correct Buber. To do so, Fackenheim returns to the difference between the concreteness of the I–Thou relation and the abstractness of our philosophical reflection on that relation. Even if the reflection on the relation must be implicit in the encounter itself and quickened by the encounter, there remains a distinction between the encounter itself and philosophical reflection on it: the former is I–Thou, while the latter is I–It. According to Buber, says Fackenheim, these are the *only* two attitudes and the only two types of knowledge, and they are mutually exclusive. Yet Buber himself engages in philosophical reflection which

49. Martin Buber, *Moses: The Revelation and the Covenant* (London: Harper Torchbook, 1958).

50. Ibid., 59.

constitutes a *critique* of I–It knowledge; it "transcends the realm of I–It in that it recognizes its limitations and, in recognizing them, points beyond them to the realm of the I and Thou,"[51] writes Fackenheim. He then quotes a passage in which Buber says that the philosopher who recognizes God as Thou, being unable to include God in his philosophical system, would be "compelled to point toward God without actually dealing with him." This is problematic, says Fackenheim: if the philosopher is necessarily engaging in I–It knowledge, and if I–It and I–Thou are mutually exclusive and are the only possible types of knowledge, how can the philosopher even "point toward" the God who is Thou?

To resolve this impossibility Fackenheim argues for a kind of philosophical reflection on I–Thou and I–It that, strictly speaking, belongs to neither of these. Belonging to neither, but flowing directly from I–Thou and the commitment that characterizes the I–Thou encounter, it mediates between I–Thou and I–It as a third kind of knowledge. (Here Fackenheim is redeploying Hegelian vocabulary in order to make his point.)

We might think of his "third thing" in the following way. It has already been said here that our encounter with Jesus Christ is not the same as our reflection on that encounter. But is not our reflection on our own encounter different from a scientific investigation of it (e.g., as conducted by any of the social sciences), and the scientific report that would emerge from that investigation? The scientific report has nothing to do with I–Thou at all, because there is no personal engagement with what is being investigated; but the doctrinal reflection that we make, born of our committed encounter with Jesus Christ, has everything to do with I–Thou. Our reflection is not I–Thou, but the encounter was I–Thou, and therefore our reflection on it is intrinsically related to the I–Thou in a way that a scientist's report is not; *our reflection on the encounter is conditioned by the commitment that characterized the encounter.* This is Fackenheim's point. In other words, from a Christian point of view, even while Christian doctrine is a human reflection on one's engagement with Jesus Christ, it is not natural human activity *merely.*

---

51. Fackenheim, "Martin Buber's Concept of Revelation," 72.

After all, we do not say of justification by faith, "That happens to be Paul's opinion. I believe in justification by moral achievement." Rather, we recognize that Paul's reflection on his encounter with Jesus Christ is quickened by the encounter itself, and cannot be substituted.

I maintain Fackenheim is correct here. Without a third kind of knowledge that mediates dialectically between I–Thou and I–It, we would have to conclude that it is impossible to express any true knowledge about the I–Thou encounter, because as soon as we talk *about* the encounter we are in the I–It world, which by definition has no access to or knowledge of I–Thou.

Fackenheim extends his point concerning Buber to Existentialist thought in general; that is, Existentialist thought mediates between *actuality* on the one hand, or the kind of knowing born of detachment, and *reality* on the other, or the kind of knowing born of radical personal commitment. Even nontheistic Existentialist thought flows directly from an existential encounter or engagement, and therefore the thought is intimately related to that encounter in a way that other philosophical thought is not. The result, however, is neither systematic (and we know that Existentialists would be the first to agree with that assessment) nor philosophical in the strict sense, because philosophy cannot be committed and remain philosophy. In Buber's case, since his existential "unargued commitment" is to "the dialogue with the ancient God of Israel," one might say that he is a "Hebrew sage"[52] rather than a philosopher.

Concluding Thoughts

In conclusion we should note that by submitting Buber's thought to the scrutiny of analytic philosophy, Fackenheim is making Buber's commitments and their implications all the clearer, locating their points of irresolvability, and sharpening the contrast between Existential philosophy and the rest of the philosophical tradition. He does so without in any way delegitimizing Buber's thought. Whatever else one might say about analytic philosophy, it is a useful tool in that it sharpens

52. Ibid., 74.

a person's thinking and guards against the slovenly use of philosophical vocabulary. At the same time, Fackenheim used to say good-naturedly of analytic philosophy, "It is a tool we all need, but can we live by it?"

We might also ask, "Can we find God with it?" Each of us must arrive at our own understanding of the place and nature of philosophy and its relationship to theology, because there is no unanimity among Christians on that question: those of a scholastic orientation would say there is every place for philosophy in theology, while those of a more existentialist approach would maintain the opposite. In Isaiah, God says to his people, "Come, let us reason together; though your sins be as scarlet, they shall be white as snow."[53] But is God speaking about a reasoning that takes place *within* revelation, within the orbit of a relationship to him, or a reasoning that brings us *into* such a relationship and *into* the orbit of revelation? Is it even possible for reasoning to bring us into the orbit of revelation? That depends on how much credence we give to apologetics and natural theology. But there is no question that it is possible to reason *within* the orbit of revelation. Of course it is: we are commanded to love God with our minds. When the writer of Acts describes how Paul goes to synagogues and other thoughtful gatherings and reasons with the people, he uses the Greek verb *logizomai* [λογίζομαι]. *Logizomai* can mean anything from speaking to discussing to interrogating, and is a rational activity; but it does *not* mean philosophical demonstration.

Fackenheim concludes his article, "Buber's own commitment, and the commitment he would ask of his reader, would simply rest on the ancient and irrefutable faith that God can speak even though he may be silent; that he can speak at least to those who listen to his voice with all their hearts."[54] It is in God's speaking to us that our heart is opened to hear, yet our heart must be open or we will not hear. That is the antinomy in which Buber lives, and in which he invites us to live also.

---

53. Isaiah 1:18.
54. Fackenheim, "Martin Buber's Concept of Revelation," 74.

10

Martin Heidegger:
Dasein in the World

Introduction

Readers may find the philosophy of Martin Heidegger the most difficult
to understand of all those discussed in this book. Sartre, for instance,
although the intellectual child of Heidegger (who nevertheless diverges
from him at a number of points in his thinking), will be easier to grasp
for most. This chapter begins with a biographical sketch of Heidegger,
proceeds to a brief overview of his philosophy, and concludes by
commenting on the introduction to Heidegger's work found in
Existentialism: Basic Writings (edited by Charles Guignon and Derk
Pereboom), the same book referred to above in the chapters on
Kierkegaard and Nietzsche.

Heidegger was born in September of 1889 to a poor Roman
Catholic family in Messkirch, southwest Germany. He attended high
school in Konstanz, where he began preparing for the priesthood, but
moved shortly thereafter to continue his high school studies in Freiburg.
There he became interested in philosophy. In 1909 he entered the
Jesuit novitiate but was discharged from the seminary within a month,
apparently on account of ill health. He entered the University of
Freiburg and began studying philosophy and scholastic theology,
terminating his training for the priesthood in 1911. Subsequently he
applied himself to modern philosophy, especially that of Husserl, a
phenomenologist. Phenomenology is a school of philosophy that
immediately underlies Existentialism. It examines the contents of
consciousness or conscious mental processes; more specifically, it probes

self-consciousness while attempting to set aside underlying assumptions—beginning "from scratch," as it were, with observations about perception, interpretation, and intention as we experience them, without seeking to formulate anything approaching a neurological theory of consciousness.[1]

Heidegger went on to graduate in 1913, married a Protestant (Elfriede Petri) in 1917, and apparently turned away from institutionalized Catholicism. He began working as an unsalaried lecturer (*Privatdozent*) at Freiburg, and there became an assistant to Husserl—who was, according to Hannah Arendt, "the hidden king of philosophy."[2] In 1923 he was appointed an associate professor at Marburg, where he became a friend of Protestant New Testament exegete and theologian Rudolf Bultmann; Bultmann, along with Oscar Cullmann, C. H. Dodd, and Joachim Jeremias, was one of the giants of Protestant New Testament scholarship in the twentieth century.[3]

Heidegger rose to fame with the publication of his first major work, *Being and Time*, in 1927. He succeeded Husserl at Freiburg University in 1929, was elected rector by the Freiburg faculty in 1933, and joined the Nazi party. A year later he resigned the rectorship over conflicts with faculty and party officials, but remained a member of the Nazi party. He

1. This thumbnail sketch of phenomenology is modestly amplified in the section "Phenomenology" in chapter 11, on Sartre. Sartre devoted even more study to this field than Heidegger did.

2. S. J. McGrath, *Heidegger: A Very Critical Introduction* (Grand Rapids: Eerdmans, 2008), 5. Heidegger had an extended affair with Arendt, a Jewish student of his, who fled Germany in 1933 and went to the University of Chicago. She was eighteen when she began studying at Freiburg; Heidegger was thirty-five and married, with two children. As a young student Arendt did not realize she was Jewish. She found out only by accident and was forced to flee Germany when the Nazis came to power. Nevertheless, she subscribed to Teutonic superiority throughout her life. Although she came to fame chiefly as a political thinker (her first major work being *The Origins of Totalitarianism*), Arendt is considered by some to be the most noteworthy thinker on the nature of thought.

3. As is so often the case, it is philosophy that influences theology and not the other way around. I am convinced that Bultmann's theology shows the profound influence of Heidegger in a way that denatures the gospel. The gospel has been denatured in various ways by theologians who were too uncritically influenced by philosophers such as Plato, Descartes, Kant, or Hegel; Bultmann has denatured it in a specifically Heideggerian way.

began a series of lectures on Nietzsche in 1936 and continued through the 1940s, eventually publishing them in 1961.

Following Germany's collapse in 1945 Heidegger appeared before the Denazification Commission in Freiburg, which banned him from teaching in 1946; among the Allied nations who opposed him, it was the United States that pressed hardest to exclude him from the classroom. However, he was reinstated in 1950 when hearts thawed, and taught at Freiburg from 1951 until 1958 without formal professorial appointment. Thereafter he lectured occasionally and continued to publish, albeit in a vein that marked a shift from *Being and Time*. He never repented of his involvement with Nazism, attempting as late as 1966 to justify his conduct during the Nazi regime.

Heidegger died in May 1976. He had joined the Lutheran church at the urging of Husserl, a Christian of Jewish background, but was buried from the Roman Catholic Church in Messkirch. The funeral service was conducted by his nephew, Father Heinrich Heidegger.

An Overview of Heidegger's Philosophy[4]

In terms of its philosophical significance, Heidegger's *Being and Time* is sometimes compared to Hegel's *The Phenomenology of Mind*, Kant's *Critique of Pure Reason*, or Plato's *Republic*. In other words, it is one of those monumental achievements the philosophical world will never be without. *Being and Time* has influenced philosophers, theologians, psychologists, and sociologists; there is a whole school of psychology and psychotherapy that comes out of Heidegger's understanding of being, and his impact on Protestant New Testament scholarship is undeniable. His later work, while exhibiting various developments that distance it from *Being and Time*, cannot be understood apart from that first and principal work.

It has already been observed (in connection with Hegel) that when we think about Being, we invariably have in mind the being *of something*, such as a car, an apple, or a rock. The entity that Heidegger

---

4. I have been assisted throughout this overview by Michael Inwood, *Heidegger* (Oxford: Oxford University Press, 1997).

chooses to reflect on is the human being, which he calls *Dasein*. In German, *sein* is the verb "to be," and *da* means "there"; hence *Dasein* simply means "being there," that is, "existence." That is what it is to be a human being: to *exist*, or to *be there*.[5] And since *Dasein* is the only being conscious of itself, the only being that asks questions about Being, the first task of the philosopher is to analyze *Dasein*.

Heidegger's first observation regarding *Dasein* is that the human being is *essentially in the world*—in the sense that without the world, the human being is not human, and without the human being, the world is not a world. Recalling the difference between corresponding and correlative entities, we can say that for Heidegger, the world and the human being are polar correlates: each presupposes and implies the other in the same way that north presupposes and implies south, or left presupposes and implies right. If one is removed, the other disappears. The human being without the world is mere animated flesh, and the world without the human being is merely an environment, as it is for other creatures such as plants and animals. The natural order is an environment for all creatures, but it is not a *world* for any creature except the human; only human beings possess a world.

Moreover, when Heidegger says that the human being is essentially in the world, his "in" refers not merely to spatial location but to an ontic actuality akin to involvement or immersion: our very humanity is embedded in the world. Being essentially in the world also means that *Dasein* continually interprets and engages other entities and their context, which in turn means that it is only because of *Dasein*'s activity that there is an integrated "world" rather than a jumble of entities. A "world" presupposes integration for the one who regards it as a world; I am always interpreting what is "out there" as a world, and specifically as *my* world. Heidegger's selection of the human being as the starting point

---

5. It is interesting to note the similarity between Heidegger's name for the human being and Buber's interpretation of the name by which God identified himself to Moses at the burning bush: *Ehyeh asher Ehyeh* [אֶהְיֶה אֲשֶׁר אֶהְיֶה], "I am what I am" or "I shall be what I shall be," which Buber translates as "I shall be there." As we observed in an earlier chapter, Buber understood this to mean that God will always be present at every moment of human existence.

of his philosophy is therefore not arbitrary; rather, it reflects the fact that there are other entities and a world *only because of* human beings.

Second, asserts Heidegger, the being of *Dasein* is "care." More will be said below about the precise meaning he gives to this term. Third, unlike Plato's notion of true human Being, which is ahistorical and atemporal, *Dasein* is essentially temporal and historical; it is embedded in world occurrence, in time, as an aspect of its being essentially *in* the world. Fourth, given this essential temporality, *Dasein* always anticipates its own death: true human being is Being-towards-death, in that death is always on the horizon of human self-consciousness. Fifth, *Dasein* contemplates its life as a whole, and such integrative contemplation Heidegger calls "Conscience." This concept will be amplified below as well; for now, it is sufficient to note that it is to be distinguished from the ordinary psychological sense of the term—namely, the faculty in our head or heart that tells us what we ought or ought not to do.

Knowing

Heidegger characterizes Western philosophy as unduly preoccupied with epistemology,[6] which attempts to answer the questions: What is it to know? How do we know? What is the scope of our knowing? This preoccupation is deleterious, according to Heidegger: "It continuously sharpens the knife," he says, "but never gets around to cutting."[7] Epistemology traditionally discusses the relation between knower and objects, and Heidegger questions all three terms of that premise: that is, he questions what is meant by *relation*, what is meant by *knower*, and what is meant by *object*. Is the knower a pure subject, a mind with a disinterested, theoretical knowledge of the object? Or is the knower an interested, embodied, temporally situated human being, with many relations other than that which the knower is attempting to know? Heidegger prefers the second. Moreover, he asserts, knowing is only one relation we take up concerning things in the world, and not the primary

---

6. The same is frequently said of Western theology, or at least of Protestant theology from the Reformation to Karl Barth.

7. Martin Heidegger, *Basic Problems in Phenomenology*, trans. Scott Campbell (New York: Bloomsbury Academic Press, 2013), 4; quoted in Inwood, *Heidegger*, 10.

one. My relation to the hammer I pick up, for instance, has entirely to do with a project I have: I want to build a bookcase. The hammer head is made out of metal, but while I know nothing about the metallurgical engineering or industrial processes whereby it was constructed, I am nevertheless profoundly related to the hammer; I am related to it in terms of its function—which is, points out Heidegger, our primary way of relating to most things in life. It is a far more profound and more primordial relation than others, such as knowing, that we subsequently adopt with respect to objects. Indeed, much knowing is taken up only later in life, and then only sporadically.

In what does knowing consist? Most of us remain wedded (even if we are unaware of it) to an Enlightenment-empiricist understanding of knowing; that is, scientific knowing. By now, however, we recognize that all the Existentialists chiefly meant something else by knowing. Heidegger observes that the knowing of the historian, for instance, is different from the knowing of the scientist. In fact, the kind of knowing in every case *is determined by the object to be known*: there is an epistemology that pertains to the investigation of objects, such as asteroids, and another that pertains to the investigation of a historical figure or event, such as Wellington's defeat of Napoleon. The philosophical question here is: How do we come to divide up the world in this way? And how, according to Heidegger, do we come to understand the world as an *integrated* world?

Being

Aristotle maintained that there is *actual* being and *potential* being, with actuality having logical priority over potentiality. According to Heidegger, however, Aristotle's scheme was too limited; Aristotle understood *that-being* (for example, the fact that a horse exists) and *what-being* (the fact that it is a horse and not a cow), but Heidegger introduces the more important *how-being*, the mode or manner of an entity's being; that is, *how it functions with respect to human intentionality*. Being, for Heidegger, is chiefly related to functionality, and this functionality pertains to the entity itself, not merely to what we do with it. In other words, it is not the case that there is this peculiar object which I am able to use as a hammer; rather, the very being of the hammer has to do with its capacity to drive nails. The Being of *any* being, therefore, is not independent of *Dasein*; *all* beings depend for their existence and for their mode of being on the fact that they are produced, interpreted, used, engaged, or asked about by *Dasein*, human being.

Every human being has a preliminary, intuitive, or pre-reflective understanding of Being; otherwise, we could not even ask or think about Being or engage with beings, including ourselves or one another. Even those who do not ask questions about it must have a preliminary understanding of Being. Clearly, this pre-reflective understanding is not the explicit account offered by the philosopher, and may be riddled with inadequacies and errors; nevertheless, insists Heidegger, every human being intuits Being. Moreover, "*Dasein* is an entity for which, in its Being, that Being is an issue."[8] That is, our Being is *problematic* for us in some respects: we must contend with our Being, and are threatened by the fact that it is going to cease.

Being is everywhere, says Heidegger—in the form of people, hammers, dogs, and stars—and at the same time Being is nowhere, because it does not inhere in beings as a discernible property. Consider a car, for instance. It may be red, it may be old or new, it may seat two people or four, it may have manual transmission or automatic—these are all properties of the car. But we do not say that the car has Being, as if Being were one of its properties. Properties define, and Being is not essential to a definition. Take Pegasus, for instance: Pegasus has a definition—it is a winged horse—but Pegasus does not exist; existence, or Being, is not part of the definition, which is the same whether Pegasus exists or not. This is equally true of a car or any other thing. That is why Heidegger says that Being is nowhere: it does not inhere in beings as a discernible property. Another way of expressing the same idea is that *there is no Being except actual beings*; Being *is* only as it is instantiated. This understanding is bedrock for Existentialist philosophy.

8. Martin Heidegger, *Being and Time*, trans. John Macquarrie and Edward Robinson (New York: Harper & Row, 1962), 236. While the numbered pages of this translation of *Being and Time* contain page numbers of Heidegger's German text, all page numbers I cite from *Being and Time* refer to the translation.

Unlike other beings or entities, however, *Dasein* has no definite essence. We can define a car; we can define a unicorn (even though it does not exist); but *Dasein* has no definite essence. This is a notion common to all Existentialists, and one of the first points made in this book: for Existentialists, the self is a self-*making*. As we will see in the next chapter, Sartre's version of this is "Existence precedes essence": in other words, there is no human nature or essence prior to our forging it. This in turn means that I can never evade responsibility for myself; if I behave badly, I cannot excuse myself by saying, "Everyone acts like this: it's only human nature," because my nature is that which I determine my self to be. By contrast, nonhuman entities cannot choose or take charge of their own being. Their being, as we shall see below, is dependent on what humans intentionally do with them—which is, in turn, limited at least partly by the physical properties of those entities.[9] Only a human being is what it *decides* or *has decided* to be. "*Dasein* is its own possibility,"[10] asserts Heidegger. In direct contradiction to Aristotle, Heidegger insists that a human being is not a substance with an essential nature, properties, and accidents; rather, *Dasein* is the *possibility* of various ways of being. We can determine the way of our being in the world; it is not pre-ordained or given to us.

"Thrownness" and freedom

While we may choose to die, says Heidegger, we cannot choose to be born, or to be born in this or that situation: I did not choose to be born to the Shepherd family in the city of Edmonton during World War II, but as a matter of fact I was. In that sense, every human being is "thrown" into the world, into an immediate situation that she has not chosen or willed. This notion of "thrownness" is central to Heidegger's thought;

9. Such properties, which are the same even when no human is using the object for anything, constitute the fixed definition of material objects, their "whatness," or essence. They limit the purpose for which humans can intentionally use the object, and in that way determine its *how-being*, its mode or manner of being. For example, while I might be able to use my wife's shoe to drive nails, in which case it is not a shoe but a hammer (about which more below), I could not use a slice of bread for that purpose. But this has nothing to do with a choice or decision on the part of either the shoe or the slice of bread.

10. Ibid.

we are just *here*. Once in the world, however, *Dasein* has a greater sphere of action open to it than just the option of suicide. While we may not have decided to be in the first place, once here we always decide *how* to be. That is the crucial point. For this reason *Dasein* alone, unlike all other beings, "exists" in the sense of "standing out" (from Greek *ek* [ἐκ] *out* + *histemi* [ἵστημι] *stand*)—an idea we have already encountered in the thinking of other Existentialists. In Heidegger's thought, specifically, we "stand out" from what he calls *fallenness*,[11] or the habit of passively allowing our context to determine us (another concept about which more will be said below).

Dasein creates its own ways of being as no other entity does. A dog does not create its way of being, and neither does an apple; but you and I do create ours, and therein lies our great freedom, according to Heidegger. In other words, we are never completely determined by our circumstances, and can always respond to them in assorted ways. Suppose I was born with a hideously scarred face, or was facially disfigured as an infant. I can try to disguise my scarred face in shame, applying cosmetics and wearing a hat with a big peak so others will not see my face. Alternatively, I can wear my scar proudly: I can seek suitable theatre parts, or volunteer for medical experiments. I can try to minister to similarly afflicted people (since it is our wound in life that gives us credibility with other wounded people). In other words, the fact that I am scar-faced—or not scar-faced—does not determine who I am, what I am, or how I am going to be; *I* am going to determine that, scar-faced or not. I cannot do anything about the "thrownness" of my existence which has left me disfigured, but that does not make it the vehicle of my determination. *Dasein*'s freedom is the capacity to view entities as possibilities rather than sheer actualities. An entity *is* an actuality: my scarred face, in our example above, is an actuality that I cannot get rid of. My freedom, however, lies in my capacity as a human being to view my scarred face as possibility.

Is this what the Christian means by freedom? On the one hand, not

---

11. German *Verfallenheit*, by which he does not simply mean what the church means when it speaks of the condition resulting from the Fall.

exactly. Theologically, the only freedom the Christian has is the freedom to obey Jesus Christ. On the other hand, from a finite, creaturely vantage point, Heidegger has identified something we cannot afford to be without. I can choose to languish in self-pity all my life because of my scarred face, and exercise the tyranny that the sick exercise over the strong;[12] or, I can respond to the actuality of my scarred face in any number of other productive and courageous ways. Part of the Christian's obedience to Jesus Christ is an attitude of trusting thankfulness in all circumstances (though not *for* all circumstances), an acceptance of weakness as an occasion for the grace and strength of Jesus Christ and an opportunity for witness and ministry.

Is it really the case, though, that I freely choose my response? Or is my response, at bottom, socially determined? Is it determined, for instance, by social convention? According to Heidegger, if I capitulate to social convention or social pressure (what he calls "the they," like Nietzsche's "the herd"), I exist *inauthentically*; that is, I am not being true to myself. This does not mean that authenticity implies contrarianism or deliberate eccentricity, so that I wear a pistachio tie just because everyone else wears a red one; eccentricity, especially of such a reactive kind, can be just as inauthentic, and conversely, one can be authentic while happening to reflect social custom. It all depends on how the decision is "owned." Thus, says Heidegger, strictly speaking, my existence may be undifferentiated in that I may have never questioned my socio-economic background, genetic history, and so on, and never reflected on the fact that I am a wartime, English-speaking, Protestant male born in Western Canada, or on the fact that these things contribute to my "throwness." If, however, upon recognizing this world of mine I reject it in favour of another one suggested by "the they," my existence becomes *inauthentic*. If, for example, I were persuaded by someone who said to me, "That's all very well, Victor, but you live in Toronto now, in academia, in the twentieth-first century—so why don't you just conform

---

12. Anyone who doubts for a minute that there is a tyranny exercised by the sick and weak over the strong need only talk to someone who is a caregiver for a querulous, complaining, self-pitying patient. Nietzsche devoted considerable writing to this issue.

to *this* world?" I would by my own choice fall victim to "the they," and my existence would be inauthentic.

Anxiety and "care"

The move out of undifferentiated existence gives rise to anxiety as I confront my freedom and the possibility of Nothing: if I repudiate one after another all the voices telling me who I am—my society, my family, my church—and cast off the roles and titles that circumscribe how I am to be, I may find in the end that I am nothing, that I do not know who I am. Can I live with that possibility? And if not, will I still be able to flee back into "the they"? Slavery is dreadful, but at least the slave eats three times a day; when the people of Israel were delivered from slavery in Egypt and found themselves in the wilderness where life was unforeseeably harsh, they complained to Moses, "Take us back to Egypt, because at least in Egypt we had enough to eat."[13]

There *is* security in enslavement to "the they," but accepting that slavery is what Heidegger means by "fallenness": when I listen to "the they," says Heidegger, and allow myself to be determined by what they say, I am "fallen." Is there an echo here of the biblical story of the Fall? Who listened to whom in the Garden of Eden, and who fell? Heidegger's *Verfallenheit*, while not the same as the Fall in Eden, suggests an overlap between the two: the influence of Genesis 3 and its place in church tradition seems difficult to deny in Heidegger.

If, on the other hand, I face up to the possibility of Nothing, become aware of my existence as a being-toward-death, and thereby become responsible for my own life despite my anxiety, I am transformed to the way of being that Heidegger calls "care." The world of "the they" has not changed or disappeared, but my relationship to it has, and the shift in that relationship in turn alters my relationship to Being. In undergoing this transformation from paralyzing anxiety to owning my mortality to caring, I exist authentically.

Heidegger's "care" embraces both ordinary senses of the word, namely "being concerned about" and "taking care of," yet is more fundamental than either. It unifies our being-with-others and being-in-

---

13. Numbers 11:4–5.

the-world-of-entities, and also integrates everything in our past, present, and future. It pertains to the future in that the human is always "ahead of itself," as Heidegger says, on the cusp of what to do next; we are our possibilities. It pertains to the past in that the human is already in the world, always "thrown" into a specific pre-existing situation with all of its attitudes. And it pertains to the present in that the human is always alongside other entities in the world, engaged in a task. In this way, "care" integrates everything about the human. Moreover, "care" correlates with the significance of the world. That is, *the world has significance or meaning only to the extent that we "care."* If we fail to care, the world is devoid of significance.

Those who exist inauthentically have not thereby become subhuman. They remain human nonetheless; they remain *Dasein.* Their being never lapses into the being of other entities. Compare this with the Christian understanding of the Fall, according to which the fallen human being remains in the image of God, however grossly disfigured, and does not become an animal or demon or mere thing. Heidegger makes a similar point: the inauthentic human is still human, and is therefore not to be mistreated.

Dasein in the World

Dasein is always embodied; it entails the indivisible unity of the human being, in contrast to a body-mind dualism in which the body drops away at death. It is crucial for all Existentialist philosophy that we are not, as Plato maintained, mind or intellect that has had the misfortune to be embodied and will throw off bodily encumbrance at death. Here, too, Existentialism overlaps with a Christian understanding of personhood, according to which the human creature is never unembodied, even at death. At death, Christians believe, we are given a resurrection body; its exact form is unknown, but it is a body. The Hebrew word *nefesh* [נֶפֶשׁ], when translated "soul," does not mean what Plato meant by *psyche* [ψυχή]. The Hebrew word means "animated body," because according to biblical thought it is impossible to be human, in this world or the next, and not be embodied. Similarly the Existentialist insists that we are aware of ourselves as *whole* human beings, and that it is only by means of deliberate abstraction that we speak of our body *qua* body rather than of our self as a unity. We do not normally say, "My body stood up," but rather "*I* stood up"; not "Her body died," but "*She* died." We recognize ourselves concretely as a psycho-physical entity. The body may be inconspicuous, depending on what we are doing—for example, when I am writing, the movement of my arm and hand is in the background while I am attending to what I am writing and why—but it is nonetheless necessary to our humanity. Even though we are not defined by or reducible to our body, we are never without our body, and cannot be who or what we are without it.

It is because *Dasein* is always embodied that it is always engaged with the world, a fact that relativizes such abstract disciplines as logic, psychology, and epistemology. Logic is the academic discipline closest to being purely mental: even the theoretical physicist must still take account of matter or energy, but logic consists entirely in the mental manipulation of symbols. Nevertheless, even such disciplines as logic and mathematics are ways of humankind's being in the world. Mathematics may be highly abstract and unrelated to body, but the mathematician who performs the mathematical operations is not unrelated to his body.

Dasein's engagement with the world is uniquely characterized by the fact that, unlike other entities, *Dasein* is aware of the world and of itself, and of other entities as related to the world and itself. As soon as I see a table, for instance, I see not merely a geometric shape, but an entity *for* something I might do: a table is what I write on or what I eat from. I do not initially see just the physical shape and then, in a second step, interpret it as a table; rather, the instant I see it I know it is a table. In other words, I simultaneously see and know it with respect to its function in the world. If I am poor and cannot afford a conventional table, so that all I have to eat or write on is an orange crate stood on end, it is still a table; it is not an orange crate at that point but a table, and if I later decide to sit on it, it is a chair. *The nature of any object in the world depends on its function with respect to the subject.*

Consequently, I also see any given entity in connection with other entities in the same setting: I see the table in connection with pen and paper, for instance. These entities contribute, with the table, to a realm of significance, and are (in Heidegger's vocabulary) "ready-to-hand" rather than merely "present-at-hand." If I am sitting at a table to make notes for an upcoming lecture, what is "ready-to-hand" are table, paper, pen, and chair. What is "present-at-hand" are crumbs on the table, left over from my breakfast: I am not even aware of them. There might also be some dust on the table, or an old hockey puck. Those items are "present-at-hand," but they are not "ready-to-hand," which always pertains to functionality. Now, clearly, the immediate world of these connected entities always points to a larger world beyond it: to the students who will hear the lecture, the lectures that preceded this one, and what I want students to grasp at this particular juncture in the course. Space and time are involved, but not in an abstract Euclidean or Newtonian sense; what matters when it comes to space is whether the table is of a suitable size and shape for my writing purposes, and what matters with regard to time is whether I can finish this task, with this equipment, before supper.

Everything that pertains to me as human also pertains to "the other" as human, whom I do not infer but recognize intuitively. This is a crucial point of Heidegger's. I do not look at another person and deduce that it is a human being because it has two legs and no wings. Rather, the human other is intuited and recognized as such instantly; to apprehend him at all is always to apprehend him *as human*. We may make a connection here with what the Bible means by "face." What is it to have a face? What is the face of God? Paul says that we see "the light of the glory of God in the face of Jesus Christ."[14] The face is the window onto personhood, and through the face we have an immediate grasp of the fellow human.[15]

---

14. 2 Corinthians 4:6.

15. This is a point that figures largely in the work of another Existentialist thinker not dealt with in this book, the French Jewish philosopher Emmanuel Lévinas. Lévinas has much to say about "the other," and specifically about the immediate recognition of humanity in the other. Since we recognize the other as human, asks Lévinas, why are we in such a hurry to kill him? What perversity is there in us that we are determined to slay the fellow human whom we recognize instantly and non-inferentially as human? I once heard it said by Jakob Jocz, a Jewish professor of Christian theology at Wycliffe College at the University of Toronto, "Fallen humankind is a killer: we are never so happy as when we are killing each other." Whenever

Mood, interpretation, language, and truth

Another central theme for Heidegger is *mood*. How we view the world depends on our mood—which is not to be confused with our emotional state at any given moment due to circumstances or biochemical processes. Emotion is a reaction to entities in the world: my car broke down in a rainstorm, for example, and I had to wait hours for a tow truck, all of which made me feel very frustrated. The Heideggerian notion of mood, on the other hand, is a habitual attitude or way of viewing the world. Moods such as angst and boredom—not temporary boredom produced by a specific occasion such as a long, dry lecture, but boredom with life in general—cast a pall on the world, whereas a mood of courage brightens the world. Earlier, in discussing Kierkegaard and Nietzsche, I observed that an increasing number of people seem to view the world from a mood of fear. Our fear of vulnerability and self-exposure makes us unable to love. People who view the world from a mood of fear may not even know what they are afraid of; they may simply be afraid, and their fear colours the world for them. Heidegger maintained that everyone has a characteristic orientation to the world. It could be apprehension or boredom, excitement or the anticipation of adventure, trust or distrust, but everyone has a way of orienting herself to the world. The human being is never moodless.

Our mood reveals to us what we are otherwise usually unaware of, but alone it does not disclose the world to us; for that, *understanding* is necessary. The world is disclosed to us, in other words, through the twofold operation of mood and understanding. *Dasein* "understands" its environment as presenting a range of possibilities, and those possibilities (as we saw before) are the source of significance; hence *Dasein* is always poised between alternative ways of engaging the world. That awareness of possibility and choice is what is meant by *understanding*. Understanding, in turn, is distinct from *interpretation*. In everyday matters, understanding is pre-conceptual and general, pertaining to the

anyone who is at all perceptive looks out at the world, and then when all of us look at the anger and malice and treachery in our own hearts, we recognize Jocz's pronouncement to be no exaggeration. Is there in fact a naïveté in Heidegger's understanding of "fallenness," in that it is not nearly fallen enough?

world as a whole, whereas interpretation pertains to particular entities in the world and to our self; for example, I interpret an object as a pen, as something I might write with, rather than as a hollow plastic cylinder. My interpretation of an object I encounter specifies its involvement with the world and with myself.

In this connection, Heidegger makes several important statements about language. "Man is not merely a living creature possessing among other faculties that of language," he asserts. "Language is the house of being, and it is by dwelling (in this house) that man ek-sists (*sic*)." As man dwells within this house, he simultaneously "protects the truth of being to which he belongs."[16] Heidegger speaks of language as "the house of Being" in some places, and as "the house of the truth of Being" in others[17] but there is no material difference, as he is using the word *truth* in the same sense as *reality*: language is the "house" in which the reality of Being resides. Interpretation, as just described above, need not be expressed in language, but language emerges from interpretation.

Heidegger rejects the correspondence theory of truth, according to which truth is correspondence between assertions and objects or facts; rather, he thinks of truth as the unconcealment or illumination of reality.[18] Moreover, truth is a matter of degree rather than simple either/or, for illumination is never complete and never entirely absent. The correspondence theory of truth presupposes assertions and facts, standing in a certain relation to each other; but what is an assertion, and what is a fact? If assertions are genuinely independent of facts, and hence capable of corresponding to them or failing to do so, then assertions are merely sounds. But we do not hear pure sounds as such; we hear waves crashing, or wind blowing, or woodpeckers pecking—or,

16. Heidegger, *Gesamtausgabe*, Vol. 9, *Wegmarken*, ed. Friedrich-Wilhelm von Hermann (Frankfurt am Main: Klosterman, 1976), 333; quoted in *The Cambridge Companion to Heidegger*, ed. Charles Guignon (Cambridge: Cambridge University Press, 1995), 118.

17. E.g., "Letter on Humanism," in *Basic Writings*, trans. HarperCollins Publishers (New York: HarperCollins, 2008), 217–219.

18. Similarly, when John's gospel reports Jesus as saying "I am the Truth," using the Greek word *aletheia* [ἀλήθεια], it is not a correspondence theory he is talking about, but ultimate reality. It is the same with the Hebrew word *emet* [אֱמֶת], translated "truth": it also means "reality."

at least, something that we think is probably woodpeckers pecking.[19] In other words, it is entirely artificial to hear pure, uninterpreted sound. And similarly, when we hear someone speaking about something, says Heidegger, "we are already with him, in advance, alongside the entity which the discourse is about."[20] Even when we hear indistinct speech or a foreign language, it is not a welter of tone-data that we hear, but words, albeit ones that are unintelligible to us. And no word has meaning independent of its "world."

Consider the word *bat*. What does it mean? It can mean at least two things: the small animal that comes out at twilight and flies around your backyard, or the implement by which a baseball player propels a baseball. We know the meaning of the word *bat* only when we know which "world" it is being used in. Words and their meanings, says Heidegger, are world-laden: every word comes with a world attached to it.

And what about the entities to which words and assertions refer? They too are meaningless apart from their involvement in a "world."[21] To return to the example of a pen: it is involved with other entities (such as paper and a table, and me writing lecture notes), and has its place in a world. However, no doubt all of us have known a pen to have other meanings. In my elementary school days I knew a girl who was affronted and disgusted by a boy who had spat on her desk; she grabbed her long-handled straight pen and shoved its inch-long nib into the boy's buttock. At that moment it was not a pen; it was a dagger, just as the orange crate in our earlier example is a chair and not an orange crate when someone is sitting on it.

In light of all of the above, the world—the nature of the world—can never be disclosed by assertions about objects, but only by our *mood* and *understanding*. Mood is our orientation to the world, and understanding is awareness of a possible way of engaging the world; both are unique

19. Heidegger, *Being and Time*, 207f.

20. Heidegger, *Being and Time*, 207.

21. This is not quite the same thing as "context," which technically speaking refers only to the verbal context in which a word is used. Heidegger is emphasizing that our understanding of words in general depends on the actual situation: the occasion and physical environment. This aligns with his insistence (see below) that the locus of truth is not assertions, but *Dasein*.

to *Dasein*, and together they disclose the world to us. Another way of saying this is that our orientation to the world and our awareness of possible ways of engaging it is what enables us to recognize the world as a world. Assertions arise from this recognition; they are not its source. According to Heidegger, because humans dwell in the house of Being as they guard the truth of Being,[22] the locus of truth is not mere assertions but *Dasein*.

What about falsehood? For Heidegger, falsehood is not chiefly lack of correspondence between assertion and fact or object (as in a correspondence theory of truth); rather, falsehood is cover-up or distortion, which may be effected without assertions at all, by non-verbal means: gesture, facial expression, body language. I can say one thing, and you look at my facial expression and know that I mean exactly the opposite. In other words, my facial expression has falsified my assertion. We do this all the time, and it is destructive—psychiatry calls it "dysfunctional communication."

In addition, says Heidegger, *Dasein* has a tendency to misinterpret itself and other beings, because *Dasein* tends to objectify itself and in so doing to capitulate to "the they." Nor is the philosopher exempt from this tendency; the human being as philosopher tends to capitulate uncritically to tradition.

Falsification, misinterpretation, objectification of oneself and others, and capitulation to "the they" are all instances of the *Verfallenheit*, or "fallenness," of *Dasein*.

The human being falls away from its authentic self, and has always tended to do so; there was never a time when *Dasein* was unfallen. We speak with others in assertions, but even at the everyday level, we struggle and usually fail to communicate what our assertions betoken for us in our engagements. Others may acknowledge that our assertion is valid, but already it has a different force and function for them; the assertion that is crucial for our *Dasein* is for them a shallow curiosity or amusement, and highly ambiguous. It does not illumine. And much of what we say is mere chatter, which consists of repeating statements

---

22. A paraphrase of "Letter on Humanism," 217–218.

severed from the context that gave rise to them. Such chatter is inert, and tranquillizes us. It is an instance of fallenness. Gossip is another.

Time and death

Time and death, finally, are two other categories that are crucial for Heidegger.

Being in time is not being in space; time is a far more important category than space. All Being finds its meaning in temporality, says Heidegger. He insists that there are no atemporal or supertemporal entities, a statement which immediately rules out the Platonic forms. Does it similarly rule out the Christian God? Is God atemporal or supertemporal? The Unmoved Mover has no involvement with history, but the God of the Bible does—supremely so in the Incarnation, which continues in the ascended and risen Lord; therefore the Christian God is not *merely* supertemporal. Furthermore, since God can be known only through revelation, and since revelation occurs only as God acts in history, God can never be known atemporally.[23]

Authentic humanity looks ahead in time to its death, as well as back into the historical past before its birth. Historical awareness enables us to survey our life as a whole in a way that no spatial travel does, and awareness of our past presents us with possibilities that are vastly richer than those afforded by awareness of what is happening now in remote places. In other words, what is part of our historical consciousness has vastly greater importance to us than what is happening right now in Antarctica.

Further, tradition is handed down through time, not over space, and the question we ask of a painting or piece of music is whether it will stand the test of *time*—that is, not whether it will look or sound as good in London as it does in Berlin, but whether it will look or sound as good generations hence as it does now.

Human beings are fundamentally temporal in a way that we are not fundamentally spatial. Our temporality renders the world temporal

---

23. We should note, too, that God can never be obeyed atemporally. We obey God only as we act in time, only as we are historical agents. An alleged inner obedience of the heart, devoid of outer instantiation, fails to be the obedience of which Scripture speaks.

as well, opening up "world-time" and allowing the assessment that some matters in world occurrence are significant while others are trivial.[24]

The temporality of human being means that *Dasein* is always "ahead of itself" (to use Heidegger's vocabulary), poised before possibilities—and always aware of the cessation of possibility in death. *Dasein*'s awareness of its own death pervades and configures life now. It also separates the authentic from the inauthentic, rescuing us from "the they," because there is no possibility of resisting "the they" unless we are first aware that we are going to die; it is only when we live in the awareness of our own imminent death, says Heidegger, that we can have the courage to extricate ourselves from "the they." In this way awareness of death confers wholeness and "resoluteness" (Heidegger's word) on *Dasein*. In short, *Dasein* that is "resolute" runs ahead to confront its death in the future, reaches back into its past, and then decides what to do in the present, the moment of "vision." Only as we grasp the past and anticipate the future can we act authentically in the present.

However, time pertains more to the future than to the past or to the present, since time is *for* something, time to *do* something. The German word for "future" is *Zukunft*, literally "to-coming" or "coming towards." *Dasein* runs ahead to its own death, and then "comes towards itself" out of the future; simultaneously, *Dasein* rebounds to the past—not *Vergangenheit*, literally "gone-ness" or dead past, but *Gewesenheit*, "having-been-ness,"[25] the relevant past that emerges from the future and bears on the present. At this point, we *act*. Such a present, however, is not the specious present of the indefinable instant between

24. In Scripture, too, time is much more significant than space. We are commanded to remember the Sabbath day, a time. We are not commanded to remember the sacred space, for there is no such thing. Jesus was crucified under the reign of Pontius Pilate, says the Apostles' Creed, but it does not mention Jerusalem, even though we know that was the place. Why does time have a significance for biblical thought that space lacks? Why is space subordinate to time, and not time to space? The idols occupy space but have no relation to time, since they are ahistorical: they neither act nor speak. Here we must be aware that the Hebrew word for word, *davar* [דבר], means both "word" and "event." When God speaks, something always happens, to which we must respond. God's speech/act in time constitutes us historical agents. History is the sphere of God's revelatory activity and no less the sphere of our obedient activity.

25. Both are German nouns meaning "past."

past and future, but rather a present in the sense of "being present"—like the Greek word *parousia* [παρουσία] used in the New Testament; it is "present" thought of as the opposite of "absent." Recall that *Dasein* means "being there," which we could also render "being present." This ability to run ahead to its death, rebound to the past, and surge into the present makes *Dasein* a unified self.

Conscience and resoluteness

Earlier we mentioned the Heideggerian notion of *Conscience* without defining it. Conscience (spelled here with a capital to distinguish it from the psychological faculty that supplies moral direction and is usually simply the voice of "the they") is related to the human awareness of impending death, of which we have just been speaking. Conscience calls us not to a specific act but to authenticity, and this call is unexpungeable: since humankind is never wholly or irrecoverably lost in "the they," even when we flee authenticity we always glimpse that which we are fleeing. As much as we flee the call to authenticity, maintains Heidegger, we can never escape it.

Conscience also renders us "guilty" in a uniquely Heideggerian sense that is not easy to grasp. When we exist authentically, exercising the power of choice, every genuine, committed choice is equally valid; there is no ground for choosing one thing over another apart from the choice itself. (This is a point made many times in this book: recall, for example, Kierkegaard's insistence that there is no objective criterion for evaluating a commitment.) Similarly, Heidegger observes that the choice which makes me authentic lacks any basis or ground outside itself—and, moreover, that to seek such a basis is to live inauthentically. This being the case, the life I project for myself without any objective justification is, from a purely rational point of view, a lack—a nullity. "Guilt," as understood by Heidegger, occurs in that I am defined by this nullity.[26]

In the face of such nullity, however, *Dasein* becomes resolute, and this resoluteness (*Entschlossenheit*) gives rise to *Dasein*'s

---

26. Heidegger, *Being and Time*, 329.

disclosedness (*Erschlossenheit*; Heidegger maintained that his philosophy could be articulated only in German or Greek). That is, resoluteness discloses or reveals *Dasein* in a new way, and with it possibilities that did not previously exist. In this connection Heidegger discusses the conversions of Paul, Augustine, and Luther, who, at the moment of resoluteness, became what they had not been before. There was a new way of existing for each of them.

While resolute *Dasein* can interpret *Dasein*'s irresoluteness, the reverse is not the case. In other words, authenticity is able to recognize inauthenticity, but inauthenticity cannot recognize authenticity—just as someone who is awake can interpret both waking and sleeping, while the sleeping person can interpret neither. In the same way, authentic *Dasein* is able to recognize inauthentic *Dasein*, but not the reverse.

This last statement is reminiscent of Plato's analogy of the cave, a feature of Platonic thought to which Heidegger returned repeatedly. In the famous analogy, the people in the cave see flickering shadows on the cave wall, cast by a fire behind them, and think the shadows are reality. It is only when they are brought out of the cave, and then taken back in, that they recognize the shadows as shadows: then they see that the light of the fire, shining past other people or objects, casts shadows of those people or objects on the wall. Until they are brought out into the light of the day, away from the cave, they mistake shadow for substance. There is a Christian parallel to this: for the Christian, the reality of Jesus Christ is the truth, and sin is the lie. The person related to Jesus Christ recognizes both, whereas the person unrelated to Jesus Christ recognizes neither; such a person fails to recognize the truth as truth, and mistakes the lie for truth.

God is not explicitly discussed by Heidegger; he does not relate the human being to the Being of God at all. Some people—including John Macquarrie, the first major translator of *Being and Time*—think that Heidegger's philosophy, suitably adjusted, is close to Christian theology.[27] However, I am convinced they are overstating the case. Heidegger is not talking about God, nor does he want to. It is true that

27. See, for instance, John Macquarrie, *Heidegger and Christianity* (New York: Continuum, 1994).

towards the end of his life, when he saw the breakdown of European culture in the 1960s and 1970s (interestingly, he failed to see that breakdown in the Nazi era), he is reported to have said repeatedly, "Only a god can save us."[28] All he meant by this, however, was that Europe needed to be remythologized religiously, since only a religious mythology could preserve European culture in the face of the technology juggernaut. Heidegger was not pleading for Yahweh to come and save us from ourselves; rather, he was calling for exactly the kind of utilitarian, faithless religion that Kierkegaard deplored. Yahweh, for Heidegger and other children of Nietzsche, was irrevocably gone.

The Heidegger of *Being and Time* speaks as an agnostic; his philosophy characteristically unfolds agnostically. The later Heidegger, following the celebrated "turn" to a philosophical expression more akin to poetics, became mystical in a way described by Emil Fackenheim as "pagan."[29] This was perhaps not such a departure for Heidegger as one might think, given that Nazism was also pagan; after all, Nazism used the religious symbolism of the swastika (variously understood as an ancient Hindu good luck symbol or a cross with arms bent) and was enamoured of Norse mythology. What about our own society? Are we secularists, or pagans? Have we rid the world of gods, or have we re-divinized our culture with pagan ones?

A Comment on the Introduction to Heidegger in Guignon and Pereboom's *Existentialism: Basic Writings*

The Guignon and Pereboom Introduction comments on excerpts from Macquarrie's translation of *Being and Time*.[30] As such it provides ready access and insight into the main points of Heideggerian philosophy; it also provides an outline that will recapitulate for us, from a slightly

28. "Noch nur ein Gott kann uns retten." Quoted in Macquarrie, *Heidegger and Christianity*, 94.

29. Fackenheim never qualified or rescinded this stark assertion. See Fackenheim, *Encounters Between Judaism and Modern Philosophy* (London: Aronson, 1994), 221.

30. In *Existentialism: Basic Writings*, ed. Charles Guignon and Derk Pereboom (Indianapolis: Hackett Publishing, 2001), 183–210.

different angle, the Heideggerian understanding of the human predicament and its solution.

The profoundest question we can address, according to Heidegger, is the question of Being, and our attempt at understanding Being is what determines our existence.[31] We already have considerable, albeit tacit, understanding of the being of entities. Not only does everyone have a pre-reflective, intuitive understanding of Being generally; in addition we also have a rudimentary understanding of entities with respect to their particular nature. For instance, even a very young child with no formal exposure to physics understands that if she spills milk it will run all over the floor, whereas spilled honey will spread out only a few inches. However untechnical the vocabulary she may use to articulate this understanding of the relative viscosity of fluids, the understanding is genuine. Indeed, every time we use any entity, such as a doorknob,[32] we display our understanding of its being. Recall that for Heidegger the essential being of any entity is its function, and this function, which depends on our intention, is what gives the entity significance in our world. A doorknob, therefore, is not a metallic sphere, but a door-opening device. Thus Heidegger moves away from the traditional, abstract discussion of Being in terms of substance that underlies accidental appearances.

The introducer goes on to draw a contrast between technoscientific approaches to Being, which maintain a rigorous subject-object *detachment*,[33] and Heidegger's view, which insists on the self-world *correlation* we have already discussed. In a technoscientific approach, meaning is something we "find" or arbitrarily fashion and apply to the material element. The result is that many people now complain of the world's meaninglessness because they do not succeed in "finding" any meaning in the material environment. Heidegger, on the other hand, insists that Being *includes* meaning: if you understand the being, you understand its meaning. For example, the meaning of the being of the woman who is my wife resides, for me, in what she is to me. The natural

31. Ibid., 184.
32. Ibid., 185.
33. Ibid., 186.

sciences describe gynecology, and the social sciences describe female behaviour and thought processes, but none of this comes anywhere close to capturing what my wife means to me, and hence what her Being is for me.[34]

Detached reflection on Being-as-substance, says Heidegger, is always abstract, and does not deal with the *concreteness* of Being.[35] It also lands us in an irresolvable dispute between Realism and Idealism. For Heidegger, what is to be examined is neither the abstract, disembodied mind of Idealism, nor the technoscientific objectivity to which Realism aspires, but rather self-in-its-world, because *self* and *world* are always correlated: there is no self without a world, and no world without a self. Therefore, Heidegger always probes the nature of the self in the context of the self's world.

The clue to understanding Being, according to Heidegger, is *everydayness*—that is, familiar, ordinary situations in which we interact with other entities in our environment.[36] Everydayness acquaints us with the givenness of the nexus of relationships in light of a "project." In other words, the relationships between everyday entities in the world, and between ourselves and those entities, depends on what we intend to *do*, and what we intend to do is our "project." The being of any entity is determined by that entity's significance for us in light of our project; the "ready-to-hand" (the pen and paper and tabletop I am going to use for writing my lecture notes) is more basic or primordial than the "present-at-hand" (crumbs left on the table), and is concrete being, *real* being.

It is not the case that the ready-to-hand is just the present-at-

34. What does this say about the Being of God as discussed by philosophers, apologists, or even theologians, as opposed to the Being of God for the believer, the person intimately related to God? Martin Luther used to say, "God is God only if he is God-for-you," and "Faith resides in the personal pronouns." In other words, as long as God is merely "God," unrelated to me, he is not God for me at all; and the Being of Jesus Christ when I say that he is *my* Saviour is different from the Being of Jesus Christ whom I declare, as a matter of mere abstract doctrine, to be the Saviour of the world. For Luther's amplification of this point see his tract, "A Meditation on Christ's Passion – 1519," in Timothy F. Lull and William R. Russell, eds., *Martin Luther's Basic Theological Writings* (Minneapolis: Fortress, 2012), chapter 16.

35. Guignon and Pereboom, *Existentialism: Basic Writings*, 188.

36. Ibid., 191.

hand with something added to it, such as significance.[37] Rather, the present-at-hand does not even *arise* until we move from the concrete to the abstract: in our example, the crumbs do not enter the picture at all until they interfere with my writing, until they intrude on the "world" or context of my project so that I withdraw from it into a stance of detachment. Here Heidegger's Existentialist outlook contrasts starkly with a technoscientific outlook in which the crumbs on my tabletop have, at all times, the same ontological significance as the pen and paper. For Heidegger, only the ready-to-hand is real Being; there is no Being apart from our intentionality, and Being occurs only because we humans are agents with projects.[38] This also means that, if I do not have a hammer to drive nails in order to build my bookcase, and use my wife's shoe for that purpose, the shoe is at that point a hammer: its being is defined by my intentionality. It is not a shoe until my wife decides to walk in it. In short, *no* entity has a meaning apart from our intention.[39] At the same time, the "project-ability" of the world defines *our* Being as agents; that is, we are agents only because the world is capable of accommodating projects. In this way, being-in-the-world is a unified phenomenon, overcoming the conflict between Realism and Idealism.

So far from dealing with the concrete, science deals with the highly abstract, since it deals only with the present-at-hand—entities considered apart from any human intentionality and hence apart from a "world."[40] Here we notice a significant overlap with Martin Buber and his two stances or attitudes, the I–It of science and the I–Thou of relationship. What Heidegger says about the abstraction of science detached from human intentionality is reminiscent of Buber's claim that I–Thou is primary or primordial, while I–It is derivative and abstract. Heidegger agrees, declaring that truth is not technoscientific pronouncement but the reality of the self-world inseparability, disclosing itself by means of

37. Ibid., 192.

38. Ibid., 193.

39. In light of what Heidegger is saying, we ought to reflect on the sorts of projects we have, since our projects define the Being of entities. From a Christian perspective, are our projects "Kingdom" projects?

40. Guignon and Pereboom, *Existentialism: Basic Writings*, 196.

our mood and understanding—that is, by our attitude to it, and by our interaction with it in the carrying out of projects.

What is the structure of human agency, our way of being whereby we engage in projects? The Guignon–Pereboom Introduction brings together and summarizes Heidegger's thinking on this question. First of all, humans are beings who "care," in the expanded sense we have already mentioned.[41] Moreover, we "care" because we "take a stand" in our lives, and it is only as we "take a stand," says Heidegger in a statement reminiscent of Kierkegaard, that we come to "understand." The only person who profoundly understands marriage is the person who has taken the stand of becoming married; the only person who profoundly understands faith is the person who exists in faith. In Scripture, it is only as we stand with Jesus as a disciple that we understand the reality of our new life in him. That is why, as we have repeatedly observed, without this stand or commitment on your part nothing I can tell you will adequately convey that reality to you, and once you are rendered a new self through your commitment to Christ, you do not need me to tell you.

In fact, declares Heidegger, humans *are* their stands; we *are* what we *do*—again, a bedrock statement for Existentialists. We do not have an "inner definition" distinct from what we do, and the self does not "find itself" through any amount of introspection, but only in what it does.[42] Therefore the self is also always an event, not a substance or an essence; the self is always a becoming. It is both a self-constituting, and a self-interpreting: what I do *is* who I am, and *discloses* who I am.

In contrast to the view held by Platonists, for whom time is not only irrelevant to the definition of the human but also an impediment to human contemplation of the eternal forms, Heidegger insists, secondly, that human existence has a temporal structure.[43] One aspect of this temporal structure is our "thrownness," already discussed above: we are "thrown" into an environment and a situation we did not determine, which we then encounter as a task to be taken up. Moreover, because we

41. Ibid., 197.
42. Ibid., 198.
43. Ibid., 200.

are "thrown," we are "already in a world" that predates us, an actuality which yields the temporal dimension of "having been," or the past. Yet at the same time, our project entails our orientation to the future; as agents we are already "ahead of ourselves," if only because we have taken a stand on our thrownness and assumed it as a task or project. This simultaneity of our past thrownness and our future intention or project gives us a present: it is by virtue of existing as "ahead-of-itself-as-already-in-a-world" that *Dasein* is able to act in the present.[44] Moreover, our actions in that present are to be understood in terms of what they *undertake*, not in terms of what they *achieve*—that is, in terms of the commitments we make and not in terms of outcomes, since we have jurisdiction over the former but virtually none over the latter.

Third, human existence is always embedded in a communal context that enables us to interpret our self.[45] We act and interpret and assess ourselves through the collective pool of interpretations in our world, or "the they."[46] But while "the they" is the *context* of our action, "the they" should not be the *content* of our action; if it is, we have conformed to our environment and tacitly accepted its outlook as truth when an outlook can never be truth. Such absorption into "the they" is what Heidegger calls "fallenness" or inauthenticity; we are helped to escape it, he claims, through awareness of our inescapable finitude (or the fact of our death) and through the "mood" of anxiety it precipitates in us. Our "mood," as observed earlier in this chapter, is our way of hearing or attuning ourselves to the world; the mood of anxiety precipitated by awareness of our death serves to alienate us from the world so that we are no longer carelessly and complacently at home in it like "the they." We become aware that we have been fleeing authenticity,[47] and that our death is not only a termination, but a confirmation and sealing of our self-definition: death will seal the self we have made, authentic or not.

Awareness of mortality, then, continually forces us to come to terms with the question: What self am I now rendering myself? It precipitates

44. Ibid., 201.
45. Ibid., 202.
46. Ibid., 204.
47. Ibid., 206.

an urgency to *own up to* our life, and hence to *own* it rather than to keep on tacitly surrendering it to "the they" as most people do.[48] Authenticity may not determine the specific action we take, but it precipitates our repudiation of "fallenness" and our acceptance of the call to own our self. This focused stance with respect to one's life is what Heidegger calls *resoluteness*,[49] and (as we saw earlier in this chapter) it discloses the human being in a new way.

Finally, in becoming authentic we become what we are as true humans.[50] As we observed once before in chapter 7 while studying Nietzsche, this statement is reminiscent of Scripture's exhortations to become who we are in Christ. Christians are those who *have already put on* Christ; now we are exhorted to *put him on.*[51] We *are* a new creation in Christ; now we are to *become* that new creation. In the orbit of faith, we understand that every day we must own afresh the truth of our existence and become what we are in Christ, as the first of Luther's *Ninety-five Theses* suggests.[52] We cannot say, "I became a new creature in Christ thirteen years ago, and that was good enough." Heidegger's similar approach to this matter would seem to point to a secularized understanding of faith.

Concluding Reflections

If Sartre is the most written-about philosopher of the twentieth century, Heidegger is the most influential. He has had an enormous influence on theology, giving rise to a whole school of Existentialist theologians such as Carl Michalson, John Macquarrie, and others. He has also profoundly affected New Testament scholarship, particularly that of Rudolph Bultmann and the form-critical school that has arisen after him. For Bultmann, Heidegger's philosophy exposed the deficits and

48. Ibid., 207.

49. Ibid., 208.

50. Ibid., 210.

51. E.g., Colossians 3:8–14.

52. Lull and Russell, *Martin Luther's Basic Theological Writings*, 8. The first thesis announces, "When our Lord and Master Jesus Christ said 'Repent', he willed the entire life of believers to be one of repentance."

contradictions in the human being, and the gospel was the answer to the Heideggerian diagnosis. However, it must be asked: If we begin with a Heideggerian diagnosis of the disease, does the gospel cure become Heidegger-shaped? If we begin with Plato or Kant, do we arrive at a gospel that is really Plato or Kant in disguise? How do we identify the gospel that is Jesus Christ *himself* acting on us and speaking to us, as opposed to us unwittingly talking to ourselves? All of these philosophers assume that philosophy acquaints us with the human predicament; but while they may indeed make insightful observations on the situation arising from our predicament, is it not the case that only the remedy of the gospel truly discloses the predicament? Earlier we reflected on the impossibility of undertaking theology without a philosophical vocabulary. The question to be asked is: How shall we use that philosophical vocabulary so as to avoid adulterating the gospel?

Psychology and psychotherapy owe a great debt to Heidegger as well: European psychiatrists Ludwig Binswanger and Medard Boss draw extensively on Heidegger's understanding of *Dasein*, the human existent.[53] A psychotherapist with a Heideggerian background makes a connection between a client's unhappiness and the fact that she is sunk in "the they," needing to recover the call to authenticity and own the truth of her existence in terms of project and intentionality. Since any school of psychotherapy relies on a particular understanding of the human, ultimately it must be driven by philosophy. To the extent that literary theory and literary analysis also assume a particular understanding of the human and our place in the world, these, too, are driven by philosophy.

Heidegger was a philosophical giant; hence his influence has been felt in virtually every field of the humanities and social sciences, and anyone who studies them studies him.

---

53. See, for instance, the rich exchanges between Heidegger and Boss, and Boss's amplification of their correspondence—more than 250 letters—between 1947 and 1971: Medard Boss, ed., *Martin Heidegger: Zollikon Seminars – Protocols, Conversations, Letters* (Chicago: Northwestern University Press, 2001). Other noteworthy sources include Michel Foucault and Ludwig Binswanger, *Dream and Existence*, ed. Keith Hoeller (Humanities Press, 1992); and Medard Boss, *Psychoanalysis and Daseinanalysis* (New York: Basic Books, 1967).

11

Jean-Paul Sartre:
Possibility, Meaning, and the Weight of Freedom

Introduction

Born in 1905, Sartre is the most famous philosopher of the postwar era. His philosophical works still sell, and he remains influential in disciplines besides philosophy, such as literature and psychoanalysis. He was the major representative of the Existentialist philosophy that dominated European intellectual life in the 1940s and 1950s, and the translation of his works served to hasten the movement's spread to other countries. University courses on Sartre and Existentialism continue to attract students, and few philosophers appeal as readily to undergraduates. Nietzsche may be more popular, but Sartre has elicited the greater response: as noted before in this book, Sartre is the most widely written-about philosopher of the twentieth century.[1]

Many of Sartre's literary works have achieved popular success and enduring critical acclaim. All of his plays continue to be studied, and his novel *Nausea* (*La Nausée*) is deemed one of the greatest of the twentieth century; at least two of his short stories, "The Wall" and "The Childhood of a Leader," are considered to be among the best in the

---

1. In attempting to expound Sartre to students who have had no previous exposure to him, my efforts at simplifying his thought have been assisted by Gary Cox, *Sartre: A Guide for the Perplexed* (New York: Continuum, 2006); David Detmer, *Sartre Explained: From Bad Faith to Authenticity* (Peru, IL: Open Court Publishing, 2008); Donald D. Palmer, *Sartre for Beginners* (Danbury, CT: For Beginners LLC, 1995); Philip Thody and Howard Read, *Introducing Sartre* (Duxford, UK: Icon Books, 1999).

world. His massive and controversial biographies of Jean Genet and Gustave Flaubert have garnered much serious attention, and the journal he co-founded and edited, *Les Temps Modernes*, remains significant in the intellectual life of contemporary France. Like all Existentialist thinkers Sartre is sophisticated in the field of literature, and so bridges naturally with it; his critical essays are a must-read guide to the literary, dramatic, and visual arts of his time.

Importantly, Sartre was politically involved not only through his writings but through his activism. Any Existentialist philosopher realizes that detached armchair thinking is cheap and ineffectual; it makes little difference to anything. Existentialism has always called for a response of the whole person rather than a merely intellectual response. It has been aptly said that the last thing Jesus wants is an admirer: he says to his admirers, "Why do you call me 'Lord, Lord,' and not *do* what I tell you?"[2] Similarly, the last thing an Existentialist philosopher wants is a flatterer: he expects those who read and understand him to *do* something.

Sartre's political activities were risky. He courted a prison sentence by signing an illegal petition condemning France's military activities in colonial Algeria, and documented atrocities perpetrated by the French against the Algerians—atrocities that the mainstream French press had declined to cover. Following World War II, France prosecuted former Nazi war criminals with a seemingly vindictive self-righteousness while overlooking its own treatment of the Algerians—which was every bit as bad as German treatment of the French during the war; Sartre (along with other thinkers such as Christian lawyer, professor, and sociologist Jacques Ellul) exposed the hypocrisy in these proceedings. He also advocated consistently for the victims of economic, racial, and political oppression, a fact that has since gained him an extensive readership among intellectuals in developing countries. He is a huge figure in many African nations to this day; Frantz Fanon,[3] for instance, maintains that

2. Luke 6:46.

3. Fanon was a philosopher, physician, and Marxist revolutionary born in Martinique in 1925. He was heavily involved in the Algerian liberation movement.

the account of anti-Semitism in Sartre's *Anti-Semite and Jew* inspired his own analysis of anti-black racism.

In his early years Sartre was exposed to phenomenology, the exploration of human consciousness. Consciousness in humans is always of the order of *self-consciousness*. The higher animals are conscious—if they are not asleep or dead—but as far as we know they lack *self*-consciousness; they do not reflect on their own activities or existence. Human consciousness, however, is always of the order of self-consciousness, and its nature and structure are the preoccupation of phenomenology. In 1933 Sartre went to Berlin to study the phenomenology of Edmund Husserl, and soon began incorporating new phenomenological insights into his own writings—most notably in his novel *Nausea*, published in 1938. Before that he wrote *Psychology of the Imagination* in 1936 and *Transcendence of the Ego* in 1937; the latter, especially, explores his phenomenological approach to consciousness.

In September of 1939 Sartre was called up for military service. The nature of his military assignment left him much free time, and he began work on a novel, *The Age of Reason*. In order to inform himself first regarding the background to European philosophy, he immersed himself in Kierkegaard. (Everyone in Europe who is serious about philosophy reads widely and deeply in Kierkegaard, even if they distance themselves from him; Nietzsche, Heidegger, and Sartre all did so. Kierkegaard is frequently called the father of Existentialism, and although he was a Christian, many agnostic and atheist Existentialists are among his philosophical offspring. Sartre is one of them.) In June 1940 Sartre was taken prisoner of war and began writing *Being and Nothingness*, which was published in 1943; it was his first major work, and the one by which he is most readily identified.

In 1941 he escaped from the prisoner-of-war camp and resumed teaching in Europe. It is puzzling that he managed to do this without being re-arrested, especially since he proceeded to write articles for underground newspapers—an exceedingly dangerous undertaking—and produced a play, *The Flies* (*Les Mouches*), that had a blatantly anti-Nazi message. There were even Nazi officials in the audience in Paris when the play was performed, yet it was not suppressed and Sartre was not arrested. In any case, his philosophy of existence not only seized the French but spread around the world, and by the end of the war in 1945 he was virtually a deity in France.

Under the influence of Merleau-Ponty, another French phenomenologist, Sartre moved politically towards Marxism—an understandable development on his part given the egregious social inequities in Europe arising from centuries of a class system more oppressive than anything we see in North America. He abandoned his plans to write a sequel to *Being and Nothingness*, thinking that Marxism had a profounder claim on him; he refused to join the French Communist party, however, finding it inconsistent in its Marxism. He nevertheless aligned himself with the Soviet Union against the United States during the Cold War—a move that distanced him from Albert Camus, who was quicker to recognize the hidden monster in Soviet Stalinism.[4]

The undeniable brutality of the Soviet Union in suppressing the Hungarian uprising of 1956 left Sartre appalled and disillusioned. The Soviet overlords shocked the whole world by simply rolling their tanks over human beings in the street—much as the Chinese authorities did in Tiananmen Square decades later. In 1960 Sartre published *The Critique of Dialectical Reason*, a book that signalled a departure from his earlier work; although still concerned with the individual and with freedom, he now sought to rescue people from molestation at the hands of Stalinist Marxism and from deception by the French Communist party. He broke entirely with the Kremlin in the wake of the Soviet intervention in Czechoslovakia in 1968. When Algeria went to war against France in order to gain its independence, Sartre sided with the Algerians, whereupon 50,000 French army veterans marched in Paris calling for his execution. He was forced to go into hiding, and his apartment

---

4. Marxism was popular with many intellectuals at the time. No less a figure than Malcolm Muggeridge thought, in the 1930s, that Marxism was a way of redressing the social inequities of Great Britain. He touted this idea until he visited the Soviet Union and observed how the people lived. Confronted by mass starvation and the Stalinist purges, he realized that Marxism would never be able to deliver on its promises.

was bombed twice. Being a philosopher—especially an Existentialist philosopher—is sometimes costly.

In 1964 Sartre was awarded the Nobel Prize for Literature, but rejected it on political grounds. Shortly afterwards he joined Bertrand Russell's tribunal to investigate American war crimes in Vietnam. In 1977 he renounced Marxism altogether, and in 1983 (at the age of seventy-eight) issued his most mature philosophical statement, *Notebooks for an Ethics*. In that work he can be observed to move away from the seemingly one-sided bleakness of *Being and Nothingness*, where, for instance, he had taken a purely negative view of "the other." In *Being and Nothingness* even the gaze of the other is understood as threatening to our own personhood, because the other person's gaze reduces us to an object. Even another who supposedly loves us has objectified us simply by confronting our personhood with her own.

More will be said about this below, but we can note immediately the contrast between Sartre's understanding of "the other" as briefly described above, and Buber's as we encountered it in *I and Thou*: for Buber, far from being inherently a threat, the other is inherently the condition of the dialogical encounter. The two philosophers' views on the *divine* Other are equally diametrically opposed. Sartre regards God as the giant who infinitely transcends us and therefore objectifies us as thoroughly as we objectify any physical artifact: if God made me, declares Sartre, I am as much an object to God as my pen is to me. Therefore, he insists, it is inherently impossible for human beings to thrive in an environment of theism; in the shadow of the deity the human entity can only shrivel. For Buber, on the other hand, not only is God ceaselessly engaged with every human being in the world, but his unwearying engagement underlies the definition of the human and is the condition of the human good. It is only *the* Person's engagement with all persons, insists Buber, that saves us ultimately from objectifying each other despite our wicked attempts to do so. While the mature Sartre never became a theist, he did move away from a one-sidedly dark understanding of "the other," arguing that his earlier observations in *Being and Nothingness* described relationships that are deficient or defective, or operating in what he called "bad faith" (about which more below).

Sartre died on April 15, 1980, and the streets of Paris were thronged with those who turned out to honour him.

A Philosophy That Sought to Be a Consistent Atheism: Overview

Existence vs. essence

One of Sartre's pithiest statements about the human being is "Existence precedes essence"—where "essence" is what a thing is, its nature or function.[5] Regarding the things we make, the opposite is true: essence always precedes existence. We have an idea of what a hammer must be, given its function of driving nails; we envisage the kind of tool needed for this purpose and manufacture it in accordance with our vision, which is almost akin to a Platonic form. The hammer's existence is *subsequent to* its essence, and its value depends on how well it conforms to that essence—how well it fulfills its function. As for things we find in nature, there, too, essence always precedes existence. Even though we did not invent or make the horse, it is possessed of an essence independent of us, as are all other natural objects.

When it comes to humans, on the other hand, Sartre maintains that the Western philosophical tradition has the sequence backwards: traditionally, it has been said with respect to humans also that essence precedes existence, but Sartre overturns this thesis. Aristotle, for instance, said that to be a human being is to be a rational animal: animal is the genus, and rationality is the species, meaning that humans are animals distinguished by the fact that they are rational and other animals are not.[6] And Plato maintained that to be human is to participate in the eternal form of the human. Even Christianity, according to Sartre, falls

---

5. Sartre, *Existentialism and Humanism*, trans P. Mairet (London: Methuen, 1960), 26.

6. From a biblical perspective Aristotle is only partly right: we are distinguished from the animals by rationality, but only because it is an aspect of "spirit"—our orientation toward God and ability to respond to God by having been addressed by God. Humans are the only creature to whom God speaks, and our rationality is directly related to that speech of God to us.

into the same category as the rest of Western philosophy with respect to the relation of essence to existence: Christianity declares that to be human is to be a creature whom God has fashioned in his image, and if God has *created* us, we arrive ready-made, forged and formed according to God's plan and purpose—which is to say that our essence precedes our existence. Our routine use of the expression "human nature," Sartre points out, confirms this outlook. Existentialists will speak of a human situation or human condition, but never of a human *nature*.

It must be asked, however, whether being created in the likeness and image of God is the same as a "human nature." An alligator has a nature: its nature is to live in a swamp and eat smaller animals that enter its orbit, and it can only ever behave in accordance with that nature. A cloud has a nature: it is water vapour suspended in the air, and cannot be anything else. We do not expect anything else of an alligator or a cloud; it is only with humans that we can remonstrate, when one of us mistreats another, "Come on, now. Be a man. Show a little humanity." Even if we are made in the likeness and image of God, does this mean there is a nature given to us that is analogous to the nature given an animal, tree, or cloud? In other words, can we only be what we are now? Christians would say that, thanks to God's effectual promise of new birth, we can become in some sense what we are not now. Regardless of any religious consideration, however, our society assumes we *can* be what we are not now. When someone is arrested for car theft, it is pointless to say to the judge, "But Your Honour, I am just being what I am: a thief. Thieving is my nature." The judge will insist, "You are a thief (since in one sense we are what we do), but you do not need to be, and everyone expects you not to be."

It is precisely here, in fact, that we have identified Sartre's understanding of what it means to be human. "*The human being*," he says in another of his pithy expressions, "*is what it is not, and is not what it is.*"[7] Leaving aside any Christian appeal to regeneration, new birth, or the indwelling of the Holy Spirit, no one in our society will endorse

---

7. Sartre, *Being and Nothingness*, trans. Hazel E. Barnes (London: Methuen, 1986), 70. See *Being and Nothingness,* Part 2, chapter 1, as well as my amplification of the same point below regarding Being-in-itself, Being-for-itself, and Nothingness, and Sartre's notion of "bad faith."

the argument that my being human means I have a defined, constituted nature for which no one can fault me. If we are going to speak of a human nature, we must be more subtle and nuanced—in which case we probably should not use the word *nature* of humans at all, since we mean by it something entirely different from the nature of any other entity. That is why, again, Existentialists insist on referring not to a human nature but to a human situation or condition.

If there is no God, says Sartre, and we deny Plato's world of forms, then there is no predetermined human essence. This is bedrock for Sartre, as it is for any Existentialist. Instead—and by now every reader can recite this refrain by heart—the human individual forges her essence through free choices and acts. Unlike animals, which are utterly constrained by instinct, human beings have drives which are undeniable but concerning which we can make choices. We saw this earlier in our study of Nietzsche: we have a sex drive, for example, but we can choose to forgo or delay its gratification. Our drives are part of what Sartre (like Nietzsche) calls "facticity," but our facticity never determines who we are, because at any given moment we can freely decide what to do with our drives. While our facticity is undeniable, its expression is not inevitable. This freedom is what underlies the fact that to be human is to be what we are not, and not to be what we are.

Sartre's view denies biological determinism, one form of which is *epiphenomenalism*, the notion that mind can be reduced to brain. Everyone agrees that there is some connection between mind and brain: if I undergo a major head injury or suffer from brain disease, I will think differently, and even apart from disease or injury my brain will shrivel as I get older, affecting my mental processes. But does this mean that mind can be *reduced* to brain, and that mental states are no more than reflections of brain chemistry? If that is the case, then what passes for thought is an illusion: we think we are thinking, but we are not. Rather, what we call "thinking" is merely the precipitate of biochemical changes in our body being projected on a screen inside us. That is the state of affairs according to epiphenomenalism. Sartre, however, denies this and all forms of determinism, whether biological or social.

He also denies, as one more form of determinism, the unconscious mind about which Freud speaks so much—for the simple reason that Freud speaks of it not as something we *have*, but rather as that which *controls* us. If our unconscious mind is controlling us, there is no such thing as human freedom.

In speaking of a human "situation," Existentialists mean our "thrownness" into existence in a particular time, place, and set of circumstances, whereas a human "condition" means something akin to human nature—Heidegger's "fallenness," or our default tendency to conform to "the they" or live inauthentically. Recall, however, that even Kierkegaard, a Christian who believes that we are made in the likeness and image of God, insists that we *choose* the sort of self we become. We cannot excuse ourselves by appealing to a predetermined 'nature.' Oddly enough, while the appeal to human nature is a frequent defence in our society, it is deemed a sufficient explanation only up to a certain point; in the criminal court system, for example, it has no currency.

Phenomenology

Being and Nothingness, the first of Sartre's famous works, was subtitled "An Essay in Phenomenological Ontology." In it Sartre explored the nature and structure of human consciousness and its relationship to the self. It may be easiest to appreciate his understanding of consciousness if we first view it alongside views espoused earlier by Descartes and Edmund Husserl.

We are all familiar with Descartes' pronouncement, "I think, therefore I am." In his pursuit of certitude, Descartes took consciousness as his starting point because he considered it to be the one indubitable thing: to wonder if you have a mind is to prove that you have one. From that indubitable premise he posited a self: if I am thinking, then there must be an I. As we observed in chapter 1, however, Descartes' pronouncement taken as a starting point also constitutes a definition of what it means, foundationally, to be human: to *be*, as a human being, is to be a thinking thing.

There are a number of objections to this from the Existentialist point of view. For one (a point we also visited earlier), "I think, therefore I am" seems arbitrary, given that humankind is the only animal that cooks its food and the only animal that buries its dead; we could just as well say, "I cook, therefore I am," or "I bury, therefore I am." Why make thinking definitive of human existence? Recall, especially, the Existentialists' bedrock assertion that existence cannot be *thought*, existence can only be *lived*, and it is in living, in doing, that one comes to be a self. This being the case, how can mere consciousness be the definition and ground of human being? Sartre had other objections to Descartes as well, about which more will be said below.

Edmund Husserl (1859–1938) is often considered the founder of phenomenology. Whereas many have said that what goes on in our consciousness has little to do with our understanding—that is, the pictures in our mind's eye have little to do with what we know—Husserl maintained that what was needed was a method that would display the subjective features of consciousness as well as its objective structure. He proposed two stages in the development of this method: (1) a detailed description of the way the world presents itself to consciousness—that is, the way it is experienced by conscious beings; and (2) a pre-theoretical description of the various acts of consciousness and their objects.[8] Note that what he is aiming at is a *description of the acts* of consciousness, not a *theory* of consciousness. Theories of consciousness always make use of entities that are not themselves present in consciousness: consider, for example, the unconscious invoked by Freud, or current neurological theories about the relation of mind to the chemistry and structure of the brain. Husserl's phenomenology, on the other hand, aimed to exclude everything that was not itself *in* consciousness; it aimed at being assumption-free, since assumptions are, by definition, not *in* conscious states but only presupposed by them.

You made assumptions, for instance, when you picked up this book and saw the title: you assumed the whole book would be in English, and also that it would use standard English orthography rather than phonetic script like the pronunciations in a dictionary. You did not think to yourself, "I bet they used standard English spelling for the text of this book," nor did you ask yourself, after flipping through the first chapter or two, "I wonder if the latter half of the book is in phonetic script?"

8. See Palmer, *Sartre for Beginners*, 34–35.

You made assumptions that are presupposed by your conscious state, but by definition you are not conscious of those assumptions. We are making assumptions all the time that are not *in* our consciousness. To take another example: if I extract a coin from my pocket and look at it lying flat in my palm, I see it is circular. If I hold it at a forty-five- degree angle, however, the image on my retina is not a circle but an ellipse; nevertheless, I interpret it as a circle because I already know that coins are circular.[9]

Husserl's phenomenology is an attempt to move *behind* these assumptions that are prior to interpretation. The terms characteristically used by him to refer to the disposing of assumption are "suspension," "bracketing," and "epoché." If we "bracket" our consciousness of time, for instance, we are aware of "clocked" time—time measured by the clock, which is conceptual time—and "lived" time, which is perceptual time. Needless to say, we live in both: when we are rushing to meet a deadline two hours away, we know what two hours is, and we know it is always the same length of time; yet those two hours seem to pass very quickly. Children, until they learn to tell time, live almost exclusively in perceptual time, where there is a constant "now." It is the same with respect to space: "lived" or perceptual space is a constant "here." Husserl maintained that perceptual time-and-space is the phenomenological epicentre of *all consciousness.* In other words, all consciousness is the "here now" experience of time and space. From the phenomenological study of pure consciousness, Husserl then tried to derive an "absolute self" or "pure ego," much as Descartes had deduced selfhood from consciousness.

Sartre, however, took the discussion in a different direction from both Descartes and Husserl. We may start with a crucial distinction

---

9. The undeniable role of assumption in interpretation reduces the force of such apologetic gambits as the "watchmaker" argument for the existence of God, according to which the complexity and order of the world bespeak a designer and creator in the same way that a watch implies the existence of a watchmaker. Whatever traction the argument might have it has only in a culture that already knows what sort of thing a watch is. If a bushman is shown a watch, he draws no conclusion about a watchmaker; he makes nothing at all of the watch. He is aware of a state of consciousness with respect to it, but what he sees is wholly uninterpreted. Similar observations have been documented by many psychologists. Children, too, are aware of many more things than they can interpret.

he made in *The Transcendence of the Ego*, published in 1937, in which he speaks of reflective consciousness and unreflective consciousness. Unreflective consciousness is my consciousness of an object such as a car turning in front of me—something of which I am aware, but about which I am not thinking; I am thinking of something else. (We all experience this on a daily basis when we drive along a familiar route and cannot remember any of the red lights at which we must have stopped. All of that is unreflective or pre-reflective consciousness.) If, on the other hand, I walk into the car turning in front of me and am knocked over, I say to myself, "I ought to be more careful! I am in pain!" This is reflective consciousness. Notice that in unreflective consciousness there is no "I," whereas reflective consciousness has the self as its object: when I walk into the car and am knocked over and feel pain, the object of my consciousness is not the car but myself. Sartre maintains that the self can be found *only* in reflective consciousness; the self can never be found in unreflective or pre-reflective consciousness.

This being the case, Sartre argues, Descartes was wrong: "I am" does not follow from "I think," since there is no self in thought except in reflective consciousness, which is clearly much rarer than unreflective consciousness. We get through most days not thinking at all about thinking, and thinking very little about our self; we get through the day with everything on the *edge* of consciousness, in pre-reflective consciousness. The light turns green, and I put my foot on the accelerator; but I do not say to myself, "The light is green. I must press my foot and trust that the car will move ahead." In fact, I have no recollection of having made any decision at all, because none of it occurred in reflective consciousness. Since unreflective consciousness is where we live most of our lives, at most Descartes should have said, "I think, therefore there are thoughts," or "I think, therefore there is thinking." Either of those conclusions would be legitimate, Sartre argued, but it is not legitimate to say, "I think, therefore I am"; after all, who is the "I"? The I may be the condition of thinking, but it is never the thing thought, never what we think of as a self, never what we mean by our "self."

Thus we do not find an "absolute ego" or "pure self" in

consciousness, as Husserl claimed; in fact, the self is absent from consciousness most of the time. Consciousness is an "impersonal spontaneity" that overflows ceaselessly, and the absent self is *discovered* only as it is *forged*. There is also no pre-existing self as Plato claimed, no noumenal self as posited by Kant, no potential self or hidden self waiting to be disclosed. There is no latent self analogous to the oak in the acorn. For this reason, all psychologies that speak of "self-realization" in fact deny a self.[10]

Note Sartre's claim that consciousness is always impersonal. He denies Husserl's personal consciousness as that which orders conscious activity. Our personal ego—our personal identity or character, or our personality—is always an *object* of consciousness, never consciousness itself. If you ask me what my personality is, and I say, "I have a personality like a porcupine," the self I am describing to you is an object of my consciousness. I am now thinking about my personality, and telling you, from conscious observation and reflection regarding my actions or thoughts, that I have a personality like a porcupine; but this personality is not consciousness *itself*, nor is it something behind consciousness. We can never think our way into "pure consciousness," or consciousness apart from some object. Even non-reflective consciousness is always conscious *of* something: while engrossed in a televised hockey game, I may pick up an apple and eat it without thinking about it, but I must be conscious of the apple or I would not have picked it up. As soon as I try to think my way into pure consciousness, I and my thinking become the object of thought: I objectify myself as "thinker." Consciousness is not personal, although it is particular in the sense that yours is not mine and mine is not yours; note the difference, in that statement, between particular and personal. Another way of making Sartre's point is to say that consciousness is not an *entity*, but an active *process*.

Unlike animal consciousness, notes Sartre, every human consciousness is self-consciousness in the sense that there is a (finite) self-transcendence to it that animal consciousness lacks. One evidence

10. For an amplification of this point see Sartre, *Being and Nothingness*, Part 2, chapter 1, "Immediate Structures of the For-Itself."

of this has to do with vocabulary. A dog may recognize and respond in a consistent manner to certain words, such as "walk" or "water"; a very intelligent dog has a vocabulary of about 200 such words. A human being, on the other hand, discounting certain disorders, has a vocabulary of thousands or even tens of thousands of words.[11] Moreover, the dog's vocabulary is entirely percept-oriented, whereas our vocabulary has a large conceptual element in it—the more educated we are, the larger it is. Concept formation requires a degree of self-transcendence, which is the ability to rise above our immediacy.

Having established this much, Sartre moves on to his understanding of the self. So far, two statements have been made about consciousness (besides the fundamental statement that it is not the self): (1) Consciousness is always consciousness *of* something; and (2) Human consciousness is self-consciousness. We can make such statements, says Sartre, only because consciousness "nihilates" Being.

"Consciousness nihilates Being" is an assertion that requires explication. By it Sartre means that, in transcending our immediacy, we look beyond the Being of that which *is*—the current state of affairs in which we find ourselves—towards a state of affairs that is currently *non-existent*, in hopes of achieving it. In other words, we introduce a "Nothingness" into Being in the form of something that does not (yet) exist but is in our consciousness.[12] The introduction of this Nothingness into Being in turn opens up *choice* as opposed to determination: because we can introduce things that *are not*, and act towards them in order to bring them about, that which *is* loses its power to determine us. Sartre insists that in the course of making choices, the self is forged and discovered, and by this process tyrants are dethroned. This is because the Nothingness just mentioned cancels the causal nexus of social and political and economic determination.

---

11. We all have far more words in our vocabulary than we are aware of having. We have a passive vocabulary of words we understand when reading or listening, and an active vocabulary of words we ourselves use when writing or speaking, the latter always significantly smaller. Of the active vocabulary, our writing vocabulary is greater than our speaking vocabulary; the active speaking vocabulary is the smallest of all.

12. See *Being and Nothingness*, Part 1, chapter 1, "The Origin of Negation."

Think of it in the following way. That which *is* is Being-in-itself, while that which we *project* as a possible eventuality or outcome is Being-for-itself. That which we project has not yet occurred, however, and this non-occurrence is a kind of Nothingness; hence Being-for-itself entails a Nothingness that we apply to Being-in-itself. And as soon as we apply the Nothingness of Being-for-itself to Being-in-itself, we have broken the causal connection because we open up a choice for our self.

Let us suppose, for example, that I am aware of hunger, meaning that I lack food. The animal that is aware of hunger instinctually eats the next edible thing it sees, whereas I, on the other hand, can postpone gratification: I can eat or not eat. My awareness of what I lack is therefore also an awareness of what I may do or not do about it in the imminent future, an awareness of possible action not yet realized. We could say it is an awareness of the "gap" between hunger (Being-in-itself, that which is) and possible fullness (Being-for-itself, that which may be in future). Sartre expresses this as an introduction of the Nothingness of Being-for-itself into my world of Being, and my awareness of this Nothingness means that *I am not determined*. Whereas an animal has no choice, and must either put up with its current situation (because food is not available) or act instinctually in response to it (eat whatever is available), a human can project a situation that is different from the current one, and make a choice with respect to it. In so doing, the human "nihilates" the current situation by negating its determinative power.

Facticity is any given element in our current situation; it is an aspect of Being-in-itself. We cannot *an*nihilate facticity, in the sense of doing away with it: I am a white male, and cannot be other than a white male. It is no use my pretending to be an Asian female. However, I can *nihilate* my facticity any time: I can say, "I am a male and I am white, and therefore have social privilege in Canada, but I don't want to exploit it; I am not going to be a chauvinist or a racist." My facticity is not changed, but I have introduced an element of Nothingness between Being-in-itself (that which is, namely, the white male that I am) and Being-for-itself (my project to be a gender-inclusive non-racist). My awareness of and action towards this project is the only way I nihilate, or avoid being driven or determined by, my facticity. It is the way I forge a self.

There are many aspects of facticity: our genetic makeup, the social environment into which we were born, and other things we did not choose. Do our gender, genetics, and social environment mean that we are so thoroughly determined as to have no choice? Or is it the case, for example, that we can say, "I was born in poverty, but I don't want to live in poverty, and will set about doing something to achieve the economic sufficiency I do not yet have"? To say this is to nihilate—not *annihilate*, but *nihilate*—the facticity of our poverty by introducing an element of Nothingness into our current situation.

Nothingness laps the Being of humans at all times, says Sartre. A student can study for the next day's test, or go to a party; it is not the case that she is driven and has no choice. She can introduce an element of Nothingness by projecting the outcome of doing well on the test, which is part of the larger project of gaining an education. Neither has happened yet, but she can allow Being-for-itself (the project of gaining an education) to nihilate Being-in-itself, and forgo the pleasure of attending the party. Nothingness does not lap the Being of the animal, on the other hand; the animal just is, and its environment just is. The Nothingness that constantly laps our Being comes from the fact of human consciousness, which is always self-consciousness. Self-consciousness is the source and the condition of the human capacity to nihilate facticity.

The corollary of this is that every choice *for* something is a choice *against* other things. If I decide to go to Winnipeg tonight, I have made a decision not to go to Montréal. Every year when it turns cold, the geese fly south, but it is not because they have made a decision to fly south rather than north; they all simply begin flying south instinctually. I, on the other hand, make a self-conscious decision to say "Yes" to the option or possibility of going to Winnipeg, and in so doing nihilate not only staying home, but going to Montréal. All human choice presupposes the power of nihilating, without which we are psychologically, socially, or biologically driven.

It may seem as though nothing that has been said so far is especially profound. What Sartre does with it, however, is indeed profound. There were people in France who saved their skins by collaborating with the Nazis, thinking it was the only course open to them, and there were others who resisted and paid the price. We can never, in any situation, say that we have no choice, because at every point in our existence we have the power of nihilation. If I have a raging headache, people might indulge my short-temperedness on the grounds that I have no choice; they would be wrong, however, because there are people who suffer atrociously and whose behaviour is nevertheless exemplary. We always have a choice as to how we will respond to our facticity. Sartre seals off the evasions that have become second nature to most of us.

This consciousness of ours, and the freedom it brings, is not without its burdensome aspect. The self is overwhelmed by the sheer superfluity of spontaneity and the welter of possibilities it brings before us; we find our freedom monstrous.[13] The anguish we feel in the face of such freedom is foundational to human consciousness, says Sartre; we experience anguish because we must make choices without ever knowing how they will turn out. I married a woman over forty-five years ago, and it turned out gloriously; several of my classmates married women, and for them it turned out wretchedly, even though we all married with the same expectations. How often do we say, "If I had only known where that action would lead, I would never have taken it"? We do not know until it is too late.

For that reason, says Sartre, anguish accompanies every decision in human existence, and this anguish in the face of freedom is foundational to human consciousness. He is talking about the Existentialist category of *Angst*, a German word now naturalized in English. *Angst* in German is usually translated "fear," but the angst spoken of by the Existentialist is different from fear. Fear is quickened by a specific object; I may be afraid of big dogs, for example, or injections. The angst of which the Existentialist speaks, however, is not fear of a specific object or outcome;

13. It may be that young people are less threatened by this than older people. Young people feel that the whole world is theirs, that there is almost nothing they cannot do, and revel in the fact. Older adults often handle the smorgasbord of possibilities by shrivelling their world so as to shut most of them down, and thereby make life manageable.

rather, it is the unremovable anxiety that accompanies our state of consciousness because of the indeterminate freedom that consciousness generates. Those who cannot live with that angst constantly try to reduce it by surrendering their freedom and looking to someone else to tell them what to do. Sartre considers such people despicable, because freedom is the very thing we cannot surrender. Even the decision to allow someone else to decide for us is a decision; hence there is no escaping responsibility at any time.

Nausea

Nausea, a novel Sartre published in 1938 about being overwhelmed by the sheer arbitrary massiveness or superfluity of existence, features a character named Mr. Roquentin. While sitting on the streetcar he puts his hand on the seat, and it suddenly feels alien to him; he feels its *existence,* not its "seatness." Since we can sit on a tree stump or a bench or a rock, "seatness" has nothing inherently to do with the object, only with our *naming* the object. "Things are divorced from their names," observes Roquentin.[14] What he notices is not the seat as a seat, but as an object among myriad other objects in his environment, one on which he happens to be sitting.

Nausea, like angst, is a major category in Existentialism. In Sartre's writing it has the force of something akin to acid reflux, the slight taste of vomit. We can "taste" ourselves as existing objects, taste the arbitrariness and absurdity of contingent Being. In the absence of God or other teleology, *all* Being is contingent and arbitrary, and we are overwhelmed by the sheer surfeit of facticity. We ask, Why is there something rather than nothing? There is no answer to this question. Even from a Christian perspective there is no answer that makes the universe logically necessary. God, who lacks nothing in himself, chose to create. Why did he choose to create? Not for companionship, because he already enjoyed relationality within the Trinity; and not to remedy any deficit in himself. We do not know why he created, but we affirm in faith that he did. Sartre says that *all* Being is contingent; since there

---

14. Jean-Paul Sartre, *Nausea*, trans. Lloyd Alexander (New York: New Directions, 2007), 123.

is no Creator, the fact that there is *anything* rather than nothing is purely arbitrary—sheer accident.

It is difficult for Christians to understand what this means to a thinker like Sartre. When we say that the world is here because God made it, we assume that God had a purpose in making it, and that it is incumbent on God's people to discern that purpose and honour it. However, if the world simply appeared by accident and was not made, then the fact that there is a world at all is purely arbitrary, accidental, and hence meaningless. Nausea attests our recognition of sheer overflowing facticity—of arbitrary, meaningless Being. And if the world as a whole means nothing, what do *I* mean? I have no meaning either, apart from the meaning I create for myself. What I mean depends on me—which takes us back to the inescapable weight of freedom of which the Existentialist speaks, and the angst surrounding it.

We may understand the force of Roquentin's experience if we look more closely at the whole issue of Being or existence in Existentialist thought—some of which we encountered in Heidegger. Consider the concepts we use for thinking: they are simply names for what members of a class have in common, and are therefore always abstractions. The concept "boat" is an abstraction of what all boats have in common. "Big" is a concept that names a quality shared by all big things. We can have in our mind an image of a boat, and an image of a big boat, which will be different in just the feature of size. *Existence*, however—and this is crucial for Existentialists—is *not* a concept: an image of a boat and an image of an existing boat are the same. This being the case, we can also say that if we have in our mind an image of a unicorn, it is identical with the image of an existing unicorn; "existing" adds nothing to the image because it does not name a concept in the way that "boat" or "big" does, and cannot be pictured. If we try to abstract the quality of "existence" from all existing things, we have nothing. *Existence* is always concrete, never abstract; therefore *Being*, strictly speaking, can only be encountered, never thought or imagined.

Now, someone may say, "I can abstract the concept of Being; I can think about Being on its own. Who says I can't? I *will* think about it: Being. There!" But recall where we started with Hegel in chapter 2: he observed that if we try to think, not about the being of any object—such as the sweater someone is wearing, the tree outside our window, or someone we saw in the street—but just try to think pure Being, we end by thinking nothing. That is why he made the statement that to think of Being is immediately to think of non-being; and when we think of the simultaneity of Being and non-being, we think of *becoming*, and so the Hegelian dialectic is launched.

Kierkegaard, we recall, disagreed with Hegel on this point, insisting that the operative dialectic is never that of *being* but always the dialectic of *choosing*. Sartre borrows from Kierkegaard here, and disallows the Hegelian notion of the dialectic of being. When we try to *think* pure Being, in the abstract, we think of nothing, but when we *encounter* Being in the being of concrete objects, we do encounter something. Hence Being can never be thought; it can only be encountered—and when we do encounter it, we are overwhelmed and suffocated by its sheer massiveness, superfluity, arbitrariness, and meaninglessness, like Roquentin in *Nausea*. All this arbitrary Being is enough to make a person sick.

We may inure ourselves to that sick feeling, suggests Sartre, in the same way that we can stretch our stomachs by overeating: by the time we reach adulthood we can easily overeat without throwing up, whereas a baby or very young child throws up immediately after overeating. Sartre's point is that if we allow ourselves to apprehend the sheer unnecessary abundance of Being instead of hardening ourselves to it, it makes us sick. People informed by a theistic perspective, even those who are not Christians, may not be sickened by this encounter with the sheer abundance of unnecessary Being, but that is because at some subtle level we understand all Being as related to the Creator's purpose in creating it. Like the apologist who developed the "watchmaker" argument, we have already interpreted what we see and have given it meaning based on our assumption of a Creator.

Just as we in this culture cannot simulate for ourselves the experience of someone who has never seen a watch, it is difficult for theists to put themselves in the position of someone who does not believe in God. As a pastor, however, I have seen numerous people who have "lost their faith" and are in exactly the same spot as Sartre. God has evaporated on them. "What is the point of it all?" they ask. And as soon as I tell them what the point of it all is, they say, "Well, that's easy for you to say, because you believe in God. I no longer do—so, what is the point of it all?" The honest answer is that, apart from God, there *is* no point.

However, Sartre insists, we can live with that if we have courage. We can do something with it: recognizing the innate awareness we have of the gap between Being-in-itself and Being-for-itself, we can nihilate our facticity, accept the radical freedom in being human, take responsibility for that freedom, and act—even if the uncertainty of the outcome makes it agony to do so. In this way we forge our self and create meaning for our own existence. If we lack courage, on the other hand, we will simply give up.

In an early chapter of this book we discussed the sense in which Nothing can be something. We observed that a lie corresponds to nothing at all, yet wields terrible power; and that a vacuum is by definition nothing, yet has the power to suck everything into itself. Similarly the Nothingness about which Sartre speaks is, in some sense, *something* in that it cancels the causal nexus of determinism and opens up freedom for us. Actuality prior to any human intervention in it he calls "Being-in-itself." Human consciousness, which is consciousness of what might be, he calls "Being-for-itself." In between is Nothing—no being, nothing that *is*. But in that gap, in that Nothing, lies human freedom.

Biblical theology makes a similar kind of statement about the origin of sin. What is the ontological status of sin? A good God fashions a good creation in which there is only blessing, and no curse. We were not created suspended between blessing and curse, or between godliness and corruption, looking back and forth at two existing options and selecting one over the other. According to the Genesis saga, we were created and placed in the Garden of Eden already in the midst of pure blessing; we were created loved by God and loving him back, and good existence was all there was. That being the case, sin is logically impossible. There is no logical explanation for the fact that, knowing blessing only, we elected curse; to explain it is to explain sin away and render it non-sin. Yet the actuality of sin proves its possibility. Sin, then, is an impossible possibility,[15] an ontological paradox like the Nothing which is something. Kierkegaard maintained that anyone who claims to understand sin has never experienced it. The absurdity of temptation is that we know what we are tempted to do is sin, and we know there is a terrible price attached to doing it, and yet we go ahead and do it anyway. The only conclusion is that we are insane—and yet we are not; we yield to temptation while quite sane.[16]

It sounds likewise ridiculous (because contradictory) to say that the difference between Being-in-itself and Being-for-itself is Nothing, and to say at the same time that there is a momentous difference between them. If there is no difference, we are determined entirely by our facticity: our biochemistry, our social environment, our genetic makeup. The glorious condition of our self-determination is the Nothing that yawns between our facticity, which exists, and the endpoint of our project, which does not.

Sartre makes a second important point in *Nausea*. Between Being-in-itself and Being-for-itself, along with our freedom, is that which militates against our freedom; namely, the world of humanly created structures fashioned to deal with reality. These structures include language, especially, but also theories, institutions, explanations, traditions, and customs. We rarely confront Being-in-itself directly; we nearly always confront it through the medium of human institutions that camouflage reality rather than disclose it, with the result that we are always living with an element of deception. Thought is rarely about reality, but rather about thought itself—the layer of human structure that covers and tames reality. In other words, thought is mostly self-referential; it does not refer beyond itself to real existence.

Once our thinking is merely about thought, we can think as long

15. See Karl Barth, *Church Dogmatics*, Vol. 4, Part 1, trans. G. W. Bromiley (Edinburgh: T&T Clark, 1961), 408–410.

16. I witnessed this absurdity often as a pastor involved in criminal court cases. I quickly learned, for example, not to ask the successful businessman with the six-figure income why he stole the screwdriver from the hardware store. He was not a kleptomaniac or psychologically abnormal in any way; he did it only once, and incurred a criminal record. There was no point in asking him why he did it, because he did not know.

and as much as we want without ever *being* any different or *doing* anything different, and that is precisely the trouble: self-referential thought leaves us inert. Most people are perfectly content to be inert; famously, in any group enterprise (including the typical church), eighty percent of the work is done by twenty percent of the people. This is because, for most people, thought is about thought; most people in church hear the sermon and say, "You know, in thinking about that sermon, I found the second point to be really good. The first and third points were not as good. Furthermore, I particularly liked the way he expressed that second point; his English is getting better every week, and so is his presence in the pulpit." Existentialists oppose this kind of self-referential thought, of course, and the inertia it produces; Kierkegaard, for instance, would say that thought about thought is just one more objectivity. In *Nausea*, Sartre forces his character to face reality head-on, unmediated: for Roquentin, the reality-taming world of language, institutions, and explanations has collapsed and he is confronted directly with the sheer, massive arbitrariness of Being.

A clergyman I knew was trying to instruct socially deprived youngsters in the Christian faith. They were inner-city children who had never been taken on a holiday to the country or seen any natural beauty. He took them to see things like Niagara Falls or the autumn colours in Collingwood, because the beauty and vastness of creation had always spoken to him about God. Such things do speak to you about God if you are already convinced that God made them, but otherwise they are just things. These beautiful and majestic sights meant nothing to the children; they were always only looking for the next ice cream cone. The clergyman suddenly realized that everything he thought would speak unmistakably to any human being about the transcendence and creative power of God was in itself absurd; it said nothing at all to the youngsters, and the only reason it said anything to him was that he was reading into it a meaning that was already in his own mind. The experience precipitated a crisis of faith for him. Such is the position of the central figure in *Nausea*, who recognizes finally that, in a world not created, we are overwhelmed by sheer facticity and absurdity is overwhelming.

There are many people in this position in our society. One consequence is that they endlessly anesthetize themselves with mindless entertainment, alcohol, sex, sports, and other occupations. Some even resort to ending their own lives: suicide is undertaken by people who are in insuperable pain—sometimes, the pain of finding life meaningless. We want to say to such people, "Don't worry; life isn't pointless. Jesus is the meaning." But they have heard such assurances many times already, and none of it has registered; merely telling them again is not the answer. At some point, the suffering person will say, "Jesus may be the meaning for *you,* but frankly, I have tried for thirty years to contact him and haven't managed it." More people around us live in the Sartrian world than we want to admit—which is one indisputably good reason for Christians to seek understanding of it.

Aristotle said that for anything that exists there must be a sufficient cause or reason. For that thing which constitutes a cause or reason, however, there must in turn be a cause or reason. Thus we can form a chain of reasons (and hence of meaning), such as: I got up today because I had to go to work; I had to go to work because I have to make a living; I have to make a living because I have to buy food: I have to buy food because I must eat in order to stay alive; I must stay alive because I am afraid of dying; and so on. The chain of reasons consisting of *contingent* being, according to Aristotle, terminates in *necessary* being. Sartre rejects this approach, however. He insists that such a chain is endlessly regressive because there is no final term that will ground all contingent being, and no necessary being underlying contingent being; rather, *contingent being is all there is.* And if there is no necessary being to constitute the ground and condition of contingent being, then there is no necessary *meaning*, either; the only meaning is the meaning we impute to anything—failing which, there is unrelieved absurdity. Meaning is not found in God, says Sartre, since God does not exist; "God" is posited by cowards in order to avoid admitting life's absurdity. Instead we should own the absurdity, develop the courage to act in spite of it, and thereby *create* meaning in an inherently meaningless world.

Crucially, however, we must remember that Sartre has already decided in advance that God does not exist, in view of his conviction that if an all-transcendent, infinitely powerful God existed, we would be so dwarfed by his infinitude that we would be reduced to the status of an object such as a stick or a stone; if God exists, in other words, the human self cannot. Having thus posited the non-existence of God as the condition of his own existence, and knowing that he himself exists, Sartre can draw no other conclusion than atheism.

We may rightly contest Sartre's understanding of God as inadequate, but unfortunately the God he rejects is the God many Christians believe in and proffer to others: a God whose "sovereignty" controls and manipulates humans as if they were objects. The God whom Scripture attests, however, is no such puppeteer. When, having created human beings in his "likeness and image," God finds they have turned out as they have, the text of the Bible implies that he was startled, taken aback, even perplexed, and that he "repented" of having created those whose relative autonomy was so shockingly misused.[17] He felt a certain regret about having made us—a response that does not sound like omni-causality or omni-control.[18] We have revisited repeatedly the truth that God's sovereignty does not consist in his control of the universe and its inhabitants, but in the limitless efficacy of his cruciform vulnerability. If the deity put forward by European Christendom had been the hemorrhaging Lamb rather than the conquering Lion, might Sartre have been a believer?

We shall never know, of course. Our speech about God can never do justice, ultimately, to God's transcendent reality. We need to use words, or we cannot communicate anything about the reality, but that reality must forever transcend our speech. Only an encounter with God can do justice to his reality. That is why "Whoever believes in the Son of God has the testimony in himself."[19] Such a person's encounter with

17. See Genesis 6:6. The King James Version uses "repented," while newer translations customarily say "God was sorry…"

18. Given that the sovereign God does not exercise control over us, we ourselves should renounce trying to control people, and recognize that our penchant for control is what ruins our relationships. Our sphere of control is in fact extremely small; we flatter ourselves if we think otherwise. Our sphere of influence, however, may be vast. To control is to be a tyrant, whereas to influence is to be a leader.

19. 1 John 5:10.

the reality is sufficient, even as her speech is halting. When we describe Jesus in order to commend him to others, what we are ultimately saying is, "He is more glorious, more attractive than anything I can describe, but you will have to meet him yourself." For this reason we can always point to God, but can never finally argue for God. Ultimately we are witnesses, not apologetes.

Not only are we mere creatures, we are sinners as well; how can what is finite and sinful effectually commend the infinite Holy One? Our witness can be effective only as God in his condescension uses our finite, stammering testimony, and in his mercy sanctifies our sin-riddled attestation.

Being and Nothingness

Crucial to Sartre's ontology is his cryptic statement, "Consciousness adds Nothing to Being."[20] He means that one of the features of human consciousness is that our awareness of being is always accompanied by an awareness of non-being, but not in precisely the same sense meant by Hegel. Sartre's point is that when we think of an object, we are aware not only of what it is, but what it is not. If I think of a ball, for instance, I am aware that it is not a cat. I am aware that a baseball is not a basketball. And when I enter a restaurant looking for my friend, my friend's absence leaps out at me; it is an actuality of which I am aware. Like a vacuum or a lie, the absence of something or someone is nothing, yet also something.

As we have noted above in the context of other works by Sartre, non-being or Nothingness is what fosters action; if being were not accompanied by Nothingness, action would be impossible. My awareness of my friend's absence is precisely what facilitates my doing something about it: I go looking for him. And if I want to play basketball, I set aside the baseball and procure a basketball. The element of Nothingness in life makes action possible because it discloses *discontinuities in causality*. Apart from non-being, in other words, there would be a continuous chain of causality, and we would be entirely determined. True human action, in the sense of something we choose to

---

20. Jean-Paul Sartre, *Being and Nothingness*, trans. Hazel E. Barnes (New York: Philosophical Library, 1992), 217.

do, would be impossible. We saw this earlier in the context of Being-in-itself and Being-for-itself, or facticity and project.

Recall the illustration of the four alpine hikers who come across a huge boulder in their path.[21] One hiker sees the boulder as an insurmountable obstacle and declares the outing over because they cannot go any further. The second hiker admires the beautiful striations in the boulder and decides to photograph it; he sees the boulder as aesthetic stimulus. The third sees the boulder as scientific object, noting and analyzing its geological formations, and the last hiker resolves to find a way around the boulder and continue hiking; he sees it as a challenge to be overcome. None of these meanings is inherent in the boulder; rather, the four different meanings come from the four different hikers. Similarly, while we cannot alter facticity or Being-in-itself, we choose and create its meaning. We do so *by taking action towards a state of affairs which is not (yet) the case*, and it is only our human consciousness of non-being that makes this action (and consequent meaning) possible.

Consider yet another case: if I am only five feet tall, I probably cannot play professional basketball, but there are a variety of responses I can make to the facticity of my height. I can grind my teeth in frustration at the sheer bad luck that I cannot play professional basketball; alternatively, I can train to be a jockey, or become a model for short men's clothing. By the choice I make, I forge the self I become and create the meaning of my life. We are never without a self-determining choice with respect to our facticity. However, making such a choice requires courage, because the project, or Being-for-itself—the state of affairs we imagine—does not exist; it is separated from our past by a gap, a non-being or Nothingness that can be terrifying. In other words, the future has no facticity; I must construct the future, and in so doing I also construct a self which is not the self I currently am. I make an appointment, as it were, to meet myself in the future.

At the same time, the fear that I may not find myself at that appointment, or will not want to keep the appointment, causes me

21. Sartre uses such illustrations frequently in order to deny fate of any sort. See *Being and Nothingness* (1992), 488–489. For the details of this example I am indebted to Palmer, *Sartre for Beginners*, 62.

anguish. And since freedom is a permanent structure of the human, the anguish to which it gives rise is also permanent. Most of us experience this anguish relatively rarely; we are in the habit of making certain choices (such as going to work day after day) that entail other routine choices. The anguish arises when we realize that there is *no necessity* and *no inherent meaning* to the routine: we could do something different, and whatever we do has no meaning apart from the one we give it. The fact that we are the source of our own meaning, of our own values, causes us anguish.

It is different, of course, for Plato, who is convinced that whatever is has value because all things are instantiations of eternal verities or forms; but the Existentialist eschews Plato's metaphysics and hence has no such assurance. It is different for the theistic tradition, too: God's Being possesses infinite value, and creaturely Being has finite value conferred on it by virtue of God's having created it. In that view, humans must choose between what is valuable (good) and what is of no value (evil). For Sartre, on the other hand, only the choice itself creates value: in choosing to do something, we confer value on that which we have chosen. To return to the story of Abraham and Isaac, for example, Sartre would maintain that Abraham's freely chosen act bestows value on what Abraham deems to be God's command. The fact that we are the sole foundation or source of value, even as our own value is without foundation, is for Sartre a burden that causes anguish.

The anguish of being the creators of our own meaning, and the anguish of having to make choices without knowing the outcome, is too much for most people, observes Sartre, and they flee it by living in "bad faith."[22] "Bad faith" is an ontological concept, not a moral one: it has to do not with willful insincerity or fraudulence towards others but with the lie that we tell ourselves, and believe and live by, regarding our own lack of freedom and responsibility. Freud maintained that we lie to ourselves unconsciously, but (as noted above) Sartre rejects Freud's notion of the unconscious mind; in fact, he considers the notion itself to be conceived in bad faith, because by definition it evades responsibility. Lying to myself unconsciously is impossible, insists Sartre, because the

22. Sartre introduces this expression in *Being and Nothingness* (1986), 67–68.

truth I am trying to repress, or hide from myself, I already possess. Is the repressor, he asks, on the side of the conscious or of the unconscious? It cannot at the same time be *part of* the unconscious and yet censoring the unconscious, while if it is on the side of the conscious, then in some way we must *know* that we are censoring. In short, Freud's insistence on repression as a purely unconscious activity is logically inconsistent.

Sartre maintains, instead, that we tend to live in a state that hovers over the boundary between conscious lying to oneself and Freud's supposed unconscious, a state Sartre describes as "being-in-the-midst-of-the-world"—that is, choosing to be an inert presence, a passive object among objects.[23] In so doing we are still choosing a self, but we believe we are escaping responsibility for it. Meanwhile we must adopt roles to facilitate social intercourse, and these roles make it easy for us to objectify ourselves, deny our freedom (without being able to escape it), and so live in bad faith. We simply reduce ourselves to our roles.

What is "good faith," then? It is living authentically; that is—to return to Sartre's comment on what it is to be human—"being which is not what it is and which is what it is not"?[24] What does this mean? It means that those who live in good faith are not content with what is, Being-in-itself or facticity; we aspire instead to the authentic selfhood of Being-for-itself, our project, that which is not yet but may be. However, such authenticity is never "our possession forever";[25] it must be constantly forged anew. Being-for-itself is always newly enacted.

All of this in turn means that authenticity or "good faith" is precisely *not* sincerity, because the sincere person tries to be just what she is, on the assumption that she really is what she is in the same ontic way that a rock is what it is. Unlike the rock, however, whose "is" pertains to its definition or essence, the human has no essence and is not defined; the human must define herself. Our human consciousness puts us in an ontically different category from the rock, because our awareness of that which is not (Nothingness) makes us able to choose it and bring

23. Ibid., 58.
24. Ibid., 70.
25. Ibid.

it into being. Hence Sartre's definition: good faith—being that is truly human—is "being which is not what it is and which is what it is not."

The self and the other

A problem arises when the self encounters other people. If, on encountering another person, I regarded her as a thing, she would simply be another item in the landscape. Seeing her would not change my relationship to that landscape. When I see her as another person, however, I suddenly recognize space and objects organized around her instead of around me, and the relationships I had established with my environment disintegrate; in other words, she steals my "world" from me. We have all observed how someone sitting on a park bench will get up and leave when someone else comes and sits down at the other end of it; the person who gets up and leaves is expressing just what Sartre has in mind. Phenomenologically, the appearance of another person forces me to reinterpret my world, with the result that her freedom destabilizes mine. I try to objectify her but cannot *fully* objectify her, as I discover when she turns her gaze on me: objects do not gaze. Now (in an echo of Hegel's master–slave dialectic) *she* is objectifying *me*. The possibility of being seen by the other is experienced as shame. In the moment of being seen, we discover ourselves as the object created by the other's gaze; we discover our being-for-others, and are forced to pass judgment on ourselves as object. This is what we feel as shame.

As well as shame, says Sartre, we may experience fear. The origin of this fear is likewise the discovery of my being-as-object, the discovery that my Being-for-itself is transcended by possibilities that are not *my* possibilities. I must then try to recover my freedom from entrapment by the other, and can do so only insofar as I objectify the other. The shame and fear we feel before God (as it were) is the recognition of our being-as-object before a subject (God) whom we can *never* objectify; hence we can *never* lose our fear and shame in the presence of God, who is the other magnified to the nth degree. This is why Sartre declares God to be the cancellation of the possibility of our personhood. Consider the contrast between this view and Buber's, according to which God—who is not the quintessential other, but the absolute and hence unique Other—is the very condition of human personhood.

Sartre makes a further point about the relationship between our being and the "invention" that is God. Recall that Being-in-itself is always a fullness, whereas Being-for-itself is an emptiness or lack, a Nothingness that gives rise to human freedom. A dialectic arises here, however: the Nothingness inherent in Being-for-itself is frightening, and we seek to overcome it by becoming Being-in-itself ultimately, with no need to forge our self and our meaning through any project. We crave a justification of ourselves as we are, a security and a guarantee of meaning in ourselves as we are, a freedom that does not lie in possibility but is its own necessary source of being. We crave, in other words, Being-in-itself-for-itself. But Being-in-itself-for-itself is the definition of "God." What we crave, then, is to be God: complete without any lack or Nothingness. Since Being-in-itself-for-itself is self-contradictory, so is our craving. Sartre concludes, therefore, that "Man is a useless passion."[26]

In his *Notebooks for an Ethics*, the older Sartre speaks differently of "the other," and even in *Being and Nothingness* he speaks of "radical conversion" that can provide deliverance from hellish, antagonistic relations with others.[27] Such radical conversion is an abandonment of the attempt to be Being-in-itself-for-itself, or God. In abandoning that attempt, we not only find our own freedom, but also give up trying to subjugate the other's freedom. In *Notebooks for an Ethics* Sartre refers to the account he gave in *Being and Nothingness* as "an ontology before conversion";[28] in other words, to live inauthentically or in bad faith, as described in *Being and Nothingness*, is to seek to become God: to seek to be, ultimately and necessarily, only what we are. Bad faith, or clinging to Being-in-itself, is the default position of humankind, says Sartre;[29] conversion is the "fundamental project," and since the self is a totality

26. Ibid., 615.

27. Sartre, *Being and Nothingness* (1992), 534, n. 13.

28. Jean-Paul Sartre, *Notebooks for an Ethics*, trans. David Pellauer (Chicago: University of Chicago Press, 1992), 6.

29. We may see in this an analogue to the Christian doctrine of original sin.

that is manifest in every act, the "fundamental project" is recreated every moment through every choice we make.

In view of the above, Sartre's freedom ethic entails our always being "on the road" and never having arrived. For this reason our value-creating freedom, relentlessly exercised, gives rise to values that are, in turn, always a work in progress rather than fixed and final. All answers give rise to new questions; all accomplishments give rise to new projects. What matters, then, is not arriving, but doing or pursuing. Sartre states, "Authenticity reveals that the only meaningful project is that of doing (not that of being).... [A]uthenticity consists in refusing any quest for being..."[30] While any value we posit might appear to be valid simply by virtue of being posited, Sartre maintains that the highest values presuppose freedom as both their source and their end; that is, freedom is the *sine qua non* of ethical action, and such action ought to facilitate the greatest freedom for others as well as ourselves. Not surprisingly, then, Sartre insists that "any ordering of values has to lead to freedom"; in a word, values are to be classified "in a hierarchy such that freedom increasingly appears in it."[31] What, then, are the highest values for Sartre? In ascending order they are passion, pleasure, criticism, and the demand for evidence, responsibility, and creation, with all of these crowned by generosity.[32]

It is in *No Exit*, one of his plays, that Sartre makes the oft-quoted statement, "Hell is other people." In *Sartre on Theater*, however, he maintains that this statement has been misunderstood: he does not mean that our relationships with other people are invariably poisoned and hellish, but that the default tendency (before "conversion" from bad faith) is to relate to others as threats to our selfhood.[33] *No Exit* should be read, then, not as the description of an inevitable way of relating, but as a caution against such relating, a call to resist the default. There is indeed an exit from inauthenticity and from hellish relationships; the thing

---

30. Sartre, *Notebooks for an Ethics*, 475.

31. Ibid., 9.

32. Ibid., 470.

33. Jean-Paul Sartre, *Sartre on Theater*, ed. Michel Contat and Michel Rybalka, trans. Frank Jellinek (New York: Pantheon, 1976), 199.

from which we have "no exit," on the other hand, is our freedom, our responsibility for what we do—and accepting the latter is the condition of the former.

Concluding Reflections

We may well ask of Sartre: For whom or to whom are we responsible? He replies in *Notebooks for an Ethics* that any one individual is responsible for all, and therefore to all: in choosing my self, I choose (for) all.[34] Since we exist and hence forge our self only in relation to others, freedom cannot be subjectivism; rather, he insists, it is a freedom that depends on the freedom of others, and on which the freedom of others in turn depends.

This philosophical conviction was one on which Sartre staked his life, and took action at great cost to himself. During his wartime activity in the French Resistance, he was aware of what was at stake for all resisters. In 1944, following the Allied landings in France that doomed the German military effort even though the war had another year to run, Sartre commented:

> A single word could have led to ten, to a hundred, arrests. Is not this total responsibility in total solitude the very revelation of our freedom? This abandonment, this solitude, the enormous risk—these were the same for everyone, for leaders and men alike. For those who carried messages without knowing what was in them and for those who directed the entire Resistance effort, the punishment was the same—imprisonment, deportation and death. In no army in the world is such an equality of risk shared by private and commander-in-chief. And this is why the Resistance was a true democracy: for the soldier as for the commander, the same danger, the same responsibility, the same absolute freedom within discipline. Thus, in the shadows and in blood, the strongest of Republics was forged. Each of its citizens knew

34. See, e.g., *Notebooks for an Ethics*, 482. The assertion is an echo of the Kantian Categorical Imperative.

he had an obligation to all and that he had to rely on himself alone. Each, in the most total abandonment, fulfilled his role in history. Each, standing against the oppressors, made the effort to be himself irremediably. And by choosing himself in freedom, he chose freedom for all.[35]

Few philosophers have insisted as compellingly that the world's horrific injustices are not inevitable but are the result of human choices, and that we have the freedom and responsibility to make changes; and fewer still have done as much to translate that insistence into action. Sartre did, and for this reason alone, if not for many others, his version of Existentialism calls for serious and respectful attention.

Sartre's understanding of freedom has evoked other criticism on the grounds that he has not adequately distinguished freedom from arbitrariness or caprice; he is left saying that choice is groundless. If our choice is unrelated to who or what we are already, then what we choose and the "freedom" it presupposes is nothing more than unmotivated accidentality, sheer contingency.[36] Is mere indeterminism proper protection against the assorted necessities to which "bad faith" appeals?

Thinkers such as Paul Tillich maintain that freedom, as opposed to the mere negation of determinism, *must* be related to "destiny,"[37] the identity we already possess on account of birth, upbringing, education, and countless additional formative influences. Without freedom, "destiny" would amount to mechanistic determinism or fate; and without "destiny," freedom (so-called) would be reduced to mere indeterminism.

I maintain we experience our selfhood as neither sheer fate nor sheer arbitrariness. We are aware of our selfhood as a dialectical tension

35. Jean-Paul Sartre, *We Have Only This Life to Live: The Selected Essays of Jean-Paul Sartre, 1939–1975*, ed. Ronald Aronson and Adrian van den Hoven (New York: New York Review Books, 2013), 84–85.

36. See, for instance, C. W. Robbins, "Sartre and the Moral Life," *Philosophy* 12 (1977): 409–421.

37. Paul Tillich, *Systematic Theology*, Vol. I (Chicago: University of Chicago Press, 1951), 174–185.

between our awareness of freedom and necessity, necessity being the countless determinations (biological, historical, national, linguistic, political, economic, social) to which we are subject. These *determinations* are factors in who we are, yet without ever becoming *determinisms*. At the same time, we are aware of the finite self-transcendence by means of which we can at least identify these determinations and, if not escape or alter all of them, at least alter their meaning.

Criticisms of Sartre's understanding of freedom are not without their cogency. Nonetheless, his understanding of the human situation needs to be heard and heeded. And his courageous exemplification of his own philosophy, with its attendant price tag, should challenge Christians who may find the dangers and costs of discipleship more than they anticipated, and may be tempted to cloak their cowardice in the "bad faith" of doctrinal affirmation or church membership.

Bibliography

Allen, Diogenes, and Eric O. Springsted, eds. *Primary Readings in Philosophy for Understanding Theology*. Louisville: Westminster John Knox Press, 1992.

Arendt, Hannah. *On Violence*. New York: Harcourt Brace & Company, 1970.

Aronson, Ronald. *Jean-Paul Sartre: Philosophy in the World*. New York: Schocken Books, 1980.

Audi, Robert, ed. *The Cambridge Dictionary of Philosophy*, 2nd ed. Cambridge: Cambridge University Press, 1999.

Balthasar, Hans Urs von. *The Christian and Anxiety*. San Francisco: Ignatius Press, 2000.

———. *Prayer*. San Francisco: Ignatius Press, 1986.

Barrett, William. *What Is Existentialism?* New York: Grove Press, 1964.

Barth, Karl. *Church Dogmatics,* Vol. I, Part 2. Translated by G. W. Bromiley. Edinburgh: T. & T. Clark, 1970.

———. *Church Dogmatics,* Vol. IV, Part 1. Translated by G. W. Bromiley. Edinburgh: T. & T. Clark, 1961.

Boss, Medard, ed. *Martin Heidegger: Zollikon Seminars – Protocols, Conversations, Letters*. Chicago: Northwestern University Press, 2001.

———. *Psychoanalysis and Daseinanalysis*. New York: Basic Books, 1967.

Bready, J. W. *England Before and After Wesley*. London: Hodder & Stoughton, 1939.

Buber, Martin. *Eclipse of God*. New York: Harper & Row, 1957.

———. *I and Thou*. Excerpted in *The Martin Buber Reader: Essential Writings*, edited by Asher D. Biemann. New York: Palgrave MacMillan, 2002.

———. *I and Thou*. Translated by R. Gregor Smith. New York: Charles Scribner's Sons, 1958.

————. *Moses: The Revelation and the Covenant*. London: Harper Torchbook, 1958.

Burnham, Douglas. *Reading Nietzsche: An Analysis of* Beyond Good and Evil. Montreal: McGill-Queen's University Press, 2007.

Calvin, John. *Commentary on John*, Part One. Translated by T. H. L. Parker. Grand Rapids: Eerdmans, 1974.

————. *Commentary on John*, Part Two. Translated by T. H. L. Parker. Grand Rapids: Eerdmans, 1994.

————. *Institutes of the Christian Religion*. Edited by John T. MacNeill. Translated by Ford Lewis Battles. Philadelphia: Westminster Press, 1960.

Cassidy, Sheila. *Sharing the Darkness*. London: Darton, Longman and Todd, 1988.

Caws, Peter. *Sartre*. London: Routledge and Kegan Paul, 1979.

Collins, James. *The Mind of Kierkegaard*. Princeton: Princeton University Press, 1983.

Cooper, D. *Authenticity and Learning: Nietzsche's Educational Philosophy*. Brookfield, Vermont: Avebury, 1991.

————. *Existentialism*. Oxford: Blackwell, 1999.

Cox, Gary. *Sartre: A Guide for the Perplexed*. New York: Continuum, 2006.

Crowell, Steven, ed. *The Cambridge Companion to Existentialism*. Cambridge: Cambridge University Press, 2012.

Detmer, David. *Sartre Explained: From Bad Faith to Authenticity*. Peru, IL: Open Court Publishing, 2008.

Dutton, Kevin. *The Wisdom of Psychopaths: What Saints, Spies, and Serial Killers Can Teach Us About Success*. Toronto: Doubleday, 2012.

Edwards, Jonathan. *The Works of Jonathan Edwards*, Vol. 2. Edited by John E. Smith. New Haven: Yale University Press, 2009.

Evans, C. Stephen. *Faith Beyond Reason: A Kierkegaardian Account*. Grand Rapids: Eerdmans, 1998.

————. *Passionate Reason: Making Sense of Kierkegaard's* Philosophical Fragments. Bloomington: Indiana University Press, 1992.

Fackenheim, Emil. *Encounters Between Judaism and Modern Philosophy.* London: Jason Aronson Inc., 1994.

———. *Jewish Philosophers and Jewish Philosophy.* Bloomington: Indiana University Press, 1996.

———. *The Religious Dimension in Hegel's Thought.* Bloomington: Indiana University Press, 1967.

———. *What Is Judaism?* New York: Summit Books, 1987.

Foucault, Michel. *Power/Knowledge.* Edited by Colin Gordon. Translated by Colin Gordon, Leo Marshall, John Mepham, Kate Soper. New York: Pantheon, 1988.

Foucault, Michel, and Ludwig Binswanger. *Dream and Existence.* Edited by Keith Hoeller. Humanities Press, 1992.

Friedman, Maurice S. *Martin Buber: The Life of Dialogue.* London: Routledge, 2002.

———. *Encounter on the Narrow Ridge: A Life of Martin Buber.* New York: Paragon House, 1993.

Frye, Northrop. *The Educated Imagination.* Toronto: CBC Publications, 1963.

Gouwens, David. *Kierkegaard as a Religious Thinker.* Cambridge: Cambridge University Press, 1996.

Grimm, Harold, trans. *Luther's Works*, Vol. 31. Philadelphia: Fortress Press, 1979.

Gritsch, Eric W. *Martin Luther's Anti-Semitism.* Grand Rapids: Eerdmans, 2012.

Guignon, Charles B., ed. *The Cambridge Companion to Heidegger.* Cambridge: Cambridge University Press, 1995.

———, ed. *The Existentialists: Critical Essays on Kierkegaard, Nietzsche, Heidegger and Sartre.* Lanham, MD: Rowman & Littlefield, 2004.

Guignon, Charles, and Derk Pereboom, eds. *Existentialism: Basic Writings.* Indianapolis: Hackett Publishing Company, 2001.

Hannay, A., and G. Marion, eds. *The Cambridge Companion to Kierkegaard.* Cambridge: Cambridge University Press, 1999.

Hegel, G. W. F. *The Phenomenology of Mind*, 2nd revised edition.

Translated and edited by J. B. Baillie. Mineola, NY: Dover Publications, 2003.

Heidegger, Martin. *Basic Problems in Phenomenology*. Translated by Scott Campbell. New York: Bloomsbury Academic Press, 2013.

———. *Basic Writings*. Translated by HarperCollins Publishers. New York: HarperCollins, 2008.

———. *Being and Time*. Translated by John Macquarrie and Edward Robinson. New York: Harper & Row, 1962.

Heschel, Abraham J. *A Passion for Truth.* Woodstock, VT: Jewish Lights Publishing, 1995.

———. *I Asked for Wonder*. Edited by Samuel H. Dresser. New York: Crossroad Publishing, 1991.

Hodes, Aubrey. *Encounter with Martin Buber*. Middlesex: Penguin, 1975.

Howells, Christina, ed. *The Cambridge Companion to Sartre*. Cambridge: Cambridge University Press, 1999.

Inwood, Michael. *Heidegger*. Oxford: Oxford University Press, 1997.

Kaufmann, William. *Nietzsche: Philosopher, Psychologist, Antichrist*. New York: Meridian Books, 1965.

Kierkegaard, Søren. *Concluding Unscientific Postscript to Philosophical Fragments*. Edited and translated by Howard V. Hong and Edna H. Hong. Princeton: Princeton University Press, 1992.

———. *Fear and Trembling / Repetition*. Translated by Howard V. Hong and Edna H. Hong. Princeton: Princeton University Press, 1983.

———. *Philosophical Fragments*. Translated by Howard V. Hong and Edna H. Hong. Princeton: Princeton University Press, 1985.

———. *The Sickness Unto Death*. Translated by Howard V. Hong and Edna H. Hong. Princeton: Princeton University Press, 1980.

———. *Upbuilding Discourses in Various Spirits*. Edited and translated by Howard V. Hong and Edna H. Hong. Princeton: Princeton University Press, 2009.

———. *Works of Love*. Translated by Howard V. Hong and Edna H. Hong. Princeton: Princeton University Press, 1995.

Kramer, Kenneth. *Martin Buber's* I and Thou: *Practicing Living Dialogue*. Montreal: Novalis, 2003.

Laurin, J. *Nietzsche and Modern Consciousness.* New York: Haskell House Publishers, 1973.

Lewis, C.S. *The Great Divorce.* Glasgow: Fontana Books, 1972.

———. *Reflections on the Psalms.* London: Fontana Books, 1965.

Loewith, K. *From Hegel to Nietzsche.* New York: Holt, Rinehart and Winston, 1964.

Lull, Timothy F., and William R. Russell, eds. *Martin Luther's Basic Theological Writings*, 3rd ed. Minneapolis: Fortress Press, 2012.

Macquarrie, John. *Existentialism.* London: Penguin, 1972.

———. *Heidegger and Christianity.* New York: Continuum, 1994.

Magnus, B., and K. Higgins, eds. *The Cambridge Companion to Nietzsche.* Cambridge: Cambridge University Press, 1999.

Mayhall, C., and T. Mayhall. *On Buber.* Toronto: Nelson Education Ltd., 2003.

McGrath, S. J. *Heidegger: A (Very) Critical Introduction.* Grand Rapids: Eerdmans, 2008.

Mendes-Flohr, Paul. *From Mysticism to Dialogue: Martin Buber's Transformation of German Social Thought.* Detroit: Wayne State University Press, 1989.

Michael, M., ed. *Heidegger and Modern Philosophy*: *Critical Essays.* New Haven: Yale University Press, 1978.

Naphy, William. *Calvin and the Consolidation of the Genevan Reformation.* Louisville: Westminster John Knox Press, 2003.

Nietzsche, Friedrich. *Basic Writings of Nietzsche*, Modern Library edition. Edited and translated by Walter Kaufmann. New York: Random House, 2000.

———. *Will to Power.* Translated by W. Kaufmann and R. J. Hollingdale. New York: Vintage, 1967.

Olson, Robert G. *An Introduction of Existentialism.* New York: Dover, 1962.

Palmer, Donald D. *Sartre for Beginners.* Danbury, CT: For Beginners LLC, 1995.

Rae, Murray. *Kierkegaard's Vision of the Incarnation.* Oxford: Clarendon Press, 1997.

Reardon, Bernard. *Hegel's Philosophy of Religion.* New York: Harper and Row, 1977.

Robbins, C. W. "Sartre and the Moral Life." *Philosophy* 12 (1977), 409–421.

Rorty, Richard. "Heidegger and the History of Philosophy." *Monist* 64 (October 1981).

Sartre, Jean-Paul. *Being and Nothingness.* Translated by Hazel E. Barnes. New York: Philosophical Library, 1992.

―――. *Existentialism and Humanism.* Translated by Philip Mairet. London: Methuen & Co., 1948.

―――. *Nausea.* Translated by Lloyd Alexander. New York: New Directions, 2007.

―――. *Notebooks for an Ethics.* Translated by David Pellauer. Chicago: University of Chicago Press, 1992.

―――. *Sartre on Theater.* Edited by Michel Contat and Michel Rybalka. Translated by Frank Jellinek. New York: Pantheon, 1976.

―――. *The Transcendence of the Ego.* Translated by Forrest Williams and Robert Kirkpatrick. New York: Noonday Press, 1957.

―――. *We Have Only This Life to Live: The Selected Essays of Jean-Paul Sartre, 1939–1975.* Edited by Ronald Aronson and Adrian van den Hoven. New York: New York Review Books, 2013.

Schaeder, Grete. *The Hebrew Humanism of Martin Buber.* Detroit: Wayne State University Press, 1973.

Shepherd, Victor. "John Wesley: A Gift to the Universal Church." *Canadian Theological Review* (2012).

―――. *The Nature and Function of Faith in the Theology of John Calvin.* Vancouver: Regent College Publishing, 2004.

Shinn, Roger L. *The Existentialist Posture.* New York: Association Press, 1959.

Solomon, Robert. *From Hegel to Existentialism.* Oxford: Oxford University Press, 1987.

―――. *Living with Nietzsche.* London: Oxford University Press, 2003.

Solomon, Robert, and K. Higgins. *What Nietzsche Really Said.* New York: Schocken Books, 2000.

Stern, J. P. *A Study of Nietzsche.* Cambridge: Cambridge University Press, 1979.

Taylor, Georgiana M. "Oh to Be Nothing." In *Victorious Life Hymns.* Dayton, OH: Heritage Music Press, 1975.

Thody, Philip, and Howard Read. *Introducing Sartre.* Duxford, UK: Icon Books, 1999.

Tillich, Paul. *Systematic Theology*, Vol. I. Chicago: University of Chicago Press, 1965.

Unamuno, Miguel de. *The Tragic Sense of Life.* Translated by J. E. C. Flitch. New York: Barnes and Noble, 1990.

Vardy, Peter. *An Introduction to Kierkegaard.* Peabody, MA: Hendrickson Publishers, 2008.

Warnock, Mary. *Existentialism.* Oxford: Oxford University Press, 1999.

———. *The Philosophy of Sartre.* New York: Hilary House, 1967.

Wartenberg, Thomas E. *Existentialism: A Beginner's Guide.* Oxford: Oneworld, 2008.

Wengert, Timothy J. *Martin Luther's Catechisms.* Minneapolis: Fortress Press, 2009.

Wesley, John. *The Works of John Wesley*, Bicentennial Edition, Vol. 1. Edited by Albert C. Outler. Nashville: Abingdon, 1984.

Wilcocks, Robert, ed. *Critical Essays on Jean-Paul Sartre.* Boston: G.K. Hall, 1988.

Index